Social Marketing

The (social marketing) Ambulance Down In The Valley

T' was a dangerous cliff, as they freely confessed,
Though to walk near its crest was so pleasant;
But over its terrible edge there had slipped
A duke, and full many a peasant.
The people said something would have to be done,
But their projects did not at all tally.
Some said, 'Put a fence 'round the edge of the cliff,'
Some, 'An ambulance down in the valley.'

The lament of the crowd was profound and was loud,
As their hearts overflowed with their pity;
But the cry for the ambulance carried the day
As it spread through the neighbouring city.
A collection was made, to accumulate aid,
And the dwellers in highway and alley
Gave euros and cents – not to furnish a fence –
But an ambulance down in the valley.

Then some people saw, there was money galore
In tickets to walk the cliff top
So billboards appeared, saying there's nought to be feared
And extolling the joys of the drop
They said 'don't remonstrate that folk take our bate
Their behaviour is quite voluntary
Just give the child, the poor the reviled
And stick an ambulance down in the valley'

'For the cliff is all right if you're careful,' they said;
'And if folks ever slip and are dropping,
It isn't the slipping that hurts them so much
As the shock down below – when they're stopping.'
When people said 'No!' to marketing so
Forth the companies' lawyers did rally
Then to keep us all sweet, they sponsored a fleet
Of ambulances down in the valley.

So let's hear no more, of the old kill or cure
Prevention's the much better way
Let's give people the skill, the hope and the will
To win the quotidian fray
With policies broad and common accord
To divvy more fairly the tally
We can help one and all, keep away from the fall
To the ambulance down in the valley

And we must also fight those with the might
To push us the opposite way
So if business does harm, by muscle or charm
The polluter will just have to pay
But also I say, we can learn from their ways
And help people and parliament rally
Not behind wealth, but long life and good health
And so dispense
…with the ambulance down in the valley

Adapted from the original, May 2005
(with apologies to Joseph Malins)

Social Marketing

Why should the Devil have all the best tunes?

Gerard Hastings

AMSTERDAM • BOSTON • HEIDELBERG • LONDON • NEW YORK • OXFORD
PARIS • SAN DIEGO • SAN FRANCISCO • SINGAPORE • SYDNEY • TOKYO
Butterworth-Heinemann is an imprint of Elsevier

Butterworth-Heinemann is an imprint of Elsevier
Linacre House, Jordan Hill, Oxford OX2 8DP, UK
30 Corporate Drive, Suite 400, Burlington, MA 01803, USA

First edition 2007
Reprinted 2008

Notice
No responsibility is assumed by the publisher for any injury and/or damage to persons
or property as a matter of products liability, negligence or otherwise, or from any use
or operation of any methods, products, instructions or ideas contained in the material
herein. Because of rapid advances in the medical sciences, in particular, independent
verification of diagnoses and drug dosages should be made

British Library Cataloguing in Publication Data
A catalogue record for this book is available from the British Library

Library of Congress Cataloging-in-Publication Data
A catalog record for this book is available from the Library of Congress

ISBN: 978-0-7506-8350-0

For information on all Butterworth-Heinemann publications
visit our website at books.elsevier.com

Printed and bound in *Italy*

08 09 10 10 9 8 7 6 5 4 3 2

Working together to grow
libraries in developing countries

www.elsevier.com | www.bookaid.org | www.sabre.org

ELSEVIER   BOOK AID
International   Sabre Foundation

Contents

Preface

Marketing is at a crossroads. For decades it has been taught uncritically in business schools to inculcate new generations of executives in the ideas and skills of the trade. Now, post Naomi Klein, it is being poked, prodded and questioned. Some are asking whether or not the apparently very powerful tools of marketing – such as branding and market segmentation – can be used to promote socially desirable goals. If billboards have sold cigarettes to generations of children, can they be used with equal success to push the counter message of not smoking? Others are questioning the right of commercial marketers to sell the cigarettes in the first place.

These twin notions of both learning from and scrutinizing commercial marketing are encapsulated in the concept of *social marketing*. This book will explain its principles, techniques and potential.

Contributors' Biographies

Frances Abele

Frances Abele teaches in the School of Public Policy and Administration at Carleton University, Ottawa, Canada. Her research interests include Indigenous-Canada relations, circumpolar political and economic change, comparative public administration, and policy- and decision-making.

Julie A. Baldwin

Julie A. Baldwin is a Professor at the University of South Florida College of Public Health, and is Co-Director of the Research Methods and Evaluation Unit of the Florida Prevention Research Center. She previously directed several community-based disease prevention projects funded by NIH, SAMHSA and the Robert Wood Johnson Foundation.

Carol A. Bryant

Carol A. Bryant is Professor and Co-Director of the Florida Prevention Research Center at the University of South Florida. She is currently developing and evaluating a community-based social marketing framework for social change. This approach teaches communities to use marketing principles and techniques to design programmes to tackle local public health problems.

Robert Burns

Recently retired from full-time academic life, Dr Robert Burns has taught applied psychology in Education, Business and Medical faculties in the UK, South Africa, Australia and Brunei. He held the Chair of Applied Psychology in the Education Faculty of Cape Town University and was head of the Post Graduate School of Education at Bradford University. He still involves himself in academic endeavours part-time at the University of the Sunshine Coast.

Lisa Cohen

Lisa Cohen was Project Manager for the West of Scotland Cancer Awareness Project. During 16 years with the NHS, she worked on social marketing initiatives ranging from breast screening to teenage mental health and active commuting. She now runs her own consultancy, XL Communications, specializing in social marketing, training and project management.

Anita Courtney

Anita Courtney (M.S., R.D.) worked as the Director of Health Promotion of the Lexington Fayette County Health Department for 25 years, coordinating programmes in nutrition, diabetes, physical activity and tobacco. She is currently the Chairperson of the Lexington Tweens Nutrition and Fitness Coalition, which is nationally recognized for its work in developing innovative programmes for youths.

Sameer Deshpande

Sameer Deshpande (Ph.D., University of Wisconsin-Madison) is an Assistant Professor of Marketing and a faculty member of the Centre for Socially Responsible Marketing in the Faculty of Management at the University of Lethbridge. Sameer has conducted research in a variety of public health contexts in the USA, Canada and India.

Violaine Des Marchais

Violaine Des Marchais is a Canadian research assistant working with the Marketing Department of HEC Montreal, affiliated with the University of Montreal. She is also a co-founder of a small business offering educational and artistic activities in the education system in Canada.

Robert J. Donovan

Robert J. Donovan is Professor of Behavioural Research in the Division of Health Sciences, and Professor of Social Marketing and Director of the Social Marketing Research Unit in the School of Marketing in the Curtin Business School. He has had a long history in research both in academia and the private sector.

Douglas Eadie

Douglas Eadie is a Senior Researcher at the Institute for Social Marketing at the University of Stirling and the Open University, where he specializes in applied consumer research in the field of mass communication and social advertising using formative, process and outcome evaluation approaches. He has contributed to numerous public health campaigns and has published widely in the field.

Danika Hall

Danika Hall has worked and studied in the fields of marketing communication, health and education. With the Centre for Health Behaviour and Communication Research, she has developed and delivered social marketing training packages and conducted research to inform social marketing interventions. She is currently undertaking a Ph.D. in public health.

Debra Harker

Before becoming an academic, Associate Professor Debra Harker worked as a Marketing Consultant with KPMG Peat Marwick Management Consultants in England and AGB McNair in Australia. Debra achieved a B.A. (Hons) in Business Studies at South Bank University, London, and evaluated the effectiveness of the advertising self-regulatory scheme in Australia for her doctorate, which was awarded by Griffith University in Brisbane, Australia. She now lectures in Marketing at the University of the Sunshine Coast in Queensland, Australia and publishes in quality journals around the world.

Michael Harker

Michael Harker is Associate Professor in Marketing and Strategic Management at the University of the Sunshine Coast in Queensland, Australia. He has a B.Sci. (Hons) in Economics from Southampton University and M.A. in Marketing from Lancaster University, both in England. His Ph.D. in Strategic Management is from Griffith University, Brisbane, Australia. His articles have appeared in journals in the USA, Europe and Australia. Before taking up a teaching and research position at the Australian University, Michael was Marketing Director for Lloyds in Europe.

Geoffrey Jalleh

Geoffrey Jalleh is Associate Director of the Centre for Behavioural Research in Cancer Control at Curtin University. His primary research interests are in health communication and social marketing. He has been involved in a variety of health areas, including tobacco control, skin cancer prevention, drugs in sport, nutrition, physical activity and road injury prevention.

Ray James

Dr Ray James is Associate Professor of the Centre for Behavioural Research in Cancer Control, Curtin University of Technology, Perth, Australia. He completed his graduate studies in education and public health at the University of California Berkeley in 1980, and has worked in population health at the community, regional, state and university level in NSW and WA. He has also worked in Asia and South-East Asia over the last 30 years.

Sandra Jones

Associate Professor Sandra Jones is the Director of the Centre for Health Behaviour and Communication Research and Associate Dean (Research) in the Faculty of Health and Behavioural Sciences at the University of Wollongong. She has published over 50 refereed articles in the areas of social marketing and media influences on health behaviour. Prior to becoming an academic, Sandra worked in senior marketing roles in the human resources and tertiary education sectors.

François Lagarde

François Lagarde is a Canadian social marketing consultant to several organizations in the health, philanthropy, development aid, environment and housing fields. He is also an Associate Professor in the Faculty of Medicine of the University of Montreal, where he teaches social marketing in the health administration and public health programmes.

Raymond Lowry

Dr Ray Lowry is senior lecturer at the University of Newcastle upon Tyne, and an Honorary NHS consultant in Public Health. His research and service interests include water fluoridation, health promotion, social marketing and oral cancer. He has published widely in the learned press.

Chad MacArthur

Chad MacArthur (M.Ed., M.P.H.) is the Director of Training and Community Education and Director of Trachoma for Helen Keller International, a non-governmental organization implementing evidence-based programmes around the world to address the causes and consequences of blindness and malnutrition.

Judith Madill

Dr Judith Madill is Professor and Chair of the Marketing Area, Sprott School of Business, Carleton University, Ottawa, Canada. She is the author of more than 50 refereed papers, and her current research focuses on social marketing and sponsorship, as well as financing small and medium-sized enterprises.

Kelli R. McCormack Brown

Kelli McCormack Brown is a health education specialist with more than 20 years of experience. As a health educator she has trained numerous public health practitioners how to successfully use social marketing to enhance their programmes.

Laura McDermott

Laura McDermott is a Research Officer based at the Institute for Social Marketing at Stirling and the Open University. Laura's research focuses on social marketing in relation to food and nutrition. She has written extensively about both the impact of commercial food marketing on diet and the potential effectiveness of using social marketing techniques to improve dietary behaviour.

Robert J. McDermott

Robert J. McDermott is a Professor at the University of South Florida College of Public Health and is Co-Director of the Florida Prevention Research Center. Since 1981 he has been an investigator on more than $19 million in grants and contracts and has contributed to over 200 articles and books.

Neil McLean

Neil McLean is Director and co-founder of Quit&Save, an emerging social enterprise based in central Scotland, which runs community and corporate smoking cessation services. Neil is a board member of the Social Enterprise Academy and has recently received a scholarship from the Scottish Forum for Public Health, exploring the role that social enterprise can play in improving Scotland's health.

Kiri Milne

Kiri Milne has been a member of the New Zealand Health Sponsorship Council's Research and Evaluation Unit since 2002. In this role Kiri has worked on a number of social marketing programmes, including the Quit&Win competition, the Smoke-free Homes campaign and the SunSmart campaign. She is currently involved in the development of a social marketing programme that will contribute to preventing obesity among New Zealanders.

Jen Nickelson

Jen Nickelson is a registered dietician and doctoral student in the College of Public Health at the University of South Florida. She serves as liaison between the Florida Prevention Research Center and the Obesity Prevention Coalition of Sarasota County, Florida, who modelled a VERB™ Summer Scorecard programme after Lexington's programme.

Norm O'Reilly

Norm O'Reilly is Director and Associate Professor at the School of Sports Administration in the Faculty of Management at Laurentian University in Sudbury, Canada. As a researcher, Norm has published in numerous refereed management journals in a variety of management disciplines, including social marketing. As a sport practitioner, Norm has occupied a variety of posts, including Senior Policy Officer at Sport Canada, Director with the Canadian Olympic Committee, Event Manager for the Toronto 2008 Olympic Bid and was on Canada's Mission Staff at the 2004 Olympic Games.

Iain Potter

Iain Potter is the Chief Executive of the New Zealand Health Sponsorship Council (HSC), a Crown Entity based in Wellington. The HSC promotes healthy lifestyles to New Zealanders through social marketing programmes focusing on Smoke-free, SunSmart, Bike Wise, preventing and minimizing gambling-related harm, and healthy eating. Iain has been with the HSC since 1992, was a member of the National Participation Taskforce, the Healthy Eating Healthy Action external advisory group, the Cancer Control Taskforce and is a past Executive Council member of the Public Health Association.

Josephine Previte

Josephine Previte (Ph.D.) is currently a Postdoctoral Fellow in the School of Advertising, Marketing and Public Relations at the Queensland University of Technology, Australia. Her doctoral research examined the role of the Internet in social marketing. In addition to a strong focus in marketing and society research, Josephine is also interested in a critical marketing analysis of consumption and e-marketplace behaviours, and has other interests in the study of government and non-profit marketing strategy.

Martine Stead

Martine Stead is Deputy Director of the Institute for Social Marketing at the University of Stirling and The Open University. She has been involved in social marketing research since 1992, and has particular expertise in substance use prevention and the evaluation of complex behaviour-change interventions. She is also interested in expanding social marketing beyond public health into other areas of social change.

Manisha Tharaney

Manisha Tharaney is the Country Director of Helen Keller International's field office in Tanzania. A career non-profit professional, Ms Tharaney holds an M.P.H. in International Health from the George Washington University and an M.S.W. in Medical and Psychiatric Social Work from the Tata Institute of Social Sciences in Mumbai, India.

Michèle Tremblay

Dr Michèle Tremblay is a medical consultant with the Quebec Institute of Public Health. For the last 10 years, she has been actively involved in the development and implementation of interventions aimed at reducing tobacco use in Quebec.

Sue Walker

Dr Sue Walker is the manager of the New Zealand Health Sponsorship Council's Research and Evaluation Unit. Before this, she managed the Research and Evaluation Services team in a major government department – Internal Affairs. Sue also has been the information manager for the Commerce Commission and the research and information manager for the Hillary Commission. Before coming to New Zealand in 1995, she worked on an extensive range of projects as a contract researcher in the public and private sectors in the UK.

Acknowledgements

There are many people I need to thank, people without whom this book would not have appeared.

First and foremost there are my colleagues at the Institute for Social Marketing, who have been invaluable: contributing cases and examples galore, commenting on drafts and putting up with my distracted state over the last few months. A particular mention should go to: Jennifer Dooley, who tamed the case studies; Aileen Paton and Kathryn Angus, who masterminded the assembling of the manuscript; and Sarah Aldred, Neil McLean, Ray Lowry and Gary Noble, who test drove and debugged it.

The many authors of the case studies have also made an enormous contribution; their wisdom and experience is distilled in the many examples of their work. They also provide an invaluable reminder that social marketing is an international phenomenon.

I also need to thank all the research funders who have supported the work of the Institute over the last two decades. It is they who have enabled us to learn. Most especially, I want to thank Jean King at Cancer Research UK; without her support and encouragement, much of the work we have done in tobacco control would not have happened.

Intellectually I owe much to Douglas Leathar, who founded the original research unit back in 1980 from which the Institute for Social Marketing grew; he employed, enthused and trained me. Three other senior colleagues should also be recognized: Michael Baker, Head of Department for my first 10 years in academia, who had that rare management gift – the ability to let people get on with their jobs; Michael Thomas, who took over as Head of Department and gave me a crucial first taste of critical marketing; and James Fleck, Dean of the Open University Business School, who helped me see that real learning comes neither from the teacher or the student, but both.

Finally, I want to mention a dearly missed friend and colleague, Lynn MacFadyen. She embodied James' insight: although I was ostensibly in charge throughout our working relationship – first as her undergraduate supervisor, then her Ph.D. supervisor and lastly as her line manager – in practice it was always a partnership. Lynn's work lives on in the book, not just in specific chapters (the discussion of ethics in Chapter 10, for instance, leans heavily on a paper Lynn and I wrote together), but on every page. Whenever I switched on the laptop and set to typing I could hear her questioning and challenging me. Thanks Lynn.

Thanks everyone.

CHAPTER 1

If it Works for Tesco …

■ The power of marketing

Think for a moment about how our everyday lives are dominated by commercial enterprise. We wake in the morning to radio and television programmes interspersed with advertising messages, perform our ablutions courtesy of Procter & Gamble and The Body Shop, breakfast with Kellogg's and Quaker, then dress ourselves with the help of Nike, Topshop and Gap. Before we have even left the house, the commercial sector has not only succeeded in getting us to listen to their messages and use their products – they have turned us into walking adverts.

Such is the power of marketing, a power which is based on a very simple idea: putting the consumer – rather than production – at the heart of the business process. Whilst Henry Ford focused on selling what he could produce, offering his customer little choice but cheapness – 'any colour that he wants so long as it is black' – modern marketers invert this rubric and produce what they can sell. This deceptively simple change has revolutionized commerce over the last 50 years, making Nike and Coca-Cola the behemoths that they are. Exxon Mobil, which became the world's biggest corporation in August 2006, has a turnover which exceeds the GNP of Sweden.

This state of affairs might alarm you. It certainly raises some challenging questions about the extent of consumption in a finite world, and the power and accountability of corporations. This book, however, takes a more optimistic slant. What commercial marketers are demonstrating is an enviable capacity to influence behaviour. They are past masters at getting us to do things – buy their products, visit their shops, attend to their messages, *deliver* their messages, buy their products again. And, crucially – for the most part at least – we cooperate voluntarily. Over a century ago, General William Booth asked, 'Why should the devil have all the best tunes?' I am not sure about his demonic metaphor, but the idea of learning from success is clearly a good one.

Moving out of the marketplace

This capacity to bring about voluntary behaviour change is far too valuable to be limited to the marketplace. The smooth running of any democratic society depends on people living their lives in a way that serves both individual and collective needs. The criminal justice system, international diplomacy, the democratic process itself all depend on voluntary, cooperative behaviour. This book shows how marketing thinking can help in all these spheres: not commercial marketing, which as we have just noted has such a dramatic impact on our consumption behaviour, but a variant on the theme called 'social marketing', which uses similar techniques to influence our social and health behaviour.

Case Study 1 on p. 229, for example, describes how marketing ideas were used to help think through issues of crime and punishment. The specific problem that needed to be addressed was burgeoning prison numbers: the UK has a particular penchant for incarcerating criminals; in western

Europe, only Portugal locks up more people per head of population. Yet prison is remarkably ineffective: 59% of prisoners discharged from prison in 1999 were reconvicted within two years of release (Home Office, 2003). The challenge then, was to find ways of reducing incarceration. The case shows how the marketing idea of segmentation (Chapter 4) was used to identify all the groups who make and influence the decision to impose custodial sentences – from judges to the general public. Then competitive analysis (Chapter 8) helped examine the attractiveness of alternative products to imprisonment, such as restorative justice, and how this attractiveness could be increased.

Furthermore, developments in public health show that social marketing is not just valuable – it is a matter of life and death. We are now entering an era where chronic, lifestyle-related illnesses are a much greater risk to life and limb than the more familiar communicable killers of yesteryear. Over a decade ago, a landmark paper in the *Journal of the American Medical Association* (McGinnis and Foege, 1993) concluded that more than half of premature deaths were, at that time, attributable to lifestyle diseases such as smoking-related cancer and alcohol-driven cirrhosis. Since then, the problems of obesity have become much more apparent, with a combination of poor diet and inactivity bringing an explosion in Type 2 diabetes, high blood pressure and heart disease. Experts (Olshansky *et al.*, 2005) are now raising the real possibility that life expectancy in the USA might actually start to dip as a result – the first such fall since the Wild West was colonized and towns stopped putting up readjusted population figures on a daily basis.

In this climate, insights into how behaviour can be influenced are at a premium: our health and longevity depend on them.

The evidence base

There is also hard evidence that marketing works. Starting first with the commercial sector, it has now been established, for example, that alcohol, tobacco and food marketing all have a significant impact on our drinking (Hastings *et al.*, 2005), smoking (Lovato *et al.*, 2003) and eating behaviour (Hastings *et al.*, 2003; McGinnis *et al.*, 2006). And remember that these are not just consumer behaviours, but important *health* behaviours. Tobacco use is the single biggest threat to public health: as Exercise 1.1 at the end of this chapter states, by 2030 up to 10 million people are likely to be killed by tobacco every year unless we can encourage significant numbers of smokers to quit or youngsters not to start.

Social marketing can both imitate this success and mitigate the harm it sometimes causes. Thus, a recent systematic review of social marketing initiatives designed to improve nutrition showed that, out of 25 interventions, no fewer than 21 had a significant effect on at least one dietary behaviour (McDermott *et al.*, 2005). Similar reviews have now been commissioned by the UK Government and shown that social marketing ideas and techniques can successfully shift exercise, drinking, smoking and drug use behaviour (Gordon *et al.*, 2006). And the potential is even more extensive. We have already noted its use to address criminal justice

Table 1.1 Social marketing cases

Number	Topic	Author(s)	Country
1	Reducing prison numbers	Stead *et al.*	UK
2	Oral and bowel cancer prevention	Eadie and Cohen	Scotland
3	Safe driving	Stead and Eadie	Scotland
4	Junk food advertising	McDermott *et al.*	International
5	Sugar-free medicines	Lowry	England
6	Smoking in pregnancy	Lowry	England
7	Physical activity	Bryant *et al.*	USA
8	Smoking cessation in deprived groups	Milne *et al.*	New Zealand
9	Social enterprise	McLean	Scotland
10	GPs and smoking cessation	Lagarde *et al.*	Canada
11	The challenge of HIV/AIDS	Deshpande	India
12	Racism	Madill and Abele	Canada
13	Doping in sport	O'Reilly and Madill	Canada
14	Suicide and domestic violence	Previte	Australia
15	Diabetes	Jones and Hall	Australia
16	Blinding trachoma	MacArthur and Tharaney	Tanzania
17	Mental health	Donovan *et al.*	Australia
18	Obesity	Harker *et al.*	Australia

The full cases are presented in the Case Studies section starting on p. 225.

problems; the Case Studies section (Table 1.1 provides a list of them) also shows how social marketing has been applied to road safety, domestic violence, doping in sport and discrimination, as well as public health.

Social marketing can also help us think incisively about the impact of commercial marketing and what to do about its less desirable effects. As social marketing understands how the engine functions, it can monitor its performance more accurately and, when necessary, judge exactly where to put the spanner in the works. Thus, it recognizes that in dealing with the activities of the tobacco industry, controlling advertising and promotion is only part of the picture; we need to think about all the ways they attract customers, including packaging, new product development, price promotions and distribution. In the last area, for instance, it is interesting to note that, in the UK, despite all the work done to reduce smoking – including an advertising ban, dramatically enlarged health warnings and smoke-free public places – which has reduced prevalence from around 70% in 1960 to less than 30% now, we still have 90 000 outlets selling tobacco.

However, restrictions on business have to be applied with caution. The engine being adjusted drives economic growth and generates wealth. This feeds the taxes that pay for schools, hospitals and social services. Indeed, most of the social marketing initiatives we will discuss in this book would not have happened without an energetic business sector. This is why, as Chapter 8 discusses, social marketing recognizes the value of new research techniques to help build a robust evidence base to guide regulation.

■ The need for clarity

Social marketing is gaining currency. Business schools and universities in the UK, New Zealand, Australia and North America now offer courses in it. The idea that skills learnt to push fast-moving consumer goods or financial services can also be used to address pressing social problems such as HIV/AIDS or drink driving is extremely appealing to students. The related discipline of critical marketing, which challenges the traditional unquestioning approach to the teaching of business, is also growing (see, for example, Saren *et al.*, 2007). Social marketing incorporates such thinking and adds to it: as well as criticisms it offers solutions – by delivering both direct social benefits and a better regulated, and therefore more benign, private sector.

The widening international interest in social marketing is further demonstrated by the case studies listed in Table 1.1, which show that experts around the world are increasingly looking to social marketing to help resolve a range of social problems. This is matched by a burgeoning global appetite for training, seminars and conferences in social marketing.

The case studies also show how the health sector is taking a particular interest in social marketing. In the UK, it has reached the heights of being mentioned in a Government White Paper, which talks of the 'power of social marketing' and 'marketing tools applied to social good' being 'used to build public awareness and change behaviour' (Department of Health, 2004, p. 21). This has led to the formation of the National Social Marketing Centre (NSMC), a collaboration between the Department of Health and the National Consumer Council, which is leading a national review of social marketing and developing the first National Social Marketing Strategy for Health in England. Similarly, the Scottish Executive recently commissioned an investigation into how social marketing can be used to guide health improvement, and the resulting report is about to be published (Stead *et al.*, in press). Australia, New Zealand, Canada and the USA all have social marketing facilities embedded high within their health services, or are in the process of acquiring them.

Commercial agencies and consultancies are also springing up claiming social marketing expertise. Not-for-profit and for-profit organizations are using some or all the sorts of practices discussed in this book to bring about social change. As Chapter 10 discusses, this, at the very least, raises important ethical issues.

Given all this enthusiasm, it behoves us to be clear about what social marketing is.

At first glance the picture is reassuring. As we discuss in Chapter 3, there are lots of well-thought-out definitions which have been produced by very able people in the field (see Box 3.1). However, further investigation uncovers a worrying phenomenon. When you actually look at the published literature and see what is being claimed as social marketing, much of it fails to live up to even the most basic precepts of the discipline. Thus, the authors of the nutrition social marketing review mentioned above

(McDermott *et al.*, 2005) hit two sets of obstacles when they began their task by simply searching for studies that used the label social marketing. First, many of the studies and interventions they retrieved, although labelled as social marketing, were in fact no more than communication campaigns.

At this point, therefore, before we clarify what social marketing *is*, let us be clear about what it *is not*. *Social marketing is not social advertising*. Social marketers may make use of communications – or they may not – depending upon the problem being addressed and, particularly, the needs of the people they are trying to influence. To equate social marketing and social advertising is as misguided as assuming that McDonald's dominance of the fast-food industry has been delivered purely by their communications activities. In reality advertising is a tiny part of their effort, which also comprises getting the right product, in the right place at the right price, as well as addressing the needs of key stakeholders such as suppliers, franchisees and, increasingly, policymakers. Social marketing is equally multifaceted.

The second problem the reviewers had was that they missed out on work that followed the relevant principles, but was not called social marketing. They wisely decided that they 'were interested in whether social marketing *ideas* work rather than whether social marketing *labels* work' (McDermott *et al.*, 2005, p. 549) and approached the task by simply selecting papers that used social marketing ideas, regardless of the nomenclature employed. They adapted these from Andreasen's (2002) criteria, and these help us to get closer to an understanding of what social marketing is. The NSMC has since refined these into its eight social marketing benchmarks (see Box 1.1).

Box 1.1 Key characteristics of social marketing

Good social marketing:

1. Sets behavioural goals.
2. Uses consumer research and pretesting.
3. Makes judicious use of theory.
4. Is insight driven.
5. Applies the principles of segmentation and targeting.
6. Thinks beyond communications.
7. Creates attractive motivational exchanges with the target group.
8. Pays careful attention to the competition faced by the desired behaviour.

Source: based on the NSMC Social Marketing Benchmarks,
http://www.nsms.org.uk

Case Study 18 on p. 343 applies similar thinking to the problem of obesity. The NSMC's benchmarks remind us of our social marketing's origins, as they reprise the key elements of good commercial marketing. We need to start with a clearly defined behaviour and target group: *what* do you want *who* to do? To deliver effectively to their needs we have to understand them and their current behaviour very well – which requires sophisticated research and sound theoretical foundations. This process needs to be insight driven to make our approaches as attractive and motivating as possible, always remembering that marketers, whether commercial or social, deal in voluntary behaviour: we cannot compel people to do business with us. Satisfying people's needs also requires a move beyond the assumption that they are all alike, opening the way for customized approaches to cohesive subgroups or segments of the wider population.

The NSMC's sixth criterion reinforces the point that social marketing is much more than communication. This breadth can also be extended to cover the very important idea that social marketing should not just focus on the individual citizen, but also stakeholders and policymakers. This is crucial because we now understand that human behaviour is strongly influenced by social context. Thus, a young person's inclination to smoke is partly a matter of personal volition, but also a function of his or her local environment (e.g. whether friends smoke and tobacco is readily available in neighbourhood shops) and wider social norms (e.g. whether tobacco advertising or smoking in public places is permitted). Similarly, road accidents are not just a function of driver and pedestrian behaviour, but also car design (manufacturer behaviour) and road infrastructure (Government behaviour).

John Donne was right: no man (or woman for that matter) is an island.

These local and wider environmental pressures are not immutable. Indeed, to a large extent they are themselves the product of human behaviour: policymakers can ban tobacco advertising, shopkeepers can be discouraged from selling to minors. It therefore follows, as Hastings *et al.* (2000) argued, that social marketers have a legitimate role and indeed a moral imperative to address what Laurence Wallack described as 'upstream' behaviours (Wallack *et al.*, 1993).

The NSMC's final criterion is that social marketing takes cognizance of the competition, recognizing that our clients, whether Government Ministers or teenage tearaways, have a choice. They can – and often do – continue with their current behaviour. It is therefore very important to look closely at this 'competition' in order to understand what benefits it is perceived to bring and how our alternative behaviour can be made more attractive. For example, it is clear that for some teenagers smoking is felt to hold a range of benefits – including coolness, weight control and sophistication – which more than outstrip the orthodox downside of lung and heart disease in years to come. The NSMC is reminding us that we need to take this perspective into account if we are to have any hope of winning these young people over.

These current behaviour patterns might be termed *passive competition*.

There is, however, an important additional sense in which social marketers need to address the competition. As well as current behaviours, there are also organizations that are actively pushing in the opposite direction. Thus, in the case of tobacco, one of the reasons so many young people continue to take up smoking is that the tobacco companies use their marketing to encourage them to do so. And, as noted above, we know that their efforts are successful – as are those of the alcohol and fast-food companies. Box 1.2 discusses why this additional dimension to social marketing – sometimes termed critical marketing – is so important.

Box 1.2 Active competition and critical marketing: three reasons why it matters

- Understanding the efforts of Philip Morris or Diageo, and consumer response to them, provides us with invaluable intelligence. As advertising guru David Ogilvy once remarked, ignoring this would be like a general ignoring decodes of enemy signals.
- Commercial activity is a crucial aspect of the environment that we have already accepted is itself an important determinant of behaviour. Ignoring the impact of commercial marketing would open up the discipline to the same criticisms as if it only focused on individual behaviour: ineffectiveness and immorality.
- The success of the tobacco, alcohol and food industries provides a rich seam of evidence that marketing works. If marketing can get us to buy a Ferrari it can also encourage us to drive it safely.

This critical dimension takes us back not just to the origins of social marketing, but to those of the marketing discipline itself. When Wilkie and Moore (2003) did their exhaustive review of marketing thought, they showed that the impact and applicability of marketing beyond the marketplace has been a significant part of academic debate ever since the discipline emerged in the early twentieth century.

Lazer and Kelley's classic definition of social marketing brings these critical and behaviour change threads neatly together:

'Social marketing is concerned with the application of marketing knowledge, concepts and techniques to enhance social as well as economic ends. It is also concerned with analysis of the social consequence of marketing policies, decisions and activities.'

(Lazer and Kelley, 1973, p. ix)

It is the definition we will use throughout the book.

■ Customers, consumers or clients?

Labels matter. Writing about social marketing inevitably raises the issue of what we should call the people we are trying to do business with: the teen smoker we want to quit, the driver we want to slow down, the politician we want to convert to restorative justice. In commercial marketing 'customer' works as a label, in that it gets across the key idea of purchase and money changing hands. But that is not the case in social marketing. Money may be involved, but often is not – and the profit motive is, to all intents and purposes, absent. Indeed, it is worth stressing that social marketing is *not* a form of commercialization.

The word 'consumer', on the other hand, presents its own problems: it suggests the ordinary citizen, the man or woman in the street. But very often in social marketing the behaviour change we seek is that of stakeholders and policymakers. Consumer also implies a passivity that belies the reality of effective social marketing, where both the marketer and the client have to be actively involved in the process. Good health, safer roads and better communities are all joint endeavours.

I have therefore settled on the term client to describe the various sorts of people with whom social marketers attempt to do business. It is not ideal, but it does not have the baggage of the other two options.

■ The book at a glance

The book starts with theoretical issues and moves on to more practical considerations.

In Chapter 2 we examine the *theoretical foundations* of the discipline. There is no single theory of social marketing, but its focus on behaviour change leads us naturally to theories of human behaviour. We will use three of these to help us think through the key social marketing questions:

- How close are our clients to making a particular behaviour change?
- What factors are influencing this positioning?
- How can these – and our clients – be moved in the desired direction?

Theory can help social marketers answer these questions more systematically by building on previous understanding and research. Specifically, we will see how *Stages of Change Theory* can help answer the first question, *Social Cognitive Theory* the second and *Exchange Theory* the third.

Chapter 3 explores three *basic principles* of social marketing thought. The first is that *learning can be transferred* from commercial to the social sphere – and vice versa. The second is that *client orientation* is crucial to success, and we will examine how this builds on Exchange Theory to help us seek out win–wins. The third marketing principle is that *strategic analysis* is the starting point for any social marketing endeavour. Good marketing starts by appraising the situation, defining the problem, assessing the competing forces and only then beginning to deduce possible solutions.

Chapter 4 moves on to practicalities and introduces the *social marketing toolbox*. As we have already mentioned, the challenge social marketers face is to determine *who* we would like to do *what* – in addition we need to know *how* we can best encourage them to do it. The *who* question leads us to 'segmentation and targeting', which helps improve our understanding of our clients and lays the groundwork for helping to meet their needs more effectively. The *what* question makes us think about our *objectives* – a crucial first step in both identifying where we want to get to and, later on, determining whether or not we have succeeded in getting there. Thirdly, we come to the crux of the matter: how do we *devise an offering* that will encourage the target group to engage in an exchange with us. The idea of the marketing mix (also known as the 'four Ps' of product, place, price and promotion) transfers a little uncomfortably from commercial marketing, but does at least provide a useful way of thinking about the problem.

As we have noted, social marketing and social advertising are not synonymous; nonetheless, mass media *communication* is often an important part of social marketing practice. Furthermore, communication theory shows that the way the media works has a lot in common with social marketing. We now know that the audience is very much an active participant in the communications process, and needs to be consulted through careful pretesting research if campaigns are to succeed; effective communication is, like beauty, in the eye of the beholder. Chapter 5 therefore focuses on communications as a way of enhancing our understanding of social marketing as a whole. It also picks up a particularly contentious issue in social marketing communications: the use of fear. Why is it that health and safety advertising will readily use very hard-hitting material that sometimes pushes the limits of public decency, whereas commercial marketers are typically much more circumspect? Furthermore, why do they put so much effort and resource into the development of evocative brands, and does this hold lessons for social marketers?

Chapter 6 picks up the idea of *moving upstream* and dealing not just with individual behaviour, but the social and environmental influences on it. Social marketers have to think through who is in the best position to have an effect on a particular social or health problem and focus their behaviour-change efforts on them. The chapter discusses the implications this has for social marketing, and how overlooking this broader picture is not only ineffective but unethical.

Chapter 7 adds the idea of length to this breadth. In this chapter we will examine how recent marketing thought has developed what was originally a focus on transactions into relationship building. The enormous potential this *relational thinking* holds for social marketing is examined using a range of different examples, including smoking cessation, drug misuse and water fluoridation.

Chapter 8 concerns *competition* in social marketing. Competitive analysis is a vital tool in commercial marketing that, perhaps surprisingly, can be equally useful in the social and health arenas. Specifically, it can help us respond more effectively to client needs and gain sustained as well as ad hoc advantage. More directly, competitive analysis can be applied to sectors of commerce whose marketing might undermine or challenge social marketing efforts. Tobacco, alcohol and food marketing can all be seen in this light, and as we have already noted there is now a strong evidence base to support the view that their marketing is having a detrimental effect.

Consumer and stakeholder *research* is a vital guide in any social marketing effort. Chapter 9 examines basic epistemological issues about how it is used in social marketing, emphasizing that it should be seen as a flexible support to decision making – as a navigational aid – rather than a rigid arbiter of success or failure. The chapter goes on to discuss both qualitative and quantitative research methodologies.

Social marketing raises many important *ethical issues*, not least *who* decides *what* behaviours need to be changed. Chapter 10 examines both theoretical and practical ways of addressing these moral dilemmas.

Finally, the Case Studies section presents a series of real social marketing *cases* from around the world. These are referred to throughout the text, but can also act as a quick way of working out how social marketing is used in practice.

■ Who should read this book?

This book is suitable for anyone with an interest in social marketing.

If you already have marketing knowledge then it will help you apply this in a social and health context. It will demonstrate how knowledge about selling baked beans can be applied to road safety, crime prevention or safer sex – and the ways in which it needs to be adapted. It will also address some of the challenging questions about marketing that may have already occurred to you, and have certainly been raised by commentators like Naomi Klein, Joel Bakan and George Monbiot. Should marketers be selling products that kill one in two of their most loyal customers? Should McDonald's bear any responsibility for the obesity epidemic? Is marketing turning us all into over-consuming pollution hazards? Social marketing can both help find the answers and provide solutions.

If you come from a public health, criminological or safety background, and have little knowledge of marketing, it will introduce you to its key principles and give you the chance to apply these ideas in familiar settings. It is not that social marketing is some sort of panacea or revolutionary super-solution, but it can provide genuinely useful insights for us in our attempts to influence human behaviour. It should be seen as complementing traditional approaches in such fields as health promotion, road safety and education – indeed, any spheres where influencing human behaviour can bring beneficial results.

The book will also provide both marketers and non-marketers with an insight into how we can tackle two of the most pressing problems in modern society: individual and corporate behaviour. As noted above, the former underpins most aspects of a modern, sophisticated society, from criminal justice to international relations, and in particular has rushed up the public agenda with the escalation of chronic disease. Corporate behaviour is also attracting notoriety from Enron to *Super Size Me*. This book will show how social marketing can help scrutinize and control the activities of what the World Health Organization dubbed the 'hazard merchants'.

■ Getting your hands dirty

This is not just a book about ideas, it is also about practice – so it is full of examples and exercises. For the most part these are real cases, many taken from our work at the Institute for Social Marketing (http://www.ism.stir.ac.uk). The Institute is a collaboration between the University of Stirling in Scotland and the Open University, and has over 25 years' experience of conducting research in social marketing with clients such as the World Health Organization, the European Union, Scottish and UK Governments, charities like Cancer Research UK and Alzheimer's Scotland, and local health bodies.

In addition, experienced and respected social marketers from North America, Australia, New Zealand and Europe have been kind enough to allow their work to be included in the book, most notably in the Case Studies section. A full list of these experts is provided at the beginning of the book, and I would just like to take this opportunity to offer them my heartfelt thanks.

The intention is that this work will demonstrate how social marketing works in practice, and by extension encourage you to try out social marketing for yourself. In this spirit, and before you go any further, have a look at Exercise 1.1 and jot down your ideas. Hang on to them and then, when you have finished the book, have another go. See if your ideas have changed in any way. Has a better understanding of social marketing introduced any new thinking?

Exercise 1.1

Social marketing and tobacco

The problem
One in two long-term smokers die as a result of their habit. Of these, half will die in middle age. This translates to 6.3 million people in the UK since 1950 (Peto *et al.*, 2005). Or in global terms, given present trends in global tobacco consumption, the projected number of deaths by tobacco will grow to 10 million per year by 2030. If the prevalence remains unchanged and children start smoking at the expected rates, in 2025 there will be almost 1.9 billion smokers consuming more than 9 trillion cigarettes (Guindon and Boisclair, 2003).

The demographics of smoking
The uptake of smoking is a paediatric phenomenon: 90% of smokers start as children. Acquiring the habit demands a degree of perseverance, and the principal reasons both for trying it and sticking at it are to do with personal image: to look older, more sophisticated and cool. A limited repertoire of premium brands provides the cigarette of choice. Adult smoking is quite different. Most (66%) want to give up (Office for National Statistics, 2004), but cannot. The principal driver of

continued consumption is addiction. Nicotine is now known to be as addictive as heroin and cocaine (Royal College of Physicians, 2000). Thus, image takes second place to nicotine delivery.

The other principal social demographic at play in tobacco consumption is social class. The further down the social scale you are, the more likely you are to smoke. Only 14% of those in higher professional occupation households smoke, compared with 32% of those in semi-routine occupation households (Goddard and Green, 2005). Studies of deprived and disadvantaged groups have shown smoking levels among lone parents in receipt of social security benefits in excess of 75% (Marsh and McKay, 1994).

The tobacco industry

Until recently, the UK tobacco industry spent around £100 million a year on advertising and promotion. Tobacco advertising has now been banned, but the rest of their marketing effort remains: product innovation, distribution, packaging and pricing strategies all play a big part in their effort. Research has shown that this both encourages uptake and discourages cessation.

The economics of smoking

Tobacco is a profitable business. Cigarettes cost pennies to make, particularly with modern production methods, and generate long-term profits. The average UK smoker will smoke a pack a day for 25 years and, at today's prices, spend about £36 000 on tobacco. Governments also do well out of tobacco. In the UK, 80% of the cost of a pack of cigarettes is tax; the Revenue netted £8093 million in 2003–4 (excluding VAT) (HM Customs and Excise, 2005).

Increasing tobacco prices through taxation also has public health benefits. There is a direct, inverse correlation between the price of tobacco and the number of smokers. The one exception to this rule is among the poor, who seem immune to price increases and will carry on smoking regardless, cutting down on essentials in the process.

Question

How would a social marketer respond to this problem?

■ References

Andreasen A.R. (2002). Marketing social marketing in the social change marketplace. *Journal of Public Policy and Marketing*, **21**(1): 3–13.

Department of Health, HM Government, UK (2004). *Choosing Health: Making healthier choices easier*. Public Health White Paper, Series No. CM 6374. London: The Stationery Office.

Goddard E. and Green H. (2005). *Smoking and Drinking Among Adults, 2004*. London: Office for National Statistics, December.

Gordon R., McDermott L., Stead M. and Angus K. (2006). The effectiveness of social marketing interventions for health improvement: what's the evidence? *Public Health*, **120**: 1133–1139.

Guindon G.E. and Boisclair D. (2003). *Past, Current and Future Trends in Tobacco Use.* Health, Nutrition and Population (HNP) Discussion Paper: Economics of Tobacco Control Paper No. 6. Washington, DC: The World Bank, March. ISBN: 193212666X.

Hastings G., MacFadyen L. and Anderson S. (2000). Whose behaviour is it anyway? The broader potential of social marketing. *Social Marketing Quarterly,* **VI**(2): 46–58.

Hastings G.B., Stead M., McDermott L., Forsyth A., MacKintosh A.M., Rayner M., Godfrey G., Carahar M. and Angus K. (2003). *Review of Research on the Effects of Food Promotion to Children – Final Report and Appendices.* Prepared for the Food Standards Agency, UK. Published on Food Standards Agency website: http://www.food.gov.uk/healthiereating/advertisingtochildren/promotion/readreview

Hastings G., Anderson S., Cooke E. and Gordon R. (2005). Alcohol marketing and young people's drinking: a review of the research. *Journal of Public Health Policy,* **26**(3): 296–311.

HM Customs and Excise (2005). *Tobacco Factsheet (February 2005).* London: HMCE.

Home Office (2003). *The Prison Population in 2002: A Statistical Review.* London: Research, Development and Statistics Directorate, Home Office.

Lazer W. and Kelley E. (1973). *Social Marketing: Perspectives and Viewpoints.* Homewood, IL: Richard D. Irwin.

Lovato C., Linn G., Stead L.F. and Best A. (2003). Impact of tobacco advertising and promotion on increasing adolescent smoking behaviours. *Cochrane Database of Systematic Reviews,* (4): CD003439.

Marsh A. and McKay S. (1994). *Poor Smokers.* London: Policy Studies Institute.

McDermott L., Stead M. and Hastings G. (2005). What is and what is not social marketing: the challenge of reviewing the evidence. *Journal of Marketing Management,* **21**(5–6): 545–553.

McGinnis J.M. and Foege W.H. (1993). Actual causes of death in the United States. *Journal of the American Medical Association,* **270**(18): 2207–2212.

McGinnis J.M., Gootman J.A. and Kraak V.I. (eds) (2006). *Food Marketing to Children and Youth: Threat or Opportunity?* Committee on Food Marketing and the Diets of Children and Youth; Food and Nutrition Board; Board on Children, Youth, and Families; Institute of Medicine of The National Academies. Washington, DC: The National Academies Press.

Office for National Statistics (2004). *Proportion of Smokers Who Would Like to Give Up Smoking Altogether, By Sex and Number of Cigarettes Smoked Per Day: 1992 to 2003, GHS 2003.* London: ONS.

Olshansky S.J., Passaro D.J., Hershow R.C., Layden J., Carnes B.A., Brody J., Hayflick L., Butler R.N., Allison D.B. and Ludwig D.S. (2005). A potential decline in life expectancy in the United States in the 21st century. *New England Journal of Medicine,* **352**(11): 1138–1145.

Peto R., Lopez A.D., Boreham J. and Thun M. (2005). *Mortality from Smoking in Developed Countries 1950–2000,* 2nd edition. Oxford: Oxford Medical Publications.

Royal College of Physicians (RCP) (2000). *Nicotine Addiction in Britain.* Report of the Tobacco Advisory Group of the Royal College of Physicians. London: Royal College of Physicians.

Saren M., Maclaran P., Goulding C., Shankar A., Elliott R. and Catterall M. (eds) (2007). *Critical Marketing.* Elsevier.

Stead M., McDermott L., Hastings G.B., Lawther S., Angus K. and Lowry R. (in press). *Research to Inform the Development of a Social Marketing Health Improvement Strategy for Scotland.* Report for the Scottish Executive.

Wallack L., Dorfman L., Jernigan D. and Themba M. (1993). *Media Advocacy and Public Health.* Newbury Park, CA: Sage.

Wilkie W.L. and Moore E.S. (2003). Scholarly research in marketing: exploring the 'four eras' of thought development. *Journal of Public Policy and Marketing,* **22**(2): 116–146.

CHAPTER 2

Making Use
of Theory

■ Overview

Theory is just the distillation of previous work in a particular field; it enables us to learn from experience. This chapter discusses how it can be used to support and improve social marketing. It starts by discussing why theory is needed, and showing that our focus on lifestyles and behaviour makes theories of behaviour change particularly relevant. It also discusses the limitations of theory. It then introduces three examples – Stages of Change Theory, Social Cognitive Theory and Exchange Theory – and shows how these can help social marketers think through the process of behaviour change.

This is not to suggest that these theories are the only ones social marketers should use; the chapter will show how many other theories of behaviour change can and have been used by social marketers. It just enables us to get to know the principles underlying specific theories and see how helpful they can be. The chapter concludes by going beyond principles and providing an opportunity to put the three theories to work on a tangible case.

Thus, the aim of this chapter is not to advocate for particular theories, but to make the more general point that, for social marketers, theory is a valuable tool which is easy to understand and straightforward to use.

Learning objectives

After working through this chapter you will:

- Be able to explain why theory is important in social marketing.
- Be familiar with three theories of behaviour change – Stages of Change Theory, Social Cognitive Theory and Exchange Theory – whilst recognizing that there are many other useful ones as well.
- Understand how these theories can help social marketers answer three key questions: where their clients are in relation to a particular behaviour, what factors influence this positioning and how it might be changed.
- Be able to apply the theories.

During this chapter you might find it useful to cross-refer to the discussions of:
- Consumer orientation and flexibility in Chapter 3
- Upstream social marketing in Chapter 6
- The limitations of research in Chapter 9
- The Theory of Planned Behaviour in Case Study 3.

LINKS TO OTHER CHAPTERS

■ Introduction: why we need theory

The word theory strikes dread into many a heart. It speaks of complex flow charts, polysyllables and abstraction. Memories return of lectures from obviously very clever but equally obtuse professors, or textbooks that lose all connection with the real world after the first couple of pages. But it need not be so. As Kurt Lewin (1951, p. 169) pointed out, 'there is nothing so practical as a good theory'. So let me start by offering three reassuring observations.

First, theory is simply a way of learning from other people's work. It is organized plagiarism, but without the copyright infringement. Newton famously remarked that he had achieved so much, not on his own, but by 'standing on the shoulders of giants', a reference to all the hard work done by fellow scientists that formed the basis for his ideas about gravity. Theory enables us to follow suit and codify past endeavours so that we too can build on solid foundations. More prosaically, it also helps us avoid the duplication of error and the reinvention of solutions.

Second, theories aim to simplify things. They model what are typically much more complex phenomena in the real world, and thereby help us to get a grip on them.

The third reassuring comment is that there is no theory of social marketing. No new labels or charts to master, no unfamiliar terminology to grapple with, no dubious claims that this is the ultimate theory.

But, make no mistake, theory is very important to social marketers. They do want to learn from history; it is just that they approach the problem like a magpie rather than a scientist and seek out existing theories that they can press into service. They also adopt a pragmatic perspective, with a keen eye for what works rather than the all-encompassing and unalloyed – but inevitably illusive – perfect theory.

As social marketing is essentially about behaviour change, the obvious place to look is at theories of human behaviour. Box 2.1 shows how an intervention on youth drugs prevention melded one of the theories we will discuss below – Social Cognitive Theory – with social marketing principles.

Box 2.1 Theory in social marketing

NE Choices used a social influences model, backed by social marketing. The former is underpinned by Social Cognitive Theory, which assumes that drug use behaviour is reciprocally determined by personal and environmental factors. As other similar programmes have done, NE Choices sought to promote drug resistance skills, and to provide participants with opportunities to rehearse social strategies and skills to deal with drug use.

Social marketing emphasizes the importance of consumer orientation, beneficial exchanges between intervention planners, target groups and other stakeholders, and continuous and strategic formative and process research, audience segmentation and targeting.

Source: Hastings *et al.* (2002)

■ The limitations of theory

Social marketers, then, respect theory – but they also recognize its limitations. Human behaviour is the most complex phenomenon we could possibly try to understand. This means that, on the one hand, we need all the theories and models we can get to help us make sense of it. On the other, we have to recognize that all these theories and models will, inevitably, be gross oversimplifications that will ultimately be found wanting if we set too much store by them. A mathematician friend pointed out that if she were to try to model a cow she would start by assuming it to be spherical; the variability and complexity of a real cow shape is just too much to handle. Her ungulate model might well have been of some help to animal husbandry, but it would fall a long way short of enabling a Martian to recognize a Friesian cow.

The continuing controversy about one of the theories we will discuss below – Stages of Change – is a case in point. This currently drives the UK's smoking cessation services, but has been applied too inflexibly and been assumed to reflect reality too well. The complexity and imponderability of human behaviour simply defies such oversimplification and rigidity.

Having argued that human behaviour is impossibly complex, however, we also need to recognize that we all spend our lives successfully engaged in responding to and *influencing* it. Every day we get our children, siblings, work colleagues and complete strangers to do things, and they do the same to us. I well remember my eight-year-old son's ability to get me to take him swimming when he wanted, a combination of diplomacy, threat and bribery that would have made the United Nations envious.

As we noted in the introduction, businesses from the corner shop to the corporation do the same thing, day in and day out. My local Indian restaurateur does a fantastic job of influencing my behaviour: he gets me to visit his restaurant, bring friends and colleagues along, order take-aways and recommend him to others. And I do all this willingly, with pleasure and indeed am happy to pay for the privilege. But I would be astonished if Jasbir has ever even looked at any theory of behaviour change.

So whilst people are undoubtedly complex, influencing them does not have to be rocket science – however much experts might wish it were. Ultimately, social marketers are interested in people – in understanding and responding to their needs. Theories are just one way of helping us think about them, but that is all they are. They can inform our decision making – about the plans we devise and the activities we engage in – but so will much else. The rest of this book talks about ideas, tools and research methods that can play an equally important role in guiding our thinking. We must also remember Jasbir and make good use of our experience and common sense.

So yes, social marketing advocates the judicious use of theory, but also guards against over-reliance and rigidity – just as one might accept that a knowledge of psychology might help you to understand the opposite sex a bit better, but recognize that it is a bad idea to take the textbook along on your first date.

■ Three to get you started

In essence, a social marketer's focus on behaviour change begs three questions:

1. Where people are in relation to a particular behaviour.
2. What factors cause this positioning.
3. How they can be moved in the desired direction.

Theory can help social marketers answer these questions more systematically. Specifically, Stages of Change or the Transtheoretical Model informs the first question, Social Cognitive Theory the second and Exchange Theory the third. Each will be discussed in turn.

Note that this is not to suggest that these are the only theories that social marketers should use. There are also many other useful theories of behaviour change. Case Study 3 on p. 245, for instance, shows how the Theory of Planned Behaviour was used very successfully to guide the development of a Scottish anti-speeding campaign. Similarly, Table 2.1 shows how social marketers attempting to influence nutrition and exercise behaviour have used a wide variety of different theories. The Further Reading section at the end of the book provides a list of articles and books you can consult if you want to find out more about any of the three theories we focus on here, or other key behaviour-change approaches.

Table 2.1 Theoretical approaches used in nutrition and exercise social marketing

Intervention	Description	Theoretical approach
CATCH	Curricular and environmental intervention to reduce fat and sodium in school cafeteria food	Organizational Change Theory and Social Cognitive Theory
Coeur en Santé St-Henri Heart Health Programme	Education, environmental and media nutrition intervention for cardiovascular disease (CVD)	Social Learning and Behaviour Change Theory
EatSmart	Education, physician endorsement and counselling intervention to increase fruit and vegetable consumption, decrease red and processed meat consumption, and replace whole-fat dairy products with low-fat products	Stages of Change Theory
GEMS Pilot Study	Child and adult targeted programmes and events to tackle obesity by promoting healthy eating	Social Cognitive Theory and Family Systems Theory
Go Girls	Interactive educational, behavioural and skills training to increase fruit and vegetable	Social Cognitive Theory

(Continued)

Table 2.1 (Continued)

Intervention	Description	Theoretical approach
	consumption, decrease fat and fast-food intake, decrease television viewing and increase physical activity	
Maryland WIC 5-a-day Promotion Program	Peer-led educational and media intervention to increase fruit and vegetable consumption	Stages of Change
Maryland WIC Food for Life Program	Peer-led educational and media intervention to increase fruit, vegetable and fibre consumption, and decrease fat consumption	Stages of Change and Social Learning Theory
Minnesota Heart Health Program (MHHP)	Community-wide educational and environmental intervention to reduce the risk of cardiovascular disease (CVD) by improving eating, smoking and exercise behaviours	Social Learning Theory and Persuasive Communications Theory
Pathways	Service-, curricula- and family-based programmes to reduce dietary fat intake	Based on elements of Social Learning Theory
Physical Activity and Nutrition Among Adolescents (PACE+)	Interactive computer program- and practitioner-based intervention to encourage healthy nutrition and physical activity behaviours	Stages of Change Social Cognitive Theory and the Relapse Prevention Model
San Diego Family Health Project	Educational programme to reduce cardiovascular risk by improving eating habits	Social Learning Theory and 'principles of self-management'
Social Marketing for Public Health Employees	Communications and promotions, environmental changes, and events to increase fruit and vegetable consumption and physical activity	Stages of Change
TEENS	Curricula and school environment intervention to increase fruit and vegetable consumption and the consumption of lower fat foods	Social Cognitive Theory

This chapter then, is not intended to be exhaustive and discuss every possible behaviour-change theory, it is just illustrative. The aim is simply to demonstrate that theory can be useful.

Stages of Change Theory

Stages of Change Theory is more formally known as the Transtheoretical Model of Behaviour Change. This rather clunky name belies the beautiful simplicity underlying Prochaska and DiClemente's (1983) basic idea: that we do not make and carry through decisions, especially complex behavioural

Current smokers

Q1 During the **past 12 months** have you, **on purpose**, given up smoking for one day or more?
(Please tick one box only)

Yes	❏
No	❏
I'm not sure	❏

Q2 Do you **plan to give up smoking** in the next 30 days?
(Please tick one box only)

Yes	❏
No	❏
I'm not sure	❏

> **If answered 'No' to Q2, ask:**

Q3 Do you think you will **try to give up smoking** in the next 6 months?
(Please tick one box only)

Yes	❏
No	❏
I'm not sure	❏

Past smokers

Q4 **When** did you give up smoking cigarettes?
(Please tick one box only)

(a)	Within the last week	❏
(b)	Within the last month	❏
(c)	Within the last 6 months	❏
(d)	Within the last year	❏
(e)	Within the last 3 years	❏
(f)	Within the last 5 years	❏
(g)	Within the last 10 years	❏
(h)	More than 10 years ago	❏
(i)	I'm not sure	❏

Precontemplation:

'No' to Qs 1, 2 & 3.

Contemplation:

'No' to Q1 & 'Yes' to Q2.
Or
'No' to Q2 & 'Yes' to Q3.

Preparation:

'Yes' to both Qs 1 & 2.

Action:

Abstinent for less than 6 months [Answers 4 (a)–(c)].

Confirmation or Maintenance:

Abstinent for 6 months or more [Answers 4 (d)–(h)].

Figure 2.1
Assessing current and past smokers' stage of change.
Source: Institute for Social Marketing.

ones, in a simple binary fashion. So the smoker does not just wake up one morning and think 'OK, I'll quit', then do so and sit down to breakfast as a non-smoker. It is much more likely he or she will spend a long time considering the possibility of giving up, think about ways of doing it, give quitting a go and then spend weeks or months adjusting to the change. Indeed, the accepted definition of a non-smoker is someone who has been smoke free for at least 12 months.

Prochaska and DiClemente suggest that we move through five stages, from ignorance of or indifference towards the idea of changing through trial to becoming committed to the new behaviour:

● *Precontemplation* – you may be aware of the new behaviour (e.g. quitting smoking or obeying the speed limit), but are not interested in it, at least at this point in your life

- *Contemplation* – you are consciously evaluating the personal relevance of the new behaviour
- *Preparation* – you have decided to act and are trying to put in place measures needed to carry out the new behaviour
- *Action* – you give it a go
- *Confirmation (or maintenance)* – you are committed to the behaviour and have no desire or intention to regress.

The Transtheoretical Model has undergone considerable field testing. Since 1983, Prochaska and his colleagues have validated 12 types of behaviour, including smoking cessation, condom use, quitting cocaine, using sunscreen and weight control (Prochaska and Velicer, 1997).

Alan Andreasen argues that, from a social marketing standpoint, three features of this model are significant. First, Prochaska and DiClemente have been able to show that it is relatively straightforward to separate consumers into these five stages by asking them a few simple questions. Figure 2.1 shows a questionnaire based on their work which was used in Scotland to map low-income smokers across the stages, along with definitions of how respondents should be allocated to the various stages.

Second, they found that the appropriate intervention strategy depends on position in the process. For example, it is important to emphasize benefits in the early stages and costs in later stages. Finally, they recognized that a social marketer's goal should not be to propel the consumer to the Confirmation stage in one step, but to move the consumer to the next stage. Only through a series of steps will the consumer reach the social marketer's goal of sustained behaviour change (Andreasen, 1995).

Have a try at Exercise 2.1.

Exercise 2.1

Measuring stage of change

Try the questionnaire in Figure 2.1 out on your colleagues. If you wish, you can adjust it to deal with another behaviour, such as speeding or diet.

Does it work? Are you convinced by the idea that decisions to change these behaviours are indeed multi-stage?

This all seems very plausible and agreeably practical: the social marketing practitioner has a nice simple rubric for enacting behaviour change. At which point we should beware: as we have already noted, nothing is that simple with human behaviour. The UK Smoking Cessation Services (SCS) has adopted Stages of Change with great gusto and applied it much as Andreasen recommends. The result is that precontemplators get ignored and only those in the action stage get referred to the service. This assumes that the model is spot on (and we know no model ever is), that our measurement procedures are perfect (which, as we will discuss in Chapters 8 and 9, they never are) and that the SCS is the only game in town.

Predictably, therefore the model has faced criticism on a number of fronts. First, it has been challenged for assuming people move in a linear fashion through the stages (Davidson, 1992). Although it was initially proposed that people would progress linearly, behaviour change is now recognized as a 'spiral' where the individual may relapse back to a previous stage, but through experiential learning may eventually reach maintenance (Basler, 1995).

Second, the model has been criticized for not considering those who change their behaviour without consciously going through all five predefined stages (Davidson, 1992). This point is refuted by the authors, who suggest that consumers may pass through some stages more rapidly than others (Prochaska *et al.*, 1992). Later versions of the model recognize these dynamics and variations (see Figure 2.2).

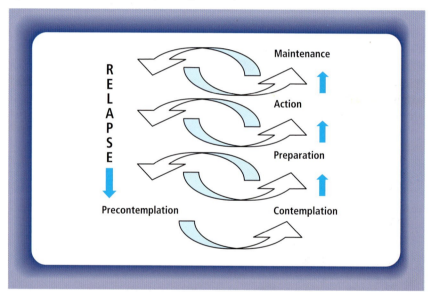

Figure 2.2
A 'spiral' model.
Source: adapted
from Buxton *et al.*
(1996).

These refinements of the model, however, still fall a long way short of providing a complete representation of our behaviour. To muddy the waters further, for instance, complex and challenging behaviours typically take several attempts to change – as the anonymous wit pointed out, 'Giving up smoking is easy – I've done it hundreds of times'. Some of these attempts will, undoubtedly, be spur of the moment. Heavy drinkers will spontaneously forswear booze and dieters cake on a regular basis. Indeed, Robert West (2005) points out that the evidence suggests that *most* smokers kick the habit in this apparently instantaneous manner. This seemingly damning failing – Robert goes on to argue that the model should be laid to rest – does not fatally undermine the theory, however; spur-of-the-moment quitters may well have gone through all the stages of change in their previous attempts.

The theoreticians will go on arguing about the validity of this model. From a social marketer's point of view, however, the discussion becomes increasingly redundant. Theories will never model human behaviour perfectly, but they can help us think about it more systematically. Stages of Change brings a useful and plausible idea to the table: that behaviour change is a process rather than an on/off switch, and it is a good idea for those interested in enacting change to start by finding out how far people have progressed along this process.

The problems that Robert West identified are real enough, but they stem more from how the theory is being applied than flaws in its basic precept. It does not provide a rigid manual on how to proceed, nor should it be used in the inflexible way it is by the SCS. As DiClemente (2005) himself recently put it, it is a mistake to treat 'the model as a religion and not a heuristic to explore the change process'. The model simply provides an intelligent way of thinking about how close our clients are to a particular behaviour.

We need to turn elsewhere to understand why people arrive at a particular stage and what moves them on to the next (Buxton *et al.*, 1996).

Social Cognitive Theory

Social Cognitive Theory postulates that human behaviour is reciprocally determined by internal personal factors (such as knowledge and self-efficacy) and environmental factors (such as levels of deprivation or availability of facilities in the local community) (Bandura, 1986; Maibach and Cotton, 1995). Exercise 2.2 explores this thinking.

Exercise 2.2

External influences on our behaviour

Consider one of your own behaviours – maybe drinking alcohol or driving, for instance. Now try to think what factors influence you other than personal choice.

Taking driving as an example, to what extent does the behaviour of other drivers affect your driving? You might get frustrated or anxious, for example, if others speed. What about your car and its capabilities and design features? Does the rally car steering wheel make you more inclined to race along the road or the much publicized safety cage make you feel inordinately safe – and therefore a tad more reckless? And do the roads affect you? Speed bumps obviously will, but what about an improved road surface or the extra lanes on the newly extended motorway?

And what factors influence you to drive at all? Is it just free will or the absence of public transport, or a desire to make the most of the money you have invested in your new four-wheel drive?

It is readily apparent that we are not quite the free agents we might like to think.

As social marketers, then, our view of health behaviour should take into account the influence not only of the individual, but also their environment. The latter can be further divided into two domains. First, there is the relatively direct influence of friends, family and the local community, what has been termed the 'immediate environment'. Second, there is the more indirect influence of social mores, economic conditions and cultural norms, which we have called the 'wider social context'. Figure 2.3 illustrates how these different influences interact.

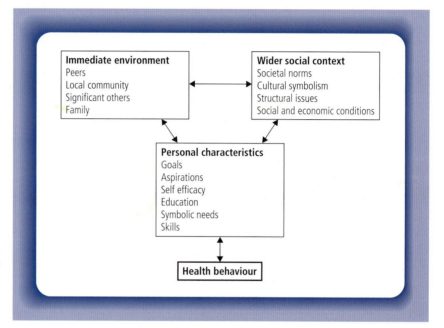

Figure 2.3
The wider determinants of health behaviour.
Source: MacFadyen *et al*. (1998).

Thus, social cognitive theory recognizes the two-way relationship that exists between personal and environmental factors: environments shape people and their behaviours, who in turn shape their environments through their behaviour and expectations (Maibach and Cotton, 1995). It emphasizes the need for social marketers to address both dimensions or risk failure. Simply telling people in poor communities to eat more fruit and vegetables if none are available in local shops is going to do little for public health. Arguably, it is also an unethical case of 'victim blaming' – putting an unfair degree of responsibility for their own predicament on people who are already suffering and disempowered.

This thinking underpins the idea of 'denormalization' – that if we can adjust people's perceptions of how common and normal a particular behaviour is, we will also be able to influence their inclination to engage in this behaviour (Sussman, 1989; Hansen, 1990). For example, young people's perceptions of the prevalence and acceptability of smoking in both their immediate peer and family group, and in society as a whole, are key predictors of their tendency to take up smoking. Accordingly, smoking uptake will be reduced if pro-smoking norms are challenged and anti-smoking norms strengthened. Normative education, or denormalization programmes, therefore, correct 'erroneous perceptions of the prevalence and acceptability of drug and alcohol use and establish conservative group norms … [they] are postulated to operate through lowering expectations about prevalence and acceptability of use and the reduced availability of substances in peer-oriented social settings' (Hansen, 1992, p. 411). Evidence reviews suggest this is a useful insight and that normative education is a valuable ingredient of effective substance use prevention (e.g. MacKinnon *et al.*, 1991; Donaldson *et al.*, 1994; Coggans *et al.*, 2003).

Social Cognitive Theory has been subject to criticisms. It assumes that knowledge is a prerequisite to behaviour change – that is, there is a hierarchical system to improving behaviour. However, some people may simply decide to eat healthier because of an increase in the price of high-cholesterol food or because new branded vegetables provide emotional benefits. The model is also criticized for not indicating how to move consumers on to the next stage of behaviour change – Exchange Theory may help here.

Exchange Theory

Exchange Theory has its foundations in psychology and economics (Houston and Gassenheimer, 1987), and assumes that we are need-directed beings with a built-in inclination to try and improve our lot. Richard Layard (2005) takes this thinking way back to the origins of our species, arguing that cooperation and mutually beneficial exchange were key to our success on the African savannah:

> 'If human beings had not been able to cooperate in this way they would probably not have survived the rigours of the savannah – or subsequently of regions much colder. At best our lives would have been, as Thomas Hobbes put it, solitary, poor, nasty, brutish and short. We survived because our genes gave us the ability to cooperate.'
>
> (Layard, 2005, p. 98)

He goes on to point out that 'the result of this cooperation is not a zero sum game; it is a win–win activity' (*ibid.*). Craig Lefebvre (1992), a social marketer of great experience, argues that the discipline can in essence be reduced to a process of seeking win–wins.

In order to increase consumer's readiness to change, therefore, social marketers must provide them with something beneficial in exchange. In this sense, exchange involves the transfer of tangible or intangible items between two or more social actors (Bagozzi, 1979). Kotler (2000) suggests five prerequisites are required for exchange to take place:

1. There are at least two parties.
2. Each party has something that might be of value to the other party.
3. Each party is capable of communication and delivery.
4. Each party is free to accept or reject the offer.
5. Each party believes it is appropriate or desirable to deal with the other party.

Central to these assumptions is the notion that the exchange must be mutually beneficial. The theory postulates that if social marketers can 'demonstrate that the perceived benefits … outweigh the perceived costs of its purchase, voluntary adoption by the consumer is most likely' (Maibach, 1993, p. 211). A tobacco advertiser put the same point more baldly when he pointed out that: 'If a brand of cigarettes does not convey much in the way of image values, there may well be little reason for a young adult smoker to persist with or adopt the brand' (Rothmans UK, cited in Hastings and MacFadyen, 2000, p. 12).

It might seem that exchange is a difficult idea to apply in social marketing, where the benefits clients can derive are often more ambiguous than in commercial marketing. In the latter sphere, goods or services with a tangible purpose are exchanged for money – a prawn sandwich which satisfies our hunger in exchange for an agreed amount of cash, for example – what Bagozzi (1975) calls 'utilitarian exchange'. By contrast, he argues that social marketing usually involves the mutual transfer of psychological, social or other intangible entities – symbolic exchange. So, he goes on to state, whilst 'there is most definitely an [mutually beneficial] exchange in social marketing relationships … the exchange is not the simple quid pro quo notion characteristic of most economic exchanges' (Bagozzi, 1975, p. 38).

This suggests that the job of the social marketer – forever selling unseen benefits such as not getting cancer or avoiding a traffic accident – is particularly challenging. However, further consideration reveals that commercial marketers also spend a great deal of time selling intangibility. They offer us services such as restaurant meals, the enjoyment of which depends on much more than the simple quality of the food or the satisfaction of hunger, insurance from which (for the most part) we hope never to get any tangible return and lifestyle benefits such as weight control. Even with physical products, we happily pay more for branded goods because we trust them, feel more fashionable consuming them or want to be seen to belong to a particular social group. Charles Revson famously argued that, whilst his Revlon factories made cosmetics, the shops sold hope; the tobacco advertiser quoted above is offering the young smoker ephemeral emotional and psychosocial benefits.

It seems then that commercial marketers do not see 'symbolic exchange' as a problem, but very much as an opportunity. Perhaps social marketers should do so too.

There is also plenty of evidence that people respond to incentives to change their behaviour. In their book *Freakonomics*, Levitt and Dubner (2005) show how schoolteachers were motivated to defy years of training and professionalism and cheat in school tests in order to gain financial rewards for good results. In the same book, they point out that inadequate rewards or penalties can actually be counter-productive. They tell the story of a nursery that instituted a system of fines for parents who were late picking up their offspring. The fines were set so low that parents saw it as a cheap form of additional child-minding! Even so, the example demonstrates how susceptible our behaviour is to an incentive; it just adds in a reminder that we need to consult the target group if we want to make it an effective one. (This theme of client orientation will recur many times in the proceeding chapters.)

Two other criticisms have been directed at exchange theory and its applicability to social marketing. The first concerns Kotler's third and fourth prerequisites: social marketers face problems in ensuring that people are capable of communication and delivery, and also have the ability to accept or reject the offer. It assumes a balance of power that is often no more than a chimera; many groups in society lack the knowledge, articulacy and power to ensure that a genuine compromise is reached. For example, those living in disadvantaged communities may not have either the money or the access necessary to eat fresh fruit and vegetables. This re-emphasizes the need to maintain a collective as well as an individual perspective in social marketing, as discussed in the section on Social Cognitive Theory. As noted there, a good social marketer should always be cognizant of both the individual and social determinants of behaviour.

More fundamentally, some commentators have strong reservations about the assumption in Exchange Theory that the social marketer (safety worker/probation officer/health promoter) as well as the target group is getting something out of the behaviour-change process. Buchanan *et al.* (1994) argue, for example, that such an analysis fundamentally undermines the essentially altruistic basis of health promotion. Exercise 2.3 explores their views in more detail. Do you agree with them?

Exercise 2.3

Is exchange unacceptable?

'We have two concerns with importing the notions of exchange and related concepts into the field of health promotion. By promoting an exchange mentality, social marketing concepts propagate radical transformations in: (i) the types of motivations thought to characterize the health promoter's work and (ii) the ways in which health promoters relate to the public. We wish to explore the implications of such a transformation. To anticipate, our concern is that such a transformation will both undermine the health promoter's commitment to the field and lead to a more antagonistic relationship to the public.

In marketing, the nature of the relationship between the two parties is characterized by the strategic pursuit of self-interest. It is an adversarial bargaining relationship. There is mutual antagonism that is captured in the primordial marketing principle: *caveat emptor*. The two parties are drawn together by a cost benefit calculus, and as soon as the costs are perceived to be too high by one or the other, the relationship is terminated.

In contrast, people have traditionally entered the health field out of a sense of caring for others, not to satisfy self-interests. The vast majority of public health personnel still feel that to be a health professional means to have a vocation, a sense of calling. They strive to create a healthy society in which no one will be handicapped from participating due to unnecessary illness and suffering ... The yardstick by which their work is measured is the realization of a collective good that flows from the elimination of disease, pollution, hunger, poverty and oppression.

A shift to the idea that it would be better to think of the purpose of health promotion in terms of exchange would mark a major transformation. If enough people can be talked around into thinking that the reason for doing health promotion is for the gains health promoters get for themselves, we believe the field will be sapped of a major source of strength ... We believe the field is better off now, while health promoters still draw inspiration from role models who give freely of themselves without self-regard. Under the logic of exchange, such people can only be considered "suckers".

Finally, if health promoters conceive of their work in marketing terms, then the ways they think about their relationship to the public will also be transformed. The uneasiness that many people feel about social marketing is that it constantly threatens to collapse into a manipulative relationship.'

Questions

How would you respond to Buchanan, Reddy and Hossain?

- Are the target groups for social marketing inevitably passive?
- Do marketers always seek to manipulate?
- Are all health professionals philanthropists who are answering a vocation?

Source: Buchanan *et al.* (1994), a critical analysis of Hastings and Haywood (1991)

From a social marketing perspective there are a number of major problems with Buchanan *et al.*'s view (Hastings and Haywood, 1994). First, the rejection of exchange seems to suggest that people have nothing of value to offer and health workers can learn nothing from them. But it is only by listening to our clients that we can understand the limitations of our initiatives and the narrowness of our own views. We need their help.

Second, Buchanan *et al.* see exchange as inevitably involving one party trying to get the better of another. They cannot envisage a mutually beneficial system or Lefebvre's 'win–win' (*op. cit.*). For them, marketing exchange is in reality based on 'mutual antagonism' and 'constantly threatens to collapse into a manipulative relationship'. Of course, there is deceit and manipulation in some marketing exchanges, but this is the exception rather than the rule, even in the commercial sector – otherwise there could be no such thing as repeat purchase, brand loyalty or customer satisfaction.

Third, Buchanan *et al.*'s view of the motivations of health professionals being 'altruism, self-sacrifice and concern for the common welfare' carries with it connotations of superiority: 'we know what's best for you and because we are such good people we are prepared to give you the benefit of our wisdom' (*op. cit.*). It is a short step from here to imposing our view on the client and condemning their (almost inevitable) ingratitude.

Relying on altruism is also questionable in a world of targets, account-ability and performance-related pay. The famous comment of Aneurin Bevan, the health minister who established the UK National Health Service (NHS) some 60 years ago, that he only got the agreement of the British Medical Association to join the NHS because he 'stuffed their mouths with gold' certainly paints a different picture.

Summary

Collectively, these three theories provide a theoretical guide for social marketers. Stages of Change aids social marketers in the identification of where consumers are in relation to the desired behaviour change. Social Cognitive Theory allows the social marketer to identify environmental and personal factors that influence behaviour. Exchange Theory deter-mines how to move the consumer to the next stage of behaviour change.

■ From theory to practice

At the beginning of this chapter we noted the adage that 'there is nothing so practical as a good theory', so, in Exercise 2.4, we will now have a go at using the three theories we have explored.

Exercise 2.4

The case of Greenville

Greenville is a town of 100 000 people with awful dental health. Children as young as five years old have significant caries and are in need of fillings. By the age of 10 years, 50% have fillings and many also have had to have teeth extracted. As their teeth are associated with so much pain and discomfort, many of these extractions take place under general anaesthetic with, inevitably, a small risk of serious side-effects – and even death. Widespread dental disease progresses into adulthood and by the age of 40 one-third of the population have lost all their natural teeth, a proportion that rises to two-thirds by the age of 60.

Question

You are a social marketing consultant who has been retained by the local health authority to tackle this problem. What additional information would you seek about the people of Greenville in order to guide your efforts? Jot down your thoughts before continuing.

The theories we have explored suggest three additional types of information would be helpful.

Where are Greenville's people with regard to dental health? (Stages of Change)

The people of Greenville know little about the principles of dental health and do not feel it to be a very important issue. Toothbrushes and toothpaste are familiar items to them but they are considered to be expensive and non-essential. Other oral health products, such as floss and fluoride drops, are unfamiliar to them. Fillings, extractions and false teeth are seen as a normal and acceptable part of everyday life. Indeed, false teeth are felt to have many advantages over natural ones – not least the absence of pain and discomfort. Sugary food is also very popular in Greenville: it provides a cheap and tasty way of getting calories into the diet.

This suggests that they are very early on in the process of improving their own dental health. They are what Prochaska and DiClemente would term precontemplators and this has obvious implications for any direct approaches you might make. It also begs questions about why the people of Greenville are so distant from the ideas of dental health.

Why are they in this position? (Social Cognitive Theory)

The people of Greenville are very poor, and dental health inevitably has a low priority compared with basics such as food, clothing and housing. The local health professionals are concerned about oral hygiene in Greenville, but feel they are fighting a losing battle. Their bosses in the nearby city of Lanchester are more concerned with issues of community safety and crime, which have a greater political priority. The oral hygiene product manufacturers see Greenville as a lost cause, with little demand for their products, so take no interest in it. Their products are not promoted or widely distributed in Greenville. The sugar industry, on the other hand, sees it as a lucrative market opportunity. High-sugar products such as candy, cakes and cookies are relatively cheap, readily available and heavily promoted as nutritious and fun.

This insight forces us to think beyond the individual and recognize the social determinants of health, reinforcing the importance of the broader perspectives encapsulated in the social cognitive school of thought. However, it leaves you wondering about how things might be improved.

How can change be encouraged? (Exchange Theory)

There are some shafts of light. The young people of Greenville put a priority on their appearance, and a good smile, with clean white teeth, is an important part of this. There are also centrally funded welfare schemes that could allow activity at no cost to the people of Greenville or Lanchester. Competition in the oral hygiene market is fierce and new markets are badly needed. At the same time, the sugar industry is coming under increasing scrutiny for its marketing practices.

The mists are now beginning to clear, and a series of mutually beneficial exchanges can be planned with both people and stakeholders alike. Only the sugar industry look like they may remain an obstacle to progress – but any marketer worthy of the name has to learn to best the competition.

■ Conclusion

Theory has a vital role to play in any human endeavour, because it enables us to learn from past experience.

In this chapter you have been introduced to three theories of behaviour change that are of potential value to social marketers:

1. Stages of Change, which shows that decisions about complex behaviour are often protracted, ranging from first beginning to consider the possibility of change through to trying to reinforce permanent change.
2. Social Cognitive Theory, which emphasizes the social as well as the individual causes of behaviour.
3. Exchange Theory, which helps us think about how people can be changed.

This is not – nor is it intended to be – an exhaustive list. It simply illustrates the potential for theory to help, and hopefully in the process has removed some of the negative connotations the word can have.

■ References

Andreasen A. (1995). *Marketing Social Change – Changing Behavior to Promote Health, Social Development, and the Environment*. San Francisco, CA: Jossey-Bass.

Bagozzi R. (1975). Marketing and exchange. *Journal of Marketing*, **39**(October): 32–39.

Bagozzi R.P. (1979). Toward a formal theory of marketing exchanges. In *Conceptual and Theoretical Developments in Marketing* (Ferrell O.C., Brown S.W. and Lamb C.W. Jr, eds), pp. 431–447. Chicago, IL: American Marketing Association.

Bandura A. (1986). *Social Foundations of Thought and Action: A Social Cognitive Approach*. Englewood Cliffs, NJ: Prentice-Hall.

Basler H.D. (1995). Patient education with reference to the process of behavioral change. *Patient Education and Counseling*, **26**: 93–98.

Buchanan D.R., Reddy S. and Hossain H. (1994). Social marketing: a critical appraisal. *Health Promotion International*, **9**(1): 49–57.

Buxton K., Wyse J. and Mercer T. (1996). How applicable is the stages of change model to exercise behaviour? *Health Education Journal*, **55**: 239–257.

Coggans N., Cheyne B. and McKellar S. (2003). *The Life Skills Training Drug Education Programme: A Review of Research*. Edinburgh: Scottish Executive Drug Misuse Research Programme, Effective Interventions Unit.

Davidson R. (1992). Prochaska and DiClemente's model of change: a case study (Editorial). *British Journal of Addiction*, **87**(6): 821–822.

DiClemente C.C. (2005). A premature obituary for the transtheoretical model: a response to West (2005). *Addiction*, **100**(8): 1046–1048.

Donaldson S.I., Graham J.W. and Hansen W.B. (1994). Testing the generalizability of intervening mechanism theories: understanding the effects of adolescent drug use prevention interventions. *Journal of Behavioral Medicine*, **17**(2): 195–216.

Hansen W. (1990). Theory and implementation of the social influence model of primary prevention. In *Prevention Research Findings: 1988, OSAP Prevention Monograph Number 3* (Rey K., Faegre C. and Lowery P., eds). Rockville, MD: OSAP.

Hansen W.B. (1992). School-based substance abuse prevention: a review of the state of the art in curriculum. *Health Education Research*, **7**(3): 403–430.

Hastings G. and Haywood A. (1991). Social marketing and communication in health promotion. *Health Promotion International*, **6**: 135–145.

Hastings G.B. and Haywood A.J. (1994). Social marketing: a critical response. *Health Promotion International*, **9**(1): 59–63.

Hastings G.B., Stead M. and MacKintosh A.M. (2002). Rethinking drugs prevention: radical thoughts from social marketing. *Health Education Journal*, **61**(4): 347–364.

Houston F.S. and Gassenheimer J.B. (1987). Marketing and exchange. *Journal of Marketing*, **51**(October): 3–18.

Kotler P. (2000). *Marketing Management – Analysis, Planning, Implementation and Control*, 10th edition. London: Prentice-Hall International.

Layard P.R.G. (2005). *Happiness: Lessons from a New Science*. London: Allen Lane.

Lefebvre C. (1992). Social marketing and health promotion. In *Health Promotion: Disciplines and Diversity* (Bunton R. and MacDonald G., eds), Chapter 8. London: Routledge.

Levitt S. and Dubner S.J. (2005). *Freakonomics: A Rogue Economist Explores the Hidden Side of Everything*. London: Allen Lane.

Lewin K. (1951). In *Field Theory in Social Science; Selected Theoretical Papers* (Cartwright D., ed.). New York: Harper & Row.

MacFadyen L., Hastings G.B., MacKintosh A.M. and Lowry R.J. (1998). Tobacco marketing and children's smoking: moving the debate beyond advertising and sponsorship. Paper presented at the 27th EMAC Conference, Stockholm, Sweden, 20–23 May 1998. In *Track 3 'Marketing Strategy and Organization': Proceedings, 27th EMAC Conference – Marketing Research and Practice* (Andersson P., ed.), pp. 431–456. Stockholm: European Marketing Academy.

MacKinnon D.P., Johnson C.A., Pentz M., Dwyer J.H. *et al.* (1991). Mediating mechanisms in a school-based drug prevention program: first year effects of the Midwestern Prevention Project. *Health Psychology*, **10**(3): 164–172.

Maibach E. (1993). Social marketing for the environment: using information campaigns to promote environmental awareness and behavior change. *Health Promotion International*, **3**(8): 209–224.

Maibach E.W. and Cotton D. (1995). Moving people to behaviour change: a staged social cognitive approach to message design. In *Designing Health Messages. Approaches From Communication Theory and Public Health Practice* (Maibach E. and Parrott R.L., eds), Chapter 3, pp. 41–64. Newbury Park, CA: Sage.

Prochaska J.O. and DiClemente C.C. (1983). Stages and processes of self-change of smoking: toward an integrative model of change. *Journal of Consulting and Clinical Psychology*, **51**(3): 390–395.

Prochaska J.O. and Velicer W.F. (1997). The transtheoretical model of health behavior change. *American Journal of Health Promotion*, **12**(1): 38–48.

Prochaska J.O., DiClemente C.C. and Norcross J.C. (1992). In search of how people change. *American Psychologist*, **47**: 1102–1114.

Rothmans UK. Young adult smokers. *Smoking Behaviour and Lifestyles 1994–1997*. The Rothmans (UK) Marketing Services, October 1998. Cited in Hastings G.B. and MacFadyen L. (2000). *Keep Smiling: No One's Going to Die. An analysis of internal documents from the tobacco industry's main UK advertising agencies*. The Centre for Tobacco Control Research and the Tobacco Control Resource Centre. London: British Medical Association. ISBN: 0727916009.

Sussman S. (1989). Two social influence perspectives of tobacco use development and prevention. *Health Education Research*, **4**: 213–223.

West R. (2005). Time for a change: putting the Transtheoretical (Stages of Change) Model to rest. *Addiction*, **100**(8): 1036–1039.

CHAPTER 3

Basic Principles

■ Overview

Social marketing adheres to some important principles; this chapter will introduce you to the three most fundamental ones.

The first is already familiar to us: the idea of transferring learning that has developed to influence consumer behaviour in commercial marketing across the profit divide, where it can be used to inform social and health behaviour change. The second concerns perhaps the most quintessential marketing idea: client orientation. Successful behaviour change is built on a thorough and well-grounded understanding of current behaviour and the people engaged in it. Exercise 2.4 in the previous chapter illustrated how attempts to improve Greenville's dental health have to begin with a detailed understanding of the population. The aim of this understanding is to identify that grail of social marketing: the mutually beneficial exchange.

Third, we will look at the vital importance of careful strategic planning. Good marketing starts by appraising the situation, defining the problem, assessing the competing forces and only then beginning to deduce possible solutions.

Learning objectives

After working through this chapter you will:

- Understand that exchange means that both the target population and the social marketer gain something.
- See that this builds mutual respect and ensures a clear focus on the job in hand.
- Recognize that consumer orientation, seeing the world as our clients see it, is the starting point for good social marketing.
- Realize that planning guides strategic as well as tactical decision making, and ensures that our efforts take account of the social context.

During this chapter you might find it useful to cross-refer to the discussions of:

- Exchange in Chapter 2
- Continuity and relationship marketing in Chapters 5, 7 and 9
- Qualitative research methods in Chapters 5 and 9
- Case Studies 1, 11 and 12 also provide helpful background.

LINKS TO OTHER CHAPTERS

■ Learning from commerce

Social marketing has its roots in the commercial sector. More than 50 years ago, an American academic called Wiebe (1951/52) started people thinking in this way when he analysed contemporaneous social advertising campaigns and argued that the best ones were those that mimicked their commercial counterparts. He concluded that it is possible to 'sell brotherhood like you sell soap' (p. 179). In 1971, Kotler and Zaltman used the term 'social marketing' for the first time in their *Journal of Marketing* article 'Social marketing: an approach to planned social change', and defined it as:

> 'The design, implementation, and control of program calculated to influence the acceptability of social ideas and involving considerations of product planning, pricing, communication, distribution and marketing research.'

(p. 5)

Since then, many social marketers have produced their own definitions (see, for example, Box 3.1). Almost all of these make reference to the use of (commercial) marketing principles and techniques. Andreasen (1994) confirmed this emphasis when he began his definition of the discipline with the words: 'the adaptation of commercial marketing technologies to programmes designed to influence the voluntary behavior...' (p. 110).

Social marketing, therefore, is all about technology transfer.

Box 3.1 Social marketing is ...

'...the simultaneous adoption of marketing philosophy and adaptation of marketing techniques to further causes leading to changes in individual behaviours which ultimately, in the view of the campaign's originator, will result in socially beneficial outcomes.'

(Susan Dann)

'...the application of marketing concepts and techniques to exchanges that result in the achievement of socially desirable aims; that is, objectives that benefit society as a whole.'

(Rob Donovan)

'...an attempt to influence consumers for the greater good, and as such, always has an ethical aspect; specifically, social marketing seeks to induce consumer change that is deemed to be inherently good, as opposed to change that is good merely because it increases profits or non-profit earnings.'

(Brian Gibbs)

'...the application of appropriate marketing tools and the systematic analysis, development, implementation, evaluation and integration of a set of comprehensive, scientifically-based, ethically-formulated and user-relevant programme components designed to ultimately influence behaviour change that benefits society.'

(Susan Kirby)

'...a programme planning process which promotes voluntary behaviour change based on building beneficial exchange relationships with a target audience for the benefit of society.'

(Beverly Schwartz)

'...a large-scale programme planning process designed to influence the voluntary behaviour of a specific audience segment to achieve a social rather than a financial objective, and based upon offering benefits the audience wants, reducing barriers the audience faces, and/or using persuasion to influence the segment's intention to act favourably.'

(Bill Smith)

Source: adapted from Albrecht (1996)

Its origins distinguish it from other approaches to behaviour change, such as health education and promotion, which come from the education and public health stables, or community and traffic safety, which also pull in engineering and enforcement ideas. Case Study 12 on p. 302 from Judith Madill and Frances Abele explores these distinctions further.

This cross-fertilization between social and commercial marketing also provides a great strength: the business sector is essentially an enormous and fabulously resourced laboratory for testing out new ways of influencing behaviour, driven by a commercial imperative which makes these experiments both pragmatic and productive.

Furthermore, as we have already noted and will discuss more fully in Chapter 8, commercial marketers are indisputably successful in influencing behaviour. There is now a very well established evidence base to show that alcohol, tobacco and food marketing all have a pronounced effect on us. Indeed, it is this evidence base that has led to such serious curtailments to commercial marketing as the recent comprehensive ban on tobacco advertising introduced in dozens of countries around the world.

However, at this point we are interested not in curtailing business, but learning from it. Exercise 3.1 will help you start thinking this through.

Exercise 3.1

Poacher turned gamekeeper

Choose an established alcohol, tobacco or fast-food marketing company or brand (McDonald's, Bacardi or Marlboro, for example), and analyse how and why they are successful. What principles guide their efforts, what techniques do they use and how do you know they are succeeding? You can do this by examining their websites, stock market statements, observing their visible marketing efforts and monitoring the business pages of the quality press. You might even try speaking to some of their customers.

Now think through what lessons this might bring for a social marketer trying to combat binge drinking, teen smoking or childhood obesity.

Everything that follows in this book is based on this notion of applying marketing learning to social rather than consumer behaviour, so the answer to the exercise is effectively a reprise of all the subsequent chapters. Arguably the most fundamental point to note, though, is that marketing is driven by self-interest. In the final analysis marketers want to survive and flourish at both a personal and organizational level, and the most successful companies meld these two agendas. It is this that gives them their edge, helps them find creative solutions, and disciplines them to define and meet clear objectives.

Consumer orientation, which we will discuss below, only enters the equation because marketers have worked out that everyone else is also driven by self-interest. The best way for me to get what *I* want is to convince you that it, or some configuration of it, or something I am offering in exchange for it, is in *your* best interests. Bagozzi (1975) explained the intellectual principles behind this some 30 years ago.

Social marketers are no different. As we confirmed in Chapter 2, we are not philanthropists. We are not doing what we do because we are inherently good people. We are doing it because it is our job, because it advances our careers, because it makes us feel good. If you have any remaining doubts on this score just consider how competitive social marketers – or, for that matter, health promoters, road safety specialists and criminologists – are in chasing tenders.

Philanthropic delusions also deflect us from our main purpose. Commercial marketers are not interested in satisfying consumer needs for the sake of it; they see this as the means to the end of profitability. By the same token, social marketers are not interested in educating people about health for the sake of it. As Alcalay and Bell (2000, p. 55) argue, the most likely outcome of this is simply better informed self-destruction. What they want to do is improve public health by, say, improving people's eating habits. This might be achieved by increasing public knowledge, enhancing public services such as school dinners or curtailing the promotion of unhealthy options – or a combination of all three. Deciding how to proceed requires strategic analysis, not missionary zeal.

This focus on doing a deal – seeking a win–win – underpins a further characteristic of social marketing: pragmatism. The focus is on getting the job done, rather than doing good. Let me give you an example. A few years ago the Institute for Social Marketing conducted some pretesting research (see Chapter 5) on the in-pack instruction leaflet for the female condom or femidom.

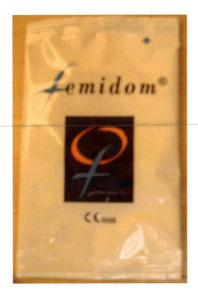

Figure 3.1
The femidom. From
The Female Health
Company.

This is the only barrier contraceptive over which the woman has complete control, as she can fit it inside herself prior to intercourse. It is a product that has particular potential in countries where women are disempowered and feel unable to influence the use of male condoms.

The leaflet required the reader to insert a finger inside herself and feel for the pubic bone, and most women we interviewed had no idea where – or even what – this was. When this finding was reported back to the client, a philanthropic organization made up of commercial marketers (who had decided they wanted to 'put something back') and health promoters (who saw a chance to go to scale), the difference in response was quite striking. The health promoters immediately became concerned about the women's ignorance and wanted to educate them about their bodies. The marketers simply said 'they don't know what the pubic bone is? – let's just call it a lump'. The former wanted to do good; the latter wanted to get the job done.

Finally, on the subject of learning from commerce, Box 3.2 makes the important point that, appropriately enough, the relationship between commercial and social marketing is mutually beneficial: it is not just that we learn from our commercial cousins, they can also learn from us. In particular, the application of marketing ideas such as consumer orientation and relationship building in extreme situations – with addictive or even criminal behaviours, for instance – tests out their robustness and clarifies their characteristics.

Box 3.2 Advancing marketing thought

It would be wrong to leave the impression that social marketing is simply the follower or pupil of commercial marketing. It shares with its progenitor an interest in influencing behaviour, but the behaviours it addresses are very different – and often much more difficult to change. Increasingly, therefore, it has a leadership role to play in testing the limits of marketing thought and the benefits it can bring to society beyond the marketplace.

For instance, when tackling behaviours such as addiction and target groups that are marginalized and disempowered, it can explore whether or not there are behaviours which are simply not susceptible to marketing's notion of voluntarism, or groups who cannot be reached by principles of mutually beneficial exchange or relationship building.

It has been argued, for example, that criminal behaviour takes us into the field of compulsion – punishment is used to force behaviour change – and therefore away from marketing (Rothschild, 1999). However, criminologists are paying increasing attention to the idea of 'restorative justice' (Umbreit *et al.*, 1997; Marshall, 1999), which encourages the offender to take responsibility for their behaviour and face up to the harm they have done to their victims and the community. The aim is to re-engage a typically alienated and marginalized group with society. Arguably, it is also a form of relationship building (see Chapter 7), introducing more strategic thinking than the conventional crime/punishment transaction and therefore falls well within marketing's domain (Hastings *et al.*, 2002).

Similarly, Donovan *et al.* (1999) show how social marketing can work in the traditionally compulsion-oriented field of domestic violence:

> 'The Western Australian "Freedom From Fear" campaign … aims to reduce women (and children's) fear by stimulating perpetrators and potential perpetrators to voluntarily attend counselling (or "batterer") programmes.'

Case Study 1 on p. 229 looks in more detail at how marketing and criminal justice can work together.

■ Client orientation

Arguably the single most important proposition that marketing has brought to the business process in the last 100 years is that of consumer orientation. It is a simple and unobtrusive idea: putting the consumer and the stakeholder – rather than production – at the heart of the business process. As noted in the introductory chapter, this deceptively simple change has revolutionized commerce and helped create the enormous corporations that now dominate business. Indeed, they dominate the globe: half the world's biggest economic entities are corporations rather than countries (Anderson and Cavanagh, 2000). This dominance has come about for many reasons, but at its heart is the idea of putting the customer first.

Consumer orientation works because, paradoxically, listening to someone and taking care to understand his or her point of view makes it easier to influence their behaviour. So, in commercial terms it makes much more sense to do the research and work out what people need and want and then set about producing this, rather than developing a product and then putting resources into trying to push people into buying it. This principle is so fundamental to marketing it has been used to define the discipline as 'producing what you can sell' instead of 'selling what you can produce'.

The lesson for social marketers is clear: we have to put great efforts into understanding and indeed empathizing with our clients' behaviour. We need to get a very clear fix not just on *what* they do but *why* they do it – what motivates and drives them. And in both the commercial and social sectors this is as much about emotion as rationality: our behaviour is not always the perfect product of rational-deductive reasoning. If it were, no one would smoke and drink-driving would be a distant memory. This is why commercial marketers put such an effort into developing evocative brands. It is also why social marketers put a particular premium on ethnographic, qualitative research (see Chapters 5 and 9).

In the early 1990s, the Institute for Social Marketing conducted a survey of 16- to 24-year-olds in Dundee. At the time, HIV/AIDS had emerged as a major threat to public health and sexual transmission by young people was a particular concern – as indeed it still is. The survey therefore concerned sexual habits. The key findings made perplexing reading. Virtually everyone knew that HIV could be passed on during heterosexual encounters; virtually everyone knew this could be prevented by using a condom – *but around one-third were continuing to practise unprotected sex.*

Many similar surveys, before and since, have repeated the findings, which begs the question: why is there such a gap between knowledge and behaviour?

Detailed qualitative research is needed to unpick this riddle, as Box 3.3 notes.

Box 3.3 The value of ethnography

Marketing is the art of ensuring your offering fits with the needs, emotions and lifestyles of your client. Quantitative research can only go so far in providing the insights you need. In addition, ethnographic techniques are needed to dig below the surface of socio-demographic statistics and help explain why people behave as they do. There is a need to explain apparent irrationalities, like taking up smoking despite the threat of lung cancer or risking unprotected sex with a stranger. As the psychologist Dick Eiser said, 'just because people do stupid things, it doesn't mean they are stupid'. Ultimately, the social marketer needs to learn to see things from the perspective of his or her client – then, and only then, will their world make sense.

Ethnographic or qualitative research typically uses smaller samples than its quantitative cousin and in-depth questioning procedures that enable the researcher to probe deeply and explore the reasons behind people's attitudes and behaviour.

Chapter 9 underlines the value of this sort of research and explains how it can be done, but in the meantime the following little exercise might help. First, remind yourself that using condoms involves talking to your partner about sex before engaging in it, and raising issues of previous sexual encounters and the protective steps you did (or did not) take. Then, next time you meet with a friend of the opposite sex, try telling them when you last had sex, whether you used a condom and why you did or did not do so. If your friend has not fled from your presence, ask him or her to do the same.

Recall again that the simple injunction to 'use a condom' (how many adverts and posters have you seen this on in the last decade?) demands exactly this behaviour from all its readers.

Suddenly, the actions of the young Dundonians do not seem so difficult to understand.

Remember, though, that the marketer's interest in understanding the client – or indeed the stakeholder – is not driven by altruism. As noted above, they take an interest because listening to them and taking care to understand their point of view makes it easier to influence their behaviour.

In this way, social marketers borrow the commercial sector's 'consumer-oriented' thinking and argue that attempts to influence health behaviour should also start from an understanding of the people we want to do the changing. The task is to work out why they do what they do at present – their values and motivations – and use these to develop an offering that is equally appealing but with healthier outcomes. Often, the picture is much more complex than mere ignorance of the facts. In public health, for example, most people know that smoking is dangerous, or how their diet could be improved. They continue to behave 'badly' because they see some other benefit in doing so – relaxation perhaps, or a treat. The secret for the social marketer is to devise a way of enabling them to get the same benefit more healthily. In this sense, social marketing has a great deal in common with good, patient-centred health care. The extensive health expertise of doctors and other health professionals is much more effectively deployed when combined with empathy for the patient. Ultimately, better health has to be a joint endeavour.

More prosaically, consumer orientation is the social marketer's means to the all-important end of finding a mutually beneficial exchange.

Commercial marketers have taken this thinking a stage further; they do not just want to define and satisfy our needs once, they want to do it again and again. Their aim is not just to create one-off exchanges, but to build ongoing *relationships* with us. Again, they do not do this out of kindness, they do it because it works. Chapter 7 will explore how this thinking can be applied in health and social behaviour.

Flexible offerings

The idea of mutual benefit, however, raises a thorny issue. Can social marketers really vary their offerings like their commercial counterparts? Can we really produce what will sell, rather than selling a predetermined offering? Exercise 3.2 presents the views of two commentators who think not.

Exercise 3.2

Can you change the product in social marketing?

If a commercial marketer's customers do not like his or her product, it will be changed. Can a social marketer do the same?

Barry Elliott (1995) argues not. He takes the view that the social marketer's product, often conceived 'outside the marketplace', is typically an unalterable given, driving the programme manager largely into the business of selling or advocacy. Keith Tones (1996) has similar concerns, contending that '(i) in general, people do not actually want to be healthy … and (ii) health education cannot abandon its product and diversify its interests just because its main product may not be very popular' (p. 32).

Do you agree with Elliott and Tones? Jot down your thoughts before continuing.

Now consider the following two questions:

1. Does the commercial sector really change its products on a regular basis, even when faced with sustained negative reactions? The tobacco industry provides an example of one that certainly has not. Despite knowing for over 50 years that cigarettes are carcinogenic (Doll and Hill, 1952, 1954), and coming under immense political and social pressure as a result, they have steadfastly stuck to their product. On the other hand, they have tried to respond to market concerns by *adjusting their products* – low-tar cigarettes and filters are two examples – but these are relatively minor alterations on the periphery of the product, rather than the full-scale abandonment of it. Neither, for example, makes their products any safer.

2. Is social marketing capable of similar flexibility? In HIV/AIDS education, for example, it has been widely accepted that messages of *absolute* safety and behaviours, such as celibacy and complete abstinence from injecting drugs, simply will not sell to many potential client. They have been replaced by offerings of *relative* safety – safer sex and safer drug use.

More fundamentally, keep in mind that an absence of flexibility or the chance to compromise strikes at the heart of social marketing. If social marketers cannot change their offerings, how meaningful are the basic marketing concepts of exchange and consumer orientation? Walsh *et al.* (1993, pp. 117–118) encapsulated this point when they concluded their overview of the field with:

> 'Social marketing … challenges health specialists to think in new ways about consumers and product design. Entering the marketing world requires abandoning the expert's mind-set that the product is intrinsically good, so that if it fails to sell, the defect must reside in uninformed or unmotivated consumers who need shrewder instruction or louder exhortation.'

More fundamentally still, if social marketers cannot change their product, how can they move forward? At the end of the day, even the tobacco industry will stop producing cigarettes if no one buys them. Saying that products cannot be changed ignores this ultimate pressure and condemns social marketers to stagnation. They will become like latter-day snake oil sellers, hawking their wares long after everyone has ceased to value them.

But remember, this is a mutual process. The social marketer needs to be flexible in his or her offering, but the other side of the coin is that the client is more open to change because of the compromise. *Indeed, marketing is essentially this process of compromise, of value exchange, that must then take place if progress is to be made.* Figure 3.2 illustrates this process with examples from the commercial, health and safety sectors.

In the commercial example the manufacturers want to sell cars. To succeed they must design and produce cars that meet their consumers' needs. If the consumer wants an environmentally safe car, the manufacturers should try to provide one – within the confines of what is practical and profitable. The result will not be perfect. The manufacturers will expend time, effort and resources in attempting to build a 'green' car, but will probably only produce one that is less environmentally harmful. Nonetheless, the more effort they make towards meeting this consumer need, the more likely they are to sell their cars.

In the health example the social marketers want to sell 'non-smoking'. To do this they too must attempt to satisfy their target group's needs. In the case of young smokers, there may be a need for social status and sophistication, which cigarette smoking is felt to offer. In response, the social marketers can change their messages from ones which, for example, emphasize the carcinogenic properties of tobacco to ones stressing the maturity and strong-mindedness of the non-smoker. In this way, just like the car manufacturer, the social marketers will increase their chances of a sale, of success.

Similarly, in the case of road safety, the social marketers want to eliminate drink-driving. To make progress they too must examine, and respond to, their consumers' needs. For example, research in Australia has shown that young people are very dependent on their cars for mobility. This led road safety advocates to make a compromise, and to change their initial intention of imposing a curfew on young drivers to one of promoting

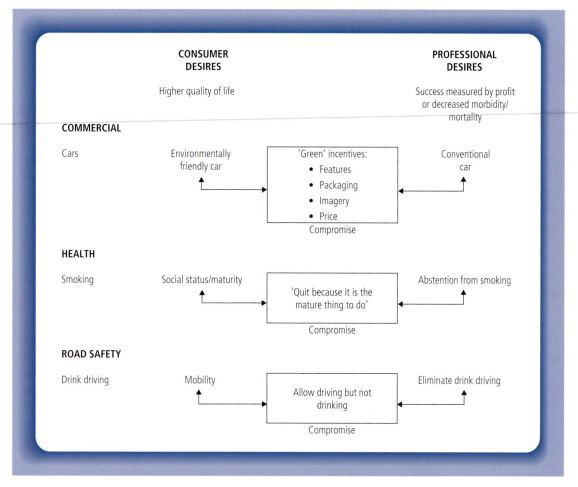

Figure 3.2
The exchange process in marketing.
Source: Hastings and Elliott (1993). Copyright OECD, 1993, reproduced with permission.

zero blood alcohol levels. This movement towards their consumers again increases the chance of success.

Thus, in each case the marketing idea of compromise, of exchanging values, leads to an increased chance of success. Social marketers can and must be able to adjust their products.

■ Strategic planning

Constructing a successful programme to change behaviour is like climbing a Himalayan peak. You need to acquire or devise a map, take careful compass bearings, check your equipment, and ensure you have the skills and resources to reach the top. Marketing therefore puts great emphasis on planning and any marketing enterprise worthy of the name begins with a marketing plan. Figure 3.3 presents a typical schema for one.

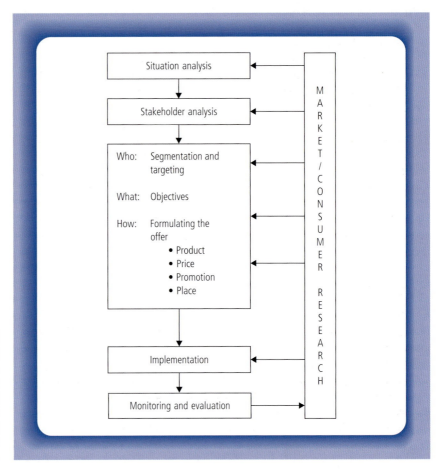

Figure 3.3
A social marketing plan.
Source: adapted from Hastings and Elliott (1993). Copyright OECD, 1993, reproduced with permission.

As can be seen, it comprises a number of standard steps that guide the marketer through accepted best practice from an analysis of the operating environment through to outcome evaluation. Before discussing the detail of these steps, two general points should be noted.

The first reflects what might be called the gestalt of marketing planning. Seen in the whole, the plan becomes more than the sum of its parts. It provides a progressive process of learning about the market and its particular exchanges. This learning takes place within particular initiatives. For example, a systematically produced and carefully researched cycling proficiency initiative for schoolchildren will enable social marketers to improve their understanding of schoolchildren and their desires, and thereby to enhance the initiative.

Second, the learning process also takes place between initiatives. The social marketer will be able to use the lessons learned from one initiative as a basis for future projects. Thus, the process is not just progressive but cyclical, hence the 'return arrow' in Figure 3.3. Furthermore, the development of understanding is not restricted to repeated cycling proficiency initiatives; social marketing efforts in quite different areas, such as pedestrian safety or sexual health, may well provide useful insights. The link between cycling and sex may seem tenuous, but both are social behaviours that are heavily influenced by perceptions and imagery. Both also have to address the competing interests of safety and social acceptability. Condoms and cycling helmets in fact have a lot in common: adolescent behaviour.

In this way, when marketing planning is seen in the whole and as an ongoing process, it can maximize the chance of success both for a particular initiative and, more importantly in the longer term, for health and safety in general. Thus, as well as providing the tactical support through various marketing tools, planning also guides strategic thinking. This idea of progressive and continuous learning is absolutely fundamental to social marketing, and we will return to it when we discuss communications in Chapter 5, relationship marketing in Chapter 7 and research in Chapter 9.

Situation analysis

Strategic vision requires breadth as well as longevity, and the second general lesson we should draw from marketing planning concerns the importance of setting our actions within a broader context. To return to our Himalayan metaphor, before choosing your mountaineers and getting them equipped, you need to check out some bigger issues. Has the mountain been climbed before? What are weather conditions at different times of the year? Do you have to get permission from the necessary authorities to undertake the expedition? Without this advance thinking you are not only less likely to succeed, but you will also put your sponsor's resources and the lives of your team in unnecessary jeopardy – you will be behaving unethically as well as unprofessionally.

The business community has long recognized that economic success is not only dependent on their own 'micro-level' marketing – getting the right product to the right people in the right place at the right price – but also on the macro political and economic environment within which the company operates. Standard marketing texts (e.g. Baker, 2002; Jobber, 2003; Kotler and Armstrong, 2004; Wilson and Gilligan, 2005) typically divide this macro-environment into four forces: political/legal, economic, social and technological (Figure 3.4).

Effective business planning includes careful monitoring of these forces. In many instances – like the weather conditions on our Himalayan peak – they are largely uncontrollable. Technological developments, for example, or social mores cannot typically be manipulated at will. However, companies still need to know about them so that they can respond to the threats

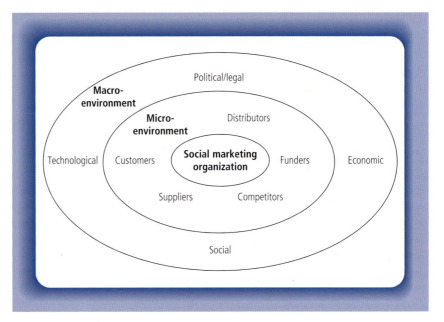

Figure 3.4
The marketing
environment.

and opportunities they present. And these forces can have a fundamental impact on decisions about marketing strategies. For example, in the USA in the early 1970s, tobacco companies were required to fund health promotion messages at a similar level to their own expenditure on television advertising. After just a few years of this, they elected to withdraw from television altogether, transferring their promotional budgets to other, unfettered media (US Department of Health and Human Services, 1989). Similarly, in the UK, television advertising for cigarettes was banned in 1965, but the decade saw a steady increase in advertising spend, reflecting the move to other media (ASH, 2006).

In other instances, however, there is at least the potential for business to exert influence. Thus, the tightening of tobacco control policy in Europe over the last 20 years has greatly influenced the tobacco industry's marketing to both consumers and stakeholders – in the latter case spawning numerous campaigns to stave off legislation in such areas as smoke-free provisions and advertising bans (Hastings and Angus, 2004).

This may include marketing to the final consumer, or it may not. For example, a UK brewer conducting a situation analysis in the late 1980s would have identified a major threat to their business in the form of a Government Monopolies and Mergers Commission undertaking a review of the industry. This ultimately forced brewers to sell off their retail outlets, but careful and sustained marketing to politicians (rather than consumers) mitigated the extent of the changes (Stokes, 1997).

Exactly the same thinking applies in social marketing. Sticking with the same sector, anyone trying to respond intelligently to the UK problem of binge drinking would need to do a careful assessment of licensing laws which have made alcohol more available than at any time since the First World War, taxation policy which has brought prices to their lowest level in 30 years and technologies that have delivered a range of new products on to the market – before considering consumer-directed efforts.

Decisions about how to respond to environmental forces are made by mapping the analysis against the strengths and weaknesses of the marketing organization. This is often referred to as a SWOT analysis – the Strengths and Weaknesses of the organizations are laid alongside the Opportunities and Threats of the environment. In this way, thinking is influenced not just by what is out there, but the capacity of the marketer to respond. To stick with our Himalayan metaphor, the weather conditions, physical environment and sheer scale of the peaks have been tackled in two distinct ways over the years. Some have chosen to invest enormous funds in very large parties of climbers and porters who effectively lay siege to the mountain. They succeed almost by a process of attrition. Others, who lack – or disapprove of using – such extensive resources opt for a much quicker in and out approach with a small, lightly equipped team. It is not that either is intrinsically wrong or right, just that two sets of factors – the external and the internal – need to be taken into account.

In the case of binge drinking, social marketers need to think about their capacity to influence policymakers or the market. This may well be considerable, and an 'upstream' approach can be contemplated. Alternatively, they may conclude that their power in this domain is actually very limited and the only thing they can do is produce downstream efforts targeting teenagers, however challenging this might be in an unsympathetic environment.

Furthermore, many social marketers are faced with a 'done deal'; they respond to a tender to do a specific task, to reduce binge drinking or some other behaviour in a particular population, and the approach is already defined – perhaps specifying a public education campaign or schools-based initiative. They have to take on trust that someone else has done the necessary strategic analysis.

In both instances it still makes sense at least to do some of this thinking themselves: at minimum it will give them a realistic idea of the task they face, as well as potentially useful insights into any shortfalls in their performance. It will also enable them to engage constructively with the funder and help them to think more carefully in the future. Gradually the result will be a very desirable increase in the strategic emphasis of all our work. Exercise 3.3 illustrates the point.

Exercise 3.3

Social marketing and HIV in India

Read Case Study 11 by Sameer Deshpande on p. 297.

You are a social marketing consultant working for a major NGO and have been charged with developing a marketing plan to tackle

HIV/AIDS in India. What will your SWOT (Strengths, Weaknesses, Opportunities and Threats) analysis look like?

If you are daunted by the result (and you should be), just imagine what it would be like trying to tackle the HIV problems of India without these insights.

The rest of the planning process

The planning process continues by assessing what is currently happening in the marketplace (or the micro-environment in Figure 3.4). We need to establish who the key stakeholders are and what they are doing or might do. In many areas of social marketing endeavour, this will uncover competing interests. In public health, for instance, the activities of the tobacco, food and alcohol industries can be of vital importance, and road safety and ecological campaigners need to take cognizance of the car industry's activities. This notion of competitive analysis is discussed in detail in Chapter 8.

Once the macro- and micro-environments have been factored in, social marketing planning focuses down on the nitty-gritty of *who* needs to do *what*, and *how* they can be encouraged to do it. Or more formally: segmentation and targeting, setting objectives and devising an offering, each of which is discussed in the next chapter. The notion of 'positioning' – how their offering sits in consumers' minds and with competing offerings – which helps marketers to think through these decisions is also considered here. Finally, completing the planning picture, the role and form of social marketing research are discussed in Chapter 9.

The crucial thing to remember at this point is that these various steps need to form a cohesive whole that will enhance our learning. Our job as social marketers is not to produce ever smarter tools, but get ever smarter about the market.

■ Conclusion

In this chapter we have considered three big social marketing ideas:

1. Exchange presupposes that there is something in the marketing process for both parties. This is as important in a social as a commercial marketing context, because it encourages both mutual respect between marketer and client and a clear focus on the job in hand. As social marketers, for example, it reminds us that we want to change behaviour, not simply raise awareness – and we will only do the latter if it helps to deliver the former.

2. Building on the notion of exchange and mutual benefit, client orientation puts a premium on understanding the people with whom we

want to do business and genuinely catering for their needs. This in turn develops into the idea of moving beyond ad hoc transactions and the building of long-term relationships.

3. Carrying forward this focus depends on a careful strategic planning, which ensures that lessons can be learnt between as well as within initiatives and that our efforts are lodged intelligently within a wider social context.

■ References

Albrecht T.L. (1996). Defining social marketing: 25 years later. *Social Marketing Quarterly*, **3**(3/4): 21–23.

Alcalay R. and Bell R.A. (2000). *Promoting Nutrition and Physical Activity Through Social Marketing: Current Practices and Recommendations*. Prepared for the Cancer Prevention and Nutrition Section, California Department of Health Services, Sacramento, CA. Davis, CA: Center for Advanced Studies in Nutrition and Social Marketing, University of California, June.

Anderson S. and Cavanagh J. (2000). *Top 200: The Rise of Corporate Global Power*. Washington, DC: Institute for Policy Studies.

Andreasen A.R. (1994). Social marketing: its definition and domain. *Journal of Public Policy and Marketing*, **13**(1): 108–114.

ASH (2006). *Tobacco Advertising and Promotion, Factsheet No: 19*. London: Action on Smoking and Health (ASH), May 2006. Online: http://www.ash.org.uk/html/factsheets/html/fact19.html (accessed 22 August 2006).

Bagozzi R.P. (1975). Marketing as exchange. *Journal of Marketing*, **39**(4): 32–39.

Baker M.J. (2002). *The Marketing Book*, 5th edition. Oxford: Butterworth-Heinemann.

Doll R. and Hill A.B. (1952). A study of the aetiology of carcinoma of the lung. *British Medical Journal*, **2**(4797): 1271–1286.

Doll R. and Hill A.B. (1954). The mortality of doctors in relation to their smoking habits: a preliminary report. *British Medical Journal*, (4877): 1451–1455.

Donovan R.J., Paterson D. and Francas M. (1999). Targeting male perpetrators of intimate partner violence: Western Australian's 'Freedom From Fear' campaign. *Social Marketing Quarterly*, **5**(3): 127–144.

Elliott B.J. (1995). *Marketing's Potential for Traffic Safety: Under or Over Stated?* Presented at the 13th International Conference on Alcohol, Drugs and Traffic Safety (T'95), 13–18 August 1995, Adelaide, Australia. Online at: http://casr.adelaide.edu.au/T95/paper/s19p2.html (accessed 16 August 2006).

Hastings G. and Angus K. (2004). The influence of the tobacco industry on European tobacco-control policy. In *Tobacco or Health in the European Union Past, Present and Future*. The ASPECT Consortium, prepared with financing from the EC Directorate-General for Health and Consumer Protection. Luxembourg: Office for Official Publications of the European Communities. ISBN: 92-894-8219-2.

Hastings G.B. and Elliott B. (1993). Social marketing practice in traffic safety. In *Marketing of Traffic Safety*, Chapter III, pp. 35–53. Paris: OECD.

Hastings G.B., Stead M. and MacFadyen L. (2002). Reducing prison numbers: does marketing hold the key? *Criminal Justice Matters (CJM)*, **49**: 20–21, 43.

Jobber D. (2003). *Principles and Practice of Marketing*, 4th edition. Maidenhead: McGraw-Hill International.

Kotler P. and Armstrong G. (2004). *Principles of Marketing*, 10th edition (international edition). London: Pearson/Prentice-Hall.

Kotler P. and Zaltman G. (1971). Social marketing: an approach to planned social change. *Journal of Marketing*, **35**(3): 3–12.

Marshall T. (1999). *Restorative Justice: An Overview. A report by the Home Office Research Development and Statistics Directorate.* London: Home Office.

Rothschild M. (1999). Carrots, sticks, and promises: a conceptual framework for the management of public health and social issue behaviors. *Journal of Marketing*, **63**(4): 24–37.

Stokes D.R. (ed.) (1997). *Marketing: A Case Study Approach*, 2nd edition. London: Letts Educational.

Tones K. (1996). Models of mass media: hypodermic, aerosol or agent provocateur? *Drugs: Education, Prevention and Policy*, **3**(1): 29–37.

Umbreit M., Coates R. and Roberts A. (1997). Cross-national impact of Restorative Justice through mediation and dialogue. *ICCA Journal of Community Corrections*, **8**(2): 46–50.

US Department of Health and Human Services (1989). Smoking Control Policies. In *Reducing the Health Consequences of Smoking: 25 Years of Progress*, Chapter 7. A report of the Surgeon General. US Department of Health and Human Services, Public Health Service, Centers for Disease Control, Center for Chronic Disease Prevention and Health Promotion, Office on Smoking and Health. DHHS Publication No. (CDC) 89-8411.

Walsh D.C., Rudd R.E., Moeykens B.A. and Moloney T.W. (1993). Social marketing for public health. *Health Affairs*, **12**(2): 104–119.

Wiebe G.D. (1951/52). Merchandising commodities and citizenship in television. *Public Opinion Quarterly*, **15**(Winter): 679–691.

Wilson R.M.S. and Gilligan C. (2005). *Strategic Marketing Management: Planning, Implementation and Control*, 3rd edition. Oxford: Elsevier Butterworth-Heinemann.

CHAPTER 4

Opening the Toolbox

■ Overview

In this chapter we move on from theories and principles to examine practicalities. Keeping in mind that social marketing is about behaviour change, the challenge is to determine *who* we would like to do *what*, and how we can *best encourage them to do it*. The *who* question leads us to 'segmentation and targeting', which helps improve our understanding of our clients and lays the groundwork for helping to meet their needs more effectively. The *what* question makes us think about our objectives – a crucial first step in both identifying where we want to get to and, later on, determining whether or not we have arrived.

Third, we come to the crux of the matter: how do we devise an offering that will encourage the target group to engage in an exchange with us not just once but, anticipating the discussion of relationship marketing in Chapter 7, repeatedly.

Finally, we note that marketers pull this thinking together – and also factor in the competition – with the idea of positioning.

Learning objectives

After working through this chapter you will:

■ Understand why segmentation and targeting are important, and how to do them.

■ Recognize the importance of setting measurable and realistic objectives.

■ Be able to use the social marketing mix as a tool for devising appealing, affordable, available and appreciated offerings.

■ Know about positioning.

During this chapter you might find it useful to cross-refer to the discussions of:
- Stages of Change and Social Cognitive Theory in Chapter 2
- Upstream social marketing in Chapter 6
- Measurement in Chapter 9
- Case Studies 2, 7, 8, 10, 15 and 17.

LINKS TO OTHER CHAPTERS

■ Segmentation and targeting

Why and how

Marketers recognize that we are all unique: we all have different make-ups and experiences, and live in varied circumstances. This means we will also have diverse needs and, because marketing is all about meeting these needs as well as possible, the ideal marketer would offer a bespoke service – a unique offering for each and every one of us. This is clearly impractical in most instances. A few (typically expensive) operators – such as tailors and architects – can offer this level of customization, but in most cases a compromise is necessary. This involves dividing the population into reasonably homogeneous segments and then choosing particular target groups to approach with an offering that better matches their needs than would one designed for the population as a whole.

There are a number of criteria that a commercial marketer can use to segment the population into potential target markets (see Box 4.1). Personal characteristics – typically subdivided into demographic, psychographic and geodemographic variables – present an obvious option. Life stage, personality and where we live can all have a fairly apparent impact on the sort of products and services we consume. For example, a car manufacturer might consider offering people carriers to families, small runabouts to single women and sports cars to testosterone-charged men.

Box 4.1 Three commonly used segmentation criteria

1. *Personal characteristics*: demographic, psychographic and geodemographic variables can all have an important link to behaviour.
2. *Past behaviour*: in commercial terms, for example, previous purchasing can provide important insights; in social marketing proximity to the desired behaviour (perhaps measured using Stages of Change) can be useful.
3. *Benefits sought*: why people do as they do at present – and how these motives vary – can be a sensible way of subdividing the population.

Previous purchase behaviours – usage of a particular product category, loyalty to a brand and related attitudes – also provide a helpful tool for sorting potential customers. Someone who has bought a BMW before is a likely prospect for another one – and a better prospect for a Mercedes than, say, a Ford customer. The benefits different customer groups are seeking can also help with categorization. As we have already alluded to, cars actually offer far more than a means of transportation: to some they represent modern family living, others independence and to a third group machismo.

From a social marketing perspective, all these segmentation approaches offer potential, but they often need extending and developing. Try Exercise 4.1 before proceeding.

Demographic characteristics have obvious implications for health. Gender, for example, provides a sensible starting point for many screening programmes, age and ethnicity are related to specific conditions such as

Exercise 4.1

Dietary segmentation

You have been charged with developing a strategy for improving the dietary health of the Scottish population. As a first step you are considering the task of segmentation. How might the three approaches we have discussed here – personal, behavioural and benefit – help? Can you see ways in which they should be developed or extended for use in a social marketing context?

Alzheimer's disease and sickle cell anaemia, and in Exercise 4.1 schoolchildren have particular needs, as do the elderly and nursing mothers. Health status itself provides a useful extension to the personal characteristics we might consider – you might want to target specific efforts at people who are obese or have Type 2 diabetes.

Psychographic methods also show potential, particularly if we think back to Social Cognitive Theory (Chapter 2), which shows that characteristics such as self-efficacy are an important determinant of behaviour.

In both Chapters 2 and 3 we noted that disadvantage is linked to damaging health behaviours such as smoking and unhealthy diet. Perhaps not surprisingly it is also linked to greater illness and earlier death. In the UK, for example, men in the deprived inner city area of Calton in Glasgow have a life expectancy of just under 54 years – that is 13 years lower than their peers in Baghdad and a full 22 years lower than the UK average (Gillan, 2006). This suggests that degree of disadvantage is a very useful extension to geodemographic segmentation, particularly because it does tend to cluster in well-defined localities such as inner city housing schemes.

Social marketing's focus on behaviour also suggests that *behavioural segmentation* has potential. Furthermore, again thinking back to Chapter 2, it can be linked into Stages of Change Theory. Populations can be segmented according to their proximity to a particular behaviour – with precontemplators being approached differently from contemplators, for instance. In our exercise, this might involve plotting the population in terms of their readiness to change their eating habits.

The final approach to segmentation, the benefit different client groups are seeking, might also help with improving the Scottish diet. Food is much more than fuel and provides many psychosocial benefits, which could generate useful segmentation variables. For example, people who are more inclined than most to use food as a way of giving themselves a treat might need to be approached with different offerings than other segments of the population. Box 4.2 shows how benefit segmentation worked for social marketers who were trying to encourage more active lifestyles.

Box 4.2 The benefits of exercise

A comparative study into younger and older people's perceptions of exercise found that different subgroups perceived different benefits in the product 'physical activity': some, typically younger men, wanted to compete against an opponent, while others aimed to better their own personal targets – to run faster or swim further, for example. A third group was most concerned with body image, and a fourth enjoyed the prospect of meeting new people, maintaining friendships and just 'getting out'.

These benefit segments formed the basis of a targeted strategy to encourage physical activity.

Source: Stead *et al.* (1997)

Choosing the target

Having chosen the segmentation variables and divided the population into groups, the next task is to decide which segments will become targets. Three principles guide this decision. First, the target should be big enough to warrant attention – it should be *viable*. In commercial terms, it must be capable of generating sufficient profit; in a social context, it must have the potential to make an impact on the problem being tackled. This will be determined by the size of the group and their level of need. Picking up the example of disadvantaged groups, these are likely to score highly on this criterion. Second, it must be *accessible*. Usable channels of communication and service delivery must exist. Again, low-income groups are likely to meet this condition – as noted above they are frequently geographically clustered, and if we focused down further to women or teenagers, then community groups and schools offer obvious channels to access them.

Third, the target should be one that the marketer is capable of serving, it should be, at least potentially, *responsive* to their efforts. There is no point in having a big and accessible target if there is nothing to offer them or they are likely to be impervious to any initiatives. Past research and the statistics of inequality suggest that low-income groups are typically unresponsive, at least in the public health arena. Arguably, however, this just points up the crucial need, which we will discuss later on in this chapter, to design an offering that genuinely meets the need of the target group. Certainly, Box 4.3 shows how targeting was successfully used to improve cancer screening rates among disadvantaged groups in the West of Scotland.

After looking at Box 4.3, have a look at the complete WoSCAP case study (Case Study 2 on p. 236) and answer Question 2.

Thinking beyond the consumer

The tendency in discussing segmentation and targeting is to assume we are concerned with grouping our end clients. But in many instances social

---

Box 4.3　Reaching disadvantaged groups with a cancer prevention initiative

There has traditionally been low awareness of both bowel (24%) and mouth (6%) cancer in the West of Scotland, particularly among working-class groups. Knowledge of the signs and symptoms of these cancers is also poor, despite the fact that presenting early to the NHS can greatly improve survival outcomes and quality of life. The West of Scotland Cancer Awareness Project (WoSCAP) aimed to tackle this. The segmentation was geodemographic and the key target working class, over 50-year-olds of both sexes. These were both numerous enough and sufficiently reluctant to present to the NHS to comprise a *viable* target group. *Accessing* them was also straightforward: this group are more likely than most to watch television (ITC (2002) viewing data show that in 2001, C2DEs watched an average of four hours of TV per day compared with three hours among ABC1s). Focusing on the correct age group was done by ensuring that the messages were delivered by people in their fifties. Furthermore, local services could be geared up to ensure that it was easy for people to act on the messages. And they were *responsive*: a high proportion of patients that were aware of the campaigns admitted that seeing them had encouraged them to seek advice more quickly (62% for bowel cancer and 68% for mouth cancer), and those who attended were genuinely symptomatic.

Source: WoSCAP (2005), ITC (2002)

---

marketers should be thinking about stakeholders as well – or even instead. Remember what Social Cognitive Theory tells us about the impact that social context has on people's behaviour and consider that we should therefore always ask ourselves whether there are any stakeholder groups who can have an impact on the relevant parts of this social context. The WoSCAP case, for example, depended for its success not just on effective targeting of individual citizens, but also local service providers.

As we discuss in Chapter 6, Wallack *et al.* (1993) described this as a process of moving 'upstream'. Carol Bryant and colleagues provide a nice illustration of how this type of thinking informed the VERB™ physical activity programme (Case Study 7 on p. 272).

Obstacles to segmentation and targeting

Two potential problems with segmentation and targeting may have already occurred to you.

First, there is an assumption in the process that our potential clients want what we are offering, and we just have to split them into groups who will want it even more. But as Tones pointed out (refer back to Exercise 3.2), this is not always the case in social marketing. Exercise 4.2 describes such a situation, where the key target is actually least likely to take up the offering. Before proceeding, consider how this impacts on our discussion so far.

Exercise 4.2

Reluctance to attend for cervical screening

A public health department wishes to encourage women within a certain age range in the health authority area to attend for cervical screening. There are a number of possible ways in which this population can be segmented, including:

- Personal – for example, socio-demographic (social class, education, income, employment) or psychographic (beliefs re. preventive health, fatalism, attitudes towards health services)
- Behavioural – health behaviour (smokers/non-smokers, etc.), previous usage behaviour (attendance for screening)
- Benefits – health protection, reassurance.

From available secondary research into the characteristics of attenders and non-attenders for cervical and other screening (e.g. Thorogood *et al.*, 1993; Sugg Skinner *et al.*, 1994; Austoker *et al.*, 1997), the public health department could make certain assumptions about the women most likely to respond positively to the programme: they will be ABC1, well educated, in work, have positive beliefs about their ability to protect themselves from cancer, favourable attitudes towards health service, and so on. If the screening programme were to be run as a profit-making service, this would be the segment to target. The screening agency could develop messages consonant with these women's beliefs, deliver them through workplaces at which the women are most likely to be employed, utilize media most likely to be consumed by them, and so forth. However, the health authority's objective is not to run the most profitable screening service, but to make the biggest possible impact on public health by reducing incidence of cervical cancer. To do this, the screening programme needs to reach those groups with the highest risk of cancer – the groups who, the same research shows, are the least likely to attend for screening.

How does this impact on our discussion of segmentation? Specifically:

- How practical is it when our clients do not want our offering?
- How acceptable is it when our offerings are life saving?

Despite initial appearances, this does not undermine the principles of segmentation and targeting – indeed, it presents a nice example of how all the variables we discussed above can be used in concert – but it does suggest that, as well as benefits, social marketers should look to perceived *barriers as a differentiating tool.* The research is not just telling us that there will be problems in reaching our target, but how we can overcome them. As we will discuss below, making our approach more appealing is not just a matter of increasing its perceived benefits, but also of reducing its costs.

The second potential obstacle is philosophical, and focuses on the fact that social marketers are typically addressing more serious issues than people in commerce. Their clients have particularly important needs – for cervical screening services, clean water or needle exchanges. Making segmentation and targeting decisions can be especially fraught as a result. Deciding which group will get life-saving services (and by extension, which will not) is much more contentious than who will get a new brand of chocolate bar.

How would you respond to this concern? Jot down your ideas before you continue; thinking about inequalities might help. You can remain focused on cervical screening or pick another example.

Lefebvre *et al.* (1995) argue that because people vary they will in any case respond differentially to generalized offers (Box 4.4). Segmentation and targeting, they point out, is an inevitable product of human diversity. If our behaviour-change efforts omit to manage it, they will simply fall victim to it.

Box 4.4 The inevitability of segmentation

'This (segmentation and targeting) often raises the concern among some public health professionals that by focusing so narrowly on certain segments of the population, others will be missed. The reality, however, is that – depending on how the health message is executed and distributed – certain groups will always be reached and others will not. The only issue is whether the targeting is done based on research and strategic analysis or by happenstance and default.'

Source: Lefebvre *et al.* (1995, p. 222)

Although they are talking specifically about communications, their view dovetails with the inequalities literature. This shows, as we have already noted, that health behaviours and outcomes are strongly linked to relative wealth. In the UK, for instance, these differentials have emerged and remain despite decades of population-wide health promotion and a universally available free health service. The most highly resourced, educated and motivated sections of society – and the least in need – seem to be best able to avail themselves of standardized provision. Thus, it seems that an egalitarian, level playing field might make the provider feel morally satisfied, but does relatively little for the most in need.

The inequalities experience also suggests that past efforts have, albeit inadvertently, actually been of most benefit to the better off, and thereby *increased* social divisions. Arguably, segmentation and targeting can help us do a bit of systematic and overdue positive discrimination.

■ Setting objectives

Measurability and realism

Once the target(s) has been determined, the next step is to clarify exactly what we would like them to do: to set our objectives. This thinking should, of course, be informed by the strategic planning process, as discussed in Chapter 3.

'Good' objectives are valuable for two reasons (see Box 4.5). First, they ensure that a clear understanding and consensus about the intent of the intervention is developed by all those involved. This includes both people within the organization and outside it. For example, if an advertising agency is being used, well-defined and agreed objectives can ensure that they are absolutely clear about what their advertising has to achieve from the outset. Similarly, good objectives facilitate communication with superiors and controlling bodies. This can be particularly important in social marketing, where funding agencies or politicians may have to be convinced of the value of an intervention.

Second, objectives provide an excellent measurement tool. They give a clear focus to intervention design, and make it possible to monitor progress and ultimately assess effectiveness.

Box 4.5　Good objectives

Clear objectives bring *two benefits*:

- *Improved communications* between the stakeholders in the initiative. Everyone knows what they are trying to do.
- *Enhanced evaluation*: if you know exactly where you are trying to reach, it is much easier to confirm whether or not you have arrived.

To provide these benefits, objectives need *two qualities*:

- *Measurability*: there must be an agreed way of calibrating whether or not they have been achieved – or at least a suitable proxy.
- *Achievability*: you need a realistic hope of success.

It follows, therefore, that good objectives are *measurable*. It may be very desirable, for instance, to run an initiative with the objective of making people happier, as Richard Layard (2005) suggests, but actually calibrating this will present great challenges. Measurability is also a function of resources. As we will discuss in Chapter 9, determining whether a particular programme has brought about a change in a population demands a complex and expensive research design that would probably swamp the budget of most small interventions. This raises the challenging question of whether or not we should set objectives – however desirable – that cannot be measured. One solution is to do so, but only if you can agree reasonable proxy measures to peg progress. Have a try at Exercise 4.3.

Exercise 4.3

Promoting safer sex

You have been awarded a contract to improve the sexual health of Brownton's teenagers. You have six months, a modest budget and a large supply of free condoms. What objectives might you set for the programme?

Direct, attributable measures of changes in the sexual health of Brownton's teen sexual health is going to be beyond your means, so setting this as an objective will not be very helpful. Indeed, measuring any change in the population is going to be very challenging, unless there just happen to be existing surveys going on from which you can benefit. Assuming not, it makes much more sense to set more modest but measurable objectives – such as encouraging a specified minimum proportion of Brownton's teenagers to access the free condoms, and do so in a way that they find empowering and acceptable.

The need for measurability leads naturally to the second key attribute of good objectives: that they are *achievable*. That is, they should be within the capability of the organization and the programme budget. Again, the strategic planning process helps here, especially the process of matching external threats and opportunities with internal strengths and weaknesses. The temptation in social marketing is to be overambitious. This may be because the jobs we are trying to do are so obviously desirable and worthy. Giving people the support they need to quit tobacco or get their baby immunized are quite literally matters of life and death, and the rewards for success are truly mind-blowing. If we really could get all the UK's 12 million smokers to give up overnight, Doll and Peto's work shows we would save around *six million* lives.

However, as we noted in Chapter 2 when discussing theories of human behaviour, changes are usually hard won. This is particularly true of the sort of engrained, lifestyle behaviours we tend to focus on, which often have an element of addiction thrown in for good measure. So it behoves us to cut our cloth accordingly. In time this may also help, as we noted in our discussion of strategic planning, to educate funders and policymakers about the long-term and systemic work that is usually needed to generate real improvements in health status.

Not forgetting the client

Ultimately, objectives, as with all aspects of effective marketing, depend on the client. They have crucial insights into a particular behaviour and can be studied to uncover valuable antecedents. Research published recently in the *Harvard Business Review* shows that consumer satisfaction is an absolutely vital measure of both current and future success in the business sector (Reichheld, 2003). This only emerged through research with customers. Furthermore, to complete the circle, Reichheld also produced a reliable and straightforward way of measuring his construct. His work is discussed in more detail in Chapter 7.

In summary then, setting objectives, like all good marketing, is a combination of strategic thinking and can-do pragmatism driven by sensitivity to client and stakeholder needs.

■ Formulating the offer

In this section we will get down to the nitty-gritty of how a marketer goes about designing and deploying an offering to a particular target segment to meet the agreed objectives. The starting point has to be the client. We need to understand why they are currently behaving as they are (e.g. speeding or binge drinking), the perceived attractiveness of behaving differently (e.g. driving safely or drinking sensibly) and how the latter might be enhanced.

The target themselves will undoubtedly have valuable insights in all these areas. For example, teenagers will be able to shed light on the challenges of practising safer sex and will have ideas about how these might be overcome. They will also be able to tell you how it feels to be faced with the task of discussing safer sex with a potential partner or how empowered they feel by a poster simply telling them to use a condom. However, there are also very real limitations to their insights into their behaviour. A smoker might not really know why they took up smoking, or whether addiction, peer pressure or tobacco advertising are playing a role in reinforcing the habit. This is no surprise – they are smokers not social scientists, and answering such questions requires more complex research procedures.

Similarly, your client group may know the answers to your questions, but be unwilling to divulge them. To take an upstream example, a politician may be reluctant to let on that their disinclination to legislate on smoking in public places is caused by a fear of electoral harm because many of their constituents smoke – that they are, in effect, putting their own interests ahead of the public's health.

So, yes, the offering is designed around the needs of the client, but the task of divining these must be approached in a subtle and sophisticated way. We will return to this topic in Chapter 9 when we talk about research.

The marketing mix

Marketers do not just think about the customer with respect to their core offering; consumer perceptions also influence decisions about what the offer will cost, where it will be made available and how they should talk about it. As Cannon (1992, p. 46) succinctly puts it:

> 'Commercial marketing is essentially about getting the right product, at the right time, in the right place, with the right price and presented in the right way that succeeds in satisfying buyer needs.'

These four variables – Product, Price, Promotion and Place – are, for some, the core tools of marketing that need to be manipulated carefully to produce the most effective 'mix'. This construct, however, has also been criticized in the marketing literature over the last 10 years for being too mechanistic and naive to handle complex marketing situations such as service provision, business-to-business networking – or, indeed, the challenging behaviours typically being addressed by social marketers. We will return to this in our discussion of relationship marketing in Chapter 7.

The criticism of the mix is justified, but does not mean that it should be completely abandoned. As with behavioural theory (Chapter 2), it is just that it needs to be used with care and subtlety. It offers a way of thinking about a behaviour-change challenge and how resources should be allocated to maximize the potential for success. It is not a pastry cutter, forcing every social marketing effort into the shape of the four Ps.

The marketer is seeking the best combination of variables to offer their consumers (Kotler *et al.*, 1999) and this is the one which comes closest to satisfying their needs – this is what Cannon means by the term 'right' in the quote above. Hence it is essential to monitor the marketing mix continually so it can be designed and developed to meet these needs. For example, research may show that a particular population is unaware of the benefits of safer sex, and so the promotional element of the mix may be given greatest emphasis. However, as the campaign proceeds, awareness may become widespread and the main problem change to one of condom availability. This is likely to increase the importance of the product and place elements of the mix.

In essence, therefore, the marketing mix is a multifaceted and flexible means of responding to client needs. Exercise 4.4 gives some illustrations of the marketing mix and gives you a chance to try it out for yourself. Whilst doing this, it will help to take a look at Kiri Milne and colleagues' work at the Health Sponsorship Council in New Zealand, where the marketing mix helped inform their Quit and Win anti-smoking initiative (Case Study 8 on p. 278).

Peattie and Peattie (2003) pick up the challenge of the social marketing mix and warn compellingly against the unthinking transference of the four Ps to a social marketing context. Indeed they argue that progress in social marketing more generally stems from recognising the differences it has from commercial marketing rather than slavishly trying to '*force-fit* ideas and practices' (p. 382).

The acid test for the much poked and prodded marketing mix is whether or not you find it useful. If you do, use it. If not, find another way of thinking

Exercise 4.4

The social marketing mix

Tool	Definition	Examples	Key marketing question
Product	The behavioural offer made to target adopters	Adoption of idea (belief, attitude, value) Adoption of behaviour (one-off, sustained) Distance from current behaviour Non-adoption of future behaviour	How appealing is the offer?
Price	The costs that target adopters have to bear and barriers they have to overcome	Psychological, emotional Cultural, social Behavioural Temporal, practical Physical, financial	How affordable is it?
Place	The channels by which the change is promoted and places in which the change is supported and encouraged	Media channels Distribution channels Interpersonal channels Physical places Non-physical places (e.g. social and cultural climate)	How readily available is it?
Promotion	The means by which the change is promoted to the target	Advertising Public relations Media advocacy Direct mail Interpersonal	How well known and appreciated is it?

Your task: choose a behaviour-change challenge – speeding in your town for instance, or teen antisocial behaviour – and design a marketing mix for it. Consider how useful the various Ps are and how they might vary given another project or the same project at a different stage.

Source: adapted from MacFadyen *et al.* (2002), reproduced with permission from Elsevier

through how you will make your offer as appealing, affordable, available and appreciated as possible. These four 'As' are the important issues to focus on, because they force us to think about what we are doing from the perspective of our clients.

Product

Social marketing products are frequently intangible and complex behaviours, which makes it difficult to formulate simple, meaningful product concepts (MacFadyen *et al.*, 2002). To take an example, 'reducing one's fat intake' involves a change in food choice, menu design, shopping behaviour, food preparation, personal habits, family routines, wider social values and so on. Furthermore, it is a behaviour which needs to be practised not just once but repeated and sustained over a long period of time.

As a first step towards formulating product concepts, social marketers need to identify and clarify their product attributes. In commercial marketing, these range from the tangible (colour, taste, shape, size, packaging, performance) to the intangible (brand, image, status). Social marketing product attributes are largely situated at the intangible end of this continuum. Some potential classifications of product attributes are suggested in Table 4.1.

Table 4.1 Social marketing product attributes	
Trialability	Can the behaviour be tried out beforehand before permanent or full adoption? (e.g. wearing a cycling helmet)
Ease	How easy or difficult is it to adopt the behaviour? (e.g. wearing a seat belt, versus giving up smoking)
Risks	What are the risks of adopting the behaviour?
Image	Is the behaviour attractive or unattractive?
Acceptability	Is the behaviour socially acceptable?
Duration	Is the behaviour to be practised once or repeatedly? Is it to be sustained over the short or long term?
Cost	Does the behaviour have a financial cost or not? (e.g. eating a healthier diet may involve more expense, drinking less alcohol does not)

Source: MacFadyen *et al.* (2002), reproduced with permission from Elsevier.

Analysing product attributes in this way helps social marketers to formulate meaningful and communicable offerings. For example, in addressing teen smoking, research may suggest that image is a key issue, rather than the avoidance of health risks. The social marketer can then put particular emphasis on producing non-smoking options that are cool and trendy – such as self-empowerment and independence – rather than ones that major on the health benefits of quitting.

Kotler provides another way for social marketers to think about their products when he distinguished the *actual* product (the behaviour change), the *core* product (the benefits it brings) and the *augmented* product (tangible objects and services to support the behaviour change). Again, it helps us think coherently about what we are offering from the perspective of the client group. Sandra Jones and Danika Hall provide a neat example of this in Case Study 15 on p. 322 (see Exercise 4.5).

Price

Only a few of social marketing's products have a monetary price, and given all we have said about inequalities this might seem to be a good thing.

Exercise 4.5

Extending our view of the product

Read Case Study 15, 'Be Well, Know Your BGL'.

How are Kotler's three constructs of 'core', 'actual' and 'augmented' product used to analyse the offering being made?

If the poor are in most need of our products, it seems crazy to start charging for them; this will surely be regressive. However, marketers remind us that price and value are closely interrelated: the value of a Rolls Royce is reinforced by its exclusive price tag and, at the other extreme, freebies are often – figuratively as well as literally – taken for granted. Condom social marketing in developing countries provides instructive lessons here. Initial efforts to encourage contraception in India involved shipping out large quantities of free condoms. However, because they were free neither the distributors or the would-be users treated them with much respect. Product ended up mouldering in warehouses, sell-by and storage instructions were not respected, and the products acquired a poor public reputation.

By contrast, it was very apparent that commercial products such as soft drinks were doing much better. They were well distributed (even the poorest village seemed to have a Coke machine), properly stored and readily consumed. Brand value was also very much in evidence. Success was due to commercialization: everyone in the supply chain stood to make money out of effective distribution. Even the final customer gained because offering had added brand value, to which price contributed. The condom social marketers decided to follow suit and charge (a very modest) amount for their products. The result has been a vastly increased condom usage and much wider availability (Dahl *et al.*, 1997; Harvey, 1997).

This does not suggest that we should rush to commercialize all social marketing efforts. But it does warn us to think carefully about what free actually means – and ensure that it does not just result in second-rate offerings.

Price also has a wider meaning in social marketing; there are almost always costs associated with behaviour change. These may be to do with time, embarrassment, effort, inertia, pain and perceived social stigma amongst other variables. Thus, the speeding driver thinks he is going to be late if he obeys the speed limit, the teenager has to overcome embarrassment to acquire a condom. These costs are balanced against the benefits of engaging in the behaviour – and both costs and benefits vary for different behaviours. Exercise 4.6 suggests a systematic way of thinking about these variations.

1. *Low cost and tangible, personal benefits*, e.g. seat-belt wearing. In this case the target perceives clear, direct benefits to themselves, and change is relatively easy (assuming reliable seat-belts are fitted as standard) relative to the four other types of initiative. Communication is likely to be a key element of the social marketing strategy.

Exercise 4.6

Thinking systematically about price

	Tangible	Intangible
Low cost	Personal benefits e.g. wearing seat-belts	Societal benefits e.g. recycling programmes
High cost	Personal benefits e.g. smoking cessation	Societal benefits e.g. avoiding use of cars

Which combination will be the toughest for the social marketer to address? Which the easiest? What are the strategic implications of your answers?

Source: based on Rangan *et al.* (1996)

2. *Low cost and intangible, societal benefits*, e.g. recycling programmes. Here the behavioural change is relatively easy to adopt, but the benefits are not perceived to be as relevant to the individual. Kash Rangan and colleagues argue that convenience is the key to this type of programme, and the ultimate benefit to the recycler and to society should be stressed.
3. *High cost and tangible, personal benefits*, e.g. smoking cessation programmes. In this case there is a very clear personal benefit to adopting the suggested behaviour, but the costs associated with doing so are high. Here the authors advocate the adoption of what they call 'push marketing' approaches: providing support services and augmented products that will reduce the cost.
4. *High cost and intangible, societal benefits*, e.g. avoiding car use. This is the hardest type of behaviour change to induce, as the costs are high and the benefits are hard to personalize and quantify. In this case, it may be necessary to adopt de-marketing approaches, use moral persuasion or social influence. Also, increasing the cost of the current behaviour (e.g. by increasing fuel tax) may help.

Place

Kotler and Zaltman (1971) suggest that place in social marketing covers both distribution and response channels, and 'clear action outlets for those motivated to acquire the product' (p. 9). Thus, where there is a communications element to a social marketing initiative, place applies to the media channels through which messages are to be delivered, but it can also apply to distribution channels where tangible products or services, such as clean needles or smoking cessation groups, are involved.

In both instances place variables such as channel, coverage, cost, timing (Kotler and Roberto, 1989), location, transport (Woodruffe, 1995) and accessibility (Cowell, 1994) are all relevant. For example, an initiative to increase uptake of cervical screening could reduce the costs of attending by manipulating the place variables of distance, time and convenience (offering screening at flexible times and in different locations).

In addition, many social marketing initiatives depend on intermediaries such as health professionals, pharmacists, teachers and community workers to act as distribution channels for media materials or as retailers for a particular behaviour-change product. For example, GPs are often given responsibility for changing smoking and drinking behaviour (Kotler and Roberto, 1989). Where intermediaries are to act primarily as distribution agents for media products, key variables such as accessibility and appropriateness should be considered. When these intermediaries have a more complex role (e.g. youth workers and teachers delivering a sex education curriculum), place variables such as source visibility, credibility, attractiveness and power (Percy, 1983; Hastings and Stead, 1999) should guide the selection of appropriate agents and inform the sort of support and training which is offered to them. For example, the drugs prevention literature has examined the relative merits of teachers, youth workers, police and peers as delivery channels for drugs prevention messages (e.g. Bandy and President, 1983; Shiner and Newburn, 1996).

Social marketers are often dependent on the goodwill and cooperation of intermediaries for access to their end targets. This is particularly the case when dealing with sensitive health issues or with vulnerable groups such as young people, where there is usually a need to communicate not only with young people themselves, but also with key groups such as parents, teachers and politicians. These groups may act as gatekeepers, controlling or influencing the distribution of a message to a target group, or as stakeholders, taking an interest in and scrutinizing the activities of the prevention agency (McGrath, 1995). If an initiative is to be effective, it needs to satisfy the information and other needs of these two groups and to maintain their support.

François Lagarde and colleagues provide a lovely example in Case Study 10 on p. 292 of how physicians were identified as a key channel for smoking cessation in Canada, and social marketing techniques, including a well-thought-through marketing mix, were used to get them involved.

Promotion

The final P is promotion, and this is discussed in the next chapter.

■ Positioning

This chapter has introduced us to the marketing toolbox, but the danger with toolboxes is that they get us too focused on the minutiae and in the process crowd out the big picture – adjusting the carburettor to the exclusion of agreeing the direction of travel. Commercial marketers help to avoid this with the idea of 'positioning' their products. Mullins *et al.* (2004), for example, in their textbook *Marketing Management*, describe how French wine was successfully repositioned in the US market from an elitist option for the *cognoscenti* to something you can quaff at your barbecue. A combination of well-targeted, down-to-earth advertising, accessible point-of-sale material, a pocket guide with supporting website and a helpline all succeeded in achieving their objective of making the product less exclusive and thereby widening appeal.

Positioning is guided by two things: how the consumer sees the product and how it measures up to the competition. In the case of French wine it was seen as high quality, but too exclusive for ordinary occasions. In terms of the competition it was losing out to more mundane alternatives, such as a can of beer; indeed, the effort to reposition it was characterized as 'trying to make Americans as comfortable with fumé blanc as they are with a Bud'.

Social marketers can do likewise. It simply provides a reminder that, in using the tools we have examined in this chapter, we have to retain a strategic view of where we want to be in our client's mind and relative to the competition. Rob Donovan and colleagues give a great illustration of how this can work in Case Study 17 on p. 335. In this instance, the aim was to reposition mental health from its current focus on illness and symptoms to a much more positive one, or as they express it:

> 'To reframe people's perceptions of mental health away from the absence of mental illness, to the belief that people can (and should) act proactively to protect and strengthen their mental health.'

Careful market research was used to understand how people currently framed mental illness and how this related to more positive concepts of mental health.

As Figure 4.1 illustrates, being active, socially engaged and feeling in control of your circumstances were widely accepted prerequisites for good mental health.

Figure 4.1
Karratha kids: young people showing how activity and socializing can bolster mental health.

■ Conclusion

In this chapter we have begun to uncover some of the practicalities of doing social marketing. Specifically, the value and functioning of three key marketing tools have been explored. Segmentation and targeting help us to get a better fix on whose behaviour we want to change and objective setting helps us pin down precisely what we want them to do. Getting them to do it forces us to think about how we will formulate a suitable offer, and make sure that, as far as our chosen target group is concerned, it is appealing, accessible, available and appreciated. This tactical activity is guided by the strategic idea of positioning.

We will continue this practical theme in the next chapter when we discuss the use of communications in social marketing.

■ References

Austoker J., Davey C. and Jansen C. (1997). *Improving the quality of the written information sent to women about cervical screening. NHS Cervical Screening Programme Publication No. 6*. London: NHSCSP Publications.

Bandy P. and President P.A. (1983). Recent literature on drug abuse prevention and mass media: focusing on youth, parents and the elderly. *Journal of Drug Education*, **13**(3): 255–271.

Cannon T. (1992). *Basic Marketing. Principles and Practice*, 3rd edition. London: Cassell.

Cowell D.W. (1994). Marketing of services. In *The Marketing Book* (Baker M., ed.), 3rd edition, Chapter 29. Oxford: Butterworth-Heinemann.

Dahl D.W., Gorn G.J. and Weinberg C.B. (1997). Marketing, safer sex and condom acquisition. In *Social Marketing: Theoretical and Practical Perspectives* (Goldberg M.E., Fishbein M. and Middlestadt S.E., eds), Chapter 11. Mahwah, NJ: Lawrence Erlbaum Associates.

Gillan A. (2006). In Iraq, life expectancy is 67. Minutes from Glasgow city centre, it's 54. *The Guardian*, 21 January.

Harvey P.D. (1997). Advertising affordable contraceptives: the social marketing experience. In *Social Marketing: Theoretical and Practical Perspectives* (Goldberg M.E., Fishbein M. and Middlestadt S.E., eds), Chapter 10. Mahwah, NJ: Lawrence Erlbaum Associates.

Hastings G.B. and Stead M. (1999). *Using the Media in Drugs Prevention*. Drugs Prevention Initiative Green Paper. London: Home Office Central Drugs Prevention Initiative, Paper 19.

ITC (2002). *Developments in the UK Television Market*. London: Independent Television Commission (ITC). Online at: http://www.ofcom.org.uk/static/archive/itc/research/industry_info_march02.pdf

Kotler P. and Roberto E.L. (1989). *Social Marketing: Strategies for Changing Public Behaviour*. New York: The Free Press.

Kotler P. and Zaltman G. (1971). Social marketing: an approach to planned social change. *Journal of Marketing*, **35**(3): 3–12.

Kotler P., Armstrong G., Saunders J. and Wong V. (1999). *Principles of Marketing*, 2nd European edition. Prentice-Hall Europe.

Layard P.R.G. (2005). *Happiness: Lessons from a New Science*. London: Allen Lane.

Lefebvre R.C., Doner L., Johnston C., Loughrey K., Balch G.I. and Sutton S.M. (1995). Use of database marketing and consumer-based health communication in message design: an example from the office of cancer communications' "5 A Day for Better Health" program. In *Designing Health Messages. Approaches From Communication Theory and Public Health Practice* (Maibach E. and Parrott R.L., eds), pp. 217–246. Newbury Park, CA: Sage.

MacFadyen L., Stead M. and Hastings G.B. (2002). Social marketing. In *The Marketing Book* (Baker M.J., ed.), 5th edition, Chapter 27. Oxford: Butterworth-Heinemann.

McGrath J. (1995). The gatekeeping process: the right combinations to unlock the gates. In *Designing Health Messages. Approaches From Communication Theory and Public Health Practice* (Maibach E. and Parrott R.C., eds), Chapter 11. Newbury Park, CA: Sage.

Mullins J.W., Walker O.C., Boyd H.W. and Larreche J.-C. (2004). *Marketing Management: A Strategic Decision-Making Approach*, 5th edition, p. 200. McGraw-Hill.

Percy L. (1983). A review of the effect of specific advertising elements upon overall communication response. In *Current Issues and Research in Advertising*. University of Michigan.

Rangun V.K., Karim S. and Sandberg S.K. (1996). Do better at doing good. *Harvard Business Review*, **74**(3): 42–54.

Reichheld F.F. (2003). The one number you need to grow. *Harvard Business Review*, **81**(12): 46–54.

Shiner M. and Newburn T. (1996). *Young People, Drugs and Peer Education: An Evaluation of the Youth Awareness Programme (YAP)*. London: DPI, Home Office.

Stead M., Wimbush E., Eadie D.R. and Teer P. (1997). A qualitative study of older people's perceptions of ageing and exercise: the implications for health promotion. *Health Education Journal*, **56**(1): 3–16.

Sugg Skinner C., Strecher V.J. and Hospers H. (1994). Physicians' recommendations for mammography: do tailored messages make a difference? *American Journal of Public Health*, **84**(1): 43–49.

Thorogood M., Coulter A., Jones L., Yudkin P., Muir J. and Mant D. (1993). Factors affecting response to an invitation to attend for a health check. *Journal of Epidemiology and Community Health*, **47**(3): 224–228.

Wallack L., Dorfman L., Jernigan D. and Themba M. (1993). *Media Advocacy and Public Health*. Newbury Park, CA: Sage.

Woodruffe H. (1995). *Services Marketing*. London: M&E Pitman.

WoSCAP (2005). *West of Scotland Cancer Awareness Project 2002–2005*. Final Report.

CHAPTER 5

Communication, Emotion and the Limitations of Fear

■ Overview

We have already noted the misguided tendency to equate social marketing with social advertising. As the discussion of the marketing mix in the last chapter underlined, communication is only a small part of the social marketing story. Nonetheless, it merits further investigation because our understanding of how mass communications work has been honed through decades of academic and applied research – and this understanding reinforces some key social marketing points. In particular, it is now clear that the audience is actively involved in the communication process: what we understand from and how we react to a particular message is as much a function of us and our experiences as it is of the characteristics of the message. It is therefore crucial for would-be communicators to use careful audience research to guide the development and monitor the impact of their efforts. Exactly the same is true of behaviour change: both marketer and client are actively involved.

Looking more carefully at communications also underlines the importance of thinking about the emotional as well as the rational. Public health and social change activity often adopts a very positivist perspective, assuming that if we are told that behaviour A has negative consequences we will respond by changing to behaviour B, that we will logically weigh up the pros and cons and do the sensible, healthy and safe thing. In reality, life is more complex than this; I will continue to eat chocolate and drink beer despite the health risks because they make me feel good – and for me, feeling good is an important part of being healthy. Similarly, my friend has bought himself a gas-guzzling SUV despite the damage he knows it is doing to the planet because it makes him feel successful and rugged, and he will speed in it on his way to work because, even though this will not get him there much faster (all the other SUVs on the road will see to that), it gives him the reassuring illusion of being in control. Life is imperfect and emotion plays a big part in the strategies we deploy to cope with it. Attempts to influence us to change our behaviour for the better must take this into account.

If we think about road safety or public health campaigns, however, where emotion is considered at all, it tends to revolve around only one sentiment: fear. And yet the evidence supporting the use of fear is chequered at best. Over-reliance on it also means that we miss out on opportunities to engage with our clients using other, more positive, emotions and puts serious limitations on our long-term efforts at behaviour, lifestyle and social change. The commercial sector is not so self-limiting. It uses branding to get across a sustained array of attractive and reassuring associations and images. Yet again we can learn from it.

Learning objectives

This chapter will reinforce the need to see communications as just part of the social marketing effort. It will also enable you to:

■ Understand that communication is a two-way process and social marketers have to recognize that the message sent is not necessarily the same as the message received – and that it is the latter that matters.

■ Recognize that this underpins the need for careful developmental, process and outcome research to guide and monitor campaigns.

■ Critique fear-based messages from a marketing perspective.

■ Understand the potential of positive emotion and branding in social marketing.

LINKS TO OTHER CHAPTERS

During this chapter you might find it useful to cross-refer to the discussions of:
- When to do what research in Chapter 9
- Ethical issues in Chapter 10
- Relationship marketing in Chapter 7
- Case Studies 3 and 5.

■ How communication works

When Orson Welles broadcast his radio production of *The War of the Worlds* in 1938 the effect was dramatic (see Figure 5.1). Around a million Americans actually believed that the science-fiction story was true, and little green men from Mars were invading Earth and about to march on New York. The result was extensive public panic, people actually getting killed in the ensuing rush to avoid the invaders and the US rules of public broadcasting being changed forever.

From our perspective the events also had a more subtle impact: they engrained a perception that the mass media are extremely powerful, and that all that is needed to get people to do as you want is to design a suitably clever message. The contemporaneous rise of the Nazi party in Germany, and the central role played by Goebbels' infamous Ministry of Propaganda, served to reinforce this omnipotent reputation.

However, the six decades of research done since Goebbels' demise suggest that this picture is actually very misleading. Early models in communication theory did characterize the process as a one-way phenomenon, involving an active message sender and a completely passive recipient. Analogies are often drawn between this model and a hypodermic syringe: just as the doctor injects the drug into the patient so the communicator

Report of a radio broadcast of The War of the Worlds from the Guardian, November 1, 1938			
A wireless dramatisation of Mr HG Wells's fantasy, *The War of the Worlds* – a work that was written at the end of last century – caused a remarkable wave of panic in the United States during and immediately after its broadcast last night at eight o'clock. Listeners throughout the country believed that it was an account of an actual invasion of the earth by warriors from Mars. The play, presented by Mr Orson Welles, a successful theatrical producer and actor, gave a vivid account of the Martian invasion just as the wireless would if Mr Wells's dream came true.	The programme began with music by a New York City hotel dance band, which was interrupted suddenly by a news announcer who reported that violent flashes on Mars had been observed by Princeton University astronomers. The music was soon interrupted again for a report that a meteor had struck New Jersey. Then there was an account of how the meteor opened and Martian warriors emerged and began killing local citizens with mysterious death-rays. Martians were also observed moving towards New York with the intention of destroying the city.	Many people tuning in to the middle of the broadcast jumped to the conclusion that there was a real invasion. Thousands of telephone calls poured into the wireless station and police headquarters. Residents of New Jersey covered their faces with wet cloths as a protection against poisonous gases and fled from their homes. Roads leading to a village where a Martian ship was supposed to have landed were jammed with motorists prepared to repel attackers. Panic evacuations were also reported around the New York area. In some cases people told the police and newspapers that they had seen the "invasion."	Mr Jacques Chambrun, Mr HG Wells's representative, stated today that Mr Wells was "deeply concerned" that last night's wireless dramatisation should have caused such alarm. Mr Wells added that the dramatisation was made "with a liberty that amounts to complete rewriting and made the novel an entirely different story". Today nerves are steadier and it is recalled that in England some years ago there was a similar reaction to the famous "spoof broadcast" by Father Ronald Knox. Many listeners took his parodied description of a riot in London seriously.

Figure 5.1
Press clipping on the response to a radio dramatization of *The War of the Worlds*.
Source: *The Guardian*. Copyright Guardian News and Media Limited 2002.

injects the message into the audience. In both cases the effects are predictable and easily measured.

This analysis presents the communicator as powerful and directly manipulative, with dramatic effects being relatively easy to achieve. The media, particularly television and radio, as channels of mass communication come to be seen as a means of controlling the population. These ideas were given added credibility when commentators like Vance Packard (1957) applied them to commercial advertising, the influence of which became greatly exaggerated and oversimplified.

The limitations on the manipulative power of advertising can be illustrated by a couple of examples. It is estimated that 80–90% of new food products fail within one year of introduction (Rudolph, 1995). If advertising were as powerful as Packard suggests, this could never be. Similarly, given the frequency of mass media efforts to dissuade people from taking up smoking (and in many countries a complete ban on pro-tobacco advertising), one would have expected an all-powerful media to have resolved the problem – and yet thousands of young people still take up smoking every year in Europe alone.

More complex explanations have been developed. These include: the two (or more)-step model initially proposed by Katz and Lazarsfeld (1955), involving opinion leaders in the process of communication; the use and gratification approaches (McQuail *et al.*, 1972; Rosengren and Windahl, 1972), which depict the consumer as deliberately using the media rather than vice versa; and, more recently, cultural effects models which place the media in a cultural context and see its effects as indirect and long term (Tudor, 1997).

Interestingly, thinking in communication theory matches that in advertising. Early models of advertising conceptualized the process as a hierarchy of effects on consumers – typically cognitive (e.g. product awareness), affective (e.g. product liking) and then conative (e.g. product purchase). However, these 'linear sequential models' have also been heavily criticized (Barry and Howard, 1990). As with early communication theory they assume a passive audience, ignore the effects of significant others and present an overly tidy picture of how communication actually works. Indeed, it has become increasingly apparent that it is at least as relevant to ask 'what do people do to advertising?' as 'what does advertising do to people?' (Hedges, 1982). English health promoters have been all too aware of this since the mid-1980s, when teenagers were found to be stealing supposedly off-putting 'Heroin screws you up' posters and hanging them on their bedroom walls (see Box 5.1).

Box 5.1 Heroin screws you up

'In the mid-1980s, the Government responded to a surge in heroin use with a television and poster campaign featuring a wasted youth with the caption: "Heroin screws you up". Dozens of posters went missing as the boy in them became a teenage pin-up. Within months "heroin chic" appeared on the catwalks.'

Source: Burke and Thompson (2000)

Linear sequential models also overlook all the thinking that has emerged from postmodernism and what it tells us about the importance of symbolism and cultural meaning to consumption, whether of products or messages (Elliot and Wattanasuwan, 1998). We now know that audiences, especially young ones, are extremely sophisticated consumers of the media and that meaning has to be negotiated, not imposed.

Thus, many plausible theories of how the mass media and advertising work have emerged. Much as with behaviour change theory (Chapter 2), social marketing does not get too hung up about which of these theories is right (they are probably all a bit right). Rather it uses the insights that result to progress campaigns, and the key insight that links all these theories is that the audience is actively involved in the communications process. As my colleague Douglas Leathar used to express it: communication, like beauty, is in the eye of the beholder. Whether in the form of opinion leaders, self-gratifiers or postmodern cynics, the audience is as important as the communicator in the process of getting the message across.

John Redmond (2006, p. 7) is talking about poetry when he argues:

'As sparks fly up when flint meets rock, so meanings fly up when reader meets poem. Sparks are contained neither by flint nor rocks but arise from their relationship. In the same way, meanings are contained neither by the reader or the poem but arise from their relationship.'

He could just as easily have been talking about advertising; the only difference is that a poem is a purely creative exercise, whereas an ad is deliberately produced to get across a particular message. The ad developer therefore has to be particularly careful to take account of the active nature of the audience as they go about their business.

Exercise 5.1 is a chance to explore the two-way nature of communication in advertising.

Exercise 5.1

Advertising and what it does

The next time you are watching television, sit through a commercial break and ask yourself the following questions:

1. What factual information do the ads provide?
2. What other messages are communicated?
3. Do any appeal to you? Why/not?
4. How do the ads compare or contrast with others you have seen?
5. What might you do as a result of seeing them?

It will illustrate that adverts – certainly television commercials – communicate a vast array of messages, many of them emotional rather than factual; that some work for you, but some do not; and, if you are watching with other people, that preferences vary from person to person, who will each bring different experiences and priorities to the communication process. This variation in response will also be accentuated if you watch commercials at different times of the day.

Question 5 in Exercise 5.1 also illustrates that even the best ad will often elicit no action from you – and those that do will depend on other forms of marketing for you to carry out any action. Let us assume a chocolate bar ad stimulates you to want to try the product: the trial will be dependent on you being able to access (effective distribution) the bar at an acceptable cost (sensible pricing) and retrial on the bar tasting good (product design). This reinforces the notion of the marketing mix we discussed in Chapter 4, and that marketing is not just about communication, but getting the product in the right place at the right price. And 'right' is defined by the client because, in both marketing and advertising, they are actively involved in what is an exchange process.

■ The crucial role of research

Exercise 5.1 and the conclusions we have drawn about the two-way nature of communication demonstrate that the only certain way of knowing what is being communicated by a particular media effort is to ask the intended audience. The more obvious manifestations of this conclusion are unlikely to be disputed. Thus, the need to check that an audience understands the language in a leaflet or that the images on a poster are decipherable needs little justification.

However, the implications are more fundamental than this. An active audience means more than testing understanding of particular words or passing verdicts on completed posters. It implies a need to design communications, from inception to dissemination and beyond, with the intended audience's needs and perspectives clearly in mind. To do this, social marketers must maintain continuous contact with the target audience – ideally through formal consumer research. This contact will provide invaluable insights at every stage and on all aspects of a campaign.

This need for continuous research is fundamental to the whole social marketing process, and Chapter 9 is devoted to discussing its whys and hows. At this point, focusing on communications, we will look at the sort of pitfalls research can help us avoid. This naturally leads us first to formative research, which can help us decide whether the media can help resolve a particular social marketing problem and, if so, what task it can perform, as well as guiding decision making about all aspects of message design.

Problem definition

At the very beginning of a project, research with the target group can help define the nature of the problem to be tackled, determine whether the media has a role to play and, if so, what objectives it might fulfil. Let us assume we are considering the possibility of developing an ad campaign for 15- to 17-year-olds to tell them about the dangers of STDs. As a first step, research could examine teenagers' perceptions about sexual health and explore what, if any, information they feel they need. This might show that teenagers know of the risks and that condoms afford the best protection; however, they feel extremely disempowered about using them – suggesting that the campaign needs to focus on safer sexual skills development rather than simply warning about the dangers.

Arguably, it might in the process suggest that this is not principally a communication problem and hence a media campaign is not the best solution here. That in fact something more engaging and better able to develop skills is needed – maybe a combination of school-curriculum development, outreach work and condom distribution. Thus, audience research can help not only to define advertising objectives, but whether media activity is needed at all.

Assuming initial contact with the consumer does define a role for the mass media, further research can help determine the relative merits of different creative ideas or approaches on which to base a campaign. For instance, the sexual health campaign could either approach the subject with a conventionally negative emphasis on the drawbacks of *not* practising safer sex – unwanted pregnancy and disease. Alternatively, it could be more positive, emphasizing the benefits of safer sex in terms of enjoying more adult and fulfilled relationships. Interestingly, when these alternative ideas were presented to young people and their views sought, an initial preference for the more familiar, negative approach rapidly changed to a preference for the positive one. In particular, teenage girls were much more able and willing to associate themselves with the benefits of using contraception than the drawbacks of not doing so (Hastings and Scott, 1986).

Research with the consumer can also provide invaluable feedback on all aspects of campaign design, including the choice of medium, language, images and links with non-media campaign elements.

Medium

'Judge Dredd' is a cartoon character (Figure 5.2). He has his own comic or magazine which is read by teenagers. A few years ago it was proposed to use him and his comic as a vehicle for drugs education material, but the idea had to be abandoned when teenagers were consulted. Many had never read the comic and saw it as puerile, assuming it to be for young children. Those who did read it rejected its use as a vehicle for such a serious topic. Judge Dredd was, for them, a fantasy character whose rather ridiculous escapades were not intended to be taken literally. He had no basis in reality, no existence off the page or outside the reader's mind.

Using him as a way of transmitting a very serious and literal message about drugs completely contradicts this. It suggests that they believe Judge Dredd to be real, much as a child might believe in Superman. It implies that they defer to him and are likely to do as he tells them. As a result, it is grossly patronizing.

A similar instance of the medium being the message – or at least greatly influencing the effectiveness of it – is provided by 'advertorials'. These are jointly written and produced by the social marketer and the producer of the host publication. When a Scottish health agency was looking for a more reliable means of delivering information-rich messages capable of engaging its audience, research showed that people were far more likely to read and attend to content that was endorsed by and written in the style of their favourite magazine. The agency went on to use this approach to deliver health messages requiring detailed information to groups who were regular readers of news and entertainment magazines – dietary advice emerged as just one area to benefit from this approach.

In Case Study 5 on p. 260, Ray Lowry makes a similar point, showing how the choice of communication channel – in this case a salesperson with customized materials – was a key dimension of a successful campaign to encourage the use of sugar-free medicines.

Language

The language used in media material must be understandable to the intended audience. Reading age tests can help in this respect, but the only

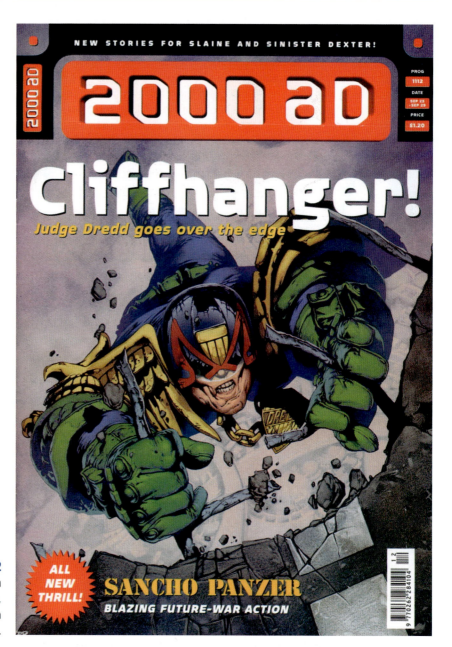

Figure 5.2
Judge Dredd. From
2000AD (1998),
reproduced with
permission.

certain check is to expose the material to your audience and ask for their reactions. This assesses not only comprehension, but equally important issues such as acceptability. For example, draft material on the safer sex campaign discussed above used the term 'bonking' for making love, in an attempt to be fashionable. Teenagers took great exception to this. They felt it implied a totally amoral and cynical attitude to sex that they rejected and found insulting.

The Foolsspeed road safety campaign, discussed in Case Study 3 on p. 245, illustrates a similar point. A pre-test using storyboards and narrative

(a)

(b)

Figure 5.3
The Foolsspeed road safety campaign. From the Scottish Road Safety campaign.

audiotapes helped avoid the inappropriate use of language and gesture. In one version of the proposed ads, road users were portrayed tapping their heads to show their disapproval of the (speeding) central character, and to encourage him to 'use his head' and slow down (see Figure 5.3a). Unfortunately, the gesture was interpreted as an act of aggression more likely to elicit a violent response than to encourage more responsible driving, or as one male respondent put it, 'it does nae mean "use your head" it means "you're a nutter!" – it's a threatening gesture'. This problem was subsequently resolved by focusing the storyline exclusively on the driver, where he was challenged to drive more slowly by his alter ego, talking to him in his rear-view mirror (see Figure 5.3b).

Images

Similar strictures apply to the visual elements of media materials. They must be decipherable and acceptable. In 2005, as part of a sexual health initiative targeting young people in deprived communities in the East of Scotland, the local health authority launched a campaign promoting respect for others and acceptance of difference.

One approach tested was to superimpose the wigs worn by court judges onto young people to signify inappropriate judgemental behaviour (see Figure 5.4a). Whilst the target audience understood the imagery and could relate this to their behaviour, the creative approach was ultimately rejected because it was seen as childish and failed to deliver a credible challenge. A different creative route was therefore adopted, which set out to challenge young people in public spaces (such as at bus stops and on board public transport), where they might be encouraged to make inappropriate judgements about people based on appearance alone (see Figure 5.4b).

In passing, it is worth noting that the quality of the graphics in Figure 5.5a is quite low. This is because we are not looking at finished material but an image produced purely for research purposes.

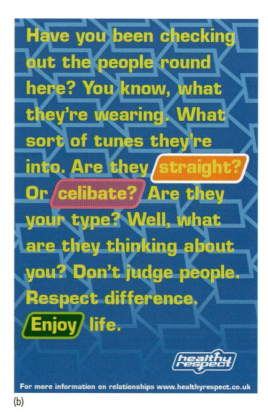

(a)   (b)

Figure 5.4
Campaign promoting respect for others. Reproduced with permission from 1576 Ltd and Healthy Respect (a Scottish Executive funded national health demonstration project for young people and sexual health) (2001–2008), http://www.healthyrespect.co.uk.

Links

As we have noted numerous times, social marketing thinking suggests that the mass media is most likely to work if it is used in conjunction with other initiatives. Target group opinion can help determine the nature of these other elements and how they should be linked to the media activity. This takes us naturally to wider social marketing research, which is discussed in Chapter 9. Issues of campaign evaluation are also discussed in this chapter.

These examples also illustrate another point that we already noted during our discussion of strategic planning in Chapter 3 and will pick up again in Chapter 9 when we discuss research in more detail. Target audience research does not just help improve individual media campaigns; because it requires continuous contact between communicator and audience throughout and between initiatives, it also enables us to increase our understanding of our clients. Some of the examples quoted above illustrate this point. The research on Judge Dredd revealed as much about teenagers and how they read comics as it did about the actual material. Similarly, young people's reaction to the word 'bonking' provides a valuable insight into their sexual feelings and attitudes. This type of understanding is fundamental to effective communication.

We have also noted a number of times now that social marketing is, in essence, a process of exchanging values. Likewise, communication is a form of exchange – it requires shared experiences, mutual understanding and empathy. If, as social marketers, we do not take the trouble to try and understand our clients, to take their ideas seriously and, at least to some extent, accept their view of the world, how can we expect them to accept ours?

■ Fear messages in marketing

Given what we have agreed about the two-way nature of communication and the need for empathy and shared understanding, it seems inappropriate to ask generic questions about whether certain sorts of messages work better than others. The answer is bound to be 'it depends' – on circumstances, past communications, available channels and so on. Above all, it depends on the audience. And yet precisely this question has been asked again and again about fear messages.

Thus, several attempts have been made to develop a theory to explain and predict how fear works, but the results are inconclusive. Three alternative models have emerged. First, the curvilinear model posits that fear *can* persuade up to a threshold of tolerance, beyond which it becomes counterproductive.

Second, Leventhal's (1970) parallel response model proposes that emotional and cognitive factors act independently to mediate behaviour, with emotional factors affecting internal attempts to cope with the threat (e.g. by rationalizing or rejecting it), whilst cognitive factors will determine the behaviour change.

Finally, Rogers's (1975) expectancy-valence model states that the effectiveness of a fear-arousing communication is a function of three variables: the magnitude of the threat; the probability of its occurrence; and the efficacy of the advocated protective response. It is proposed that these three variables will interact to produce a level of 'protection motivation' within an individual and that this will determine the level of change.

The research into the effectiveness of fear appeals is inconclusive, but the majority of studies show a positive relationship between fear arousal and persuasion (Higbee, 1969). More specifically, the following conclusions have been drawn:

- Fear appeals can raise awareness of an issue and bring it to the fore-front of people's thoughts
- Fear appeals can make people re-evaluate and change their attitudes
- Fear may be successful in stimulating an intention to change behaviour sometime in the future
- In some cases *immediate* behaviour change takes place shortly after exposure to a fear communication.

In summary, therefore, whilst the findings do vary considerably between studies, broadly speaking it is true to say that the research supports the use of fear appeals. The problem, however, is that the research has been very narrowly focused, typically using experiments in laboratory settings, to ask very specific and short-term questions. As we have seen, the resulting answers can, with some difficulty, be resolved into a coherent picture, but many other questions are left begging. Most importantly, it is not clear what happens outside the laboratory, where there is much less control, or what the long-term and wider effects of fear appeals are.

Marketing provides a rubric for asking these bigger questions. Have a try at Exercise 5.2.

Exercise 5.2

Fear in traffic safety

You have just been appointed as Head of Communications at the Transport Accident Commission in Victoria, Australia. They have used fear messages consistently for the last 15 years. Log on to their website (http://www.tacsafety.com.au) and click on 'Campaigns' followed by any of the campaign topics to view some of the road safety ads. As a social marketer, what questions does their approach raise? You might like to consider the following more specific questions:

(a) What will our clients do with the message?
(b) What benefits will they get from it?
(c) How will it affect our brand name?
(d) How will it affect their feelings for our other products?
(e) What about our non-targets who will also see the message?
(f) What are our competitors doing?
(g) Where do we go from here?
(h) What about alternative approaches?
(i) Is our message ethically acceptable?

(a) What will our clients do with the message?

Outside the laboratory, audiences can choose whether or not to accept our messages; they cannot be compelled to pay attention any more than they can be compelled to drive safely or give up smoking. This creates several potential barriers: the audience may not look at the message at all; they may look at it, but ignore it; they may look at it and accept it, but misunderstand it; they may look at it and understand it, but rationalize it (e.g. 'that couldn't happen to me', 'there are other greater risks' or simply 'life is risky'). All of these barriers – especially the last – can be accentuated by fear appeals (look at point 1 in Box 5.2). In a world where mass media messages are an optional extra, it may make more sense to use subtlety and compromise than brute force.

At a more fundamental level, it is arguable that campaigns employing extreme fear appeals, such as those used in Victoria by the Transport Accident Commission (Exercise 5.2), undermine the whole notion of voluntary behaviour. The ads literally say accept our message or 'you're a bloody idiot'. The danger is that people will reject such uncompromising approaches, or like characters in David Cronenberg's movie *Crash*, even do the opposite of what is proposed. This latter response is not as far-fetched as it may sound. Recent focus groups conducted at the Institute for Social Marketing suggested that certain young men enjoy gory road safety ads in the same way as horror movies: 'that was a cracker that one', 'that's brilliant that, when you saw her face get smashed up', 'really clever', 'and you hear it go bang, crack!'. Social change practitioners would no doubt be appalled to discover they are competing with violent pornographers!

(b) What benefits will they get from it?

Voluntary behaviour is benefit driven, so paying attention to mass media messages, just like buying Coca-Cola or driving safely, must provide the target with something they want. As Barry Day, vice-chair of McCann-Erickson Worldwide, expressed it: 'I believe an ad should be a reward.' The question then is 'what reward does a fear appeal offer?' and, by extension, is being upset, scared and/or discomfited much of a reward?

(c) How will it affect our brand name?

Coca-Cola, Nike and Marlboro will all be very careful to ensure that any ads they produce not only work effectively in their own right, but also enhance or (at the very least) do no damage to the company and the product's good name – typically encapsulated in the brand. Most successful brands are the result of decades of careful effort and design.

Social marketing organizations have their equivalents of brands; they have an image and reputation with the public. The question then is how do fear appeals affect this reputation? Do claims that are felt to be exaggerated, or at least not to reflect people's everyday experience, discredit the communicator?

Do messages that cause short-term offence, but which might be justified by high awareness figures, do long-term damage to the sender's good name?

(d) How will it affect their feelings for our other products?

Fear messages say something about the absolute risk of the behaviour being addressed, but also imply things about the relative risk of other behaviours. Take traffic safety as an example: a very fearful anti-drink campaign may lead audiences to assume that other driving behaviours, such as speeding, are less dangerous. Focus groups with young drivers conducted recently at the University of Wollongong in New South Wales (see Box 5.2) showed that whilst drink-driving and speeding were recognized as risky behaviours, others such as driving at night and driving whilst under the influence of marijuana were not. Indeed, some respondents interpreted the constant messaging on drink-driving as implicitly endorsing the alternative of marijuana use. The option of extending the traffic topics addressed by fear messages to cover all potential risks is equally problematic. It would likely lead to overload and rationalization: 'I know the roads are dangerous, but I have to get on with my life.'

Box 5.2   Young Australian drivers and the use of fear

Focus groups with young (18- to 24-year-old) drivers conducted recently at the University of Wollongong in New South Wales revealed worrying tendencies in their response to fear-based messages. The discussions examined response to ads they had seen on television in the last few months and years, which had been dominated by hard-hitting messages on drink-driving and speeding. Three findings stand out:

1. The young drivers were becoming inured to fear messages and numerous comments were made about being tired of being told what to do and that speeding and drink-driving are dangerous.

'The ads are all the same, can't speed, can't drink and drive or you will crash – so what? Everyone knows that … they don't stop me.'

(male, 18)

'Ever since I can remember the ads have been about what happens when you speed … I stopped taking any notice of them ages ago.'

(female, 21)

'The ads are silly, the latest ad shows a guy crashing this big powerful car after speeding and killing people, then right after is an ad for the same car showing these young guys enjoying themselves in it … I just turn off from the anti-speeding ads now.'

(male, 23)

2. Other risky driving behaviours such as driving at night or with lots of friends in the car were not even on their radar. As long as they did not speed or drink they felt they were okay.

'I guess other things are dangerous but not as bad as speeding and drink-driving.'

(male, 17)

'I don't think there is a problem if you have four or five of your mates in the car with you.'

(male, 18)

'No one has said that driving at night is more dangerous than driving at daytime … have they?'

(female, 22)

3. Dysfunctional solutions emerged from the narrow focus on alcohol – most notably, the less well educated of the young people were inclined to see no problem with marijuana use and driving. The broader idea of mind-altering substances in general impairing driving had been lost.

'Smoking some weed then driving home isn't as dangerous as having a heap of beers at a party.'

(female, 17)

'When I go out and if I'm driving and I had a choice between dope and alcohol then it's a no brainer … you're safer with the dope.'

(male, 20)

'I have a friend and he thinks his driving improves when he has had some herb.'

(male, 24)

It is also worth remembering that road use is only one source of danger in people's life (and danger is only one source of problems). For example, tobacco use kills more people in Europe than traffic, crime, and accidents in the home and workplace combined.

Fear messages need to reflect this reality, if only for ethical reasons.

(e) What about our non-targets who will also see the message?

Targeting is an important aspect of marketing: only well-targeted products and messages can really satisfy customer needs. However, messages transmitted in the mass media will inevitably reach other people as well as the intended target. Sticking with road safety, TV ads aimed at 18- to

24-year-old 'boy racers' will also reach older drivers. The use of fear in these circumstances can have two untoward effects. First, it may breed complacency among older speeding drivers by implying that deaths on the roads are the fault of other inexperienced and unskilled drivers. Second, it may cause unwarranted anxiety among other road users, perhaps discouraging parents from letting their children play outside or walk to school.

(f) What are our competitors doing?

As we will discuss in Chapter 8, social marketers frequently have to compete with commerce. Tobacco, alcohol, fast-food, car producers – amongst others – frequently push in the opposite direction. Even a cursory look at their advertising shows that they make relatively little use of fear.

(g) Where do we go from here?

Fear appeals present both creative and strategic problems. On the creative front, once fear has been used, there is a need to increase it on each subsequent occasion to have the same impact. At what point does this cross the threshold of acceptability? On the other hand, is there a point at which people become inured? (Have another look at Box 5.2.)

Turning to strategy, if marketing tells us that success is dependent on building long-term relationships with the customer, the strategic question becomes: is fear a good basis for a relationship? Even parents rapidly abandon it as a pedagogical option as their offspring leave early childhood.

(h) What about alternative approaches?

It is clear then that fear approaches present considerable costs to social marketers. The main benefit it offers is a high profile: strong emotional messages attract a lot of attention. But other approaches can also have a strong emotional pull – love, excitement, sex, hope, humour and sophistication are all used successfully by commercial advertisers. The key issue therefore is not 'should fear appeals be used?' but 'will they do the job better and more efficiently than alternative approaches?'

(i) Is our message ethically acceptable?

The final question a marketer will ask (or be compelled to ask by the relevant regulatory authorities) is 'do our messages meet normal ethical standards?' Will people be hurt or damaged by them? The fact that we social marketers tend to fight on the side of the angels does not absolve us from this responsibility. The end cannot be used to justify the means.

■ Emotion and branding

From a social marketer's perspective, then, fear messages leave many questions unanswered. However, the one thing they do confirm for us is that our behaviour is driven by both rational and emotional factors. As Joan Bakewell (2006) put it recently:

> 'For many people reasoned argument is not the final arbiter of how they choose to live their lives. They are swayed by feelings, moved by loyalties, willing to set logic aside for the sake of psychic comfort.'

Their recognition of this encourages commercial marketers to produce lots of advertising which focuses on feelings, promotes a product's or a company's image, generates positive associations and generally makes the potential customer feel good.

Research suggests that three other factors make emotional messages particularly persuasive:

- They are better able to gain consumers' attention than factual messages. Audiences are under pressure from an increasing clutter of advertising and promotional messages, and it becomes impossible to cognitively process them. They therefore attend selectively to those messages which are relevant, comprehensible and congruent with their values (Ries and Trout, 1981; Ray and Batra, 1983).
- They encourage deeper processing of the message and as a result tend to be remembered better (Dutta and Kanungo, 1975; Ray, 1977).
- People buy products (and engage in behaviours) to satisfy not only objective, functional needs, but also symbolic and emotional ones, such as self-enhancement and group identification (Hirschman and Holbrook, 1982; Park *et al.*, 1987). The most obvious example of this is cigarette smoking. When they first take up the habit, the prospective smoker does not have an objective need for nicotine, but rather a symbolic need to display independence or rebellion (Barton *et al.*, 1982).

Lefebvre *et al.* (1995) also remind us that all social marketing communications have an emotional dimension – a 'personality' or 'tonality' – whether the sender intends it or not. They caution that we – just like our commercial counterparts – must use research, design and careful targeting to ensure that the tonality matches the needs of their target audience. Leathar (1980) and Monahan (1995) go a step further and argue that we should actively promote positive images about health:

> 'Positive affect can be used to stress the benefits of healthy behaviour, to give individuals a sense of control, and to reduce anxiety or fear. All of these tactics are likely to enhance the success of a communication campaign.'
>
> (Monahan, 1995, p. 96)

On a more specific level, qualitative research conducted by the Health Education Authority in England with pregnant women (Bolling and Owen, 1997) also emphasizes the importance of emotional communication, concluding that messages have to be sympathetic, supportive and non-judgemental. The primary need, the research suggested, is to establish a sense of trust. This resonates with the discussion of relationship marketing in Chapter 7.

Branding

The brand is the marketer's most advanced emotional tool. It combines and reinforces the functional and emotional benefits of the offering (Murphy, 1987; de Chernatony, 1993) and so adds value, encouraging consumption and loyalty. In essence, a good marque facilitates recognition, makes a promise and, provided the full marketing back-up is in place, delivers satisfaction. This last point is vital: promise without delivery is extremely damaging. As Wally Olins put it, it is like painting the toilet door when the cistern is broken. Inevitably, therefore, the brand is developed not just using communications, but the whole marketing mix.

The process also needs care and time, and to be driven by customer needs which will be both individual and social. At an individual level, a brand will be chosen because it is liked and matches the person's self-image. At a social level, brands can be used by consumers to tell other people more about themselves, particularly with conspicuously consumed products (Murphy, 1987). Moreover, brands can also provide very practical benefits, making consumption easier. They can act as guarantees of quality or reduce risks by confirming that 'this product is for you' (de Chernatony, 1993). For example, for young people, quick and clear brand identification can make both the buying and smoking of forbidden products such as cigarettes much less risky.

Over time, brands become a fast and powerful way of confirming the synergy between marketer and customer. Indeed, it can be argued that successful brands are only part owned by the company – the customer also has a share. When Coca-Cola changed their formulation a few years ago, its ultimate failure and the need to scurry back to Coca-Cola Classic was partly put down to consumer displeasure at *their* brand being adulterated.

There is also evidence that branding may be a particularly effective way to reach people in deprived communities. Research into how working-class populations use cultural symbols in advertising found that these groups are often poorly informed about the objective merits of different products and therefore tend to rely more heavily than other groups on 'implicit meanings' – context, price, image – to judge products (Durgee, 1986). Similarly, de Chernatony (1993) and Cacioppo and Petty (1989) found that people in deprived communities are less likely to evaluate products on a rational, objective basis, but look for clues as to the product's value in terms of its price or its image. They argued that the symbolic appeal of brands is particularly effective in targeting those individuals who do not have the time, skills or motivation to evaluate the objective attributes and benefits of a particular campaign. Alternatively, it may simply be that straightened budgets make the quality assurance of branding more valuable.

A more recent review, conducted on behalf of the UK's National Institute for Health and Clinical Excellence (NICE) also suggests that brands can be an effective way of reaching information-deprived communities (Stead *et al.*, 2006).

This branding seems to hold considerable promise. Exercise 5.3 explores whether it can work in social marketing.

Exercise 5.3

Branding in social marketing

The Scottish Health Education Group (SHEG) was the Government body responsible for health education in Scotland in the 1980s and early 1990s. Over a number of years they commissioned a full range of research on their mass media activity, from basic problem definition work, through concept and pre-testing to evaluation. This began to reveal a number of recurrent problems, including a tendency for the advertising to be:

- Negative rather than positive. Smoking campaigns emphasized the dangers of smoking, not the benefits of non-smoking; contraception advice threatened people with unwanted pregnancies, rather than stressing the advantages of safer sex.
- Authoritarian rather than empathetic. Material seemed to be telling people what to do and how to run their lives, rather than enabling and encouraging them to make their own informed health decisions.
- Long-term rather than short-term focused. Anti-smoking material emphasized the health risks of cigarettes, many of which are very long term and probabilistic.
- Fragmented from other non-media activity. It did not connect with other types of intervention, such as local services or policy changes – in marketing parlance there was only one P in the marketing mix.
- Topic-based rather than whole-person orientated. Separate campaigns were run on drinking, smoking and contraception, seemingly ignoring the fact that these activities can overlap and often reflect the individual's overall lifestyle.

How might branding help resolve these problems?

Source: Hastings and Leathar (1987)

Some of the weaknesses highlighted by SHEG's research could be removed during pre-testing of individual campaigns, but others, such as fragmentation and the tendency to be topic-based, could not. It was therefore decided to produce an 'umbrella' campaign that could communicate a general lifestyle message of empowerment – 'promoting good health in much the same way as a marketing company would promote its corporate identity' (Hastings and Leathar, 1987). In addition the campaign needed to connect with both primary and secondary prevention, linking the positive imagery to clear solutions and real health problems – that is, provide branded health products. The result was 'Be All You Can Be', a communication campaign which ran in broadcast and print media, promoting a theme of empowerment and positive health. Interestingly, the same slogan has been used quite independently by the US army.

An extensive communication and awareness monitor showed that it became familiar to, and was strongly endorsed by, the Scottish population (Leathar, 1987a, b). For example, around two-thirds of people were aware of the campaign; over 90% of these felt it was fulfilling its objectives of encouraging people to live fuller lives and take a greater interest in their health, and there was very strong support for its positive and empathetic tone.

There were problems with the campaign. First, the links between the media push and service delivery modes were weak. In essence, the campaign was succeeding in promoting a brand identity for health, but not offering the branded products that enabled people to buy into it; Be All You Can Be was social advertising, not social marketing. The campaign also suffered from a lack of targeting. No attempt was made to shape it to the needs of particular groups; it was intended to appeal to everyone in a way that would now be considered naive.

Nonetheless, it did show considerable promise and certainly suggests that branding can play an important role in social marketing. Other more recent campaigns confirm this optimism. NE Choices (have a look forward to Exercise 7.3), a drugs prevention brand, built up an impressive degree of trust with adolescents in the north of England and the anti-tobacco brand Truth delivered significant behaviour change in the USA.

Sadly, in each case the additional vital ingredient of time was missing. Be All You Can Be was given only four years – the wink of an eye compared to a centenarian like Coca-Cola or Lucky Strike. The campaign stopped, not because it had failed (it was never properly evaluated but, as noted above, what data existed were encouraging), but because political changes in Scotland demanded a return to campaigns of a more conventional and didactic nature. Similarly, NE Choices was designed as a time-limited initiative and funding for the Truth Campaign has petered out.

We will return to the ideas of branding and campaign longevity in Chapters 7 and 9.

■ Conclusion

Communication is a complex process in which both communicator and audience are actively involved. This means that careful audience research is needed to decide whether, how and with what combination of other marketing activity it should be used. This vital role of research in social marketing communications reflects its importance to the discipline as a whole, which we will discuss in Chapter 9.

The picture becomes more complex when the vagaries of human decision making are factored in – especially our tendency to decide things on emotional as well as rational bases. It is a bit disappointing that the principal acknowledgement of this emotional dimension of our lives in the health and safety sector comes in the form of fear-based communications, which raise many marketing questions.

A more interesting line of thought is that other emotions could be engaged more effectively through branding with much greater strategic potential.

■ References

2000AD. (1998). Program 1112, Cover Judge Dredd by Kevin Walker. 23–29 September.

Bakewell J. (2006). *The Guardian Review*, 23 September, p. 7.

Barry T.E. and Howard D.J. (1990). Review and critique of the hierarchy of effects in advertising. *International Journal of Advertising*, **9**(2): 121–135.

Barton J., Chassin L., Presson C.C. and Sherman S.J. (1982). Social image factors as motivators of smoking initiation in early and middle adolescence. *Child Development*, **53**: 1499–1511.

Bolling K. and Owen L. (1997). *Smoking and Pregnancy: A Survey of Knowledge, Attitudes and Behaviour*. London: Health Education Authority.

Burke J. and Thompson T. (2000). Rachel: shock photo backed by boyfriend. *The Observer*, 3 March, p. 10.

Cacioppo J.T. and Petty R.E. (1989). The elaboration likelihood model. The role of effect and affect laden information processing in persuasion. In *Cognitive and Affective Responses to Advertising* (Cafferata P. and Tybout A., eds), pp. 69–90. Lexington, MA: Lexington Books.

de Chernatony L. (1993). Categorizing brands: evolutionary processes underpinned by two key dimensions. *Journal of Marketing Management*, **9**(2): 173–188.

Durgee J.F. (1986). How consumer sub-cultures code reality: a look at some code types. *Advances in Consumer Research*, **13**: 332–337.

Dutta S. and Kanungo R.N. (1975). *Affect and Memory*. New York: Pergamon Press.

Elliot R. and Wattanasuwan K. (1998). Brands as symbolic resources for the construction of identity. *International Journal of Advertising*, **17**(2): 131–144.

The Guardian (date unknown). From the Archives: Report of a Radio Broadcast of the War of the Worlds from *The Guardian*, 1 November 1938. Online version: http://www.guardian.co.uk/fromthearchive/story/0,12269,1075343,00.html

Hastings G.B. and Leathar D.S. (1987). The creative potential of research. *International Journal of Advertising*, **6**: 159–168.

Hastings G.B. and Scott A.C. (1986). *Pretest of the 'Options' Family Planning Campaign*. Glasgow: University of Strathclyde, Advertising Research Unit: September.

Hedges A. (1982). *Testing to Destruction: A fresh and critical look at the uses of research in advertising*. London: Institute of Practitioners in Advertising.

Higbee K.L. (1969). Fifteen years of fear arousal; research on threat appeals. *Psychological Bulletin*, **72**(6): 426–444.

Hirschman E.C. and Holbrook M.B. (1982). Hedonic consumption: emerging concepts, methods and propositions. *Journal of Marketing*, **46**(3): 92–101.

Katz E. and Lazarsfeld P. (1955). *Personal Influence*. New York: The Free Press.

Leathar D.S. (1980). Images in health education advertising. *Health Education Journal*, **39**(4): 123–128.

Leathar D.S. (1987a). The development and assessment of mass media campaigns: the work of the Advertising Research Unit – Be All You Can Be Case Study – Part 1. *Journal of the Institute of Health Education*, **26**(1): 6–12.

Leathar D.S. (1987b). Be All You Can Be Case Study – Part 2. *Journal of the Institute of Health Education*, **26**(2): 85–93.

Lefebvre R.C., Doner L., Johnston C., Loughrey K., Balch G.I. and Sutton S.M. (1995). Use of database marketing and consumer-based health communication in message design: an example from the office of cancer communications' "5 A Day for Better Health" program. In *Designing Health Messages. Approaches From Communication Theory and Public Health Practice* (Maibach E. and Parrott R.L., eds), pp. 217–246. Newbury Park, CA: Sage.

Leventhal H. (1970). Findings and theory in the study of fear communications. *Advances in Experimental Social Psychology*, **5**: 119–187.

McQuail D., Blumer J.G. and Brown J.R. (1972). The television audience, a revised perspective. In *Sociology of Mass Communications* (McQuail D., ed.). Harmondsworth: Penguin.

Monahan J.L. (1995). Thinking positively: using positive affect when designing messages. In *Designing Health Messages. Approaches From Communication Theory and Public Health Practice* (Maibach E. and Parrott R.L., eds). Newbury Park, CA: Sage.

Murphy J. (ed.) (1987). *Branding: A Key Marketing Tool*. New York: McGraw-Hill.

Packard V.O. (1957). *The Hidden Persuaders*. London: Longmans, Green & Co.

Park C.W., Assael H. and Chaiy S. (1987). Mediating effects of trial and learning on involvement-associated characteristics. *Journal of Consumer Marketing*, **4**(3): 25–34.

Ray M.L. (1977). When does consumer information processing research actually have anything to do with consumer information processing? In *Advances in Consumer Research* (Perreault W.D. Jr, ed.), Volume 4, pp. 372–375. Atlanta, GA: Association for Consumer Research.

Ray M.L. and Batra R. (1983). Emotion and persuasion in advertising: What we do and don't know about affect. In *Advances in Consumer Research* (Bagozzi R.P. and Tybout A.M., eds), Volume 10, pp. 543–548. Ann Arbor, MI: Association for Consumer Research.

Redmond J. (2006). *How to Write a Poem*, p. 7. Oxford: Blackwell Publishing.

Ries A.L. and Trout J. (1981). *Positioning: The Battle for your Mind*. New York: McGraw-Hill.

Rogers R.W. (1975). A protection motivation theory of fear appeals and attitude change. *Journal of Psychology*, **91**: 93–114.

Rosengren K.E. and Windahl S. (1972). Mass media consumption as a functional alternative. In *Sociology of Mass Communications* (McQuail D., ed.), pp. 166–194. Harmondsworth: Penguin.

Rudolph M.J. (1995). The food product development process. *British Food Journal*, **97**(3): 3–11.

Stead M., McDermott L., Angus K. and Hastings G. (2006). *Marketing Report (Behaviour Change: Marketing Review)*. Report prepared for the National Institute for Clinical and Health Excellence. Stirling: Institute for Social Marketing.

Tudor A. (1997). On alcohol and the mystique of media effects. In *The Media Studies Reader* (O'Sullivan T. and Jewkes Y., eds), pp. 174–180. London: Edward Arnold.

CHAPTER 6

Moving
Upstream

■ Overview

No man (or woman) is an island. What we think, feel and – most importantly for social marketing – what we do is greatly influenced by our social and economic circumstances. Speeding drivers are partly deciding for themselves that they want to go faster, but are also encouraged by cars that are made and sold to deliver speed, road-building programmes that provide good racing conditions, and a culture that equates such behaviour with machismo and power.

As we discussed in Chapter 2, Social Cognitive Theory takes this wider perspective into account and reminds us that, if we are serious about changing behaviour, we have to ask ourselves *whose* behaviour we need to address. Is it the speeding driver, the car manufacturer or the road builder? In this chapter we will see how the answer often lies beyond the individual.

Learning objectives

After working through this chapter you will:

- Understand what is meant by moving upstream.
- Recognize how important it is for social marketers to think beyond the individual and ask 'whose behaviour needs to change?'
- Be sensitized to the ethical desirability of this broader vision.
- Be able to put this thinking into practice.
- Understand that whoever's behaviour we are trying to change – whether it be a cabinet minister or a juvenile delinquent – the same basic social marketing principles apply.

During this chapter you might find it useful to cross-refer to the discussions of:
- Social Cognitive Theory in Chapter 2
- Social marketing planning in Chapter 3
- Case Studies 1, 3 and 4.

LINKS TO OTHER CHAPTERS

■ Upstream

Social marketing focuses on behaviour. While commercial marketers measure success in terms of shareholder value, sales or profitability, for the social marketer 'consumer *behaviour* is the bottom line' (Andreasen, 1995, p. 14). Laurence Wallack uses the metaphor of a river (see Box 6.1) to remind us how important it is, in maintaining this focus, to ask whose behaviour we should be trying to change.

Box 6.1 Lawrence Wallack's river

A man out walking happens across a river in which people are being swept along and in danger of drowning. His immediate desire is to help them and he considers various options – throwing in lifebelts, diving in himself and pulling some to shore or even shouting out instructions on how to swim. Each of these certainly has the potential to help, but it is equally clear that some people will drown – he has neither the time nor resources to reach them all. He begins to question why this calamity has arisen. Why are so many people in the river in the first place? To find out he has to go upstream. When he does so he finds that a few hundred metres further on there are huge and evocative billboards extolling the virtues of the river – how clean and refreshing it is – and calling on people to 'jump on in, the water's lovely'. A beautiful new diving-board has been provided to make the prospect even more enticing, and it costs only 10 cents a go. Kids are daring each other to give it a try.

The man shakes his head and carries on upstream.

After a few more minutes walking the bank begins getting wet, muddy and treacherous. He becomes anxious about falling in the river himself. Then he sees houses built on these poor foundations. They are cheap and dilapidated, more like shacks than houses, and some are clearly in danger of collapse. As he is watching a small child slips down the bank and only just manages to save itself from falling in the river.

The man is left pondering about how he can best do something about the drowning people: should he help the people who have already fallen in, stop advertisers encouraging others to jump in or move right upstream and change macro-economic policy so that the poor can afford better housing. Whose behaviour does he need to change: the individual's, the marketer's or the Chancellor's?

Source: based on Wallack *et al.* (1993)

Should we focus our efforts on influencing individuals to give up smoking, drive more safely or eat less fat (what Wallack would term 'downstream' behaviour change)? Or should we also be trying to influence the policymakers, politicians, regulators or educators to restrict access to tobacco, make roads slower and cars safer, or improve the nutritional value of food products ('upstream' behaviour change)?

Decades of research has shown, for example, that the decision to take up smoking is influenced by many factors. These include: gender (Jarvis, 1997); academic achievement (Goddard, 1990; Jackson *et al.*, 1998); the smoking behaviour and attitudes of young people's friends and family (Morgan and Grube, 1989; Barton and Janis, 1997; Jackson *et al.*, 1998); family structure (Goddard, 1990; Patton *et al.*, 1998); socio-economic background (Graham and Hunt, 1998); media portrayals of smoking (Amos *et al.*, 1998); and tobacco marketing (Pierce *et al.*, 1999). Most of these influences are beyond the control of young people, but are the legitimate concern of social marketers. What is true for smoking is also true for other behaviours; try Exercise 6.1(a).

Exercise 6.1

Whose behaviour needs to change?

(a) Think for a moment about a problem in your neighbourhood – it may be antisocial behaviour by teenagers (vandalism, petty crime, intimidating street behaviour), racism or something as simple as dog fouling. Think through what the causes might be (in a real instance you would use research to help with this). What impact do your answers have on determining a solution? Whose behaviour needs to change?
(b) Why is moving upstream important? Your answer to (a) will help think this through, but also consider what we have already learnt about social marketing. Theory (Chapter 2) and strategic planning (Chapter 3) both point us upstream. The nature of human behaviour is also important: it is volitional, complex and often multifaceted.

■ Why move upstream?

Exercise 6.1(b) poses this question; think through your answers before proceeding.

Box 6.2 gives seven reasons for at least considering the idea of moving upstream.

Box 6.2　Seven reasons for thinking upstream

  (i)　Theory tells us it is necessary.
 (ii)　Social marketing planning demands it.
(iii)　It can greatly increase efficiency.
(iv)　It can tackle hidden needs.
 (v)　It can be the only option.
(vi)　It reflects the complexity of our task.
(vii)　Not to do so is unethical.

(i) Theory tells us it is necessary

We discussed Social Cognitive Theory in Chapter 2, and how this demonstrates that our behaviour is only partially under our own control. The social environment in which we live will also have a marked impact on our choices. Furthermore, this broader perspective is supported by many other behaviour-change theories. Critical theory (Goldberg, 1995) and media advocacy (Wallack *et al.*, 1993) call for us to raise our eyes above the individual horizon. Alcalay and Bell (2000, pp. 15–24) add Social Learning Theory, the Community-Organization Model and the Social-Ecological Approach to the list.

These theories have each emerged from extended streams of research. They are, as we noted in Chapter 2, our chance to learn from the experience of others. We cannot afford to ignore them.

(ii) Social marketing planning demands it

In Chapter 3 we examined strategic planning and the need to start this with a broad 'situation analysis' to establish the nature of the problem being addressed and how best to tackle it. The key question answered by this analysis is 'whose behaviour needs to change?' In our antisocial behaviour example, for instance, is it the young people, the local authorities or the Government?

(iii) It can greatly increase efficiency

Moving upstream has the capacity to greatly increase efficiency. Consider the example of water fluoridation. This involves water providers adjusting the natural level of fluoride in the public water supply so as to produce substantial improvements in the dental health of the population, especially among children and those living in deprived communities.

It is not the only option for improving dental health. At least four alternative approaches are possible. We could:

(a) Run campaigns to encourage good oral hygiene.
(b) Increase the resistance of the tooth enamel to decay by fissure sealing and the application of fluoride solutions.
(c) Encourage the use of fluoride supplements such as tablets, drops and fluoridated salt.
(d) Remove sugar from the diet.

All of these are less effective than water fluoridation. They are also much less efficient. The underlying reason is the same: they depend for their success on far more people doing something. In the case of water fluoridation the provider has to act, then the health benefits simply flow through the tap. In option (a) campaigns have to be funded on an ongoing basis and everyone in the target population has to respond. In option (b) all dentists have to apply these measures to all their patients, and even then coverage will be partial. In England and Wales, for example, only 46% of adults even have a dentist (NHS Statistics, 2006). Option (c) requires everyone to buy and use these products forever, and option (d) demands revolutionary changes in everyone's diet – again forever.

Furthermore, uptake of (a)–(d) will inevitably be greater amongst the better off; these options will increase inequalities. Fluoridation does the reverse.

(iv) It can tackle hidden needs

Moving upstream can also help us to tackle problems that people do not even know they have. Spina bifida provides an evocative illustration. It is known that the occurrence of this debilitating and sometimes fatal birth defect can be prevented if women consume adequate quantities of vitamin B folate before and during the early stages of pregnancy. An individualistic social marketing solution to the problem would be to inform women of the risk and advise them to eat foods, such as broccoli and brussel sprouts, that are rich in folates. The marketer could add to this communication measure which ensures that these foods are available readily (place) and cheaply (price), and make them more palatable (product) – perhaps by getting celebrity chefs to promote tasty recipes. In this way he or she might get 50% of women who are intending to get pregnant eating a preventative diet.

This leaves 50%, however, rejecting the offering. One response to this is to increase the cost of their intransigence by running campaigns on the awfulness of spina bifida. (This is not quite as daft as it sounds; we still do it for lung cancer.) Alternatively, a more enlightened social marketer might scan the technological environment and suggest that, instead of pushing unpopular vegetables like broccoli, the solution is to market folic acid supplements. This might get 75% of intending mothers to cooperate.

However, a large proportion of the target do not even know they *are* the target. Last year in Britain, 50% of pregnancies were unplanned. Who is going to take steps to prevent a risk to which they have no intention of exposing themselves? Pedestrians do not wear crash helmets.

In the USA this problem has been resolved by moving upstream. Since 1998, all US wheat, rice and corn flour has been fortified with folic acid. The Food and Drug Administration ordered the measures after research showed that only about 25% of women of child-bearing age regularly consume enough folic acid in the form of a vitamin supplement. The measure worked. By 1999, the Centers for Disease Control and Prevention (CDC) found that the average red blood cell folate concentration had increased by over 50% (BMJ, 1999). And, by 2001, the CDC were able to show a decline in spina bifida and anencephaly rates (Mathews *et al.*, 2002).

In this case, therefore, moving upstream is not just more effective and efficient. For about half the target population it is the only option. And inevitably the burden of spina bifida falls disproportionately on the least well off.

(v) It can be the only option

The problems of inequality reveal a more fundamental way in which moving upstream can prove to be the only alternative. Inequality, as we have noted on regular occasions throughout this book, has an enormous impact on health and welfare. As we saw in Chapter 4, even in a highly developed country like the UK, the poor die over 20 years before their wealthier peers. Furthermore, it is becoming increasingly apparent that it is not absolute poverty that matters, but relative poverty. What really harms our health and welfare, it seems, is knowing that people round the corner have so much more than we do.

As Steven Lansley (2006, p. 202) points out:

'Successive studies have shown that high levels of inequality are associated with higher rates of illness and death amongst the poorest. This is because more egalitarian societies display higher levels of general well-being while unequal ones suffer from higher levels of stress and depression at the bottom of the social ladder. This is the result of the growing psychological importance attached to relative as opposed to absolute positions in modern societies. Above subsistence levels, what seems to undermine our personal sense of well-being most is not our absolute living standard, but "psychosocial" factors that are related to the size of the gaps between us and those above us. In modern highly visible societies driven mainly by money, poor children and the low paid are only too aware of their lowly status.'

So poverty is not just a problem of the poor, but also of the rich. Lansley goes on to say that in Britain it is now clear that we are:

'... paying dearly – in higher crime rates, diverging mortality rates and widening levels of education achievement – for the soaring inequalities that began in the early 1980s.'

(Lansley, 2006)

The scenes in New Orleans following Hurricane Katrina show that Britain is not alone.

We have known for a long time that absolute poverty is disempowering, making it difficult for the disadvantaged to improve their lot without structural support. We now know that the real bugbear is relative poverty. Tackling this is completely beyond the capabilities of the poor. It is up to policymakers to act, not just to make the poor richer, but the rich poorer.

(vi) It reflects the complexity of our task

Addressing the upstream agenda also reflects the complexity of the social marketer's task. It is not a matter of either up- or downstream, but both and everything in between. If we were to shift our focus exclusively upstream we reduce people to the status of passive recipients of our enlightened ideas and policies – and previous chapters have underlined the dangers of this. Rather we need action at all sections of the stream.

At a recent conference on obesity in San Diego the full extent of the challenge facing us had been revealed: changes were needed in the behaviour of individuals, farmers, corporations, local authorities, government and international bodies. An elderly man stood up at this point and said, as a veteran of the protests against the Vietnam War, he recognized what we needed to tackle obesity: a movement. Movements intervene at all levels of the stream. To return to Wallack's analogy, they help people to swim, shut down the unscrupulous advertisers *and* get the Government to improve housing.

(vii) Ethics

Finally, moving upstream also has ethical dimensions. On the one hand, it may raise concerns about freedom of choice. Are water fluoridation and flour fortification unacceptable examples of mass medication? Why should men, for instance, who will never get pregnant, have to eat bread with, albeit harmless, folic acid supplements? As we will discuss in Chapter 10, there are few absolutes in morality. This apparent injustice needs to be balanced against the wrongs of withholding a known benefit from other sections of the population.

The bigger moral dilemma with upstream activity was touched on in Chapter 2: if we keep focused on the individual whilst ignoring the environmental determinants of their behaviour we are effectively blaming them for their predicament – a predicament that is in many ways beyond their control. As social marketers we have to avoid this tendency towards victim blaming (see Box 6.3).

Box 6.3   The baby camel's story

A baby camel approached his mother one day and asked 'Mummy, why do we have such hard bony tails?' His mother replied 'So that, when we move through the desert, we can protect ourselves from the biting and poisonous insects.' 'Mummy,' came the second question, 'why do we have such big, flat feet?' The mother replied 'So that we can move with ease over the treacherous shifting sands of the desert.' And again the little camel asked 'Why do we have a hump?' The explanation: 'So we can travel even into the Empty Quarter, where no other animal can pass, because we have with us all the food and water we need.'

Finally, the small voice asked: 'Mummy, why are we in the zoo?'

Source: Martin Caraher

We are all like the baby camel. We have lots of potential, but as long as we are encaged and restricted by our environment our hopes of fulfilling this are greatly reduced. It is immoral as well as ineffective for social marketers to ignore this reality.

■ The practicalities of upstream social marketing

What forces are at play?

As we noted in our discussion of Social Cognitive Theory (Chapter 2), environmental influences divide naturally into two domains. First, there is the relatively direct input of friends, family and the local community: the 'immediate environment'. One impressive example of this influence at work has emerged from research done by the MRC Social and Public Health Sciences Unit at the University of Glasgow (Henderson, 2006). This shows that substance misuse varies enormously between schools – smoking, for instance, veered from 6% to 36% in the study – depending on the policies and systems in operation in each establishment. Specifically, the school with the most supportive, health-promoting regime had the healthiest pupils – regardless of the individual characteristics of those children.

A longer-term and more extensive study conducted by the same team further supports the idea that the institution, as well as the pupil, is an important determinant of health behaviour (West *et al.*, 2004). The researchers argue that their findings support the need not just for health-promoting curricula, but health-promoting schools. We will return to this point in Chapter 9, when we discuss social marketing research.

Second, on a larger scale, there is the more indirect influence of social mores, economic conditions and cultural norms: the 'wider environment'. The influence of these wider forces is perhaps most dramatically demonstrated with indigenous peoples whose way of life, whose culture, has been undermined by colonization – the Maori in New Zealand, Aboriginals in Australia and the Native Americans are obvious examples. These peoples have an unenviable record of alcohol and drug misuse. Jane Middleton-Moz (2004) explains the problem in evocative terms:

> 'Loss of cultural meaning is why so many native peoples drink or take drugs or take their own lives. Often they blame themselves because they have internalized victim-blaming. Really, the fault lies with a cultural denial and disempowerment imposed by historical circumstances from the outside.'

Speaking as a Scottish academic these influences come closer to home than one might think. Alistair McIntosh (2004) argues that it is the loss of the traditional Hebridean and Highland crofting culture that has driven the alcohol abuse which is so prevalent in the glens. He describes a conversation with a local crofter called Torcuil:

> ' "These Red Indians, if that is what you call them," Torcuil continues, gazing directly into my eyes, monitoring every unconscious flicker as he tells me about the television programme that has made such an impact on him. "They said their culture is dying. They said it is because the circle, the Sacred Hoop, is broken." Long pauses punctuate every statement. This is not snappy, soundbite culture; this is where meaning lies more between

the words than in them. "Well I'll tell you this Alistair. I'll tell you this, my boy! It's the same for us. It's the same for the Gael. At least, that's what I think. Because when I heard them on the television, those Indians, I understood instantly what they meant." '

Addressing such powerful forces is daunting indeed, but nonetheless it is vital to be aware of them – and they can at least inform our approach to behaviour change. Box 6.4 describes Tane Cassidy and colleagues' impressive attempt to do so in New Zealand.

Box 6.4　The wider environment – trying to address cultural depletion

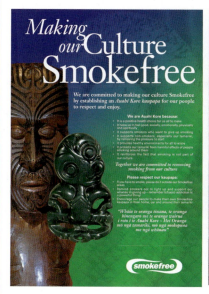 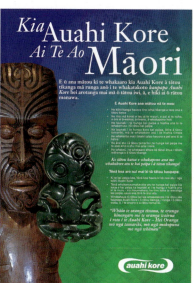

Auahi Kore was positioned as a specifically Maori offering. The core product – *Auahi Kore* – encapsulated Maori identity, Maori aspirations for development and control, pride in their culture, and Maori achievement. The actual products varied according to the consumer. One product was for upstream audiences, those people in control of significant Maori settings and/or activities. This product established Auahi Kore (Smokefree) places and policies on the basis that Maori development/achievement of Maori potential cannot occur alongside smoking and that young Maori should be provided with every opportunity to succeed. The 'Making Our Culture Smokefree' image (above) could be utilized across a range of settings – Marae Auahi Kore (smokefree marae – traditional Maori meeting places), Auahi Kore Kapa Haka events (traditional Maori performing arts), Kura Auahi Kore (smokefree schools and pre-schools), etc.

The second product focused on the downstream audience – the Maori public – and offered some of the same aspects of the first product as well as an 'Auahi Kore' experience (below). This experience equates to a demonstration that these special Maori places, events and activities could exemplify not only high quality traditional performances and/or fun or serious debate and discourse and/or family and community interaction – but they could also exemplify traditional life without tobacco – *Ao Maori, Ao Auahi Kore*.

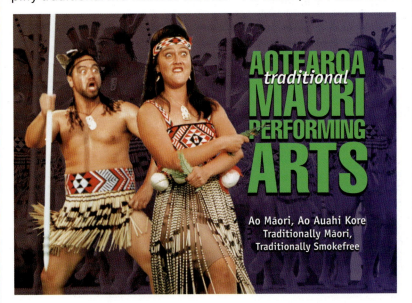

To build the personality of *Auahi Kore* strong Maori images were used and also association with uniquely Maori events and places. *Auahi Kore* is a Maori brand, not a smokefree brand.

Source: Tane Cassidy, Health Sponsorship Council, New Zealand

How can we address these forces?

Tane and colleagues help us begin answering this question. First, we need to recognize that immediate and wider environmental forces interact with each other and the individual to influence behaviour. Have a go at Exercise 6.2.

Exercise 6.2

The influence of tobacco advertising

Consider how the idea of the *immediate* and the *wider* environment might help explain the role of tobacco advertising in young people's smoking, as well as any impact it may have on them as individuals.

At the level of the *individual*, advertising can create brand awareness and appreciation. In the *immediate environment*, it reinforces the social and peer-driven aspects of smoking uptake. Advertising on billboards in the local community and at the point of sale in their favourite shops strengthens beliefs about the attractiveness and normality of smoking. It will also undermine the efforts of the local health-promoting school that the University of Glasgow research (*op. cit.*) shows is potentially so helpful.

At a *wider environmental* or societal level, the fact that tobacco advertising is allowed at all (whereas advertising for heroin or cocaine, for example, is not) communicates a very important message regarding our society's acceptance of cigarette smoking and underlines the notion that it is culturally endorsed and 'normal'. Many studies have shown that young smokers are inclined to downplay the hazards of smoking on the grounds that if it were all that dangerous, advertising would not be allowed. Figure 6.1, which is a development of the schematic we examined when discussing Social Cognitive Theory in Chapter 2, expresses the same points visually.

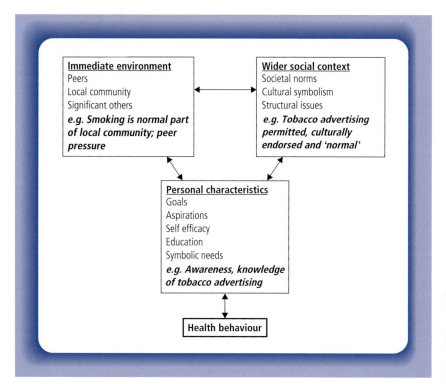

Figure 6.1
The wider determinants of health behaviour.
Source: MacFadyen *et al.* (1998).

Addressing these immediate and wider social domains involves exactly the same processes and mindset as social marketing which targets the individual. Client orientation, mutually beneficial exchange and strategic planning, all informed by careful research, are essential. First, research is conducted to identify key stakeholders, and to understand their needs, wants and motivations. Then, key market segments are identified and, having understood their needs, strategy is formulated based on an 'exchange' of values between the social marketer and the target group. Finally, the plan is implemented and evaluated.

Two examples illustrate how social marketing programmes can target the immediate and wider domains:

Example 1: The immediate environment – a sweet case

A recent attempt to redress the appalling oral health record of five-year-old children in the West of Scotland addressed an immediate environmental influence on confectionery consumption: the availability of sweets and chocolate at supermarket checkouts.

Scotland is renowned for its sweet tooth and Scottish children consume 28% more confectionery than their counterparts in the rest of the UK (Keynote, 1996). Sweets are frequently used to reward or pacify children, who come to associate comfort or praise with these sugary and familiar foodstuffs – thereby reinforcing their liking for them (Birch, 1980; Birch and Marlin, 1982). Obstreperous young children often successfully 'pester' their parents for confectionery in supermarkets and shops, especially in low-income communities. The strategic positioning of these products at the till-points greatly exacerbates this problem (Isler *et al.*, 1987).

The social marketing solution was not to tackle the challenge of changing children's liking for confectionery, or the parents' regrettable (but understandable) inclination to give in. In particular, there was a strong disinclination to make the lives of an already disadvantaged group more difficult or add guilt about inadequate parenting to their burden. Instead, it was decided to try and make their lives easier by getting confectionery removed from till-points. The target population, then, was not parents but retail outlets and, in particular, the staff who influenced in-store product positioning.

Research was conducted to inform a social marketing programme which would influence a change in policy. The research comprised an observation audit of confectionery positioning in stores and a series of in-depth interviews with key decision makers in retail organizations.

It was found that space planning decisions were rigorous and predictable: confectionery was placed at the point of sale to maximize profits from the available space. The research identified three broad groups of retail staff with a vested interest in confectionery policy: marketers, space planners and buyers. Each group had different strategic objectives and the barriers to adopting a new confectionery policy reflected each party's needs.

The research concluded that any initiative to remove confectionery at till-points must offer an exchange to each of these target groups (Table 6.1). It must demonstrate customer loyalty (to satisfy marketers), be profitable (to satisfy space planners), and offer long-term profitability for the products and alternative merchandising arrangements (to satisfy buyers).

Example 2: Regicide can be justified

'Reg' was a deliberately downbeat, ostensibly unattractive poster and press campaign for Imperial Tobacco's Regal brand of cigarettes, featuring

Table 6.1 Upstream exchange			
	Marketing staff	**Space planners**	**Buyers**
Exchange	Customer loyalty	Profitability	Supplier relationships
Intervention	Endorsement schemes Public opinion surveys	Immediate profits Competitive advantage	Long-term profitability Alternative merchan- dising strategies

fat, ugly, middle-aged men called Reg and Al (derived from the brand name). The adverts cracked facetious jokes about serious issues of the day, such as taxation and greenhouse gases. Anecdotal evidence suggested that the campaign, in fact, had a great appeal to adolescents and, given what is known about the effects of tobacco advertising, was encouraging children to smoke.

Social marketing provides a way of solving the problem.

Poster and press advertising in the UK at this time was regulated by the Advertising Standards Authority (ASA), so it became the *target*, and the *behaviour* desired of it was the removal of the Reg campaign. The ASA Code dictated that tobacco advertising must not appeal more to children than adults. To act on this it needed, in *exchange*, rigorous evidence that the campaign appealed more to children than adults. Given this, it could require the ads to be removed – indeed, it had no choice but to do so.

Audience research commissioned by the Health Education Authority (HEA), which had its rigour confirmed by publication in a major, peer-reviewed medical journal (the *intervention*), met this need. The research showed that Reg appealed to teenagers' rebelliousness, humour and peer-group values and, using branding, reinforced their smoking. It made them feel good about both their habit and themselves. Meanwhile, the campaign antagonized many adult smokers because they did not understand or relate to it (Hastings *et al.*, 1994).

Thus, the ASA's need was met and the result was a mutually beneficial exchange: the 'Reg' advertising campaign disappeared. The precise mechanisms of this removal remain unclear: the advertiser claimed they removed it voluntarily and would have done so anyway as the campaign was complete; the HEA was convinced that the pressure had delivered a good public health outcome. For our purposes it matters not; either way, it provides a good example of how social marketing can tackle the wider social environment, and that in doing so the principles are identical to those used to encourage individual behaviour change.

In Case Study 4 on p. 254, Laura McDermott and colleagues show how a much broader and more comprehensive effort to marshal the evidence base has been used to animate and inform the debate about childhood obesity and food advertising.

■ Moving further upstream

Social marketers can move further upstream. As we noted above, there are other influences on people's health, safety and quality of life that are completely beyond their control (except perhaps through the ballot box). Case Study 1 on p. 229, for instance, concerns the counter-productive tendency for the UK Government to lock up excessive numbers of criminals. By 2010, the prisoner numbers are set to reach 93 000: that is the equivalent of locking up every man, woman and child in Indianapolis. The result is overcrowded and ineffective prisons, and depressingly high levels of reoffending: Scottish figures match those for England quoted in Chapter 1 and show that almost 50% of prisoners return to prison within two years of being released. For young offenders, that return rate can be as high as 60% (SPS, 2005). Or, as Wilde put it in the *Ballad of Reading Gaol*: 'some grew mad, and all grew bad'.

The case explains how the public's need for safer communities is not being met, but at the same time there is little they can do about it. It requires action from policymakers and sentencers, and to get this both groups have to be convinced that lower prison numbers are in their interests. Politicians, for example, have to feel that voters will think better of them if they take a more enlightened stance on criminal justice, but as long as being draconian is seen as having electoral advantage little will change.

The case goes on to show how pricing, communications and product design are all useful concepts in thinking through how to tackle the problem (see Table 6.2).

Table 6.2 Reducing prison numbers: upstream social marketing in action

Objective	Marketing offering
Create consensus that current sentencing practice is increasing prison numbers	*Price*: Grants awarded to respected academics to research and publish on this issue, thereby showing the high cost of the current system; active dissemination of conclusions through peer-to-peer channels.
Increase dissonance about prison as a sentencing option for many offences	*Marketing communications*: Independent enquiry led by senior judge into the drawbacks of community sentences and the adequacy of alternatives; restorative justice seminar held in Downing Street; senior ministers invited to visit community sentence projects; RCP-funded* research on women, children, problem drug users and the mentally ill in prison to demonstrate the costs to society of imprisoning these groups, and the role of alternatives to custody such as drug treatment and testing orders.
Improve the perceived and actual effectiveness of restorative solutions	*Product*: 2005 Sentencing Review (independent of RCP) created a single, flexible community penalty; funded and disseminated demonstration projects; major cost-effectiveness review commissioned; public awareness and education.

* 'Rethinking Crime and Punishment' initiative.
Source: Case Study 1, p. 229.

In Case Study 1 on p. 229, Martine Stead and colleagues also identify an important role for the media in social marketing, not as a channel for pre-crafted messages as we discussed in Chapter 5, but as a target in themselves. In public health this is typically referred to as 'media advocacy' and involves encouraging the media to cover particular issues with a view to putting pressure on policymakers to take action. The encouragement can take the form of conventional press releases ('new research shows ...'), attention-grabbing events (e.g. public protests or celebrity appearances) and networking with journalists. Stead *et al.* (2002), for example, describe how these methods have been used to address drink-driving.

In the world of commercial marketing, this is known as public relations (PR) and has a long history. A recent enquiry by the UK Government's Health Select Committee into the pharmaceutical industry showed how networking with journalists and employing experts to write papers for publication in scientific journals are important aspects of their promotional activity (Devlin *et al.*, 2005). The tobacco industry has used similar methods over many years. In this context, media advocacy or PR raises obvious ethical concerns. When does putting a positive gloss on a story tip over into lying? At what point does a cultivated journalist stop doing his job properly? We will discuss ethics in much more detail in Chapter 10, but at this point it is just worth remembering that, as with the rest of marketing, the techniques themselves are largely amoral – it is *how* we use them and *for what purpose* that matters.

In social marketing, Andreasen (2006) has framed this type of activity as part of the movement upstream: the media are just one of the gatekeepers we should consider addressing, and this is the approach used in Case Study 1 on p. 229. It is a helpful perspective, because it reminds us that our use of media advocacy needs to be as systematic and well thought through as our other social marketing activities, even though the rather imprecise nature of the process makes this difficult. Stead *et al.*'s paper (2002), for example, shows how challenging it is to evaluate media advocacy, but argues that we have to try, and goes on to show how thinking imaginatively about research makes it possible to do so.

Similarly, despite the complexities of media advocacy, sophisticated marketing tools like segmentation and targeting can be used (see Box 6.5).

Box 6.5 Segmentation and targeting in media advocacy

In the late 1980s, the UK's Chancellor of the Exchequer bumped into a well-known and brilliant economic analyst in the corridors of the House of Commons. 'Peter,' he said, 'I very much enjoyed your editorial in the *Financial Times* on Thursday, but I didn't quite understand the point you were making about exchange rates in the third paragraph.' 'Chancellor,' came the reply, 'that editorial was aimed at three people, and you were not one of them.'

> Not perhaps a good way of making friends, but it does show how well thought through media advocacy needs to be.
>
> *Source*: Prof. Mike Saren

■ Upstream, downstream, midstream

All the examples in this chapter underline the range and complexity of the challenges social marketers have to face. Ultimately, as we have noted, it is not a matter of whether to go upstream or stay downstream, but of recognizing that all the possibilities have to be considered as part of any social marketer's strategic planning. Garry Noble (2006) suggests using an adaptation of Polonsky *et al.*'s (2003) 'harm chain' to do this systematically. Polonsky *et al.*'s thinking focuses on the potentially harmful impact of commercial marketing 'that might occur throughout pre-production, production, consumption and post-consumption' chain, and allows 'public policymakers to fully consider all who are harmed, as well as all those that can address harm'. Polonsky *et al.* go on to argue that 'this broader holistic approach to harm may ensure that more comprehensive public policy solutions are developed'. Noble takes matters a stage further and suggests that social marketers should think through the aetiology of a particular social or health problem to identify all the possible client and stakeholder groups who may be causing, being effected by or have a capacity to influence these outcomes. Combining this with a network perspective (tracing back who influences who) will make sure all those involved – whether directly or indirectly – will be identified. This broadens the picture to include the full complement of stakeholders and gatekeepers, including the media and community groups, as well as policymakers. Exercise 6.3 will help you try out his ideas.

Exercise 6.3

Fast-food advertising – who is involved?

The harm chain concept is a means of systematically 'linking' together all the stakeholders involved in a social or health issue and identifying suitable points for intervention.

Thinking in terms of four groups – those being harmed; those causing harm; regulators and significant others who can address harm; and those who influence regulators and significant others – consider all those involved in the issue of fast-food advertising to children. Then examine the diagram below and think through what intervention strategies could be placed where.

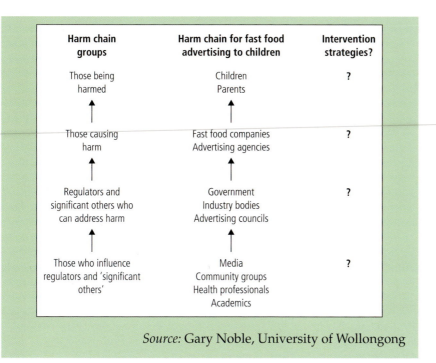

Harm chain groups	Harm chain for fast food advertising to children	Intervention strategies?
Those being harmed	Children Parents	?
↑	↑	
Those causing harm	Fast food companies Advertising agencies	?
↑	↑	
Regulators and significant others who can address harm	Government Industry bodies Advertising councils	?
↑	↑	
Those who influence regulators and 'significant others'	Media Community groups Health professionals Academics	?

Source: Gary Noble, University of Wollongong

Reading Case Study 4 on p. 254 will help you think through the exercise.

For parents and children, media literacy training might be an option, or informational campaigns to inform them that there is a problem. For example, in Case Study 4 the publicity surrounding the review of the evidence on food advertising and obesity helped inform parents that they should be concerned about the impact of advertising on their children. For advertisers and fast-food companies, the need may be for hard evidence to establish that there are real concerns in this area; without this, arguments will just go back and forth on the basis of opinion. The needs of regulators will vary depending on their constitutions and rules of engagement. In the case of Reg (above), for instance, incontrovertible evidence was needed, but other factors such as public opinion and media support may also be important, suggesting that media advocacy could be useful. The final group, the media and other stakeholders, will have various needs – a story, ammunition or funding.

Ultimately, though, the value of the harm chain is not that it will enable us to intervene successfully at every level – this is rarely possible – it just helps us to think systematically and realistically about the challenges we face. Indeed, the purpose of this chapter is to broaden our view of social marketing so that we never neglect the bigger picture, the social context that forms such an influential part of all our lives. Exercise 6.4 underlines how important this is.

Exercise 6.4

Who can save the planet?

Global warming is a very real threat. We are using too much of the wrong sort of energy, and as a result ice caps are melting, sea levels are rising and scientists of the stature of Stephen Hawking are suggesting that the only solution is to move to a new planet.

Let us see if we can come up with a less dramatic response. Consider how the broader perspective we have explored for social marketing in this chapter might be applied to the problem.

Then have a look at Figure 6.2.

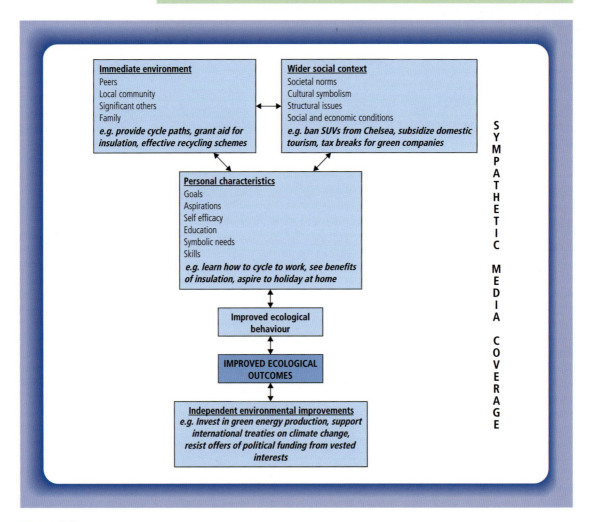

Figure 6.2
Comprehensive social marketing to tackle global warming.
Source: adapted from MacFadyen *et al.* (1998).

Conclusion

Social marketers are focused on behaviour change; it is just that when faced with any social, safety or health issue they must first ask *whose* behaviour needs to change.

To return to Wallack's metaphor, moving upstream is vital in social marketing. Addressing the individual has its place, and earlier chapters of this book have presented many examples of success with this type of intervention, but social marketers must also adopt a broader perspective. We have to be concerned with changing the social context in which individuals make decisions about their behaviour, and recognize that there will be occasions when these strategies will provide more effective and efficient social marketing solutions. There are also many health and social problems that can be mitigated without any consumer involvement, simply by targeting policymakers and implementers. In both these upstream arenas, standard social marketing techniques can be as effective as they are in changing the behaviour of individuals.

The reality, though, is that all levels of intervention are needed if social marketing is going to move from isolated behaviour change to ongoing social change. The next chapter picks up this idea of adding length to the breadth we have discussed here.

References

Alcalay R. and Bell R.A. (2000). *Promoting Nutrition and Physical Activity Through Social Marketing: Current Practices and Recommendations*. Prepared for the Cancer Prevention and Nutrition Section, California Department of Health Services, Sacramento, CA. Davis, CA: Center for Advanced Studies in Nutrition and Social Marketing, University of California, June.

Amos A., Currie C., Gray D. and Elton R. (1998). Perceptions of fashion images from youth magazines: does a cigarette make a difference? *Health Education Research Theory and Practice*, **13**(4): 491–501.

Andreasen A. (1995). *Marketing Social Change – Changing behavior to promote health, social development, and the environment*. San Francisco, CA: Jossey-Bass.

Andreasen A.R. (2006). *Social Marketing in the 21st Century*. London: Sage.

Barton J. and Janis L. (1997). *Smoking among Secondary School Children in 1996: Scotland*. London: ONS Social Surveys Division.

Birch L.L. (1980). Effects of peer models' food choices and eating behaviors on preschoolers' food preferences. *Child Development*, **51**: 489–496.

Birch L.L. and Marlin D.W. (1982). I don't like it; I never tried it: effects of exposure to food on two-year-old children's food preferences. *Appetite*, **4**: 353–360.

BMJ (1999). Fortification of flour raises folate levels in US women, says CDC. *British Medical Journal*, **318**: 1506.

Devlin E., Hastings G., Noble G., McDermott L. and Smith A. (2005) *Pharmaceutical Marketing: A Question of Regulation*. ISM Working Paper.

Goddard E. (1990). *Why Children Start Smoking*. London: HMSO/OPCS.

Goldberg M.E. (1995). Social marketing: are we fiddling while Rome burns? *Journal of Consumer Psychology*, **4**(4): 347–370.

Graham H. and Hunt K. (1998). Socio-economic influences on women's smoking status in adulthood: insights from the West of Scotland Twenty-07 Study. *Health Bulletin*, **56**(4), July: 757–765.

Hastings G.B., Ryan H., Teer P. and MacKintosh A.M. (1994). Cigarette advertising and children's smoking: why Reg was withdrawn. *British Medical Journal*, **309**: 933–937.

Henderson M. (2006). *School Effects on Adolescent Pupils' Health Behaviours and School Processes Associated with these Effects*, p. 299. Glasgow: MRC Social and Public Health Sciences Unit, University of Glasgow.

Isler L., Popper E. and Ward S. (1987). Children's purchase requests and parental responses: results from a diary study. *Journal of Advertising Research*, **27**(5): 28–39.

Jackson C., Henriksen L., Dickinson D., Messer L. and Robertson S.B. (1998). A longitudinal study predicting patterns of cigarette smoking in later childhood. *Health Education and Behaviour*, **25**(4): 436–447.

Jarvis L. (1997). *Smoking among Secondary School Children in 1996: England*. Office for National Statistics. London: The Stationery Office.

Keynote Report (1996). *Confectionery*. London: Keynote Publications.

Lansley S. (2006). *Rich Britain: The Rise and Rise of the New Super-Wealthy*. London: Politico's Publishing.

MacFadyen L., Hastings G.B., MacKintosh A.M. and Lowry R.J. (1998). Tobacco marketing and children's smoking: moving the debate beyond advertising and sponsorship. Paper presented at the 27th EMAC Conference, Stockholm, Sweden, 20–23 May 1998. In *Track 3 'Marketing Strategy and Organization': Proceedings, 27th EMAC Conference – Marketing Research and Practice* (Andersson P., ed.), pp. 431–456. Stockholm: European Marketing Academy.

Mathews T.J., Honein M.A. and Erickson J.D. (2002). Spina bifida and anencephaly prevalence – United States, 1991–2001. *MMWR Recommendations and Reports*, **51** (RR13): 9–11.

McIntosh A. (2004). *Soil and Soul: People versus Corporate Power*. London: Aurum Press.

Middleton-Moz J. (2004). Quoted in McIntosh A., *Soil and Soul: People versus Corporate Power*, p. 49. London: Aurum Press.

Morgan M. and Grube J.W. (1989). Adolescent cigarette smoking: a developmental analysis of influences. *British Journal of Developmental Psychology*, **7**(May): 179–189.

NHS Statistics (2006). *Registrations (GDS and PDS) Percentage of Population Aged 18 Years and Over who are Registered with a Dentist for England and Wales for the Quarter Ending March 2006*. Online at NHSBSA Dental Practice Division website: http://www.dpb.nhs.uk/gds/latest_data.shtml (accessed 14 August 2006).

Noble G. (2006). Maintaining social marketing's relevance: a dualistic approach. Paper presented at the 2006 ANZMAC Conference, Brisbane, Australia, 4–6 December.

Patton G.C., Carlin J.B., Wolfe C.R., Hibbert M. and Bowes G. (1998). The course of early smoking: a population-based cohort study over three years. *Addiction*, **93**(8): 1251–1260.

Pierce J.P., Gilpin E.A. and Choi W.S. (1999). Sharing the blame: smoking experimentation and future smoking-attributable mortality due to Joe Camel and Marlboro advertising and promotions. *Tobacco Control*, **8**(1): 37–44.

Polonsky M.J., Carlson L. and Fry M.-L. (2003). The harm chain: a public policy development and stakeholder perspective. *Marketing Theory*, **3**(3): 345–364.

SPS (2005). *SPS Return to Custody Bulletin 2001*, 5 May 2005. Published online: http://www.sps.gov.uk

Stead M., Hastings G.B. and Eadie D. (2002). The challenge of evaluating complex interventions: a framework for evaluating media advocacy. *Health Education Research Theory and Practice*, **17**(3): 351–364.

Wallack L., Dorfman L., Jernigan D. and Themba M. (1993). *Media Advocacy and Public Health*. Newbury Park, CA: Sage.

West P., Sweeting H. and Leyland A. (2004). School effects on pupils' health behaviours: evidence in support of the health promoting school. *Research Papers in Education*, **19**(3): 261–291.

CHAPTER 7

Relational
Thinking

■ Overview

Chapter 6 demonstrated that the behaviours social marketers want to change have multiple influencers, and this compels us to broaden our vision and ask who needs to do the changing. This chapter continues the focus on the nature of social marketing behaviours and reminds us that our interest is not usually in ad hoc acts. We do not want people to wear a seat-belt once, refrain from hitting their partner every now and then or eat five portions of fruit and vegetables occasionally. We want them to do these things again and again – indeed, forever more. Actually, our interest is very often in lifestyles rather than isolated behaviours.

Commercial marketers reached a similar conclusion some 20 years ago and began to think less in terms of individual exchanges with their customers and more about building relationships with them. Tesco does not just want us to do our shopping at its stores once, it wants us go every week; so, if we do, it rewards us with a loyalty card and discounts, and regularly sends us a nice magazine. It tries to build a relationship with us. And all the evidence is that, despite the obvious mercenary motivations of its charm offensive, it works. We do respond with brand loyalty and regular visits. This relational thinking can be applied equally well – if not better – in social marketing.

This chapter therefore emphasizes the need for social marketers to add length to the breadth discussed in Chapter 6. It also shows how these ideas dovetail well with behaviour change theory (Chapter 2) and reinforce the idea of the strategic planning process (Chapter 3). It is this kind of strategic thrust that will enable social marketing to deliver not just behaviour and lifestyle change, but social change.

Learning objectives

After working through this chapter you will:

- Be familiar with the origins of relational thinking in commercial marketing.
- Recognize its potential value to social marketing.
- See how this can be applied in practice.
- Be able to combine this thinking with upstream social marketing (see Chapter 6) into an understanding of strategic social marketing.

During this chapter you might find it useful to cross-refer to the discussions of:
- Strategic planning in Chapter 3
- The marketing mix, objective setting and segmentation in Chapter 4
- Branding in Chapter 5
- The harm chain in Chapter 6
- Case Studies 9 and 14.

LINKS TO OTHER CHAPTERS

■ Back to basics: learning from commercial marketing

Over the last 20 years the commercial sector has increasingly recognized the importance of continuity and sustainability, and this has resulted in the development of relationship marketing. The story begins in the 1980s with concerns emerging about the marketing orthodoxy.

This orthodoxy, and the basic ideas underpinning it, were laid down some three decades previously, and based on research in the fast-moving consumer goods (FMCG) sector. They used military metaphors such as 'campaigns' and 'targets', and a set of tools, typically comprising the 'four Ps' (promotion, pricing, place and product) of the marketing mix. Objectives had to be realistic, measurable and focused on sales and profits: successful transactions. This thinking has much to commend it, as we have discussed in previous chapters. It provides us with a clear and systematic way of thinking about voluntary behaviour change.

However, it also has a fundamental limitation in its focus on transactions, which are by their nature ad hoc. In the business sector it also clashes with experience in the service (e.g. banks) and business-to-business (e.g. marketing between component manufacturers and car producers) sectors. Services differ from tangible products in that they are not pre-prepared and packaged, but are, to a large extent, 'manufactured' at the point of delivery. This makes the 'four Ps' less easy to apply. Specifically, it fails to give sufficient emphasis to that most crucial of service industry constructs: customer service. In business-to-business marketing, the mass, transactional assumptions in FMCG marketing conflicted with a day-to-day reality of long-term, cooperative alliances between buyers (Rajagopal and Bernard, 1993). The experiences of sales staff and buyers showed that their success was built more on mutual understanding, cooperation and even friendship than on some prefabricated marketing toolkit.

Similar difficulties arise with social and health behaviours, which have much more in common with services marketing than the FMCG sector.

In both cases a more continuous and sophisticated model is needed.

Business has also become increasingly conscious that customer loyalty matters. It is, for example, much more efficient to keep existing customers than win new ones – one study suggests that a 5% increase in customer retention can generate a 20–80% increase in profits (Reichheld, 1996). The emphasis has therefore shifted from one-off transactions to ongoing relationships and companies thinking not just about immediate, but long-term, profitability. Indeed, individual transactions may lose money, provided the 'lifetime value' of the customer is positive.

This has fundamental implications for the business function, greatly increasing the importance of customer service and satisfaction. In this context, sales are a poor measure of performance because they put the focus on yesterday rather than tomorrow. The fact that you bought a brand X washing machine once is no guarantee you will do so again; in fact, if the experience is bad – if the shop overcharges, for example, or the machine fails to work properly – the chances are you will not repurchase. So, from a planning perspective, finding out about that experience, about customer satisfaction, is much more helpful than studying the sales graph.

Sales targets also encourage unscrupulous selling practices; if you have to sell 10 washing machines a week to get promotion, you are more inclined to twist the customer's arm or fabricate returns. From a consumer's perspective, therefore, it is much better to shop at a store where the sales force gets promoted for giving good service. A recent review of the methods used by commercial marketers to reach low income consumers – who, because of their lack of funds, are particularly canny shoppers – noted that commission-based selling met with resistance and should be avoided (Stead *et al.*, 2006). A survey conducted in 2001 by the Economics Intelligent Unit suggests that this lesson is generally well accepted in the commercial sector. It showed that customer satisfaction is taking over from profitability as the prime determinant of performance-related pay in leading companies across Europe, Asia and North America (Richardson, 2001).

The social sector is not immune to these kinds of subversions: as we noted in our discussion of exchange in Chapter 2, even schoolteachers can be corrupted by the wrong kind of incentive (Levitt and Dubner, 2005). And, as we will note below, too great an emphasis on 'sales' targets has created problems for the UK's Smoking Cessation Services.

A recent review of the methods used by commercial marketers to reach low income consumers – who, because of their lack of funds, are particularly canny shoppers – noted that commission-based selling met with resistance and should be avoided (Stead *et al.*, 2006).

More recent research has taken this thinking a stage further. Measuring good service would seem to be more challenging than measuring sales; however, a study published in the *Harvard Business Review* (Reichheld, 2003) has demonstrated that satisfaction can be measured using just one simple question: would you recommend this service to a friend? Furthermore, not only does this reveal how well you are doing now, but it predicts how fast you will grow by identifying not just satisfied, but 'delighted' customers. These *will* recommend the service to a friend. Indeed, Reichheld suggests that, on average, they will tell four other people of their pleasure, effectively becoming the company's marketing department.

In the introductory chapter we noted the commercial marketers' ability to turn us into logo-festooned billboards through branded clothing, and that we are quite willing to cooperate in this way because we benefit from doing so. We gain an association with attractive brand values: our Nike trainers or Berghaus fleece help us acquire the very imagery we are transmitting on the marketers' behalf. And these benefits are ongoing: one-off image fixes become lifestyle statements. Reichheld's research simply shows that our collaboration can become more active. This is exactly the type of mobilization or 'full engagement' that Derek Wanless (2004) called for in his recent review of UK public health. Unless people become actively involved in their own health improvement, he argues, we will make no significant impact on health status or inequalities.

In essence, with relationship marketing, the aim is to simulate the kind of service, and the resulting loyalty, that exists in a small community shop or bar. This demands an intimate knowledge of your customer, covering not just their response to your offering, but also their psychographics, past experience with the company, hopes and aspirations, and much more. It means making and keeping promises, accepting that some of the individual transactions that make up the relationship will be unprofitable and ensuring that the process, as well as the offering, provides customer satisfaction.

In this way, the emphasis moves from *marketer*- to *customer*-defined quality. This does not abandon the idea of technical expertise on the part of the marketer, it just recognizes that when dealing with human behaviour the customer's perspective is central. Box 7.1 explores this thinking using the example of a driving school.

Box 7.1   The driving school

As a driving school customer you are putting your trust in the skill and professionalism of the instructor. You know that their knowledge of driving and the Highway Code far exceeds yours. And yet you would expect them to consult you and take the time to assess your needs before they fix on a learning regimen. You would be very disconcerted, for example, to be told that you – like everyone else – had six lessons to learn to drive, then you would sit your test whether you felt ready to or not and, pass or fail, the driving school would wash their hands of you.

You would not be happy with a standardized, predetermined offering. It is not that you doubt their abilities, it is just that you have a legitimate contribution to make to decisions about your own learning.

Nor would you be comfortable with such an ad hoc service. The fact is, you are not really there to buy driving *lessons* at all, what you really want is a driving *licence*. And if the driving school is on top of its job it will sell you exactly that: the support you need to pass your test, however long that might take.

This holds important lessons for the case of the UK's Smoking Cessation Services, which we will discuss below.

Until recently, such insights were only possible on a small scale – a buyer dealing with a couple of dozen suppliers, or a local pub, for instance. But information technology has changed things. Data mining, mobile communications, vastly enhanced computers, opportunistic and endemic data-gathering all provide even the biggest operators with the potential to understand and respond sensitively to their customers. Exercise 7.1 discusses how the alcohol industry has used 'customer relationship marketing' through the Internet and mobile communications to build relationships with young people, and asks you to consider how social marketers might use similar techniques to combat binge drinking.

Exercise 7.1

Building customer relationships with young people in the alcohol market

The opportunity

Young people are the biggest users of 'new media'; many have access to the Internet at home or at school (Buckley, 1998) and 50% have mobile phones – a figure that rises to 77% of 14- to 16-year-olds (BBC News Online, 2001). The technology is evolving very quickly and young people both enjoy and succeed in keeping well abreast of the changes (*New Media Age*, 1998).

The opportunities for the marketer are considerable: the chance to produce flexible and customized messages, interact directly with individual consumers, and get them involved in generating and passing on messages. The last idea has been termed viral marketing and creates 'the potential for exponential growth in the message's exposure and influence' (Wilson, 2000). Furthermore, the process becomes a social experience, involving the peer group and taking place in young people's own leisure space. This in turn provides the opportunity to tie in with other aspects of marketing, such as sales promotions and new product development. Being at the technological cutting edge adds credibility to the process.

Example 1

Anheuser-Busch made effective use of viral marketing in their 'Whassup?!' campaign for Budweiser. Prior to any ads appearing, text messages were sent to a database of key customers giving them advance information about the campaign. Once they had appeared, the slogan was then sent out so that it could be passed on by the receivers to their friends (*Precision Marketing*, 2000). This was supported by a website offering interactive activities, including further opportunities to forward the slogan, messages and characters from the adverts to friends using both email and text messaging. The campaign was very successful: 'Whassup?!' became a popular catchphrase in many languages (*Brand Strategy*, 2001) and a musical version of the ad made it into the UK chart listings.

Example 2

In Glasgow, owners of mobile phones could register details of their favourite city bars at a website called barbeep.com, which sent text messages as and when they chose, alerting them to the latest promotions in these establishments (Ward, 2001).

How might a social marketer use similar techniques to combat binge drinking? Jot down your ideas before continuing.

Now read Josephine Previte's Case Study (number 14 on p. 315). It describes how the Internet is used to reach young people at danger from suicide and domestic violence, and provides an excellent exposition of relationship marketing. She talks about using the medium not just to provide information, but to generate 'interaction', 'participation' and 'engagement'; of creating 'a safe place that they return to frequently'; and how young people set the agenda, generate and deliver the messages, and introduce additional issues of concern.

As with other human relationships, business relationships depend on a degree of trust and commitment. Tesco has to deliver on its promises, make amends when things go wrong and develop a reputation for doing both. Relationship marketing and branding (see Chapter 5) begin to link up. One commentator even went as far as likening marketing relationships to marriage, though for many this is a metaphor too far – the motives of Tesco are clearly selfish. Tesco is not building relationships with us because it has fallen in love, but because it is good for business.

And there are indeed many commercial benefits to relationship marketing: stability and better long-term planning because you get to know your customers; lower price sensitivity because service quality and trust provide valued compensations; and the opportunity to 'up sell' (sell more) and 'cross sell' (sell alternative products). Previte's Case Study shows the applicability of these constructs to social and health issues.

The thinking can also be extended vertically, horizontally and internally. Relationships can be built with suppliers, stakeholders and even (in the case of strategic alliances) competitors (Palmer, 2000). All these groups therefore become involved in marketing, which in turn means that all employees are inevitably drawn into the equation. Total quality management demands a customer focus throughout the supply chain, and so relationship building is as important internally as externally. Morgan and Hunt (1994) suggest a total of 27 different sorts of relationship that are open to companies, which they group into four categories: lateral (e.g. competitors), buyers (e.g. customers), internal (e.g. employees) and suppliers (e.g. research or advertising agencies).

All this, it is argued, delivers the vital ingredient of successful marketing: sustained competitive advantage (we will return to this in Chapter 8). Furthermore, the idea of relationships is a more convincing articulation of the marketing concept than the transaction and the toolbox; it characterizes the marketer as doing things *with* their customers, not *to* them. Customer orientation should involve partners, not targets, and partners call for relationships, not just transactions.

It also provides an intelligent way of thinking about what happens in the real world. Customers are increasingly empowered and active in the marketing process; the media are becoming fragmented and much more interactive, undermining the traditional hegemony of advertising; and symbolic consumption is a reality that forces marketers to negotiate, rather than impose, meaning on their customers.

Many of these advantages are equally valuable in the social and health sectors.

■ From Tesco to smoking cessation

Exercise 7.2 will help you think through the possibilities using the example of England Smoking Cessation Services (SCS). This was established in 2002 to support smokers who want to quit. Smokers are referred to the service through a health professional – usually their GP. They are encouraged to set a quit date within two weeks, then supported for a further four weeks with either group or individual counselling.

Exercise 7.2

Relationship marketing and quitting smoking

The Smoking Cessation Service (SCS) have made enormous progress in recent years. Greatly improved funding, professionally defined standards and clear targets have focused effort and ensured rigour. The result is a high-quality, standardized service with six weekly sessions, a quit date set within two weeks, which is then monitored for fidelity in a further four. And it works: 12-month cessation rates jump to 15% (Ferguson *et al.*, 2005), compared with 4% (Hughes *et al.*, 2004) for those who battle on alone. The SCS is also 10 times more cost-effective than the UK Government's NICE guidelines demand (Godfrey *et al.*, 2005). In 2003, no fewer than 235 000 smokers used the service. Perhaps most impressively of all, the SCS has succeeded in reaching into low-income communities. Last year alone it helped no fewer than 4000 of the UK's poorest smokers to quit (Ferguson *et al.*, 2005).

So, a great success story.

However, there are clouds on the horizon. Whilst the 15% 12-month quit rate is impressive, the 85% who lapse (45% by week 4 and a further 40% between week 4 and 12 months) get little or no follow-up. There is a perplexing mismatch between the service (which typically lasts six weeks) and the outcome (cessation at 12 months) – what Robert West (2004), one of the world leaders in the field, calls 'latency'. The targets for throughput and quit rates are onerous and may even be encouraging cheating, which will introduce a dangerous contamination into the evidence base (Raw *et al.*, 2005). Most fundamentally, the SCS remains a 'bit player' in the real public health game: prevalence. Even its greatest advocates accept its impact can only ever be marginal. Estimates vary, but typically it is put at well under 1% – which means, if we were to depend on the SCS alone, the UK smoking pandemic would continue for at least another century.

Your task

As a marketer, how would you advise the SCS? In particular, what role can you see for relationship marketing ideas?

In considering your answers to the questions in the exercise, two additional insights might be helpful. First, as we have noted elsewhere, giving up smoking can be a formidable challenge demanding sustained and sometimes arduous effort. The counterweight is that success brings very positive rewards. The comments in Figure 7.1 are from ex-smokers and show just how uplifting and even life-changing it can be.

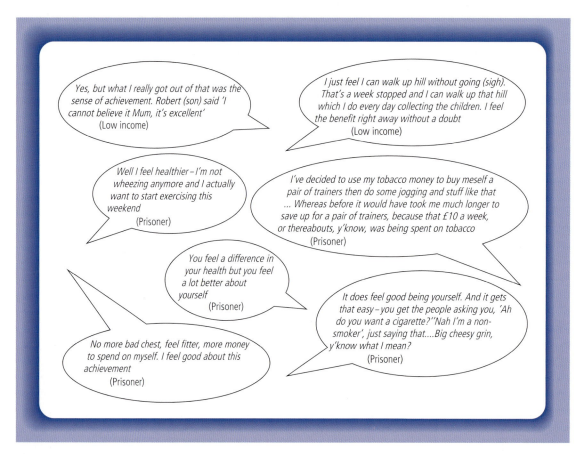

Figure 7.1
Delighted clients: quitting smoking is difficult but tremendously rewarding, especially for the most disadvantaged groups.
Source: MacAskill and Eadie (2002), MacAskill *et al.* (2002).

Second, smoking is strongly related to social class and deprivation. The poorer you are, the more likely you are to smoke. Low-income communities like Castlemilk in Glasgow still have prevalence rates of over 50%, compared to a national average of around a quarter. However, as Exercise 7.2 points out, the SCS has been remarkably successful in reaching into our poorest communities. And keep in mind the comments in Figure 7.1 came from very disadvantaged smokers.

Consulting Case Study 9 on p. 284 by Neil McLean and answering the questions will also help.

For the marketer the SCS's considerable successes to date give cause for optimism, but also suggest that to achieve its potential it will have to develop and innovate. First, the current notion of a 'one size fits all' service needs to be reassessed. Standardized practice is well suited to clinical interventions or drug therapies – areas where individual volition is relatively unimportant or even a distraction – but makes much less sense when dealing with human behaviour, even an addictive one. Furthermore, research shows that smokers' needs do vary: second-time service users differ from first timers (Hajek *et al.*, 2005) and low-income smokers differ from those in other social groups (MacAskill *et al.*, 2002; Ferguson *et al.*, 2005). Similarly, for a marketer, there is a very obvious need to address the problem of 'latency' and begin to support smokers beyond the four-week quit point. Relapse prevention, for example, is an obvious gap in provision.

This thinking is supported by even the most cursory competitive analysis (see Chapter 8), which will show that the tobacco industry actively customizes its offerings. It segments and targets with gusto, producing trendy Marlboro Lights for young aspirants or cheap and cheerful Royals for low-income jobbing smokers. For example, a segmentation analysis prepared for the UK tobacco company Gallaher, divided young smokers into four types: 'slobs', 'young aspirants', conservatives' and 'worriers'. Figure 7.2 shows how the first of these segments got its rather offensive sobriquet, and how offerings were matched up with their needs.

'Describing members of this cluster as "Slobs" may seem unkind, but this title is particularly earnt by their low concern with their appearance and the little effort they make to keep themselves informed. The latter is supported by the low status they attach to their work (a job, rather than a career) and their below average likelihood of buying a daily newspaper.'

'Hedonistic slobs' is arguably a better description of this cluster with their "head in the sand" approach to the smoking and health issue and to their diet. Their clear requirement is for a stronger cigarette, and hence both B&H Special Filter and Kensitas Club KS (this cluster being well represented in Scotland) do well amongst this cluster, whilst not surprisingly this is the weakest cluster for Silk Cut KS and low tar brands generally.'

Figure 7.2
Matching offerings to target segments in the tobacco market.
Source: TobaccoPapers.com (http://www.tobaccopapers.com/PDFs/0500-0599/0571.pdf).

A social marketer would argue that we must follow suit, though taking care to avoid such a pejorative and judgemental mindset. Offerings need to be honed to meet our customers' differing needs. This does not mean abandoning current services, but it does mean extending and developing them. Service provision must at least partly be informed by client satisfaction.

To do this, far more needs to be known about why people do or do not try and quit smoking, and the role that cessation services might play in their decision making. And for those who do try and quit, and do use cessation services, what is the experience like? How does it make them feel? Would they do it again? Would it work for other health behaviours?

This brings us naturally to the concept of customer-defined quality, which is as relevant in social as commercial marketing. Much as with the driving school example (Box 7.1), the quitter has a lot to offer in helping to define the optimal service. This does not deny the contribution of the expert (in this example, the cessation professional), but it does put it in context. It also reminds us that the focus here should be on the client's desired outcome (becoming smoke free), not the delivery of a preordained, standardized service or meeting throughput targets – just as with the driving school, it is about driving licences, not lessons; becoming smoke free, not attending cessation sessions.

And remember, it is this focus on customer satisfaction that has led business to shift their thinking from transactions to relationships. So what does the SCS do with its clients when they come to the end of their standard six-week service? Well, because it has throughput targets to meet and a standardized service to deliver, it measures whether they have quit or not and records the data. Occasionally, it will go back after 12 months and repeat the measure. But mostly it just says 'goodbye'. And it is a terrible waste.

Of the 235 000 smokers who used the English SCS in 2003, 45% failed to quit at four weeks; the SCS recorded their failure and sent them on their way. But to have got that far they must be very committed to kicking the habit; half of those assessed and assigned to the SCS do not make it to the first appointment, let alone the week 4 quit date. Surely it would make sense to hand these people on to a continuing service of some kind – maybe through links with the third sector as Wanless (2004) suggests? Putting them back to the standard SCS clearly is not appropriate; though at the moment that is effectively all the NHS offers them. At the very least they comprise a valuable list of promising potential quitters.

The 55% who succeed are also sent on their way, with no support or help through the ensuing ten and a half months of struggle, after which they get a call to check to see if they have indeed succeeded. Most – three-quarters of the 55% – will confess failure. Again, they are deeply committed to quitting and nearly made it, but the SCS severs links. Not so much as a card of commiseration and a word of encouragement to keep trying – although we know that most smokers need several attempts before they quit successfully.

If they are part of the chosen few, the 15% who have successfully quit, they will probably be asked to provide a saliva sample to verify that they have really quit – because the demands for rigorous outcome evaluation mean their word is not good enough. And then links are severed. And yet these are the Service's greatest successes, their most loyal customers. They will be extremely pleased with themselves (look at Figure 7.1 again) and – chances are – the SCS. In short they are Reichhield's (*op. cit.*) delighted customers.

Social marketing, with an emphasis on relationship building and customer satisfaction, would not be so profligate. For the 85% who do not make it, it would want to make sure the service was not getting the blame, if only because dissatisfied customers can do a lot of harm by telling other people about their dissatisfaction. More positively, they would see great opportunities for growth. These are people who are definitely in the market for cessation support, they just have not found the right product yet. At the very least, a direct marketing effort would be warranted. The 15% who succeed present an even more encouraging scenario: as delighted clients they can become the SCS's marketing department. Building relationships with them will not just enhance their experience of the SCS, but can generate real growth.

As the example of ReachOut! in Josephine Previte's Case Study shows, such relationship building and mobilization is perfectly possible for social marketers:

> 'Building and sustaining relationships is a core strategy for ReachOut!. They achieve this by providing programmes where ReachOut! participants elect to become "youth ambassadors" for the programme, and participate in decision making, developing new ideas for the service and promotional activities.'

Inequalities

Adding some segmentation and targeting (see Chapter 4) increases the potential. As we have noted, smoking is particularly prevalent in low-income communities, suggesting that previous efforts to encourage cessation have not been very successful. But, as we have also noted, the SCS is succeeding with these groups. The formal evaluation of the service estimated that around 4000 low-income smokers use the service to quit every year. That is 4000 delighted clients who will already be telling others of their own success and (hopefully) that of the SCS. They have unbeatable source credibility. And they are embedded in the communities we most want, and yet so often fail, to reach.

Just suppose the SCS did not sever links with these people, but built relationships with them. Encouraged and supported them. Recruited them as volunteer – or even paid – helpers. They could boost attendance at the SCS, increase empowerment (they are living, breathing testimonials) and even set up additional services such as self-help groups. And why stop at smoking? A bit of joined-up thinking (or to use the rather ugly relationship marketing jargon, 'up selling' and 'cross selling') and a whole raft of health improvement issues could be put on the agenda: 'Want to lose those pounds you gained when you kicked the weed? Come along to the community hall on Tuesday at 7.00 …' Indeed, it is interesting to note that Weight Watchers is largely staffed by volunteer ex-customers who find the work helps them maintain their own behaviour change (see Case Study 9 on p. 284).

■ Relationship thinking in social marketing

The Smoking Cessation Services example, along with Case Studies 9 and 14, show that relationship thinking has much to offer social marketing. As in business it can deliver strategic success by:

- Focusing effort on client satisfaction
- Supporting long-term rather than intermittent change
- Building trust and showing commitment
- Engaging and mobilizing target populations.

The emphasis on client satisfaction has fundamental implications for social marketing. It means that Andreasen's (1994) injunction to focus on behaviour change needs to be matched with an equal commitment to service quality. Otherwise promising programmes that do not result in rapid behaviour change are liable to be written off as failures. Try Exercise 7.3.

Exercise 7.3

NE Choices – failed behaviour change or incomplete relationship marketing?

NE Choices was a three-year drugs prevention intervention built around a high school drama initiative, with additional community, school governor and parent components. It had four behavioural objectives:

- To reduce prevalence of drug use
- To delay the age of onset of drug use
- To reduce the frequency of drug use among those who use drugs
- To reduce mixing of drugs (including with alcohol) by those who use drugs.

The programme adopted a social influences approach, backed by social marketing, and was thoroughly researched with all the stakeholder groups using a design that incorporated a two-year pilot, along with formative, process, impact and outcome evaluations. The last comprised a rigorous experimental design.

An action-research model meant that the pilot and formative research informed the initial programme design, and ongoing process and impact findings guided its development. The result was therefore extremely consumer oriented and the young people – as well as other stakeholders – strongly endorsed it. The impact evaluation showed, for example, that the vast majority of children felt the programme was enjoyable (89%), thought-provoking (88%) and credible (84%), and that the drama was realistic (79%) and non-didactic (e.g. 88% agreed that 'it encouraged us to speak our own minds'). In addition, the young people trusted the programme and its brand. For example, the last stage of research had to be conducted by mail, as a proportion of the young people had, by then, left school. The vast majority were prepared to provide contact details, and 70% completed the sensitive and complex (40-minute) questionnaire. However, despite three annual follow-ups, the outcome research showed no changes on any of the four behavioural objectives.

According to social marketing lore, and the programme's own objectives, NE Choices had failed.

From a relationship marketing perspective, is such a judgement justified?

Source: Hastings *et al.* (2005)

NE Choices delivered excellent customer service and built up a marked degree of trust with the young people, as well as other stakeholders, as was demonstrated by the success of the final survey. A valuable database of a vulnerable and normally elusive group was also developed, providing a unique opportunity to develop these putative relationships further. (Indeed, the programme delivery team was approached by more than one commercial operator wanting to buy the database.)

Furthermore, three of NE Choices' impact evaluation successes – reaching a range of stakeholders and settings, as well as the core clients (Fortmann *et al.*, 1995; Pentz *et al.*, 1997; King, 1998); the successful use of drama in education to engage the audience (Blakey and Pullen, 1991; Denman *et al.*, 1995; Bouman *et al.*, 1998; Orme and Starkey, 1998); and being non-didactic (Blakey and Pullen, 1991; ACMD, 1993; JRF, 1997; Allott *et al.*, 1999; Orme and Starkey, 1999) – are known to be linked to effective knowledge, attitude and behaviour change. This does suggest, as well as good relationships being established, that the first signs of behaviour change were also emerging.

Arguably, therefore, from a relationship marketing perspective, NE Choices offered a great deal of promise, but transactional thinking cut it off in its prime. As Morgan and Hunt (1994) express it:

'Understanding relationship marketing requires distinguishing between the discrete transaction, which has a "distinct beginning, short duration, and sharp ending by performance", and relational exchange, which "traces to previous agreements [and] … is longer in duration, reflecting an ongoing process".'

NE Choices was judged by the former school of thought, but had the potential to deliver the latter.

Furthermore, we know that long-term health improvement is dependent on much more than the short-term avoidance of illicit substances. It requires a broadly based positive lifestyle, which in turn demands supportive individual knowledge and attitudes, and a constructive environment. These are gradual, continuous goals not time-limited objectives, and they pull us towards relational thinking. Like the Smoking Cessation Services discussed above, NE Choices had the potential to become a long-term and trusted source of help and advice for the young people of northern England, not just on substance misuse, but all aspects of positive lifestyle.

Time and again, the types of behaviour social marketing seeks to change make relational ideas particularly appropriate. Think back to Stages of Change Theory (Chapter 2), which tells us that changes do not, for the most part, occur overnight. They involve a series of steps from initial contemplation through to reinforcement after the fact, a process that is both dynamic and precarious: the individual can regress or change heart at any point.

Even when they are apparently ad hoc, such as with one-off immunizations during a sudden outbreak of infectious disease or temporary speed restrictions following a road traffic accident, relationship issues such as source credibility and trust are going to be crucial. The scare over the MMR (measles, mumps and rubella) vaccine in the UK, for example, which has bedevilled childhood immunization efforts over the last decade, is driven by a lack of trust of the health authorities among parents (Evans *et al.*, 2001).

Furthermore, as we noted in Chapter 5, social marketing behaviours often have emotional as well as rational drivers. Feelings matter. We know, for example, that young people smoke despite their knowledge of the health consequences because it makes them feel adult and fashionable. It is this that explains the tobacco industry's huge – and extremely long-term – investment in evocative brands. It also suggests that constructive relationships are needed not just in their own right, but to counteract these abusive ones.

Social marketing also has a built-in advantage on the trust front. It is driven not by profit but, notwithstanding our discussion in Chapter 2 about mutual benefit, a desire to improve things for the target group. It therefore has a very different – and arguably a morally higher – base than commercial marketing on which to build mutual respect with its clients. So, if commercial marketers can seriously argue that 'the presence of relationship commitment and trust is central to successful relationship marketing, not power and its ability to "condition others"' (Morgan and Hunt, 1994, p. 22), then social marketers have to listen.

These benefits – satisfaction, sustainability and trust – underpin the potential for ideas like social enterprise (we will return to this in Chapter 8), and thereby can help to deliver the growth and popular engagement that is needed to deliver social change. Relationship marketing is being used all too effectively by commercial marketers to lock people into consumption; in a finite world we have to use the same tools to push more sustainable, healthy and socially desirable behaviours.

Relational thinking, then, fits social marketing like a glove. It should not be seen as just another optional tool. Like consumer orientation, it is fundamental to all marketing efforts; as Sheth and Parvatiyar (1995, p. 414) said, 'Relationship marketing has the potential for a new "General

Theory of Marketing", as its fundamental axioms better explain marketing practice'. As so often in this book, I would argue that what is true for commercial marketers is true for us in social marketing.

■ Upstream relationships

Picking up the theme of breadth from the previous chapter, relationship building is just as relevant for 'upstream' targets, such as policymakers and health professionals, as it is for downstream clients. This type of advocacy is a key dimension of Josephine Previte's Case Study which, amongst other things, led 'a call to action' for the government to 'change its approach to domestic violence campaigns'.

As always in marketing, the behaviour in question has to be seen from the perspective of the targeted change agent as well as the marketer, and relevant benefits for changing identified. For instance, as Exercise 7.4 discusses, water companies are not particularly motivated to fluoridate by

Exercise 7.4

Water fluoridation

Water fluoridation involves adjusting the natural level of fluoride in the public water supply so as to produce substantial improvements in the dental health of the population – especially among children and those living in deprived communities. Water fluoridation is a classic example of health promotion – safe, simple, effective – but, in the UK at least, not happening. No new water fluoridation schemes have gone ahead since the necessary legislation was passed in 1985.

Introducing water fluoridation in the UK is a complex process. Local health authorities request (but do not tell) water companies to start adding fluoride to the water once they have formally consulted the public and the relevant local government authorities. Research with the general public found that they were largely supportive of fluoridation and wanted to be kept informed of developments, but confirmed that they had little role to play in actively progressing the initiative. Furthermore, they were quite happy with this state of affairs, seeing it as a job for the health professionals, to whom they were prepared to defer.

Thus, fluoridation is an example of a valuable public health measure which will not be progressed by any behavioural change in the general population. Nonetheless, social marketing has a key role to play: its concepts of consumer orientation, voluntary involvement and mutually beneficial exchange are still very useful. In this case the key consumers are local authorities and water companies, whose cooperation can be encouraged by emphasizing the benefits *to them* of fluoridation.

For example, the private water companies were not interested in public health. They wanted to provide their customers with clean, wholesome water and their shareholders with a reasonable return. However, they were interested in helping the government carry out its policies, retaining good relationships with public health professionals in their area and positive public relations.

How might relational ideas be put into effect with the water companies?

Source: adapted from Hastings *et al.* (1998)

public health arguments – they are private companies, not arms of the health service. However, they are interested in providing good customer service, and evidence from public opinion surveys that their customers want fluoridation is therefore likely to be influential. How might relational thinking extend the potential of a fluoridation project?

The opportunity clearly exists to build a relationship with water companies, rather than focusing just on the once-only transaction of agreeing to add fluoride to the water. For example, the water companies could become long-term partners in ongoing health promotion campaigns. Water is, after all, probably the only liquid that all health professionals would agree is good for us! Databases used to generate bills could be adapted and customized to deliver positive health messages or products. Association with such messages and the health organizations that generate them could help make billing a less negative process and improve the company's corporate image.

Moving from transactions to relationships adds the vital dimension of time to the social marketing exchange, which turns trust into commitment and enhances strategic planning. Fluoridating the water supply is no longer a one-off maybe for the water company, but the start of a profitable long-term relationship with both key stakeholders and their customers.

Relationships can be built with many different stakeholders. Figure 7.3 adapts Morgan and Hunt's representation of these for commercial firms to a social marketing context.

This shows that social marketers need to think about building relationships in the same four domains as commercial companies:

● *Buyer partnerships*. In the original model a distinction is drawn between intermediate and ultimate customers. However, in social marketing a more important distinction is between the ultimate customer (the beneficiary of the social marketer's endeavours), such as the smoker, and the funder of their activities, such as the Government health department (Bagozzi, 1974). With the latter, good relationships can ensure that projects are set realistic objectives and that evaluation feedback will be

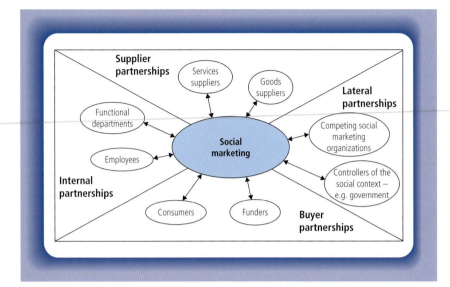

Figure 7.3
A multi-relationship model of social marketing.
Source: adapted from Morgan and Hunt (1994).

in a form that aids policy decision making. The resulting trust and commitment also reduce the tendency to determine renewed funding purely on the basis of bottom-line results.

More fundamentally, building relationships with funders enables the social marketer to influence the setting, as well as the implementation, of the policy agenda, which strengthens not just the discipline's effectiveness, but also its ethical foundation. Without it, social marketers run the risk of becoming political pawns, who might deliver micro effectiveness but ignore macro issues.

- *Supplier partnerships.* In the case of suppliers, such as advertising agencies or market research providers, in addition to the benefits discussed by Morgan and Hunt, long-term relationships help bridge cultural differences between the private and public sectors, and ensure that progress is built on consensus, matched agendas and clearly agreed long-term goals (Hastings and Leathar, 1987; Leathar, 1987; Eadie and Smith, 1995).

- *Lateral partnerships.* The benefits of working with governments and other controllers of the social context have already been discussed. Strategic alliances with competing social marketers can facilitate efficiency savings and improve competitiveness, just as in commerce. They can also help prioritize issues. This is vital given the current fragmented social marketplace, where organizations compete for public attention by highlighting the danger of their particular concern (Leathar, 1988). At any given moment, the public has to choose between the varying threats of speeding drivers, environmental tobacco smoke and alcohol abuse (none of which are completely in their control). A combined approach, based on long-term alliances, could transform this raft of capricious threats into a multifaceted opportunity to improve health and well-being.

- *Internal partnerships.* Finally, Figure 7.3 also shows the importance of internal marketing. As in commerce, fulfilling relationships with external stakeholders depend on the whole organization pulling together. Great data mining and strong interactive communications will be undermined if the dispatch office is unresponsive or the receptionist is obstructive.

This multiplicity of potential relationships presents challenges as well as opportunities. Decisions have to be made about which stakeholders to prioritize and how to handle them. As we discussed in Chapter 6, the concept of the 'harm chain' can help with this thinking.

■ Conclusion

In this chapter we have thought through the nature of the behaviours social marketing seeks to change and recognized that these are quintessentially long-term. This in turn calls for sustained rather than intermittent interventions. Commerce has reached similar conclusions over the last couple of decades, and developed relationship marketing to meet the resulting challenge.

Relational ideas fit well in social marketing, not least because the commitment and trust it needs to succeed is more attainable in a non-profit context. Ultimately, Tesco is nice to you because they want your money; the Smoking Cessation Services (at least ostensibly) want to help you. Furthermore, when combined with the upstream thinking discussed in Chapter 6, they can begin to help social marketing to deliver not just individual behaviour and lifestyle change, but full-blown social change.

■ References

ACMD (Advisory Council on the Misuse of Drugs) (1993). *Drug Education in Schools: The Need for a New Impetus.* London: HMSO.

Allott R., Paxton R. and Leonard R. (1999). Drug education: a review of British Government policy and evidence on effectiveness. *Health Education Research Theory and Practice*, **14**(4): 491–505.

Andreasen A.R. (1994). Social marketing: its definition and domain. *Journal of Public Policy and Marketing*, **13**(1): 108–114.

Bagozzi R.P. (1974). Marketing as an organised behavioral system of exchange. *Journal of Marketing*, **38**(4): 77–81.

BBC News Online (2001). Half UK children own mobiles. 29 January; http://news.bbc.co.uk/hi/english/uk/newsid_1142000/1142033.stm

Blakey V. and Pullen E. (1991). You don't have to say you love me: an evaluation of a drama-based sex education project for schools. *Health Education Journal*, **50**(4): 161–165.

Bouman M., Maas L. and Kok G. (1998). Health education in television entertainment – 'Medisch Centrum West': a Dutch drama serial. *Health Education Research Theory and Practice*, **13**(4): 503–518.

Brand Strategy (2001). Watchin' the game, havin' a Bud …. 20 February, p. 11.

Buckley M. (1998). Why Web is the perfect zone for youth marketing. *Marketing Week*, **21**(30): 42.

Chesterman J., Judge K., Bauld L. and Ferguson J. (2005). How effective are the English smoking treatment services in reaching disadvantaged smokers? *Addiction*, **100**(Suppl. 2): 36–45.

Denman S., Pearson J., Moody D., Davis P. and Madeley R. (1995). Theatre in education on HIV and AIDS: a controlled study of schoolchildren's knowledge and attitudes. *Health Education Journal*, **54**(1): 3–17.

Eadie D.R. and Smith C.J. (1995). The role of applied research in public health advertising: some comparisons with commercial marketing. *Health Education Journal*, **54**: 367–380.

Evans M., Stoddart H., Condon L., Freeman E., Grizzell M. and Mullen R. (2001). Parents' perspectives on the MMR immunization: a focus group study. *British Journal of General Practice*, **51**: 904–910.

Ferguson J., Bauld L., Chesterman J. and Judge K. (2005). The English smoking treatment services: one-year outcomes. *Addiction*, **100**(Suppl. 2): 56–69.

Fortmann S.P., Flora J.A., Winkleby M.A., Schooler C., Taylor C.B. and Farquhar J.W. (1995). Community intervention trials: reflections on the Stanford Five-City Project experience. *American Journal of Epidemiology*, **142**(6): 576–586.

Godfrey C., Parrott S., Coleman T. and Pound E. (2005). The cost-effectiveness of the English smoking treatment services. *Addiction*, **100**(Suppl. 2): 70–83.

Hajek P., Stead L.F., West R. and Jarvis M. (2005). Relapse prevention interventions for smoking cessation. *Cochrane Database of Systematic Reviews*, (1): CD003999.

Hastings G.B. and Leathar D.S. (1987). The creative potential of research. *International Journal of Advertising*, **6**: 159–168.

Hastings G.B., Hughes K., Lawther S. and Lowry R.J. (1998). The role of the public in water fluoridation: public health champions or anti-fluoridation freedom fighters? *British Dental Journal*, **184**(1): 39–41.

Hastings G.B., Devlin E. and MacFadyen L. (2005). Social marketing. In: *ABC of Behaviour Change: A Guide to Successful Disease Prevention and Health Promotion* (Kerr, J., Weitkunat, R. and Moretti, M., eds). Oxford: Elsevier Churchill Livingstone.

Hughes J.R., Keely J. and Naud S. (2004). Shape of the relapse prevention curve and long-term abstinence among untreated smokers. *Addiction*, **99**(1): 29–38.

JRF (Joseph Rowntree Foundation) (1997). Young people and drugs – findings. *Social Policy Research*, **133**; http://www.jrf.org.uk/knowledge/findings/socialpolicy/sp133.asp

King A.C. (1998). How to promote physical activity in a community: research experiences from the US highlighting different community approaches. *Patient Education and Counselling*, **33**(1, Suppl.): S3–S12.

Leathar D.S. (1987). The development and assessment of mass media campaigns: the work of the Advertising Research Unit. *Journal of the Institute of Health Education*, **25**(2): 65–72.

Leathar D.S. (1988). Be All You Can Be Study – Part 1. *Journal of the Institute of Health Education*, **26**(1): 6–12.

Levitt S. and Dubner S.J. (2005). *Freakonomics: A Rogue Economist Explores the Hidden Side of Everything*. London: Allen Lane.

MacAskill S. and Eadie D. (2002). *Evaluation of a Pilot Project on Smoking Cessation in Prisons*. Glasgow: University of Strathclyde, Centre for Social Marketing.

MacAskill S., Stead M., MacKintosh A.M. and Hastings G.B. (2002). "You cannae just take cigarettes away from somebody and no' gie them something back": can social marketing help solve the problem of low income smoking? *Social Marketing Quarterly*, **VIII**(1): 19–34.

MacFadyen L., Stead M. and Hastings G.B. (2002). Social marketing. In *The Marketing Book* (Baker M.J., ed.), 5th edition, Chapter 27. Oxford: Butterworth-Heinemann.

Morgan R.M. and Hunt S.D. (1994). The commitment–trust theory of relationship marketing. *Journal of Marketing*, **58**(3): 20–38.

New Media Age (1998). Knowing how to set the video finally pays off for British youth. 19 November, p. 18.

Orme J. and Starkey F. (1998). *Evaluation of HPS/Bristol Old Vic Primary Drug Drama Project 1997/98*. Full report. Bristol: Faculty of Health and Social Care, UWE.

Orme J. and Starkey F. (1999). Young people's views on drug education in schools: implications for health promotion and health education. *Health Education*, **4**(July): 142–152.

Palmer A. (2000). Co-operation and competition: a Darwinian synthesis of relationship marketing. *European Journal of Marketing*, **34**(5/6): 687–704.

Pentz M.A., Mihalic S.F. and Grotpeter J.K. (1997). *Blueprints for Violence Prevention: Book One – The Midwestern Prevention Project* (Elliott D.S., series ed.). Boulder, CO: University of Colorado.

Precision Marketing (2000). Budweiser text messages its customers. 18 September, p. 3.

Rajagopal S. and Bernard K.N. (1993). Strategic procurement and competitive advantage. *Journal of Purchasing and Materials Management*, **29**(4): 13–20.

Raw M., McNeill A. and Coleman T. (2005). Lessons from the English smoking treatment services. *Addiction*, **100**(Suppl. 2): 84–91.

Reichheld F.F. (1996). *The Loyalty Effect: The Hidden Force Behind Growth, Profits and Lasting Value*, p. 33. Cambridge, MA: Harvard Business School Press.

Reichheld F.F. (2003). The one number you need to grow. *Harvard Business Review*, **81**(12): 46–54.

Richardson F. (2001). Packages: the money or the options. *Business Review Weekly*, **23**, 20. Source: http://www.brw.com.au

Sheth J.N. and Parvatiyar A. (1995). The evolution of relationship marketing. *International Business Review*, **4**(4): 397–418.

Stead M., McDermott L., Angus K. and Hastings G. (2006). *Marketing Report (Behaviour Change: Marketing Review)*. Report prepared for the National Institute for Clinical and Health Excellence. Stirling Institute of Social Marketing.

Tobacco Papers.com (2003). *UK Tobacco Industry Advertising Documents Database*. Online at http://www.tobaccopapers.com.

Wanless D. (2004). *Securing Good Health for the Whole Population*. London: The Stationery Office.

Ward M. (2001). Turning mobile phones into portable billboards. *BBC News Online*, 23 April. http://news.bbc.co.uk/1/hi/in_depth/sci_tech/2000/dot_life/1287980.stm

West R. (2004). *Stop Smoking Service Quality and Delivery Indicators and Targets*. A briefing for the Healthcare Commission, July. Available at: http://www.ash.org.uk/html/cessation/smqtargetsbrief.pdf (accessed 20 December 2005).

Wilson R.F. (2000). The six simple principles of viral marketing. *Web Marketing Today*, 1 February 2005. Online at: http://www.wilsonweb.com/wmt5/viral-principles-clean.htm (accessed 24 February 2006).

CHAPTER 8

Competition and Critical Marketing

■ Overview

Competitive analysis is a vital tool in commercial marketing: it helps a company to respond more effectively to customer needs and gain not just ad hoc but sustained advantage, thereby driving growth. This is no great revelation when we think of the cut-throat rivalry of Wall Street or the City of London: red in tooth, claw and braces. Perhaps surprisingly, however, competitive thinking can also be applied in social marketing. We can, as with other aspects of behaviour change, learn from commerce in this area as well.

Competition disciplines commercial marketers to raise their game and focus more accurately on customer needs. The fact that, as the airline staff put it, they know we have a choice does concentrate their minds on matters of customer service. And the choice is not just between airlines, but other forms of transport (the Train à Grand Vitesse may get me from Paris to Marseille more comfortably than the red eye) – or even recreation (a domestic holiday rather than flying to foreign climes) or communication (a video conference rather than a face-to-face meeting). Similarly, the fact that in social marketing we have to compete with attractive alternative behaviours – taking it easy rather than exercising, a calming nicotine fix rather than an arduous quit attempt – puts us on our mettle and can provide a useful fillup. This chapter will discuss the insights and techniques that business can provide to help us respond to the challenge.

In this chapter, however, we also confront business. Our examination of competitive forces compels us to recognize and respond to the fact that there are direct challenges to many social marketing efforts – the alcohol, tobacco and fast-food industries offer obvious examples. The same commercial sector from which so much can be learnt also, at least in some guises, represents very direct competition to social marketing. We will examine the evidence base that supports this analysis and discuss the implications for social marketing. Is cooperation an option, for example? And at what point does cooperation end and confrontation begin? When does it become necessary to advocate for – and guide policymakers and the legal system about – suitable sanctions and controls on commercial marketing?

In this way, the discipline moves into the field of critical marketing: the debate about the role and values of commercial marketing in a modern democracy. It examines the sort of concerns raised by commentators like Naomi Klein, George Monbiot and Joel Bakan, about power, integrity and consumption in a finite world. Because we understand marketing, and its capacity, if properly used, to do good as well as harm, we are ideally positioned to make a constructive contribution to this debate, to offer solutions as well as find fault.

Learning objectives

This chapter will enable you to:

- Conduct a competitive analysis.
- Understand how the resulting capacity to see the competition through our clients' eyes helps us get a better fix on the needs we are addressing.
- Identify the limits of cooperation and the need for confrontation when the competition is pushing in the opposite direction.
- Understand the contribution that social marketing can make to the critical marketing debate – most notably, that it can provide solutions as well as criticisms.

LINKS TO OTHER CHAPTERS

During this chapter you might find it useful to cross-refer to the discussions of:
- The practicalities of upstream social marketing in Chapter 6
- Customer-defined quality and sustained effort in Chapter 7
- Case Studies 4 and 16.

■ Competitive analysis

Who are our competitors?

Competition is a clear and present force in commercial marketing: Burger King and McDonald's, Nike and Adidas, Coca-Cola and Pepsi are proverbial rivals; stock market ratings are the equivalent of sports leagues, takeovers and company failures the obvious results for the winners and losers in this jockeying for position. Amongst us gentle herbivores of the marketing world, by contrast, such rivalry seems counter-intuitive. Surely social marketers are all on the same side, trying to do good – not knock each other down? In reality, however, competitive analysis can be a useful tool.

Marketing is concerned with profitably addressing needs, and we have already examined how this operates as far as the company and the customer are concerned, but there is a third C in the equation: the competition. Like the natural world, business is also driven by the law governing the survival of the fittest. However, in this case the forces are not hidden Darwinian genes, but an overt managerial process guided by deliberate planning. Marketers seek to understand the behaviours of their competitors, just as they do those of their customers, so that they can control, influence or at least adapt to the resulting forces.

The ultimate aim is to establish sustainable competitive advantage, with the emphasis on sustainable. Above all else, studying your rivals informs your strategic planning; it helps define where you want to be not just in the next year, but the next decade. And this long-term vision is invaluable. Rumour has it that one Japanese car manufacturer is more than happy to show its competitors around its factories and give them as much information as they want about its production methods. By the time they have copied them, its erstwhile host will have moved on, made improvements and left them far behind. The story is apocryphal, but its thrust is correct.

Good competitive analysis, as with so much else in marketing, starts by looking at the world through the eyes of the customer. What need are *they* trying to satisfy? What products do *they* use to satisfy the same need? What do *they* buy instead? Who do *they* see as the competition? Box 8.1 presents a simple competitive analysis for McDonald's.

Box 8.1 What customer needs does McDonald's meet?

Think for a few moments about what needs the fast-food outlet are satisfying for a father and his two small children. As a good marketer you would seek to answer this question with a bit of market research, asking the father and his children why they have come to the golden arches.

The obvious answer you are likely to get is food; a McDonald's has to satisfy their hunger – but it is very likely that this is only part of the picture.

Competitive analysis suggests questions specifically about what they consider to be the alternative options. This can usefully extend your research. Questions like:

(i) Where might you have gone today if not to McDonald's?
(ii) What other places do you like going together?
(iii) How good are these alternative offerings?

The answers may produce predictable responses, such as KFC or Burger King (because they have better free toys). A little more unsettlingly, but still reasonably predictably, the answer may be a new juice bar (because the food is healthier). However, the father and his children may also suggest less obvious alternatives, like a picnic in the park (because you can also feed the ducks and try out the swings) or a trip to the cinema to see the latest Disney movie (because it has been trailered on children's television and all their friends have seen it).

This simple exercise has two great benefits for McDonald's: it helps it think more incisively both about its rivals and (more importantly) its customers. As far as its rivals are concerned, the answers in Box 8.1 will enable McDonald's executives to see who they are up against – Burger King, the juice bar or the cinema. They can then think through how they should respond. Is it straight them or us rivalry or are there also cooperative opportunities? For example, in the case of the juice bar, direct competition is probably needed, perhaps by adding healthier options to the menu; the picnic option, on the other hand, may suggest that opening a franchise in the park has potential. Similarly, in the case of the cinema, the best strategy may not be to compete head on, but form an alliance and begin serving McDonald's meals to theatregoers.

As far as its customers are concerned, the answers in Box 8.1 start to give McDonald's a much better fix on the precise customer need it is seeking to meet. It becomes clear, for example, that this is about much more than food and hunger. Fun, entertainment and a child-friendly atmosphere are all in there also. Indeed, some people actually patronize McDonald's *despite* the food: a nutritionist friend living in Geneva takes her children there although she has grave reservations about the menu, because it is one of the few child-friendly restaurants in town.

Thus, our small competitive analysis has helped us uncover a valuable marketing insight: the distinction between the offering made (in this case, ostensibly at least, a meal) and the need satisfied (child-oriented entertainment). This is a vital distinction.

Consider for a minute this question inspired by Theodore Levitt, 'what do Black & Decker make?' Drills? Do-it-yourself equipment? Tools? No. They make holes. Drills happen to be the best way of doing this, but it may not always be so. New technology may, for instance, produce a laser-driven machine that can do the job better. Unless Black & Decker realize they are in the hole business rather than the drill business they will be as vulnerable to the competition as buggy-whip manufacturers were to the new technology of the internal combustion engine.

Browning's poem about three heroic horsemen bringing good news from Ghent to Aix (Exercise 8.1) helps reinforce this point. In the poem, three riders set out to deliver 'the news which alone could save Aix from her fate'; two of their horses die during the gallop and Roland – our hero's mount – expires on the streets of Aix as the tidings are delivered. What

Exercise 8.1

How they brought the good news from Ghent to Aix

I sprang to the stirrup, and Joris, and he;
I galloped, Dirck galloped, we galloped all three;
'God speed!' cried the watch, as the gate-bolts undrew;
'Speed!' echoed the wall to us galloping through;
Behind shut the postern, the lights sank to rest,
And into the midnight we galloped abreast.

… By Hasselt, Dirck groaned; and cried Joris, 'Stay spur!
Your Roos galloped bravely, the fault's not in her,
We'll remember at Aix' – for one heard the quick wheeze
Of her chest, saw the stretched neck and staggering knees,
And sunk tail, and horrible heave of the flank,
As down on her haunches she shuddered and sank.

… 'How they'll greet us!' – and all in a moment his roan
Rolled neck and croup over, lay dead as a stone;
And there was my Roland to bear the whole weight
Of the news which alone could save Aix from her fate,
With his nostrils like pits full of blood to the brim,
And with circles of red for his eye-sockets' rim.

… And all I remember is, friends flocking round
As I sat with his head 'twixt my knees on the ground;
And no voice but was praising this Roland of mine,
As I poured down his throat our last measure of wine,
Which (the burgesses voted by common consent)
Was no more than his due who brought good news from Ghent.

In Browning's famous poem (abridged here) what did Joris, Dirck and our nameless hero really need? What sales opportunity would you, an entrepreneurial marketer living in nineteenth century Ghent, have been able to exploit? What would you have sold them?

sales opportunity would you, an entrepreneurial marketer living in Ghent in the nineteenth century, have been able to exploit? What would you have sold them?

The obvious answer is better horses. Or even a motorbike. But what they really needed – and any marketer worthy of the name would recognize this – was a telephone. Joris, Dirck and co. were not looking for a means of transport at all, but a means of communication.

Competitive analysis aids this type of lateral thinking. McDonald's analysis of its customers' views on its business stops it becoming obsessed with the product and keeps it focused on the need it is satisfying.

Competitive analysis also broadens beyond commercial rivals. McDonald's will take careful readings of how its customers see the current obesity debate. Do they have any sympathy with the New York teenagers who tried to sue the company for making them fat, or support a ban on fast-food advertising? This will help inform its consumer marketing – perhaps they should employ celebrity chefs or include healthier options on the menu. It also guides its stakeholder marketing. The rise in public concern about obesity has pushed the fast-food industry to engage much more actively with policymakers.

This need to engage with policymakers is even more apparent in the tobacco business. We noted in Chapter 3 when discussing strategic analysis that, as David Jobber (2004, p. 145), a leading business academic explains, 'close relationships with politicians are often cultivated by organizations both to monitor political moods and also to influence them'. The importance of doing this is increased by the activities of tobacco control NGOs, as Jobber goes on to note: 'The cigarette industry, for example, has a vested interest in maintaining close ties with government to counter proposals from pressure groups such as ASH.' In this sense, competitive analysis is a natural progression from environmental scanning. We have already seen how our behaviour is influenced by social context; the actions of competitors are a key element of this context.

Exercise 8.2 applies our discussion about the competition to a social marketing example.

Exercise 8.2

School dinners: which is the competition?

Imagine that you are a social marketer and have been asked for help by Oldsville High School. Only about one-third of their pupils eat school dinners; the others make alternative arrangements, either bringing their own or going out of school to local cafés. The school wants you to make their new healthier lunches more popular.

Competitive analysis suggests that the following sorts of questions may be revealing:

(i) Where do the two-thirds of non-school diners eat at the moment?
(ii) What do they like about these alternatives?
(iii) Why do the one-third remain loyal?

Think through what sort of answers might result and how they would help. If you get stuck, ask a friendly teenager.

As with our McDonald's example, you may well find that the answers take you well beyond food and hunger. Local cafés, for instance, may offer a chance to rebel, to hang around with friends in an unstructured environment or simply to save money on the allowance disbursed by parents. On the other hand, the one-third who remain loyal are presumably rejecting the competitors' offerings, so asking them why they do so may uncover some hidden strengths in the school's dinners.

Porter's competitive forces

The nature of the competition is not just influenced by what other companies do, but by more fundamental forces in the marketplace. Michael Porter (2004) divides these into four categories (see Box 8.2).

Box 8.2 Porter's competitive forces

1. The power of the *buyer* or customer is, of course, crucial. Do they have access to alternative offerings that will satisfy their needs?
2. The *power of suppliers* and the extent to which they can control what the marketer does. The room for manoeuvre of BP, for example, may be significantly constrained by OPEC.
3. The degree to which offerings can be *substituted*. Generic, easily produced commodities like potatoes or paper are much more vulnerable to competition than are branded snacks or a unique piece of software.
4. Finally, *new entrants* to the market can also increase competition, and the number of these will depend on how difficult it is to start up in a particular business. Setting up a new pharmaceutical company is, for example, much more challenging than a new beauty salon.

Source: adapted from Jobber (2004, pp. 678–680)

First, as you would expect, the buyer or customer has potential power. We have already explored this in some detail, but Porter reminds us that the amount of power the buyer has will vary according to market conditions. In a monopoly situation or a time of shortage, for instance, their power can shrink dramatically. The second force, the power of suppliers, is essentially the corollary of the first. The third force concerns the potential for substitution: are there alternative products or services available that can do the same job? In the commercial sector, branding is used to capture this sort of power – a trainer is a trainer, but a Nike Air Max is unique.

Finally, Porter considers the threat from new entrants to the market. The extent of this will be determined by how easy it is for others to move in and start satisfying the same consumer needs. In some sectors, such as pharmaceuticals and nuclear energy, the barriers are very high. In others, such as the small businesses service sector (e.g. hairdressers and cafés), entry is much easier and competition much more widespread – with a resulting tendency for businesses to appear and disappear on a regular basis.

As with other strategic decisions, a company's options for engaging with and tackling competition are going to be influenced by its internal capacity. What skills and resources can it call on? What strategic approaches can it realistically adopt? Can it compete on price, for example, or will differentiation (offering a valued alternative), focus (servicing a particular area or group), pre-emption (offering some innovation) or synergy (exploiting particular strengths) be feasible? This capacity will ultimately depend on the potential to develop a workable and effective marketing mix.

The final dimension marketers add to their competitive activities is time. For the company to flourish, competitive advantage needs to be *sustainable over time*. This emphasizes the importance of two additional concepts: people and relationships. People include customers and other stakeholders who are important for the organization's marketing offering. It also takes in staff; without their enthusiastic support, delivering good service becomes very difficult. This enthusiastic support will depend on them feeling valued by the organization. The word relationship highlights the need to think strategically and move beyond isolated transactions with all these groups. Thus, breadth and continuity are as important when developing, implementing and evaluating the competitive response as they are in marketing more generally (see Chapters 6 and 7).

■ Competition in social marketing

Again, the thinking can be applied to social marketing. The fact that social marketers deal with *voluntary* behaviour means their clients always have a choice – they have 'buyer power' (see Box 8.2) – and hence there is always competition. Client power is a valuable concept in a discipline that also competes professionally with expert-driven approaches like public health and road safety, and reminds us of the need to satisfy our target's inherent self-interest by providing *real* benefits. In this context, *real* must incorporate both the objective (technical benefits such as symptom relief or greater safety) and the subjective (what the recipient feels about consuming the offering). This harks back to our discussion about customer-defined quality in Chapter 7.

In competitive terms, there is what seems to be a natural tendency for social marketing offerings to be worthy, hard work and, as a consequence, inherently unattractive. Thus, a bad diet is fun and indulgent, a good one Spartan and dissatisfying; a sedentary life is restful and relaxing, exercise hard work and tiring. Furthermore, we always seem to be asking people to give things up – chocolate, cigarettes, the rugged manliness that comes with driving an SUV. But as Richard Layard (2005) points out, we put a greater premium on loss than gain: we get more upset from a £100 bill than we get happiness from a £100 windfall. This suggests that the Health Sponsorship Council in New Zealand were right to turn the negative offering of giving up smoking into a positive in the Quit&Win campaign (Case Study 8 on p. 278).

Similarly, social marketing seems doomed to offer long-term, probabilistic benefits (or often the absence of awful repercussions), whereas the competition brings short-term, definite ones. The immediate pleasure of chocolate competes all too effectively with the deferred (and often illusive) advantage of weight loss; more dramatically, today's nicotine fix competes easily with the possibility of a heart attack in a couple of decades. 'Discounting' exacerbates this problem: rewards lose their value and costs are less onerous in the future.

This again compels us to think about what we are offering and the extent to which it meets people's real needs. If deferred gratification is such a weak product, why do we focus on it? Especially when a little consideration shows that it is far from being the only benefit of a healthy lifestyle. It is worth looking again at Figure 7.1 and the sense of achievement that successfully giving up smoking can bring to the most disadvantaged populations. Similarly, in Box 4.2 we saw that exercise is not by definition unpleasant – whole swathes of the population get a variety of (short-term) benefits as a result. Certainly, the World Health Organization's definition of health – 'a state of complete physical, mental and social well-being and not merely the absence of disease or infirmity' – pushes us in a very positive direction.

Furthermore, if people want an enjoyable life today rather than the probability of more life tomorrow (and it is hardly surprising that they do), should we not be making sure that our products deliver this? Competitive analysis and customer power, just as with McDonald's, pushes us to think about our core business: is it just freedom from physical illness or a more fulfilled and rewarding life? Is public health and safety about avoiding threats or realizing opportunities? Competitive analysis reminds us if we do not get this right, others surely will. Exercise 8.3 shows how the tobacco industry is working hard to provide attractive short-term offerings to potential new smokers.

Exercise 8.3

The importance of competitive analysis in smoking prevention

Market research from the UK tobacco industry makes it clear that the young are a key target and that image and emotion are vital appeals:

'To smoke Marlboro Lights represents having passed a *rite of passage*.'

'Young adult smokers are *looking for reassurance* that they are doing the right thing, and cigarettes are no exception. Any break with a brand's heritage must be carefully considered in order not to throw doubt into the minds of young adult smokers.'

'Young adult smokers are also *searching for an identity*. Cigarettes have a key role to play as they are an ever-present statement of identity.'

'Smoking for these people (*young smokers*) is *still a badge*. A sign of maturity, discernment and independence.'

'Younger smokers give *more weight to imagery of cigarettes* and pay more attention and are open to fashionable brands and up-to-date designs.'

Successful brands exploit these emotional needs and insecurities:

'The success of Marlboro Lights derives from its being *the aspirational lifestyle brand … The Diet Coke of cigarettes*.'

'To be successful any Gallaher brand will have to tackle *Marlboro's coolness of image* – smokers do smoke the image as well as the taste.'

'We want to engage their aspirations and fantasies – "I'd like to be there, do that, own that".'

How well will long-term, probabilistic health warnings compete here? Are there more attractive offers we could make?

Source: House of Commons Health Select Committee (2000)

Ray Lowry's work on smoking cessation services (Case Study 6 on p. 265) demonstrates how careful and empathetic research can provide the sort of insights needed to devise offerings that meet psychosocial needs. Only when health visitors were exposed to role-playing actors did they appreciate the sensitivity that was needed to approach this issue with low-income women.

In a similar way, the Foolsspeed anti-speeding campaign (Case Study 3 on p. 245) had to compete with highly evocative ads and offerings from the car industry that, whilst they may not overtly encourage us to break the speed limit, certainly associate a lot of attractive imagery with sleek, high-performance cars. In this context, simple fear inducement seems, at best, a limited response.

As we noted when discussing Exchange Theory in Chapter 2, insurance companies, like social marketers, have the problem of deferred gratification; they offer a benefit tomorrow that is both probabilistic and inherently unattractive. Very few of us want to actually claim on our household insurance because it assumes some misfortune has visited us first. The same is even more true of life insurance. The benefit that insurance companies push, then, is not so much financial paybacks later, but peace of mind now. They do not sell *in*surance, they sell *reas*surance.

Porter's other three forces (Box 8.2) also have something of interest to offer, as Exercise 8.4 explores.

Exercise 8.4

Applying Porter's forces in social marketing

Have another look at Box 8.2. How well do Porter's other three forces – *substitution*, the *power of suppliers* and *new entrants* – help us think about social marketing problems? Jot down some ideas under each heading before continuing.

Substitution is an obvious development of customer power. There are many easily substituted products for ours on offer. Celebrity diets present an attractive alternative to lifestyle change, and cleverly promoted four-wheel drives can deflect us from more ecologically sound modes of transport. Similarly, almost any other television channel is preferable to the one showing yet another tediously graphic speeding or drink-driving ad.

More broadly, our issues compete for attention. Chad MacArthur and Manisha Tharaney's work in Tanzania (Case Study 16 on p. 329) shows how blinding trachoma has to compete with numerous other diseases and issues – including HIV/AIDS, tuberculosis, malaria and malnutrition – for government attention.

In social marketing the *supplier* is, in many instances, very powerful – often more so than in the commercial sector. There are two reasons for this. First, the supplier is frequently also the funder, with a resulting inclination to call the tune. Second, they do not have the laws of the market breathing down their neck as a commercial company does. They will not go bust if they get things wrong. As a result, in social marketing the demands of the supplier can sometimes supersede the needs of the client. For example, speed cameras might be imposed on a community despite the public's suspicions about the purity of the motives behind them or morning-after contraception discouraged because of the supplier's religious beliefs. Similarly, as we saw with Be All You Can Be in Chapter 5, a campaign can be terminated at a politician's behest, despite its evident popularity with the client.

The absence of a profit motive means they cannot just buck the market, but create it. Thus, governments will often decide what the priorities are for social marketers. This may seem like no bad thing in a democracy, but serious problems can result. Recall how, in the UK, during the 1980s the Conservative Government of Margaret Thatcher refused to accept any connection between inequalities and ill-health, and how today George Bush's focus on the 'war against terror' is pulling in resources that might otherwise be used in more conventional public-safety initiatives. More recently still, in the UK, Directors of Public Health have become concerned about public health funds being raided to fill deficits elsewhere in the health budgets (Department of Health, 2006).

These pressures put an additional onus on social marketers. There is a need to question and, if necessary, challenge the social marketing agenda being set by suppliers. This can be difficult to do, but is essential for the discipline's long-term survival. It also reinforces the points made in Chapter 7 about the importance of building relationships with suppliers.

Porter's fourth force – *new entrants* – brings us to a perhaps uncomfortably selfish notion of competition. Social marketers do compete with each other and other behaviour-change specialists for funding and work. The recent upsurge of interest in the subject has brought a range of new providers into the market. This presents real threats, not just in terms of work, but to the discipline itself. If anyone can set up in business as a social marketer – if, in Porter's terms, the barriers are too low – there is a risk that prices, and then standards, will plummet. When medicine faced this threat a century or so ago it responded by setting up very considerable barriers to entry. I would not advocate such a strategy in social marketing, but we do need to set professional standards and agree reasonable quality qualifications.

The UK's National Social Marketing Centre (http://www.nsms.org.uk) has raised similar concerns, which is why it has put such an emphasis on the need for consistency and clarity about the nature of social marketing. It is this that underpins the NSMC's social marketing benchmarks that we discussed in Chapter 1 (see Box 1.1). Similarly, Paul White of the Social

Marketing Practice warns that there is a need for clear standards and training (see Box 8.3).

Box 8.3   The need for standards in social marketing

Current UK policy interest in social marketing presents a massive opportunity for the profession and the societal policies it benefits, *provided that skills and training are developed to professional standards, and that recognizable qualifications result*. To ensure success, the social marketer needs competency skills in social research (and understanding of the breadth of social research undertaken in this area), strategic intervention planning, piloting techniques, segmentation and targeting, the social marketing mix (top-down and community-based approaches) and measurement techniques. Moreover, there are different qualities of skill required for policy strategists, social marketing campaign designers and managers, and delivery (including grass roots) practitioners. Commercial marketing communication skills themselves do not naturally translate to the social dimension.

A major gap currently exists between a latent societal policy need for social marketers and the availability of a strategic and practitioner skill base. Our estimates indicate a potential market need for over 10 000 practitioners in the UK. Early development of professional standards is needed in line with growth in skills demand, to ensure that training courses are developed to a recognized framework, and that national qualifications emerge which distinguish true social marketing expertise that delivers positive societal change.

Source: Paul White, http://www.socialmarketingpractice.co.uk (2006)

Judith Madill and Frances Abele also discuss how important it has been to encourage the accurate diffusion of social marketing in the Canadian fight against racism (Case Study 12 on p. 302).

■ Going for growth

In commercial marketing, competitive activity is one of the key drivers of growth. In a social marketing arena, however, typically dominated by targets and budget limitations, the idea of growth can be something of an anathema. And yet, if we really have pretensions to make people's lives healthier, safer and more fulfilling – if we want to generate not just behaviour but social change – then growth is essential.

As we noted in Chapter 7, a recent review of public health in the UK concluded that serious improvements would only result if the populace could become 'fully engaged' in the process of change (Wanless, 2004). It also concluded that the National Health Service will never achieve this alone. Rather we need alternative delivery methods that motivate providers not just to meet targets but expand geometrically so that people have every opportunity to get involved.

The idea of the 'social enterprise' or 'Community Interest Company' may present a good way forward here. This is an attempt to replicate the success of commercial companies – particularly their capacity for growth – in the social and health sectors. Small companies grow up because people are motivated to use their initiative, ingenuity and skills to make a living by generating profits. Growth results in two ways. First, because so many people engage in this activity there is enormous proliferation of small companies. Second, a proportion of small businesses grow into medium-sized and big companies. The result is an extremely extensive small business sector: in the UK, for instance, in 2004 it accounted for 58% of all employment (ONS, 2005).

The performance of these companies is honed by competition.

The thinking behind social enterprise is to harness all this entrepreneurial energy, along with the competitive pressure, for social good (see Figure 8.1). Whilst the ultimate aim of a small business is to produce profits, the aim of a social enterprise is to reinvest any surplus back – once salaries and costs have been paid – into the cause being addressed (Pearce, 2003).

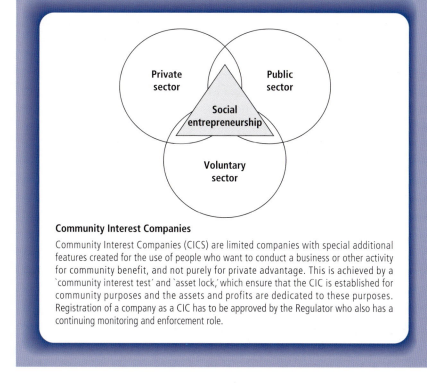

Community Interest Companies

Community Interest Companies (CICS) are limited companies with special additional features created for the use of people who want to conduct a business or other activity for community benefit, and not purely for private advantage. This is achieved by a `community interest test´ and `asset lock,´ which ensure that the CIC is established for community purposes and the assets and profits are dedicated to these purposes. Registration of a company as a CIC has to be approved by the Regulator who also has a continuing monitoring and enforcement role.

Figure 8.1
Social enterprise.
Source: Diagram after *Enterprise and Small Business: Principles, practice and policy*, 2nd edition, Carter and Jones-Evans, reproduced with permission. Text from http://www.cicregulator.gov.uk

A social entrepreneur is one driven by a social mission, a desire to find innovative ways to solve social problems that are not being or cannot be addressed by either the market or the public sector (Bornstein, 2004). Good British examples range from the Appin Community Cooperative in the Scottish Highlands to Coin Street Community Builders in London. Social enterprises have a growing role to play in the economy, not as a 'cranky' subset of the private sector, but as part of a truly alternative economic system – a third way, distinct from both the private and public systems of ownership and management. The standing of social enterprises is considerable. Often, they have what the governments and populations seek – credibility, expertise and public support.

In the UK, this potential has been encouraged by legislation (http://www.cicregulator.gov.uk), making the Community Interest Company a formally recognized legal entity (see Figure 8.1).

This thinking fits neatly with social marketing ideas about learning from commerce. Case Study 9, by Neil McLean, gives an illustration of a recently established social enterprise in the field of smoking cessation. The case demonstrates some of the benefits of the model – including flexibility of service and responsiveness to consumer need.

■ The hazard merchants

There is, of course, also a very direct way that we can think about competition in social marketing: in some instances, other organizations – typically companies selling unhealthy products like tobacco, alcohol and energy-dense foods – push in completely the opposite direction. The WHO dubbed them the 'hazard merchants' a few years ago. Thus, one simple and compelling answer to the question why so many people take up and continue smoking is because a raft of large and extremely powerful multinational tobacco corporations encourage them to do so. And they undoubtedly succeed, as study after study has demonstrated. Box 8.4 presents one fragment of this evidence base, the conclusion of a systematic literature review on the impact of tobacco advertising and promotion by the world-renowned Cochrane collaboration.

Box 8.4   Tobacco advertising does have an effect

'Longitudinal studies consistently suggest that exposure to tobacco advertising and promotion is associated with the likelihood that adolescents will start to smoke. Based on the strength of this association, the consistency of findings across numerous observational studies, temporality of exposure and smoking behaviours observed, as well as the theoretical plausibility regarding the impact of advertising, we conclude that tobacco advertising and promotion increases the likelihood that adolescents will start to smoke.'

Source: Lovato *et al.* (2003, p. 1)

Similar evidence bases are emerging for the promotion of energy-dense food and alcohol. Recent reviews conducted by the Institute for Social Marketing for the Food Standards Agency (Hastings *et al.*, 2003) and the World Health Organization (Hastings *et al.*, 2005) have concluded that in each market commercial promotion is contributing to the public health burden.

Thinking beyond the WHO's hazard merchants, other industries may also present obstacles to social marketers. Car manufacturers may encourage speeding, mentioned earlier – and certainly have a vested interest in encouraging ecologically damaging forms of travel. The toy and entertainment markets may contribute to the sedentary lifestyles of young people. The armaments business has a role in human conflict. The evidence base in these fields may be less well formed than for tobacco, alcohol and food, but social marketers involved in ecological transportation, exercise promotion and conflict resolution would be unwise to ignore their potential influence.

So how should social marketers respond to this competitive activity?

First, let us note that competitive analysis confirms that it is perfectly legitimate – indeed necessary – for us to respond. This reinforces our discussion in Chapter 3, that commercial marketing is part of the social context and that we not only *can* but *have* to make this context our business. Indeed, our insights into marketing make our role in this arena particularly valuable. We understand the forces at work here – that there is, for example, so much more than advertising involved. It is the whole of the marketing mix – the products being developed, the pricing strategies used and the well-resourced promotion campaigns and distribution networks that makes commercial marketing so successful. For example, whilst it is known that alcohol advertising contributes to youth drinking, product innovation (see Box 8.5) is probably an equally important driver (Jackson *et al.*, 2000). The advent of alcopops, heavily branded 'FABs' (flavoured alcoholic beverages like Bacardi Breezer) and shots has undoubtedly had an impact on drinking.

Similarly, tobacco, alcohol and energy-dense foods are available at every turn. Figure 8.2 gives one illustration of this; it shows posters offering special deals on snack food at an Australian cinema. It is worth bearing in mind that in its recent investigation into obesity, the UK Government's Health Select Committee pointed out that a king-size Mars bar has as many calories as a three-course meal. Incidentally, the promotion material was on display at a cinema screening *Super Size Me*!

The most immediate response to Box 8.5 and Figure 8.2 is to recognize, as we did in the last chapter, that we social marketers have to match our competitor's game: we too need ubiquity, convenience and seductive branding.

Another response for the social marketer is to address the customer and warn them about the activities of the hazard merchants. The Truth campaign in the USA did exactly this for tobacco companies, highlighting their unscrupulous business practices and deliberate attempts to attract youngsters to the habit. The ads were completely uncompromising – showing, for example, body bags being delivered to tobacco corporation headquarters to represent the numbers killed by smoking and ambushing executives with

---

Box 8.5 Alcoholic drinks

The intention was to show examples of alcoholic drinks that have appeared on the UK market in the last few years. However, some of the manufacturers were (unaccountably) concerned that this might show their products in a bad light, so were reluctant to give permission. The pictures would have included:

- **Big Beastie** A vodka based mix in a garish red and yellow bottle, described by the maker as *'Terrifyingly Tasty!'* and packing a 5.4% abv punch. (The cartoon spider that originally appeared on the bottle had to be removed.)
- **Frosty Jack's** A strong white cider that comes in handy screw-capped, blue plastic bottles up to three litres in size and boasting a 7.5% abv kick on its red, white and blue label.
- **Sidekick Shots** A short that comes in a wide variety of sophisticated flavours, including honeycomb, chocolate mint and lemon meringue creams at 14.5% abv; and fruit flavours such as blueberry and orange at 20% abv. It is designed to be drunk as a chaser and so comes in a convenient plastic capsule that clips to the top of bottle or side of the glass containing your main drink.

Sorry that the pictures could not be shown. UK readers can go into corner shops up and down the land to see them and a range of similar products – as, of course, can UK teenagers.

Figure 8.2
Energy-dense foods.

embarrassing questions. The result was a very-high-profile social market-ing campaign which worked: it brought about a marked reduction in youth smoking rates (Farrelly *et al.*, 2002). So we can compete and win.

■ To compete or cooperate?

When faced with a direct competitor like this, however, some form of cooperative response is also a possibility – as we noted in our McDonald's example. This is sometimes rather clumsily called 'co-opetition'. Some com-mentators suggest that this is the way forward for tobacco control: a tobacco industry-funded academic quoted in the journal *Science* recently argued that 'the real enemy' in tobacco control 'is the death and disease smokers suffer', not the tobacco industry (Grimm, 2005). Given the insights of com-petitive analysis, this is a simplistic argument – akin to suggesting that the mosquito is a distraction in the fight against malaria. The problem is that for cooperation to work, as with relationship marketing, two conditions have to be present:

1. There must be some capacity to find mutual benefit.
2. The partners must have at least roughly equal power.

Neither is present with tobacco.

This is an instance where the competitive analysis throws up the con-clusion that a head-to-head fight is the only solution: as long as we have tobacco corporations we will have smoking, along with its toll on life expectancy and inequalities. This sort of competitive analysis has led pub-lic health researchers to conclude that tobacco companies will have to be bought out and replaced by social enterprises (see above) which will con-tinue to ensure a supply of tobacco to dependent smokers, but will do so with a clear public health agenda (Borland, 2003; Callard *et al.*, 2005).

Instead of the current system, where tobacco companies are required by law to maximize returns to their shareholders – and hence to increase sales of tobacco – they would have the specific remit of reducing the public health burden from smoking. Thus, they would procure only tobacco prod-ucts that meet stringent public health goals (e.g. of reduced nitrosamines or with specified nicotine content) and produce generic cigarettes that meet only the nicotine needs of smokers. They will not be incentivized, as corpo-rations are, to produce evocative brands or try to meet any of the psycho-social needs of smokers discussed in Exercise 8.3.

Other competitors present a more complex picture, however. There is a convincing evidence base to show that both food and alcohol marketing have a significant and unhealthy impact, especially on the young, as the Food Standards Agency and the World Health Organization reviews dis-cussed above show.

At the same time, however, the issues in other sectors are less black and white than for tobacco. Taking alcohol as an example, most public health pro-fessionals would accept that this is not an irredeemably unhealthy product, that there is a harmless, if not positively beneficial, level of consumption. Similarly, whilst we should always remember that the majority of the world's population does not use alcohol, in many societies it is an acceptable and normal part of life. The problem is one of abuse rather than use. This suggests that one of our two criteria for cooperation is being met: most alcohol manufacturers would argue that they share public health's interest in the safe use of their product.

The second criterion, of equal power, is less clearly present. The alcohol industry is very big business and the main producers such as Diageo are amongst the wealthiest of our global corporations. We need therefore to proceed with caution. Exercise 8.5 describes a collaborative project between a social marketer and Miller Brewing. How do you feel about this? What are the strengths and weaknesses of the collaboration?

Exercise 8.5

To compete or cooperate?

In a rural, blue-collar community in the northern USA, drink-driving among young men is common practice. Forty per cent of 21- to 34-year-olds drive themselves home after an average of seven drinks at least twice a week. The competition has a monopoly: there is no other way of getting home, and its leading brand 'I can drive myself home' has huge market share. This is reinforced by the fact that brand consumption typically does not result in the negative consequences threatened by social marketers. Most of the men, on most occasions, do manage to drive home without mishap.

However, the brand also has at least one weakness. The men know they are taking unreasonable risks and feel guilty about it. An alternative offering might have potential, provided it did not come at too high a cost or interfere with their self-interest in having a good night at their local bar. The offering made was a free ride service, customized to each community and promising 'no hassles, no worries, more fun'.

It succeeded. Some 20 000 rides have now been given. Analysing the competition, and the target's perception of the competition, enabled the build-up of sustainable competitive advantage.

This case emphasizes the need for social marketing to offer 'unique meaningful benefits', which both present better value than the competition and accommodate the client's self-interest more effectively. Specifically, it underlines the value of emphasizing the short-term benefits and reducing short-term costs in this process.

But did it also create problems?

Source: Rothschild *et al.,* 2006.

The example provides a good illustration of the dilemma. On the one hand, it could be seen as a great example of the effective use of competitive analysis to deliver a simple and powerful intervention, and a major threat to public health – drink-driving – was reduced. On the other, we might have concerns about the potential repercussions of a collaboration that effectively reinforced drunkenness – and actively delivered these drunks home to their families. From a competitive perspective it also enables the brewery to promote its products as actively as ever, with an undesirable implication that getting drunk is both acceptable and fun. This theme would ordinarily get them into trouble, but in this case they actually stand to get very positive public relations benefits from it.

Thinking more strategically, what impact do these sorts of collaborations have on the standing of social marketing? Any company entering such an agreement would think very carefully about the impact it might have on its brand image – so should social marketing. This is not necessarily an argument against the Miller collaboration, just a reminder that we need to think strategically about relationships with business on the one hand and civil society on the other. And in the case of alcohol, this thinking has to be particularly careful, because the division made above, between use and abuse, is simplistic. The evidence shows that the two are in fact intimately related: the wider the availability and use of alcohol in a given jurisdiction, the greater the abuse that will result (Edwards *et al.*, 2004, 2005).

■ The limits of corporate social responsibility

The idea for cooperation with industry has its most obvious manifestation in corporate social responsibility (CSR): the principle that companies should not just keep an eye on their financial bottom line, but also monitor and control their impact on health and social welfare. This is an attractive-sounding option; business is causing problems so it is right that it should be responsible for limiting these and cleaning up any mess that results. At first glance, it seems like a pleasing variant on the 'polluter pays' principle.

CSR is indeed a good thing. There is no doubting the genuine motives of many business leaders in this area. Furthermore, business is probably in the best position to self-regulate the minutiae of its activities. Advertising content, for example, or selling methods need technical and professional insight to guide control. However, CSR also has very real limitations. First of all it can only deal with the specific, not the general. Thus, whilst it can identify and remove an alcohol advert that transgresses a code of conduct, it can do nothing about the fact that there is simply too much alcohol advertising.

Second, and more fundamentally, corporations are required by law to put the interests of their shareholders – not society – first. The social bottom line will always be trumped by the fiscal one. As Niall FitzGerald, former CEO of Unilever, succinctly put it:

> 'Corporate social responsibility is a hard-edged business decision … [We do it] not because it is a nice thing to do or because people are forcing us to do it … [but] because it is good for our business.'
>
> (Elliott, 2003)

Cooperation, then, may get us so far but it has real limitations. Sometimes the solution has to be direct regulation of the competition. This takes us back to the idea of stakeholder marketing discussed in Chapters 6 and 7. Social marketers have to build relationships with policymakers and politicians that will encourage them to take action. And in a chapter on competition it is worth bearing in mind that the hazard merchants – as Jobber reminded us above – certainly put a great deal of effort and resource into such lobbying.

■ Critical marketing

Interestingly, the idea of addressing the social consequences of business is far from being a new issue for marketing. It takes us back to the origins, not just of social marketing thought, but of marketing thought. An extensive review of the field, published recently in the *Journal of Public Policy and Marketing*, points out that what the authors call 'marketing and society' has been a key part of marketing since it first became a distinct discipline at the turn of the twentieth century. They go on to note that well before the Second World War marketers were not limiting themselves to studying managerial issues, but addressing much wider social questions, such as whether advertising is desirable or certain industries should exist at all (see Box 8.6). They were interested in how the relationship between consumers, marketers and Government could 'facilitate the maximal operations of the system *for the benefit of the host society*' (Wilkie and Moore, 2003, p. 118).

Box 8.6 Marketing and society

Wider social issues have always been a concern of marketing thought, as Wilkie and Moore's summary of the broader questions early marketers were addressing shows:

● Are there too many middlemen? Does distribution cost too much?
● Does advertising raise or lower prices?
● What control, if any, should be exerted over new combinations in distribution?
● Of the total costs paid by consumers, which elements are desirable? Indispensable?
● What about 'non-essential' services such as credit availability – should these be eliminated?

Source: Wilkie and Moore (2003)

Their review goes on to conclude that this interest in the social impact of marketing needs to continue, and indeed strengthen, a call reinforced by the discipline's premier *Journal of Marketing* in its millennium edition.

Social marketing has a crucial role to play in this renaissance. Just as our knowledge of marketing can help us deconstruct the practices of the hazard merchants, so we can contribute to the wider debate about the role and values of commercial marketing in a modern democracy. Naomi Klein and Joel Bakan (see the Further Reading section) have led an onslaught of commentators pointing out the deficiencies of corporate capitalism, from sweat shops to inflationary branding. Indeed, Bakan (2004) concludes that the modern corporation is nothing more or less than a psychopath. Others have responded defensively, pointing out that corporations do a lot of good, not least by underpinning much of the wealth that funds modern medicine, social services and education. They also point out that whilst Bakan and Klein make a great job of flagging up deficiencies, they do not present much in the way of solutions – good box office, but light on direction.

Social marketing can help plug this gap with its combination of balance and practical solutions. In terms of balance, this whole book points out that the marketing used by corporations and so despised by its critics is not intrinsically harmful. On the contrary, it can be used to great social benefit, as the case studies at the end of the book show. Helping disadvantaged smokers to quit, combating racism and making our roads safer are all very desirable social outcomes. Social marketing demonstrates that marketing is an amoral technology that, provided it is controlled properly, can bring about great good.

Turning to practical solutions to corporate misbehaviour, Heath and Potter (2006, p. 11), in their critique of the more vainglorious attacks on capitalism, point out that we should instead put our trust in the more prosaic and methodical process of 'making arguments, conducting studies, assembling coalitions and legislating change'.

As Heath and Potter intimate, popular uprisings and revolutionary change are unlikely to provide a solution (unless some of the doomsayers' predictions start to come true); rather, we need tighter and better regulation. Such regulation will be key to redressing the power imbalance that caused any unease with the Miller Brewing drink-driving case in Exercise 8.5.

■ Building the evidence base

Regulation needs a solid evidence base. Policymakers will not act unless they are confident that they can bring about genuine improvements; regulation necessarily means the infringement of liberty and there has to be credible justification for doing this. This high principle is reinforced by vested interest. We have already noted how companies actively cultivate policymakers, and their approaches become more energetic when regulation is on the cards. Indeed, in the case of tobacco it has resulted in litigation: the tobacco industry recently took the UK Department of Health to court, arguing that its new regulation on point-of-sale (POS) advertising was disproportionate. They lost because there is a rigorous and convincing evidence base to show that POS advertising does influence young people to smoke.

Building this evidence base involves both primary and secondary research. The International Tobacco Control Policy Evaluation Project (http://itcproject.org), for example, is a longitudinal research programme designed to assess the impact of different tobacco-control policy options, such as advertising bans, on pack warnings and price increases. It uses a multi-country design – originally four countries were involved (the UK, the USA, Canada and Australia), but has now been extended to more than a dozen – and natural experiments to track policy impact. For example, it has been possible to show how the ban on tobacco advertising in the UK has resulted in significant public health improvements that are not evident in the USA, where no such ban has been enacted (Harris *et al.*, 2006).

An alternative approach to building the evidence base is to analyse secondary research, which because of the degree of contention involved presents particular challenges. The medical community, which also has to make challenging, consensual decisions about a contested evidence base, has responded by developing the concept of 'evidence-based decision making' (Mulrow, 1994). This is built around the 'systematic review' (SR) (Boaz *et al.*, 2002), which strengthens traditional literature reviewing by making it comprehensive, rigorous and transparent. The process starts by laying down a clear protocol for searching all relevant databases, the content and quality criteria that will be used to determine inclusion in the review, and the methods used to assess the relative quality of the included studies and their synthesis into conclusions. The contents of this protocol are included in the completed review and can therefore be subjected to detailed scrutiny and, if necessary, replicated by other researchers.

Case Study 4 on p. 254 describes how SR methods were, for the first time, recently applied to a marketing problem: the impact that food promotion may or may not be having on childhood obesity. Have a read of the case and consider how the SR procedures used made the work proof against criticism and helped it have a considerable influence on stakeholders.

Two factors were important in strengthening the review. SR procedures backed by consistent peer review made it largely unassailable to criticism. In particular, the transparency about the methods used meant that critics have to point out precise flaws or omissions – blanket disagreement or dismissal is untenable. Second, there was a clear acceptance that no final proof is possible. As with all social science research, we can only reduce uncertainty by testing hypothesis and judging the balance of probabilities.

SR, then, provides a useful and robust way of building the regulatory evidence base. It is, however, very resource intensive. The example discussed in Case Study 4 took a team of researchers 18 months to complete. In addition, it is inherently conservative. Only the most obvious and well-proven effects will be acknowledged. These are useful qualities in a public policy debate, where the stakes are high. As we noted in the introduction to the book, business is the engine of wealth creation, which means it effectively funds all our health and social services – and indeed social marketing. Checks and balances need to be applied with considerable caution.

However, as we will discuss in Chapter 9, social marketers would argue that the value of SR in other areas, such as intervention design, is more limited.

■ Building the social marketing brand

Finally, returning to the idea that self-interest is at the core of marketing (Chapter 3), bringing social marketing to bear in the critical arena also benefits and reinforces its brand image. It is no longer a bit player in the field of health education, but a contributor to some of the greatest concerns facing our society. Furthermore, the fact that it can successfully take on and counteract the prodigious power of commercial marketing serves to reinforce its potential.

In the final analysis, social marketing is concerned with behaviour change, whether in the playground or the boardroom. The behaviour of corporations is one of the key issues facing society. Why would we do any other than address it with rigour and determination?

■ Conclusion

In this chapter we have examined how competition, which is a defining characteristic of business, also has resonance for social marketers. Competitive analysis can help us think more effectively about our clients' needs, the vital strategic importance of relationships with our suppliers and the very nature of the discipline.

It has also brought us into the crucial area of direct competition: social marketers can and must address the activities of the 'hazard merchants' if they are serious about facilitating beneficial social change. This does not preclude collaboration with commercial partners, but it does warn us to proceed with caution.

We have also seen how this links with critical marketing and the wider debate about how business and civil society interrelate. In particular, social marketing presents solutions to the problems this sometimes fractious relationship can generate by (a) building the evidence base and (b) showing that marketing can be applied to socially desirable behaviours.

Thus, competitive analysis has led us to the very core of the discipline and one of the most pressing problems facing our world – an interesting end point given that we began by raising the concern that competition may be more relevant to commercial than social marketing.

■ References

Bakan J. (2004). *The Corporation: the Pathological Pursuit of Profit and Power*. London: Constable.

Boaz A., Ashby D. and Young K. (2002). *Systematic Reviews: What Have They Got To Offer Evidence Based Policy and Practice*, Working Paper 2, ESRC UK Centre for Evidence Based Policy and Practice. London: Queen Mary, University of London.

Borland R. (2003). A strategy for controlling the marketing of tobacco products: a regulated market model. *Tobacco Control*, **12**(4): 374–382.

Bornstein D. (2004). *How to Change the World: Social Entrepreneurs and the Power of New Ideas*. Oxford: Oxford University Press.

Callard C., Thompson D. and Collishaw N. (2005). *Curing the Addiction to Profits: A Supply-Side Approach to Phasing out Tobacco*. Ottawa, ON: Canadian Centre for Policy Alternatives and Physicians for a Smoke-Free Canada.

Community Interest Companies (2006). Community Interest Companies (CICS) Website Homepage. Online at: http://www.cicregulator.gov.uk (accessed 24 August 2006).

Department of Health (2006). *On the state of the public health: Annual report of the Chief Medical Officer 2005*. London: Department of Health.

Edwards G., West R., Babor T.F., Hall W. and Marsden J. (2004). An invitation to an alcohol industry lobby to help decide public funding of alcohol research and professional training: a decision that should be reversed. *Addiction*, **99**(10): 1235–1236.

Edwards G., West R., Babor T.F., Hall W. and Marsden J. (2005). The integrity of the science base: a test case. *Addiction*, **100**(5): 581–584.

Elliott L. (2003). Cleaning agent. Interview: Niall FitzGerald, Co-Chairman and Chief Executive, Unilever. *The Guardian*, 5 July, p. 32.

Farrelly M.C., Healton C.G., Davis K.C., Messeri P., Hersey J.C. and Haviland M.L. (2002). Getting to the truth: evaluating national tobacco countermarketing campaigns. *American Journal of Public Health*, **92**(6): 901–907.

Grimm D. (2005). Ethics. Is tobacco research turning over a new leaf? *Science*, **307**(5706): 36–37.

Harris F., MacKintosh A.M., Anderson S., Hastings G.B., Borland R., Fong G.T., Hammond D. and Cummings K.M. for the ITCPES Research Team (2006). Effects of the 2003 advertising/promotion ban in the United Kingdom on awareness of tobacco marketing: findings from the International Tobacco Control Four Country Survey. *Tobacco Control*, **15**(Suppl. 3): iii26–iii33.

Hastings G.B., Stead M., McDermott L., Forsyth A., MacKintosh A.M., Rayner M., Godfrey G., Carahar M. and Angus K. (2003). *Review of Research on the Effects of Food Promotion to Children – Final Report and Appendices*. Prepared for the Food Standards Agency, UK. Published on Food Standards Agency website: http://www.food.gov.uk/healthiereating/advertisingtochildren/promotion/readreview

Hastings G., Anderson S., Cooke E. and Gordon R. (2005). Alcohol marketing and young people's drinking: a review of the research. *Journal of Public Health Policy*, **26**(3): 296–311.

Heath J. and Potter A. (2006). *The Rebel Sell: How the Counter Culture Became Consumer Culture*. Chichester: Capstone Publishing.

House of Commons Health Select Committee (2000). *Second Report – The Tobacco Industry and the Health Risks of Smoking*. Volume II, *Minutes of Evidence and Appendices* (October 2000). London: The Stationery Office.

Jackson M., Hastings G.B., Wheeler C., Eadie D.R. and MacKintosh A.M. (2000). Marketing alcohol to young people: implications for industry regulation and research policy. *Addiction*, **95**: S597–S608.

Jobber D. (2004). *Principles and Practice of Marketing*, 4th edition. Maidenhead: McGraw-Hill International.

Layard P.R.G. (2005). *Happiness: Lessons from a New Science*. London: Allen Lane.

Lovato C., Linn G., Stead L.F. and Best A. (2003). Impact of tobacco advertising and promotion on increasing adolescent smoking behaviours. *Cochrane Database of Systematic Reviews*, (4): CD003439.

Mulrow C.D. (1994). Rationale for systematic reviews. *British Medical Journal*, **309**(6954): 597–599.

ONS (2005). *Statistical Press Release URN 05/92*. DTI News Release, 25 August. London: Small Business Service Analytical Unit, Office for National Statistics.

Pearce J. (2003). *Social Enterprise in Anytown*. London: Calouste Gulbenkian Foundation.

Porter M.E. (2004). The Structural Analysis of Industries. In *Competitive Strategy: Techniques for Analyzing Industries and Competitors*, pp. 3–33. New York: Free Press.

Rothschild M.L., Mastin B. and Miller T.W. (2006). Reducing alcohol-impaired driving crashes through the use of social marketing. *Accident Analysis & Prevention*, **38**(6): 1218–1230.

Wanless D. (2004). *Securing Good Health for the Whole Population*. London: The Stationery Office.

Wilkie W.L. and Moore E.S. (2003). Scholarly research in marketing: exploring the '4 eras' of thought development. *Journal of Public Policy and Marketing*, **22**(2): 116–146.

CHAPTER 9

Research and the Art of Navigation

■ Overview

Almost everything that has been said so far in this book depends on research. Client orientation, relationship building, stakeholder marketing – indeed, every step of the marketing planning process – needs to be informed by up-to-date intelligence about the people with whom we want to do business and the world that they and we inhabit. In this chapter we will examine social marketing research. The intention is not to provide a comprehensive guide on how to do research; there are many other good sources for this. Rather it looks at research through a social marketing lens: the thinking that underpins it; the purpose it serves; the potential and pitfalls it presents. In the process we will discuss methodology, but only in so far as it serves our main purpose.

I will start by arguing that research should be seen as a navigational aid, to guide progress and aid decision making. We will then consider what decisions we as social marketers have to make, and examine the qualitative and quantitative research methodologies that can be used to inform them.

The chapter concludes by warning about the potential downsides of research if it is misused or overused. It can, for example, become a way of avoiding hard choices or smothering intuitive thinking. It can also encourage what might be termed the 'intervention mentality', which focuses efforts on perfecting materials and mechanisms for intervening, rather than the more important task of improving our understanding of people and their behaviour.

Learning objectives

After working through this chapter you will:

■ Be able to explain the navigational role of research and how important this is in social marketing.

■ Have a clear idea of what decisions social marketers have to make, and the research steps and methodologies that can help guide them.

■ Recognize the danger that an over-reliance on research can stultify decision making and hinder progress.

During this chapter you might find it useful to cross-refer to the discussions of:

- Strategic planning in Chapter 3
- The role of research in social marketing communications in Chapter 5
- Building relationships in Chapter 6
- Systematic review in Chapter 8
- Case Studies 2, 6 and 8.

LINKS TO OTHER CHAPTERS

■ The purpose of research in social marketing

Two basic characteristics of social marketing drive its use of research. First, as we discussed in Chapter 3, building successful behaviour-change programmes is like climbing a Himalayan peak – with a resulting need for maps, compasses and careful route planning. Research fulfils the role of these *navigational aids*. It helps us get our bearings, establish achievable objectives and staging posts towards these, check on progress, adjust our route and determine when we have reached the summit. Furthermore, because our ultimate goal is relative rather than absolute (improved, rather than perfect, health; a better society, not an idyll), our Everest is infinitely high.

This emphasizes the need for progressive learning, not just within but between initiatives, and ties in with our discussion of social marketing planning in Chapter 3 and communications in Chapter 5. The implications for research methodology feed back to the work of Kurt Lewin, who coined the term 'action research' and emphasized the need for empirical study to go beyond the production of books and articles, and help us take action on social phenomena. This is the same man whose much-quoted aphorism 'there is nothing so practical as a good theory' we noted in Chapter 2 when we discussed theory.

Lewin emphasized the notion of incremental learning using a range of methodologies and expressed this as a cyclical research process (Figure 9.1).

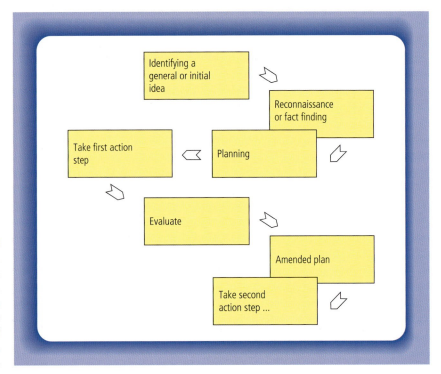

Figure 9.1
Action research.
Source: based on
Smith (1996).
Reproduced with
permission from the
Encyclopedia of
Informal Education,
http://www.infed.org.

This feeds into a plan of action that will define ultimate goals as well as immediate and intermediate steps, all of which will be honed and adapted as the plan is implemented. At the same time, however, the sequential model should not be applied too rigidly; because social phenomena are complex and subtle, the researcher has to be both flexible and sensitive. All these lessons transfer neatly into social marketing thinking, which sees research as a process (see Figure 9.3 later in the chapter) that provides progressive learning, not just about how we should intervene, but about the people with whom we want to intervene.

The second basic characteristic of social marketing that fundamentally influences thinking about research is that it addresses *voluntary behaviour*. As we have already noted, clients, stakeholders and competitors are all free to choose whether or not they do business with us. The decisions we make about constructing our marketing plan therefore have to be driven by an understanding of these actors, their motives and lifestyles. In *To Kill a Mockingbird* (see Box 9.1), Harper Lee suggests that to really understand why people behave as they do you have to 'get inside their skin'; she is making the point that you need to be able to empathize with them.

Box 9.1 Empathy – a simple but crucial trick

Atticus (the father) is explaining to his daughter (Scout) how she can get on better with her new teacher:

'Atticus stood up and walked to the end of the porch. When he completed his examination of the wisteria vine he strolled back to me.

   "First of all," he said, "if you can learn a simple trick, Scout, you'll get along a lot better with all kinds of folks. You never really understand a person until you consider things from his point of view – " "Sir?" " – until you climb into his skin and walk around in it."

   Atticus said I had learned many things today, and Miss Caroline had learned several things herself. She had learned not to hand something to a Cunningham, for one thing, but if Walter and I had put ourselves in her shoes we'd have seen it was an honest mistake on her part. We could not expect her to learn all Maycomb's ways in one day, and we could not hold her responsible when she knew no better.'

Source: Harper Lee, *To Kill a Mockingbird* (1960, p. 35–6)

These two ideas, of *navigation* and *empathy*, encourage social marketers to draw on both positivist and humanist research traditions. The first builds on the notion that there is an objective reality out there that we are trying to measure and influence. This pushes us towards quantitative methods, theory to build on previous insights, establishing cause and effect, and hypothesis testing. The second recognizes that the world – or at least the social and behavioural bits of it in which we are interested – is actually much messier than this, and will not succumb to scientific analysis however rigorous and highly powered. As a result, social marketers, like their commercial cousins, adopt a pragmatic mix of methodologies that they feel will best aid decision making and help them get a better (though always imperfect) understanding of what makes people do what they do.

Case Studies 2 and 6 provide good illustrations of action-oriented, empathetic social marketing research.

■ Pragmatism and precision

All too often with behaviour change, however, the focus is on testing the *intervention*, which pushes things towards a more positivist research approach. In public health, for example, such thinking is exemplified in the randomized controlled trial (RCT). The RCT adopts the classic experimental design, randomly ascribing subjects to either an experimental or a matched control group. The first group is exposed to the intervention and both are monitored before and after the trial. Inferential statistics are then used to determine whether or not the intervention had any effect. The overriding aim is to separate out the effects of the intervention from any other possible change agents – most notably there is a need to discount the impact of the characteristics of the different populations.

This makes very good sense when the problem at hand is to determine whether or not a new drug therapy is effective. In these circumstances it is vital that we determine what impact a new substance has, not least – as thalidomide will always remind us – because it can do all too apparent harm as well as good. As the UK's Medical Research Council (MRC) makes clear, the great virtue of the RCT is that it helps to separate out the 'active ingredients' in an intervention. We can find out precisely what the drug is doing by using placebos and double-blind procedures to factor out any contribution from the human beings involved (MRC, 2000, p. 1).

However, social marketers, as do many in health promotion, get uneasy when the same methods are advocated as the 'optimal study design' for 'complex interventions to improve health', which includes 'media-delivered health promotion campaigns' (*ibid.*, p. 2). In similar vein, the US Department of Education (2003, p. 1) argues that:

> 'Well-designed and implemented randomized controlled trials are considered the "gold standard" for evaluating an intervention's effectiveness, in fields such as medicine, welfare and employment policy, and psychology.'

It is not that we can be less cautious about our offerings than a surgeon or pharmacist. A badly conceived drugs prevention programme that hectors and patronizes might actually increase the attractiveness of illicit substances. In addition, the programme will typically use public money, so it is important to know this is being well spent. Furthermore, as we will discuss in the next chapter, there are serious ethical issues to consider in behaviour change. All of this demands that we treat our offerings with great care.

On the other hand, the Hippocratic principle, advising us first and foremost to do no harm, can be too limiting a guide when inactivity is also dangerous.

We should also recognize that caution and precision are not the same thing. Focusing in on testing the intervention before we proceed underrates the importance of the target group in the behaviour-change process. Think back for a moment to our discussion of relationship marketing in Chapter 7, and pick up the idea that satisfaction and loyalty are key outcomes. How people feel about what we are doing will help determine what behaviour change results. Add to this the idea that our clients are not just recipients but co-producers of improved health or community safety, that communication, like beauty, is in the eye of the beholder. From these perspectives, limiting our studies to the isolated influence of the intervention seems perverse to the social marketer. Or as Stead *et al.* (2002) put it:

> 'The traditional biomedical approach to evaluation, with the randomized controlled trial as its gold standard, has limited relevance for the analysis of complex health promotion interventions.'

RCTs are also extremely expensive and time-consuming. They typically cost hundreds of thousands of pounds and several years to complete. As a result, the research process becomes distorted and decision making ponderous. The question 'did it work?' dominates all. Even in this arena, the findings will be of limited value; they may tell us that intervention A worked with population B at time C – when we need to intervene with population D at time E and, in any case, would find it very difficult to replicate intervention A because the world has changed. Then imagine our desired outcomes are long term; suppose we want to intervene with primary schoolchildren so we can pre-empt adult obesity or drug use. Now we need an RCT lasting 25 years.

The research tail is well and truly wagging the intervention dog, and probably consuming the entire budget in the process. More importantly, the people we want to persuade, influence and build relationships with get marginalized, which both limits our effectiveness and causes alienation. As the songwriter Jez Lowe (1985) expresses it:

> 'So you people in power and position I tell you beware
> I tell you beware
> Of your facts and your figures to tell you what, when and where
> 'Cos your facts and your figures are the likes of me
> And don't try and tell me how my life should be
> – or you won't make old bones ...'

The lyrics have a sweet symmetry about them, as the last line turns the threat, so beloved of public health and safety campaigns (see Chapter 5), back on us.

A myopic focus on the intervention also undermines the great opportunity to learn on the hoof. The dominant brands in our lives – Marlboro, Coca-Cola, Nike – have an enormous impact on our behaviour. We know, for example, that tobacco brands are one of the key drivers of youth smoking, and the latest research we are doing at the Institute for Social Marketing suggests that this influence, though diminished, persists even after complete bans on advertising (Grant *et al.*, 2007). But these brands do not emerge from randomized control trials. They come from a mixture of happenstance, intuition and bright ideas that are guided by a variety of different research exercises and traditions, ranging from the ethnographic to the heavily quantitative.

It is not that commercial marketers reject RCTs and experimental designs. In the guise of pharmaceutical companies they probably do more of them than most. It is just that they do not limit themselves to this research methodology, or see it as the gold standard, the Rolls Royce approach. Perhaps they remember that the gold standard had to be abandoned and Rolls Royce cars went bust!

Figure 9.2, for example, shows how, having used RCTs to develop them, pharmaceutical companies go about selling their new drugs in the UK. This gives us a useful glimpse of how a marketer sees the task of behaviour change. Bear in mind that, as this document concerns prescription medicines in the UK, so the marketing is aimed at doctors not patients (in the UK, prescription medicines cannot be promoted directly to the public).

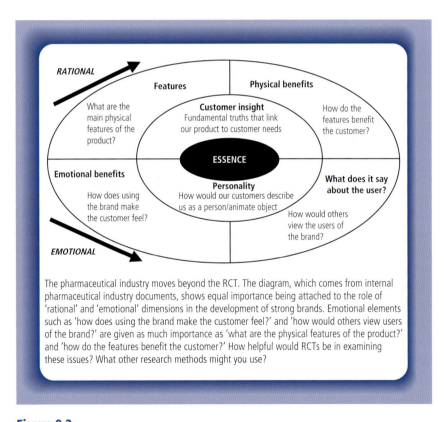

The pharmaceutical industry moves beyond the RCT. The diagram, which comes from internal pharmaceutical industry documents, shows equal importance being attached to the role of 'rational' and 'emotional' dimensions in the development of strong brands. Emotional elements such as 'how does using the brand make the customer feel?' and 'how would others view users of the brand?' are given as much importance as 'what are the physical features of the product?' and 'how do the features benefit the customer?' How helpful would RCTs be in examining these issues? What other research methods might you use?

Figure 9.2
Pharmaceutical marketing.
Source: Devlin *et al.* (2005). Parliamentary material is reproduced with the permission of the Controller of HMSO on behalf of parliament.

It seems that even when trying to influence the behaviour of highly trained professionals, whom it might be thought would be susceptible to hard-nosed, positivist arguments, softer, more flexible appeals are needed. They want to engage 'emotional' as well as 'rational' drivers, and determine how 'using the brand makes the customer feel' and 'how others would see the users of the brand'. This is one of a number of internal documents that go on to talk about the need to make doctors feel reassured, 'energetic' and even 'sexy' about prescribing particular drugs (Hastings *et al.*, 2005).

RCTs are unlikely to help here. They might be able to disentangle cause and effect, but they will say little about the personality of a brand. More flexible methods are needed to do this.

Figure 9.2 also illustrates a more basic truth: human behaviour is just too complex to succumb to the RCT. The MRC's comments extolling their virtues for public health researchers overlook a crucial point for social marketers: that, when it comes to behaviour change, the most important 'active ingredients' are people. Or as Jez Lowe puts it: 'your facts and your figures are the likes of me'.

In the final analysis, for the social marketer, using RCTs to guide our efforts at behaviour change feels a bit like using a ruler to measure the circumference of an orange.

■ Research methodology

Social marketers, then, will do all sorts of research at every juncture of the marketing planning process. The point is to get the best possible grip on the client's perspective (both rational and emotional), so that we can make intelligent decisions about how to build and maintain good relationships with them. To guide our decision making the trick is to work out *what* sort of information we need *when*.

Before looking at these issues in detail, however, we need to know more about methodology. This section will touch briefly on secondary research (the use of existing research data), and then qualitative and quantitative interviewing. It is not intended to provide a comprehensive discussion of methodology or provide a do-it-yourself guide; there are other sources for this (e.g. Kent, 2007). Rather I just want to demonstrate that there are a range of techniques available, each of which has its strengths – and that the best social marketing uses them in conjunction with one another.

Secondary research

Any research exercise should begin by seeking out and analysing existing relevant studies. This can be done with great rigour and precision using the systematic review (SR) procedures we examined in Chapter 8, or more flexibly using more conventional narrative reviews (NRs).

In Chapter 8, we noted how the rigour and precision SRs provide are invaluable when we need to resolve specific issues of cause and effect (e.g. does tobacco advertising encourage teen smoking?) that are likely to be hotly contested – and can even finish up in the courtroom. The same qualities are also useful when trying to establish whether a particular behaviour-change approach produces results. For example, as mentioned in the introduction to the book, the Institute for Social Marketing has recently undertaken a series of SRs looking at whether social marketing works in three specific fields: nutrition, exercise and substance misuse. Because the reviews were systematic, the (positive) results are much more credible than they would have been had we conducted standard reviews. The principal aim is to disentangle cause and effect, so SR is again the best solution.

However, SRs can be less helpful when we are trying to answer broader questions of not just what works, but in what circumstances, how and why. Like RCTs, they can be too inflexible for the task. This is perhaps not surprising: the rigorous quality controls that SRs apply mean that they frequently limit inclusion to RCTs.

For example, the UK's Advisory Council on the Misuse of Drugs (ACMD, 2006) summarizes the evidence from SRs on schools-based sub-stance misuse as follows:

> 'While many of the evaluations were poorly designed, those that were conducted to an acceptable standard found that even carefully designed, resourced and implemented programmes resulted in, at best, small and short-lived delays in the use of tobacco, alcohol or other drugs by pupils. Indeed many studies showed no effect at all, and some programmes were found to be counterproductive.'

One is left feeling that nothing works.

Reassuringly, the same report goes on to wholeheartedly recommend the much broader and strategic idea of health-promoting schools, despite the absence of RCT standard data to support it. The absence of such evidence is not a surprise; as the ACMD says earlier in its report (p. 76):

> 'The reviewers underlined the difficulties in evaluating community-wide programmes. The unique nature of each community also makes it difficult to know how readily even a successful intervention could be translated to other areas or countries.'

And a school is essentially a small community. There *is* evidence to support school-wide initiatives – as we noted in Chapter 6 in our discussion of the immediate environment, research in the West of Scotland (West *et al.*, 2004; Henderson, 2006) has shown that levels of substance misuse in schools are closely related to the policies in place for supporting both staff and pupils and rewarding good behaviour in the latter – it is just that the evidence is not rigorous enough to meet RCT or SR standards. Furthermore, it is worth noting that a key component of a health-promoting school is (again not surprisingly) an active health education and substance misuse programme – the very activity that systematic reviews are so pessimistic about.

In this arena, narrative review is a more flexible and practical option. The focus can move beyond identifying what previous efforts have worked, and towards helping us define the problem and identify potential solutions. Thus, secondary sources can help answer crucial questions about the prevalence and prominence of a particular social or health problem. They can shed light on the extent of the drugs or youth disorder problems in a particular locality, for instance, and show how these stack up against other issues. They may show that drugs are indeed a problem, but that alcohol is much more of one, suggesting that funders are less comfortable with addressing this issue head on (perhaps because of industry interests). This echoes our discussions in Chapter 5 on communications research, and the need not just to determine the form of an initiative, but whether it is needed at all.

Using narrative review, secondary sources can also reveal how previous campaigns and initiatives have fared, providing valuable clues about the best way forward. Note that we are not now talking simply about whether previous interventions worked, but the broader questions we identified above about how they were received and why.

Thus, both SR and NR have a role to play in social marketing research: the rigour of the former helps identify cause and effect; the flexibility and pragmatism of the latter helps us move forward. Furthermore, it is wasteful and risky to start on primary research until existing secondary sources have been exhausted. However, primary research is usually essential once we need to know about how today's target group will respond to a specific intervention, the objectives it can realistically fulfil and how it should set about doing so.

Broadly speaking, primary research comes in two forms: qualitative and quantitative.

Qualitative methods

Qualitative research can cover anthropological, observational and interviewing procedures. This section will concentrate on the last of these; if you want to know more about observation and other methods, standard market research textbooks (e.g. Kent, 2007) are a good source. Qualitative interviewing is typically done in-depth with small samples that have been selected through non-random procedures. Detailed questionnaires are not used, although interviews may be guided by a schedule of 'points to be covered' or 'questions to be asked'. Respondents can be interviewed individually or in 'focus' groups of four to 12 people.

The main advantage of qualitative interviewing comes from the depth or quality of the data that it provides. It enables the researcher to approach a subject in a completely open-ended manner, starting from the perspective of the respondent, using their language and concepts to develop the discussion, and relying on their experiences to illustrate it. Thus, in contrast to questionnaire-based research, there is no need to make assumptions about what the important issues are, how to label these or the type of responses that might be expected.

Qualitative interviewing procedures also allow a range of responses to be examined. For example, as we discussed in Chapter 5, in checking reactions to media materials, fairly straightforward matters such as understanding of the language used or its ability to communicate clearly can be assessed, as well as more complex issues such as likes and dislikes, audience identification, and other emotional responses. For instance, in examining response to fear-inducing anti-AIDS advertising (Hastings *et al.*, 1990), qualitative research revealed a tendency for people to distance themselves from the message that only became apparent after detailed probing. Similarly, researching material that aims to promote images as well as facts is very difficult without the flexibility of qualitative interviewing.

Thinking back to the pharmaceutical marketing discussed in Figure 9.2, how would we go about exploring brand image, and how would prescribing particular medicines make a doctor feel? What is the best way to approach elusive phenomena such as reassurance, fashion and sexiness? See Exercise 9.1.

Exercise 9.1

Measuring hopes and dreams

In Figure 9.2 we saw the complex and subtle ways in which pharmaceutical companies promote their prescription medicines to doctors. We noted that branding, and the capacity of a particular product to make a GP feel reassured, fashionable and even sexy, introduces elusive constructs and ideas that are not susceptible to rigorous positive methodologies such as the RCT. Indeed, even qualitative methodologies struggle to plumb these depths. How might you go about doing research to provide these insights? What questions might you ask and how? What obstacles might you meet?

One option would be to address the issues directly and simply ask GPs how they feel about prescribing different medicines, and how this varies depending on whether it is a branded or generic product. The problem you will face, however, is that GPs may be reluctant to admit their prescribing is influenced by anything other than the best science. It is also possible, of course, that this behaviour is unconscious, that they do not realize their prescribing is affected by something as subjective as brand image. You would likely meet the same problem if you asked most men why they bought a particular car. They would tell you about engine size and performance, not the feeling of superiority they get from piloting a four-wheel-drive BMW, which is perfectly capable of crossing the Serengeti, to the local supermarket.

We therefore have to approach our GPs in a much more indirect way, probably using some sort of 'projective' technique, where the answer is projected away from the respondent to a third party. This makes it both safer and easier to answer. So you might like to ask a GP 'what sort of doctor would prescribe medicine A?' or 'how would they feel in doing so?' Taking it a step further, you might try showing them pictures of doctors who just happen to be prescribing generic or branded versions of a particular drug, and ask them to describe the scene. Box 9.2 presents some other

---

Box 9.2 Five useful projective techniques

1. **Personification:** *'If the product (image / slogan) was a person, how would you describe him / her? What kind of life would they lead? How would they be different from each other?'*
   An adaptable method that is easy to use.
2. **Choice Ordering:** *'Place these products (images / slogans) in order from the one you like best to the one you like least.'*
   This technique provides a way of understanding the factors that differentiate subjects or items which is straightforward to use.
3. **Mapping:** *'Position each product (image / slogan) on the two dimensional grid to indicate how much you like each product and how popular each is.'*
   A more sophisticated version of Choice Ordering that allows you to explore the relationship between different attributes, however it is more difficult to administer.
4. **Clustering:** *'Position the products (images / slogans) according to how closely related they are to each other.'*
   A useful way of understanding the dimensions people use to judge products but can be difficult to administer.
5. **Completion:** *'So . . . ? What springs to mind . . . ? What about that one . . . ?'*
   A useful technique for understanding the factors that shape a person's view about a product (image / slogan). It is a naturalistic form of enquiry; simple and extremely adaptable.

   Source: Douglas Eadie, Institute for Social Marketing

---

examples of projective techniques; the list was produced by my colleague Douglas Eadie, an experienced qualitative researcher.

The quality of the data produced by these methods is also enhanced by the fact that they enable the interviewer to delve for the motivations and reasons underlying responses. They make it possible to ask 'why?' This point is illustrated by a Scottish anti-smoking campaign that was misinterpreted by its 10- to 14-year-old target audience (see Box 9.3). They assumed that bogus products such as a hairspray called 'Ashtré' and an aftershave called 'Stub', which were intended to highlight the drawbacks of smoking, were actually real. Focus groups revealed that this was not because they lacked intelligence or were unsophisticated, but because they could see real benefits in the bogus products. In particular, they seemed to be offering a good means of smoking surreptitiously. From the audience's perspective, this was the *sensible way* to interpret the ads. It is difficult to imagine quantitative procedures uncovering this explanation.

Qualitative procedures also improve the quality of the data collected by enabling the researcher to monitor *how* things are said. Tone of voice, context and non-verbal cues can all be important here. For example, when

> ### Box 9.3   Stub and Ashtré
>
> A television advertising campaign targeting 10- to 14-year-olds aimed to emphasize the benefits of not smoking by promoting a number of bogus products, including an aftershave called 'Stub' and a hairspray called 'Ashtré', both of which made the user smell of cigarettes and thereby much less attractive to the opposite sex.
>
> Qualitative research with 10- to 14-year-olds revealed problems. When they saw the commercials, the anti-smoking message was lost. They believed the products would be real and available in shops. To understand why they reacted in this way, it was necessary to understand what it is like to be an underage smoker. The research showed that, for them, smoking is: forbidden by parents, teachers and other adults, expensive and a difficult habit to acquire. Initially it is unpleasant – youngsters complained that their first cigarettes had caused sore throats and sickness – and only after considerable perseverance does it become enjoyable. The bogus products in the anti-smoking commercials would overcome these problems. For the respondents, the products offered obvious benefits that justified their existence; and the strap-line for the ads 'all the fun of cigarettes, without the drag of smoking' inadvertently confirmed this.
>
> *Source*: Hastings (1990)

researching the potential for using the female condom as a contraceptive among Glasgow women, their hilarity at the idea spoke very articulately about how awkward the product made them feel and how unlikely they were to use it without a considerable amount of persuasion. Again, it is difficult for quantitative methods to provide this kind of insight.

Finally, in terms of data quality – as the last example illustrates – qualitative procedures permit the examination of delicate and embarrassing topics because they enable the researcher to build a rapport with the respondent. This makes it possible to discuss topics that are socially unacceptable – or even criminal – such as shoplifting or vandalism, as well as very personal ones such as sexual behaviour. It is difficult to delve into areas like these without the trust that in-depth interviewing can generate. However, as we will discuss in Chapter 10, the licence these methods give also raises serious ethical issues.

As well as the quality of the data it provides, qualitative interviewing also has at least three important practical advantages. First, because it is flexible, a range of unfinished materials can be researched. Everything, from rough drawings and concept boards through to polished television commercials, can be used to stimulate response. This makes qualitative interviewing particularly suitable for developmental research on new initiatives. For example, focus groups to guide the development of an initiative to promote fruit and vegetable consumption in a major Scottish city

(Anderson *et al.*, 2005) tested out the idea of distributing these through primary schools. Initial reactions were favourable. Only when a storyboard depicting a small child carrying the fruit and vegetables home did the parents hit on the sheer impracticality of the idea: visions quickly emerged of veggies being thrown around the school bus, bananas getting squashed and tomatoes sat on!

Second, research projects can be conducted quickly – within a week if necessary. Third, because small samples are involved, qualitative research is often relatively cheap.

The main disadvantages of qualitative research concern its statistical validity. In statistical terms, both the sampling and interviewing procedures are flawed. The former is typically too small and selected incorrectly to be representative and the latter is not standardized, thereby precluding the summation of responses. Consequently, it is not possible to use qualitative methods to produce estimates of population prevalence to any calculable degree of accuracy.

Qualitative procedures are also criticized because they put respondents in an artificial situation. For example, in asking them to respond in great detail to a particular leaflet or service, you are probably asking them to do something they would not normally do. However, this criticism is true of any research procedure – qualitative or quantitative – that examines response to an initiative by prompting the subject with examples. It does not invalidate such methods, it just means findings have to be interpreted with caution.

A final criticism commonly levelled at qualitative interviewing is that it is very dependent on the researcher conducting the interview well and analysing the data correctly. All too often, it is argued, excessive subjectivity contaminates the process. In the case of data analysis, for example, the fact that qualitative researchers rely on their own selection and interpretation of the findings is contrasted with the quantitative researchers' production of apparently independent and hard statistics (see below). These problems are most apparent with projective techniques. How do we interpret people's responses to the pictures? How reliable is word association as a means of revealing underlying and unconscious associations? And how do we begin to calibrate the influence of such associations on decision making?

Two points can be made in response to this criticism. First, the objectivity of statistical data is often more illusory than real. Just as with qualitative data, they are greatly influenced by the researcher – he or she designs the questions, attributes meanings to the answers and numbers to the meanings. Second, it is questionable whether researcher influence is a bad thing. Researchers are typically highly qualified, skilled and intelligent – surely we should be encouraging rather than discouraging their deep involvement in every aspect of the research process. A bit like with extreme positivism, we end up so distrusting the subjectivity of humankind we overlook its benefits.

However, the main point to note here is not that there is an overall conclusion to be drawn for or against qualitative research, it is that qualitative procedures have both strengths and weaknesses. The former make them a valuable tool for certain research tasks, but the latter should always be kept in mind.

Individual versus group interviews

Exactly the same 'horses for courses' point applies when choosing between individual and group interviewing. Both approaches have strengths and weaknesses. Individual in-depth interviews provide a clear and longitudinal view of each person's perspective, avoid the problems of peer and group pressure, and permit the discussion of extremely intimate issues.

The strengths of focus groups, on the other hand, stem from the interaction that takes place between respondents. This can take many forms. Respondents can question each other's claims. A group member might remind a fellow respondent that although he claims to have given up smoking, he accepted a cigarette immediately prior to the group. Respondents might also seek information and guidance from each other – 'what is that new doctor like?' and 'how do you find using condoms?' are both questions asked by one respondent of another in groups I have moderated.

They can also provide reassurance and group identity that facilitates the discussion of otherwise difficult topics. For example, groups on drink-driving only came to life when one respondent admitted committing a serious drink-driving offence. The other members of the group then felt able to admit to similar behaviour. In these instances, the respondents are essentially interviewing each other. It is this dynamic process that contributes to the 'gestalt' of group discussions – the tendency for the whole to amount to more than the sum of the parts. It has a number of benefits – for example, it generates data, avoids respondent intimidation, makes it possible to exploit differences in opinion and examines peer interaction.

So, again, individual and group interviews each have strengths and should be used as appropriate. Indeed, in many instances, a combination of the two approaches may be the best option. Exactly the same points apply when considering quantitative methods.

Quantitative methods

Quantitative methods put a great emphasis on *sample selection* and *questioning procedures*. Samples have to be collected in a way that ensures they are representative of a particular population. Ideally, random selection procedures should be used, because this ensures that each potential respondent has an equal chance of being included in the study. This can be a complex and expensive process; at the very least it assumes you have an accurate 'sampling frame' or list of the population in question – which may not be too difficult to find if your interest is in all adults or schoolchildren, but if you want to sample sex workers and their clients, or illegal immigrants, it becomes much more difficult.

Quota sampling methods sidestep this issue by identifying the key variables (e.g. gender or ethnic origin) and ensuring that these are adequately represented in the final sample. As a result, they lack a certain degree of statistical rigour, but provide a pragmatic way through. As with RCTs, marketers tend to veer to the pragmatic end of the argument and will readily use quota sampling methods.

Representative sampling also requires large numbers. Whereas a qualitative study might typically measure its sample in dozens, a quantitative one will do so in hundreds or thousands.

The key issue with quantitative questioning is standardization. It is vital that each respondent is asked exactly the same set of questions, in the same order and, as far as possible, in the same way. Hence, we move from the free-flowing interview sequences of focus groups and in-depth interviews, to carefully constructed and piloted questionnaires, combined with detailed interviewer instructions. Standardization is so important because answers will be summed. If we want to know how many people used a particular service, or exactly how pleased they were with it, we have to be able to add up the answers to our questions. The questions and answers therefore have to mean the same thing – otherwise we are adding up apples and oranges.

Again, it is worth emphasizing that my purpose here is just to give a flavour of quantitative research that will enable our discussions about the purpose of social marketing research. Readers who want to go into more depth on, say, questionnaire design or sampling can consult standard market research texts (e.g. Kent, 2007).

■ When to do what sort of research

Social marketers, then, have a range of methodologies to choose from. To select the right one – or, more likely, the right combination – is going to depend on the decisions we have to make. Exercise 9.2 will help you think through what these decisions might be.

Exercise 9.2

Social marketing research questions

You are a consultant who has been commissioned to use social marketing to try and reverse the rise in antisocial behaviour amongst the adolescent boys of Brownesville. You will be working with the local social work department and an advertising agency. The initial proposal is to use a combination of a youth outreach centre, mass media activity and police liaison, but nothing has yet been firmly agreed.

How will you use research to guide your decision making? Specifically: *when* during the campaign will you want to answer *which questions*, and *what methodologies* will provide the best insights?

Reading Case Study 8 on p. 278 will also be useful. Kiri Milne and colleagues clearly gained a breadth of insights from a range of different research efforts in designing and implementing their Quit&Win intervention in New Zealand. Note also how they conclude by recognizing that their studies will stand them in good stead for a repeat exercise in 2008 – thereby emphasizing the strategic benefits of research.

Figure 9.3 presents the answer to Exercise 9.2 as a diagram which we will now explore step by step.

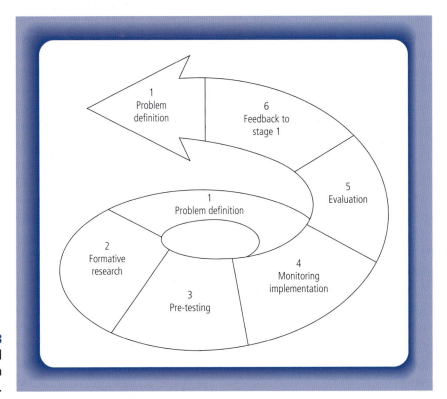

Figure 9.3
The social marketing research process.

Problem definition

In the first place, research can help define the problem (stage 1 in Figure 9.3) from the target group's perspective, exploring their perceptions of the particular issues being considered, such as smoking, sex or cancer – or in this case, antisocial behaviour. More specifically, it examines what role, if any, a particular intervention might perform and, assuming it has a role, campaign objectives can be clarified and a precise brief be given to the production and delivery teams.

Problem definition research can also clarify who the key target and stakeholder groups are. In Exercise 9.2, for instance, the latter may include parents, youth workers, civic leaders and neighbours of the proposed youth centre, all of whom may have useful insights to offer at each decision-making stage.

Methodologically, the first step here is with secondary research (see above) to check what is already known from past studies and official statistics about the problem. For example, in our case it might tell us something about the extent of the problem, the age and demographic background of offenders, and whether previous research tells us anything about their motives or patterns of behaviour. Equally, it might inform us about past efforts to tackle the problem and how the target groups responded.

If existing sources are inadequate, new primary research might need to be commissioned: qualitative to give us ideas about the target group's perceptions and quantitative to reveal more statistical data, such as the prevalence of particular behaviours.

Formative and pre-testing research

Assuming this problem definition research suggests the need for an intervention, further primary research can guide its development. Figure 9.3 divides this into formative and pre-testing (or decision-making) research (stages 2 and 3), but this is perhaps overly neat and tidy. In reality, several stages of research – typically qualitative – may be needed to perfect and hone the campaign. Essentially, the need is to identify key intervention ideas and work out how they can best be executed.

For example, qualitative research could be used to compare the potential of two different ideas for a youth outreach service on the one hand, or a more conventional communications effort designed to encourage young people to be more considerate on the other. These methods would enable you to show examples of materials and visuals of potential services. They would also make it possible to assess complex emotional reactions. A youth club might seem a plausible option and make sense on a rational level – if the kids are playing five-a-side they are not fighting in the town square – but it may be more valuable to determine what sort of youngster would actually use the service. Would they be middle-class 'goody-goodies' or those with 'street cred'? This type of issue typically calls for not just qualitative methods, but projective techniques (see Box 9.2).

This same research approach can be used to guide decisions about both the nature of the initiative (youth service or media effort) and how it should be executed. Thus, if the youth service shows most potential, it can help us determine what form it should take, where it should be located and how it should be promoted. There may also be some demand for quantitative research at this stage to determine the extent of demand or the prevalence of opinions.

In essence, these formative and decision-making stages of research mirror the discussions about developmental research to guide the design of media materials in Chapter 5. It is just that the focus has broadened to multifaceted initiatives and all elements of the marketing mix are subjected to the same degree of scrutiny.

Monitoring implementation

During implementation (stage 4 in Figure 9.3) our questions concern *what* is being delivered (how many training courses were run or leaflets handed out) and the extent to which it matches the programme objectives and expectations (Flora *et al.*, 1993). It also assesses the extent to which implementation is internally consistent across different sites and over the duration of the intervention period, and identifies the factors which can aid or hinder delivery. This is particularly important where there are many contextual and other factors that can affect how a programme is run – and, in turn, how effective it is. Box 9.4 illustrates some of the benefits of what is also called process evaluation, using a drugs prevention initiative as an example. It also illustrates how the monitoring of implementation fits in with both formative and evaluation research.

Box 9.4   The benefits of monitoring implementation

Think, for example, about a drug education package designed to be taught by classroom teachers in 20 different schools, by 50 different teachers. Even if teachers are supplied with exactly the same package, the same written instructions on how to use it and the same training in its methods, how they teach the package is likely to vary widely depending on how confident they feel about drug education, whether they agree philosophically with the approach taken in the package, whether they volunteered to teach the package or are doing it unwillingly, whether their classroom space is suitable for the activities, whether their head-teacher values drug education and makes them feel it is worthwhile, whether parents support or oppose teaching their children about drugs, and many other factors.

Process evaluation of programme implementation is an essential part of any social marketing research study, not only because it yields valuable learning in itself (for example, about the challenges of doing drug education in schools), but also because it can help explain the final results of a research study. Supposing our drug education research study finds that the package does not seem to have produced any changes in pupils' attitudes towards drugs: without process evaluation, we cannot know whether this is because the package was a bad package or whether it was just poorly implemented.

Source: Martine Stead

All the points made in Box 9.4 apply to our youth initiative. Monitoring implementation will, for instance, help us establish whether a youth centre has been successfully set up, is being used and matches the requirements established in the formative research. It can also give feedback on the sort of young people using the club and their experiences of doing so.

In terms of methodology, both qualitative and quantitative research can be used. In addition, a technique we mentioned briefly under methodology, observation, can also be useful. For example, the process evaluation in Box 9.4 included systematic classroom observation of lessons taking place.

Evaluation

Research with the target group and stakeholders can help evaluate an initiative after it has been run (stage 5 in Figure 9.3). The starting point for any evaluation of effectiveness must be our objectives, as noted in Chapter 4. It is not possible to measure achievements without clear original intentions. This reinforces the importance of clearly defining objectives at the problem definition stage.

There are essentially two kinds of objectives. First, there are those concerned with the target's reactions to an initiative – whether they are aware of it, have participated in it, understood it and so on. Second, there are objectives concerned with changes in the target population – whether, for example, there are fewer accidents as a result of an initiative, or whether, following a seat-belt promotion campaign, the target population has become more aware of the value of seat-belts, more in favour of them or more likely to actually use them. These two types of objectives require different evaluation procedures.

Measuring reactions to an initiative is fairly straightforward. Once the initiative is complete, the target audience simply has to be asked the relevant questions (e.g. have they seen the relevant advertising or visited the youth centre?). Provided that the research methodology is sound, reliable data will result. However, it may be argued that objectives and evaluations that are restricted purely to response are too limited. Furthermore, if social marketing aims to bring about social change, then, arguably, change is what should be measured when evaluating its effectiveness. Surely we need to know whether antisocial behaviour has declined?

However, measuring effect is much more difficult than measuring response. Done properly, it demands a full-blown RCT, with all the drawbacks and distortions we discussed earlier.

These problems of attribution and measuring change become most prevalent when we are trying to judge the success or failure of an individual initiative. Social marketing suggests that there is a need to look beyond one-off judgements in research. Instead, it should be *long term, integrated* and *constructive*.

Long term means putting the emphasis on strategic thinking and recognizing that change is likely to be gradual. The average change to be expected from road safety campaigns is less than 10% improvement in the measure, whether it be knowledge, attitude or behaviour (see Elliott, 1992). In our example, the impact of a new youth centre on antisocial behaviour is likely to be gradual and dependent on numerous other interventions taking place. Elliott reminds us, as we noted in Chapter 4, that our objectives must be correspondingly realistic.

Integrated means that the evaluation of effectiveness should, as in Figure 9.3, be seen as only one part of a research function that takes place throughout the development and implementation of initiatives – that evaluation is just one stage in a research process. Figure 9.3 does more than provide a schema for responding to our exercise and matching up the decision-making and research stages in developing a social marketing intervention. It also underlines the fact that these are not isolated steps, but part of a coherent process.

More fundamentally, it underlines the point that social marketing research is action-oriented and progressive. Like the strategic planning processes described in Chapter 3, it is an ongoing and fluid process. Note again how Milne and colleagues see their research on Quit&Win (Case Study 8 on p. 278) as guiding the current effort – but also ones in years to come. This strategic purpose is also underlined by the spiral design of Figure 9.3 and the fact that stage six focuses on feedback.

The Swiss response to the challenge of HIV/AIDS provides a good example of the value of this type of integrative, strategic research model. In 1987, they were faced with an urgent problem of having the highest prevalence of HIV/AIDS in Europe. A wide-ranging prevention programme was instigated, and after an initial assessment of the first wave of publicity, a comprehensive and ongoing evaluation strategy was adopted. They describe this as a 'comprehensive, utilization-focused evaluation' that 'seeks to produce results of immediate value to the development of the prevention strategy, and includes a continual process of questioning and feedback between the strategy makers and other potential users of the findings and the evaluators' (Dubois-Arber *et al.*, 1999, p. 2573).

They conclude that this approach to research:

> '... allows for a "real world" verification of strategic choices that in turn can guide further resource allocation and, last but not least, can help to maintain a high level of commitment of the different stakeholders.'
>
> (*ibid.*, p. 2580)

Social marketing suggests that this thinking can be applied not just to HIV/AIDS prevention programmes as in Switzerland, but to behaviour change more generally.

Finally, *constructive* means that the ultimate purpose of the research process is not just to test interventions, but to provide a better understanding of the stakeholders and clients with whom we want to engage.

■ The dangers of overdoing it

Given what we have agreed about the importance of doing plenty of research in social marketing, it is perhaps surprising to have a section warning against becoming too dependent on it. But there are such dangers, and they stem from misunderstandings about: (a) how research and decision making fit together, and (b) the strategic purpose of research.

Research and decision making

As we have seen, a mix of research methodologies is used to guide decision making in social marketing. However, it is important to recognize that research does not make decisions for us; it is not a matter of delegating the tough choices to the focus group or the questionnaire. The target group's expertise is in responding, not social marketing or intervention design. For example, as we discussed in Chapter 5, fear campaigns are frequently justified on the grounds that target audiences ask for them, opting for some variant on the blackened, cancerous lung or bloody car smash – the gorier the better. This misses the point of pre-testing. Smokers and drivers have a great deal to tell us about what it is like to be on the receiving end of our interventions, but they do not know which ones are most effective. They are clients, *not* consultants.

In other, closely related, spheres we readily accept this argument. We recognize, for instance, that most people are not experts in human behaviour, not even their own. So we would not simply ask smokers why they smoke and take their answers at face value. Indeed, in the 1980s, when the tobacco industry did precisely this to try and show that advertising had no effect on children's smoking (Jenkins, 1988), their research was rightly dismissed.

Indeed, there are times when decisions have to be made without any research. Good marketing has to cope when there is no data available and good marketers leave space for imagination, lateral thinking and educated guesses, even when there are data. For the truth is, as we noted at the end of Chapter 8, all research can do is lessen the risk that we get things wrong. It can reduce uncertainty; it cannot produce certainty.

Malcolm Gladwell (2005), in his book *Blink*, reminds us of the power of intuition. He tells the story of a Kuoros, an ancient Cretan statue, that was offered to the John Paul Getty museum in California. The museum subjected the potential exhibit to 14 months of very careful and high-powered scientific analysis to try and ascertain whether or not it was genuine. Their research provided reassurance, and they were on the verge of buying the Kuoros when a visiting expert looked at it and immediately warned against the purchase. He had done no research, no science, but just felt the statue was dubious. Other experts then responded in a similar negative way, again on the basis of intuition.

The statue was a fake.

Gladwell does not conclude that we should therefore abandon science and go back to guesswork. Indeed, he points out that gut feeling can be just as misleading, and in any case the experts will have educated their instincts with years of scientific rigour. He simply argues that we should leave space for intuition in our decision making. Marketers agree.

Strategic purpose

Social marketing research also suggests we should try and move beyond what might be called the 'intervention mentality' that dominates much behaviour-change activity, and instead think in terms of building long-term strategies. Three points flow from this.

First, extended time-frames are essential. Indeed, the lesson from commercial marketing is that we should opt for an *indefinite* time-frame. Ford have been successful for nearly 100 years; their basic product, cars, has remained the same, whilst the design and performance of these has improved exponentially in careful response to consumer need on the one hand and advancing technological know-how on the other. Or, closer to home, the UK's National Health Service brand has flourished for 60 years, and although it is frequently reviewed and reorganized, few would advocate closing it down. Despite its flaws and difficulties, we know it is much better than nothing. Why should social marketing programmes not have similar longevity? The Swiss HIV/AIDS experience certainly supports this notion.

It is worth reminding ourselves how rare such longevity is in the behaviour-change world. Take the UK approach to health promotion as an example. In Scotland, during the last 25 years, the body responsible for health promotion has changed its identity no fewer than four times. The English have fared even worse: having changed their national body a couple of times, they then closed it down altogether in 1997. What hope for strategic vision amid such turbulence? Certainly, if the current interest in social marketing is genuine, it calls for much less chopping and changing. The picture in New Zealand is a little more encouraging. The Health Sponsorship Council was established in 1993 and is still in business. As Box 9.5 describes, it has built brands and relationships with its key publics. Its use of social marketing principles has helped ensure its survival.

Box 9.5 The Health Sponsorship Council of New Zealand: social marketing in action

The Health Sponsorship Council (HSC) was established in the early 1990s by the New Zealand Government to buy out the then newly prohibited tobacco industry sports sponsorship deals. This job was completed by 1999, but the HSC continued and is now involved with social marketing programmes in tobacco control, sun safety, healthy eating and problem gambling. Why has it survived?

Certainly not by dictat: the HSC has no formal authority over regional or local organizations. Nor is it a funder, so cannot take the piper's prerogative and simply call the tune. Rather it works on the basis of reciprocal benefit. Thus, it provides mechanisms, resources, information and systems that assist others to achieve their objectives – it 'adds value' – while, at the same time, progressing its own aims.

This began with the provision of support services such as research and data assimilation, marketing advice, and promotional support materials like leaflets and posters. Gradually, this ad hoc activity developed into strategic gain, with, for instance, the promotional materials evolving into recognized and valued brands. For example, the 'Smoke-free' marque was developed and promoted by the HSC at a national level, but it is also utilized (with simple brand guidelines) by any local or regional organization involved or interested in tobacco control. Thus, it has become both a national emblem and a symbol of tobacco control at all levels of New Zealand society. Note that it is tobacco control that takes precedence, not the organization, so that the priority is clear: it is about the issue not the entity.

The process is very much a voluntary one. If local bodies do not like what the HSC produces they can walk away, and the HSC loses its distribution network. On the other hand, the local body stands to lose a range of support services. This encourages all those involved to build ongoing and mutually respectful relationships. It requires sharing of knowledge, collaborative workforce development through joint training and conferences, and an acceptance that cooperating often requires that something be given up by both parties – most fundamentally, power and control.

Experience shows that local and regional workers do want consistency (one brand, national themes, a common sense of direction); they do want assistance – but they do not want rigid, centrally imposed control. The structure has assisted the development of what is a customer focus – without the power to impose on others the HSC has had to discover and respond to the needs and wants of a workforce that will only enlist when they see how doing so will assist them with their objectives.

Thus, the HSC has succeeded by *doing* social marketing *using* social marketing principles.

Source: Iain Potter, CEO Health Sponsorship Council, New Zealand

Second, and related to this, we need to have faith in previous research and the idea that if we stick at it we can get it right. In point of fact this does not require a big leap of faith. Think back to the example of the NE Choices drugs prevention effort (Exercise 7.3), which was based on well-established principles that were, in turn, reinforced. One of its major lessons is that, as we noted above, we *do* know what works.

Third, we need to attribute much more importance to so-called intermediate measures. In the case of NE Choices, for instance, making young people feel more confident and empowered in their drug-related choices is a real achievement, and providing valued support at a vulnerable time of their lives is extremely worthwhile. Furthermore, these intermediate measures are known to be linked to behaviour change. Similarly, when we discussed relationship marketing in Chapter 7 we saw how customer satisfaction can be the best indicator of success. And from a research perspective it can be easily measured; as we noted, Reichheld's research suggests one simple question helps us identify our most satisfied clients: 'would you recommend this service to a friend?'

■ Conclusion

In this chapter we have emphasized the importance of research in social marketing, using the metaphor of a navigational aid. Its role is to guide our decision making from project inception through to completion, and illuminate the strategic fit between initiatives. We have also looked at the strengths and weaknesses of qualitative and quantitative methods, and how they complement each other. Both have a role in guiding social marketing decision making.

Finally, we also acknowledged the dangers of being over-dependent on research. It guides but does not replace decision making, and should not preclude intuition.

Pulling these ideas together, we concluded that systematic research acting as the servant of social marketing helps to improve our understanding not just of our marketing tools and techniques, but our target groups and their behaviours. Like good carpenters we come to understand the wood as well as the chisels. In this way, it can move us beyond the stop/start of interventions and towards a process of continuous health, safety and welfare improvement.

■ References

Advisory Council on the Misuse of Drugs (ACMD) (2006). London: Central Office of Information.

Anderson A.S., Porteous L.E.G., Foster E., Higgins C., Stead M., Hetherington M., Ha M.-A. and Adamson A.J. (2005). The impact of a school-based nutrition education intervention on dietary intake and cognitive and attitudinal variables relating to fruits and vegetables. *Public Health Nutrition*, **8**(6): 650–656.

Devlin E., Hastings G., Noble G., McDermott L. and Smith A. (2005). *Pharmaceutical Marketing: A Question of Regulation*. ISM Working Paper.

Dubois-Arber F., Jeannin A. and Spencer B. (1999). Long-term global evaluation of a national AIDS prevention strategy: the case of Switzerland. *AIDS*, **13**(18): 2571–2582.

Elliott B. (1992). *Road Safety Mass Media Campaigns: A Meta Analysis*. Canberra: Federal Office of Road Safety, Department of Transport and Communications.

Flora J.A., Lefebvre R.C., Murray D.M., Stone E.J., Assaf A. *et al.* (1993). A community education monitoring system: methods from the Stanford Five-City Project, the Minnesota Heart Health Program and the Pawtucket Heart Health Program. *Health Education Research Theory and Practice*, **8**(1): 81–95.

Gladwell M. (2005). *Blink: The power of thinking without thinking*. London: Allen Lane.

Grant I.C., Hassan L.M., Hastings G.B., MacKintosh A.M. and Eadie D. (2007). The influence of branding on adolescent smoking behaviour: exploring the mediating role of image and attitudes. *International Journal of Nonprofit and Voluntary Sector Marketing*.

Hastings G.B. (1990). Qualitative research in health education. *Journal of the Institute of Health Education*, **28**(4): 118–127.

Hastings G.B., Eadie D.R. and Scott A.C. (1990). Two years of AIDS publicity: a review of progress. *Health Education Research*, **5**(1): 17–25.

Hastings G., Devlin E. and Anderson S. (2005). Dealing in Drugs: An analysis of the pharmaceutical industry's marketing documents. In: *House of Commons Health Committee Report – The Influence of the Pharmaceutical Industry*. 4th report of session 2004–5, Vol 2, 22nd March, Appendix 33. London: The Stationery Office.

Henderson M. (2006). *School Effects on Adolescent Pupils' Health Behaviours and School Processes Associated with these Effects*, p. 299. Glasgow: MRC Social and Public Health Sciences Unit, University of Glasgow.

Jenkins J. (1988). Tobacco advertising and children: some Canadian findings. *International Journal of Advertising*, **7**(4): 357–367.

Kent R. (2007). *Marketing Research. Approaches, Methods and Applications*. London: Thomson Learning.

Lee H. (1960, 1974). *To Kill a Mockingbird*. London: Pan Books Ltd.

Lowe J. (1985). *Old Bones* (song).

MRC (2000). *A Framework for Development and Evaluation of RCTs for Complex Interventions to Improve Health*, April. London: Medical Research Council.

Smith M.K. (1996). *Action Research*. Published online by *The Encyclopedia of Informal Education*, http://www.infed.org/research/b-actres.htm (accessed 13 September 2006).

Stead M., Hastings G.B. and Eadie D. (2002). The challenge of evaluating complex interventions: a framework for evaluating media advocacy. *Health Education Research Theory and Practice*, **17**(3): 351–364.

US Department of Education Institute of Education Sciences National Center for Education Evaluation and Regional Assistance (2003). *Identifying and Implementing Educational Practices Supported by Rigorous Evidence: A User Friendly Guide*, December. Prepared for the Institute of Education Sciences. Washington, DC: Coalition for Evidence-Based Policy.

West P., Sweeting H. and Leyland A. (2004). School effects on pupils' health behaviours: evidence in support of the health promoting school. *Research Papers in Education*, **19**(3), 261–291.

CHAPTER 10

Ethical Issues

■ Overview

Social marketers interfere with people's lives, so ethical considerations abound. We decide what they should do, devise strategies to encourage them to do it, choose who should get the benefits of our efforts (and who should not), criticize other people's campaigns and conduct endless research. All of these steps present moral issues that have to be acknowledged and addressed.

This chapter starts by discussing why ethics are so important in social marketing and examines the principal dilemmas we face. Inevitably, there are no simple solutions, but we go on to see how practical and theoretical approaches reinforce each other and help us to pick our way through the maze.

Learning objectives

After working through this chapter you will:

- Recognize that there are many important ethical dilemmas facing the social marketer.
- Understand some basic points about ethical theory.
- Be able to address practical ethical problems.

During this chapter you might find it useful to cross-refer to the discussions of:
- Strategic planning in Chapter 3
- The fluoridation example in Chapter 7
- Case Studies 9 and 13.

LINKS TO OTHER CHAPTERS

■ Why we need ethics in social marketing

Ethical dilemmas arise because we deal with people and try to change what they do: our target clients, stakeholders, competitors and wider society are all impacted by our efforts. Furthermore, we focus on behaviours that are illegal, taboo or culturally sensitive – just over the last couple of years, our work in the Institute for Social Marketing has covered illicit drug use, sex, addiction, speeding, domestic violence, prisoner health and childhood immunization.

As a result, the social marketing solution often requires difficult and stressful behaviour-change options of people. For example, giving up addictive substances carries severe physiological and psychological repercussions, while encouraging increased fruit and vegetable consumption can have implications for the cost of a family's weekly shopping basket and for family relationships, particularly with fussy children.

Due to concerns about inequalities, social marketers also tend to be working with particularly vulnerable and hard-to-reach target groups. These groups include those in poverty, ethnic minorities, children and those with disabilities or pressing health needs. This poses challenges for research, segmentation and targeting.

However, the most fundamental reason that social marketers should be concerned with ethics is because ultimately their business is 'messing with people lives'. It is imperative that we take time out and consider the morality and relevance of our values for others, and the effects (intended or otherwise) our campaigns have on those who engage with them.

One example of such a campaign that was compounded by difficult ethical dilemmas was a social marketing initiative to fluoridate the water supply of north-east England. As we noted in Chapter 7, fluoridation is a remarkably simple and effective public health measure; it involves adding a small amount of fluoride to the water, the technology is foolproof and the benefits immense. Most strikingly, it ensures virtually perfect dental health for everyone, regardless of social background. But it also raises concerns about mass medication and 'nannying'. Box 10.1 gives a flavour of exactly how strongly some people feel about these issues.

> ### Box 10.1   Social marketing can raise very serious moral concerns
>
> During a campaign to fluoridate the public water supply, a letter was received from an old soldier expressing very grave reservations:
>
> '... We believe that neither you nor anyone else has the right to tell us what to consume – would you like us to tell you what to consume? Of course you wouldn't! Don't try to hijack the democratic system and individual rights in pursuit of ideological goals. Never try to deny consumers the right of choice in anything, choice also comes with democracy. Those rights were hard won on the battlefields of Europe, would you condemn those sacrifices to oblivion in your pursuit of self-gratification? ...'

However, there are no easy answers; the option of not fluoridating also presents moral dilemmas. Is it right to deprive a community of known public health benefit, especially one that has a proven effect on inequalities?

And all this assumes our social marketing efforts are successful. What happens when things do not work – do we just reinforce the negative behaviour, creating bad social marketing which makes the original problem worse? Do, for example, fearful messages about the side-effects of

smoking just provide teenage boys with a better prop for demonstrating how tough and rebellious they are? Is it unethical to make less than optimal use of limited government resources or charitable funds?

So yes, we need to address ethical considerations. In the commercial field, this forms an integral part of strategic thinking – good ethics are ultimately good business. The same thinking should apply in social marketing. But the first task is to pin down the ethical issues we face.

■ The key ethical challenges facing social marketers

In essence, every stage of the marketing planning process discussed in Chapter 3 raises ethical as well as managerial challenges. As Figure 10.1 shows, we need to address seven questions. (1) Which behaviours to address? (2) Are there potential competitors and how should we deal with them? (3) Which consumer groups to target? (4) What products/services to offer in their exchange? (5) How to use the marketing mix to make this offering? (6) Are there any unintended effects? (7) How to conduct research to inform this process?

Each of these ethical questions is now addressed.

What behaviour?

Social marketers must make informed judgements about what problems to address or what behaviour to influence. These decisions have clear moral dimensions – should restricted budgets be spent on encouraging behaviours which are likely to improve the health and well-being of small numbers of people (e.g. intensive cessation counselling), or on large campaigns which reach large populations but with uncertain results (e.g. mass media anti-smoking campaigns).

More fundamentally, social marketers must make moral judgements about what behaviours are important to endorse or discourage, and for which groups of society particular behaviours are appropriate. Legislation provides obvious guidelines, but in other areas matters are less clear-cut. For instance, in Exercise 10.1, addressing the sexual behaviour of teenagers below the age of consent, or to young people of certain religious backgrounds, presents particular problems.

It is important not to arrogantly assume that we social marketers ('experts') know best. There may, for example, be situations where, on balance, certain 'dangerous' or undesirable behaviours may be permissible. Who determines that the best and only correct life choices should be that we all become non-smoking, moderate drinking, blood donating, vegetarian, recyclers who live to become centenarians? Perhaps people do have the right to decide to take risks. It is important that, as social marketers, we avoid the easy trap of assuming that ours are the only legitimate priorities.

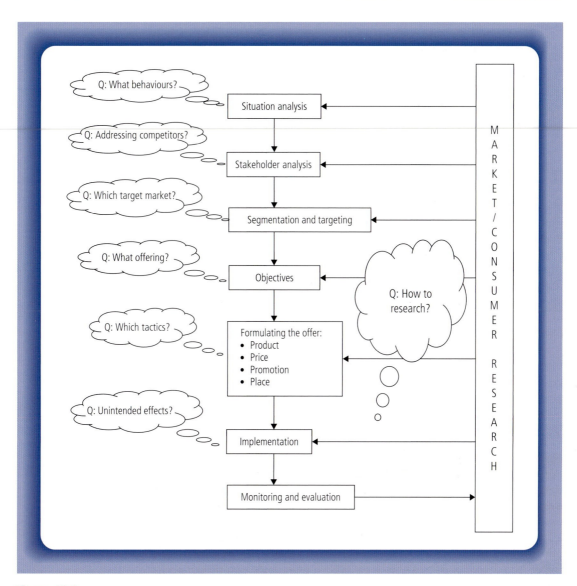

Figure 10.1
Ethical dilemmas in social marketing planning.
Source: adapted from MacFadyen and Hastings (2001).

The competition

The letter in Box 10.1 actually gives a glance into a small but typically well-organized anti-fluoridation movement. The reality is that any fluoridation programme, at least in the UK, is going to have to be progressed in the teeth of this opposition group. Difficult judgements have to be made about the legitimacy of their objections – are they based on sound science,

Exercise 10.1

Ethical challenges in sexual health

You are a social marketing consultant who has been commissioned to undertake and evaluate an initiative on teenage sexual health in Dundee. You already know that there are above-average levels of teenage pregnancy and sexually transmitted infections among 14- to 16-year-olds in the area.

What ethical dilemmas will you face with this project?

Looking back at the discussion of marketing planning in Chapter 3 will help.

for example, or just prejudice and emotion? Then there are questions about how we deal with the competition – do we try to ally with them, as in the Miller Brewing-funded drink-driving initiative (see Exercise 8.5), or oppose and defeat them?

In Exercise 10.1 the Catholic Church may well represent serious opposition to, say, the promotion of condoms. As a social marketer you will need to think through how you respond to this.

Which target market?

Segmentation in social marketing poses unique ethical problems. Despite the superiority of segmented versus undifferentiated campaigns, the decision to target (i.e. help) certain social groups to the exclusion of others can be extremely difficult. There may be an important trade-off between reaching less needy but easy-to-reach groups (geographically or strategically) or very needy but hard-to-reach groups. For example, consumers in geographically isolated islands, very-low-income communities or convicted prisoners may be difficult to 'reach' with mainstream initiatives, but can you really afford to ignore their needs?

Testing the efficacy of social marketing initiatives using an experimental research design shares this problem. The initiative is administered to one group but not another. Arguably, the control group participants sacrifice the opportunity for better health or safety to benefit others.

On the other hand, being targeted by a social marketing campaign may have deleterious consequences. Being publicly singled out for special support because of gender, poverty, disability, race, etc. may leave consumers open to stigmatization. For example, a Government drugs prevention initiative in the north-east of England was unable to target young drug users for fear of stigmatization. The programme had developed a range of intervention components for young people already using drugs. However, it would have been impossible to secure the necessary cooperation of

schools, communities and parents who would not have wished their children labelled as drug users (Stead *et al.*, 1997). A partial solution was found by combining blanket targeting with self-selection, where young people with similar interests (and presumably, similar attitudes/experiences of drugs) could opt-in to certain components (Home Office, 1998).

In Exercise 10.1 there are similar dilemmas. Will youngsters targeted with sexual health clinics suffer embarrassment or worse? Do girls come under pressure to have sex if boys are targeted with safer sex programmes?

What offering?

Ethical questions are also likely to occur when making decisions about the social marketing offering. As we noted in Chapters 2 and 3, social marketing is based on the principle of 'exchange'. A common point of understanding and fulfilment of needs must be reached for an exchange to take place. This ultimately results in some form of compromise between the principal actors. Since the behaviours involved are often deep rooted, this may result in adopting more modest objectives or advocating behaviour which, whilst reducing risk, does still have negative repercussions. This level of compromise may seem defeatist and unethical.

For example, in our exercise Dundee is not exceptional; the UK as a whole has one of the highest rates of teenage pregnancy in Europe (House of Commons, 2003). As so many young people are already sexually active, many would advocate that it is more important to prioritize safer sex than complete abstinence. This and other harm minimization campaigns, including the safer or more informed use of illegal drugs, raise key dilemmas in social marketing. Is it more important to have fewer people engaging in an undesirable behaviour, or to have more people doing it, but doing it more safely? Also, does it help to remember that in both cases we are also running against the spirit, if not the letter, of the law?

Another ethical question that may arise when deciding on a suitable offering is the level of involvement required on the part of the consumer. Some solutions, such as practising safer sex or going for cancer screening, require very active participation. Others do not require the consumer to do much, or indeed anything at all: a fluoridated water supply delivers better dental health without any action on the part of you or me. Indeed, most people do not even know whether or not their water is fluoridated. This raises a crucial ethical issue: informed consent. Regardless of how much active participation a given programme demands, people have a right to know what is being done to them. This right applies however well intentioned and benevolent the programme.

Which marketing tactics?

In Chapter 4 we considered the value of the marketing mix as a management tool, helping us think through the effectiveness of different tactics: of

getting the right product, in the right place at the right time – and saying supportive things about it. We emphasized that 'right' in this context means in close alignment with consumer needs, but here we are concerned with it in an ethical sense – and there can be conflicts between these two perspectives. For example, in Exercise 10.1, a distribution strategy of putting condoms in school toilets may well encourage boys to think more seriously about using them, but at the cost of putting pressure on girls to have sex.

A closely related problem is that of ends and means. Because social marketers are typically involved in doing good, there is a temptation to assume that otherwise unacceptable tactics are justified. This type of thinking is most apparent in communications. Fear-based messages, the vagaries of which we discussed in Chapter 5, depend for their effectiveness in portraying alarming repercussions from a particular behaviour. Paradoxically, problems can then arise if these outcomes are not upsetting enough.

The result can be a tendency for 'risk proliferation' which raises ethical issues. Is the underlying assumption that our clients are ignorant, reckless and irrational children behaving in dangerous and unhealthy ways, and our job is to goad or trick them into behaving better? The additional danger here is that, in our rush to put them right, we forget that behaviour is not just caused by the individual, but – as we noted when we discussed Social Cognitive Theory in Chapter 2 – by their social circumstances. In this way, an over-reliance on threatening messages may simply be adding to consumers' feelings of stress and disempowerment. Whether it actually changes a particular behaviour or not, this is a serious moral concern.

Unintended effects

As we noted in Chapter 9, it can be difficult enough to establish whether your campaign has done what you wanted with the intended target group. From an ethical perspective, though, it is equally important to think about people who may respond to your campaign because they misunderstand it, or are simply the wrong target. For example, in Scotland a smoking helpline established to assist adult smokers to quit was unexpectedly popular with underage smokers (Network Scotland, 1997). This was not problematic in itself, but the system was not equipped to deal with the very particular needs of young smokers; as a consequence, a demand had been created that could not be met.

Mission creep of this type can have very unfortunate results. The early attempts to warn people of the dangers of HIV resulted in a phenomenon dubbed 'the worried well', with people like children and the elderly, who could not possibly be at risk, becoming alarmed. Similarly, in Exercise 10.1, having wrestled with your conscience and decided that it is justified for 13-year-olds to receive a programme on safer sex, how comfortable would you be if 11- and 12-year-olds were also exposed to it?

There is a related issue here about keeping stakeholders informed and involved in your work. If you have indeed had to wrestle with your conscience to make decisions about the ethics of your campaign, are there other groups – such as parents or teachers – who have a right to be consulted or at least informed of developments.

Upstream interventions can also have unforeseen outcomes. Increasing the tax on – and thereby the price of – cigarettes has played an important role in reducing the UK's smoking prevalence (Townsend, 1987). However, this proved a regressive policy, having most impact amongst the more privileged social groups, whose circumstances mean that they have found it easiest to quit. The least well-off continue to smoke and the policy just makes them poorer (Marsh and McKay, 1994).

Research issues

Conducting research into the sensitive, taboo and, at times, illegal behaviours of social marketing business requires careful consideration. The research process, particularly qualitative methods that depend on the intensive involvement of participants, may enhance fears, whether justified (e.g. discussion of cervical screening amongst those with experience of disease) or not (e.g. other respondents in a focus group hyping unreal risks), or cause embarrassment. It can also prompt risky behaviour by, for instance, creating the impression that everyone is smoking tobacco or using drugs, encouraging impressionable participants to subscribe to a spurious norm. This is particularly problematic when the behaviour being researched is illegal, such as drug use, drink-driving or underage sex.

On the other hand, research is certainly necessary, as we have discussed throughout this book, and it would present equal if not greater ethical dilemmas if we were to proceed without conducting it at all. By the same token, research has to be as reliable and rigorous as possible. This means researchers do have to probe, put respondents under pressure and check their answers for veracity.

In this sense, research ethics is a microcosm of all the ethical dilemmas social marketers face: a tension between individual vulnerability and overall effectiveness, a balance between means and ends.

■ How do we respond?

Let us leave aside complex issues of social marketing for a moment. How would you decide on a more everyday ethical problem? Try Exercise 10.2.

Exercise 10.2

A sweet dilemma

You are in your local newsagent when you see a small child of 8 or 9 years steal some sweets. Do you intervene? And if so how – by telling the shopkeeper, the parent or confronting the child directly?

The chances are you will have used a combination of two ways of thinking about the dilemma: whether the action itself is right or wrong and whether the results of the action (intended or not) are desirable or not. You may also have considered the idea of human rights. Interestingly, these echo the principal strands of ethical theory that we will discuss in a moment. I say this with some confidence, because that is typically what happens in the seminar room.

In addition, you probably looked for clues in the actions of others – what would your friends or peers do in the same situation? Or, more generally, are there any codes of conduct or rules that give us some guidance about the correct course of action? Again, you are not alone. Our responses to ethical dilemmas – just like our behaviour more generally – are influenced by our environment and social norms. This lies behind the increasing inclination in business, medicine and research to lay down formal rules and procedures to guide practice.

■ The theory

As with human behaviour (Chapter 2), there are many theories in the study of ethics. We will focus on the three that are of most immediate use: Deontological Theory, Teleological Theory and Theories of Rights.

Deontological Theory

This view of ethical conduct is based on the principle of duty – the actual behaviour is emphasized, rather than its consequences. It institutes rules of good behaviour by focusing on motives rather than outcomes and assumes that a good intention is likely to produce good results. Kant expressed this in his 'categorical imperative': 'I ought never to act except in such a way that I can also will that my maxim should become a universal law (Guyer, 1998).' Kant argues that we should act in ways that we hope all others would do.

Deontologists have been criticized for not focusing on the consequences of actions and ignoring the situational context of particular courses of action. For example, most would agree that it is, in many instances, wrong to lie, but can easily imagine circumstances when such a transgression would be justified – and many more where, whilst an outright lie is unacceptable, avoiding telling the whole truth would be.

It is important not to lie to consumers in social marketing, but there may be decisions to make regarding which truth to tell. For example, research to inform an initiative to encourage older men to climb stairs instead of taking the escalator found that the key message for this target was weight loss, rather than disease prevention. In cases such as this, social marketers have to choose between a traditional public health message (to take exercise to avoid a heart attack) or a more superficial, but motivating, message (take some exercise to be more slim and attractive).

Teleological Theory

Teleological Theory (or utilitarianism) describes the morality of a particular decision in terms of its consequences, rather than its motives. An action or decision is argued to be ethically correct if it delivers the greatest good to the greatest number. This perspective rests on the assumption that morality is to promote human welfare by maximizing benefits and minimizing harm. To assess the consequences of actions, it is necessary to conduct a social cost-benefit analysis.

However, this perspective begs the question 'who decides what is good?' For example, there are some who believe that only pleasure and happiness are intrinsically good, while others believe that there are other 'good' values, such as friendship, knowledge, health and beauty (Beauchamp and Bowie, 1988). Furthermore, the drive to maximize total good may produce morally doubtful consequences. For example, in the UK, greatest health benefits can be delivered most easily to those not in poverty. The health divide between rich and poor would likely be exacerbated if we relied only on teleological reasoning.

Theories of Rights

Alternatively, decision making can be framed in terms of its duty to ensure human rights (Waldron, 1984). Theories of Rights assume that there exist some universal human rights to which we should all have equal access. These rights include: rights to life, safety, truthfulness, privacy, freedom of conscience, freedom of speech and private property. Arguably, social marketers have a corresponding duty to ensure these rights are not infringed.

This perspective may offer some clarity in the resolution of ethical questions. Take, for instance, the case of access to a database of children's contact details, which would be of great use for research on health behaviours, such as smoking or drug use. Should this database be given to researchers to conduct research that will allow them to construct a random sample and produce new data that would contribute to evidence-based public policy? Or is this unethical use of confidential information? Deontological and Teleological Theories offer competing resolutions. Teleological Theory would suggest that in the interests of the greater good – in this case, the better public policy to protect children – access to the database should be agreed. Deontological reasoning, however, would focus on the wrong being done to those on the database, and therefore militate against access. Human rights thinking provides a way through this impasse. If we accept that everyone has equal rights to privacy, then a system of informed consent emerges as a solution.

■ The practice

This theory needs to be backed up by systems. As we noted in Exercise 10.2, we depend on social cues and guidance from those around us when making and carrying through ethical judgements.

These systems are being developed and increasingly it is difficult to get very far with a social marketing idea before you trip over not just ethical issues, but requirements to address these issues. Most typically, this is driven by research ethics, which has now become a mainstream aspect of any modern study. Prior to even starting, ethical approval by a formally constituted Ethics Committee is a prerequisite for funding.

As yet, interventions themselves do not have to be scrutinized in this way and so require careful thought on behalf of the social marketer.

■ Conclusion

Every step of the social marketing process raises ethical dilemmas, but marketing itself is amoral. As we have seen throughout this book, it can be used as readily to encourage consumption of lethal and addictive drugs as it can to promote road safety. Social marketers therefore have to engage actively with ethics.

Theory and practice unite to help with this task. Thus, we are naturally inclined to think about both the inherent rights and wrongs of a particular action, and about the relative merits of its outcomes, thereby, even if unwittingly, picking up on the thinking of both Immanuel Kant and John Stuart Mill. An increasing sense that we all have certain basic human rights also helps us make progress. None of these philosophies provides the whole answer, but between them they can certainly help us analyse the challenges. The context in which we make our judgements, the views of our colleagues and peers, and formal systems such as Research Ethics Committees help us carry this thinking into practice.

There are no easy or clear-cut answers. We will make mistakes, people will get hurt – but as long as we try and apply ethical thinking to our work there is a better chance of doing good than harm. And, by way of consolation, if doing social marketing presents ethical dilemmas, not doing it presents more.

■ References

Beauchamp T.L. and Bowie N.E. (1988). *Ethical Theory and Business*, 3rd edition. Englewood Cliffs, NJ: Prentice-Hall.

Guyer P. (1998, 2004). Kant, Immanuel. In: *Routledge Encyclopedia of Philosophy* (E. Craig, ed). London: Routledge.

Home Office Drugs Prevention Initiative (1998). *Managing a Drugs Prevention Initiative: The experience of NE Choices 1996–98*. Newcastle-upon-Tyne: Northumbria Drugs Prevention Team.

House of Commons (2003). *Health Committee Sexual Health Third Report of Session 2002/2003*, Vol. 1, HC69-I, 11 June. London: HMSO.

MacFadyen L. and Hastings G.B. (2001). First do no harm: the case for ethical considerations in social marketing. Presented at: Academy of Marketing Science 10th Biennial World Marketing Congress – *Global Marketing Issues at the Turn of the Millennium*, jointly organized with Cardiff University, 30 May–2 June.

Marsh A. and McKay S. (1994). *Poor Smokers*. London: Policy Studies Institute.

Network Scotland (1997). *Calls to Smokeline: Weekly Report 267*. Unpublished.

Stead M., Mackintosh A.M., Hastings G., Eadie D.R., Young F. and Regan T. (1997). *Preventing adolescent drug use: design, implementation and evaluation design of NE Choices*. Paper presented at Home Office, DPI Research Conference, Liverpool, 3–5 December.

Townsend J.L. (1987). Cigarette tax, economic welfare and social class patterns of smoking. *Applied Economics*, **19**(3): 355–365.

Waldron J. (1984). *Theories of Rights*. Oxford: Oxford University Press.

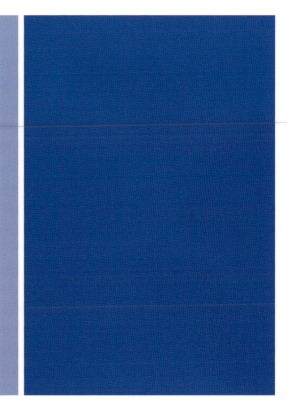

End Note

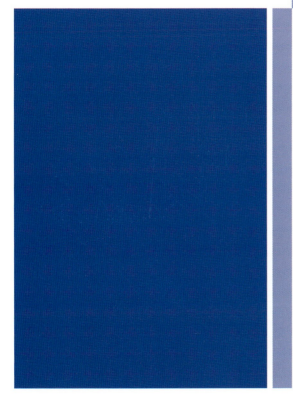

This book started by showing how marketers can get us to do things – to buy their products, visit their stores, wear their brands. We cooperate with them because we see a real gain for ourselves. Their products and services provide valued tangible and intangible benefits: trainers keep our feet warm and make us feel cool, SUVs get us to Tesco's, whilst helping us retain a sense of freedom and the wilderness.

Companies that deliver these benefits consistently and with good customer service build up a positive reputation with us, and this typically accretes in the brand. Over time, a series of mutually beneficial transactions, combined with evocative and familiar branding, can be developed into supportive relationships. We come to be trusting of, and committed to, particular brands or companies, even – as in the case of tobacco – when they are actually killing us in truly alarming numbers.

These same techniques are applied with equal enthusiasm to stakeholders – policymakers, suppliers, competitors and staff – anyone who can make the business environment more supportive.

All this just to provide us with trainers, cars and groceries.

And it works. The corporations that use marketing in this way have enjoyed unparalleled success and become some of the most powerful organizations on Earth.

Social marketing takes two lessons from this. First, that we need to recognize and tackle the competition; big tobacco is part of the smoking problem and needs hobbling if we are to succeed. Similarly, the marketing of other products that impact on health and safety – from cars to computer games – should, at least, be carefully scrutinized.

Second, the social and health sector can do its own marketing. The thinking which has proved so good at shifting consumer behaviour can be applied just as well to health and social behaviour. Indeed, given that these sectors are dealing (quite literally) with matters of life and death and are not driven by a need to make profits and satisfy shareholders, the concept of mutually supportive relationships has even greater resonance.

We have seen throughout this book that this can work – in the systematic reviews we cited in the introduction and in numerous examples and case studies from around the world. Social marketing has been successfully used to address a host of social and health issues, from fighting racism to empowering adolescents. This is not, however, to suggest that it is a silver bullet that supersedes all other efforts at behaviour change; it is not and does not – it just adds some useful ideas to the mix.

But now is the time to see if it has worked for *you*. Go back to Exercise 1.1 and have another go at it. Have your answers changed at all? Has a better knowledge of social marketing helped you tackle the UK's tobacco problem? Has it given you new ideas or insights? If not, I suggest you return to the bookshop and demand your money back (hopefully they will see it as a relationship building opportunity). If it has helped, try and think through what the most important lessons have been for you. What would be your equivalent of the National Social Marketing Centre's benchmarks? What, for you, is good social marketing?

There is no right or wrong answer, but I will finish by giving you my top 10 principles. For me, good social marketing recognizes that:

1. The evidence base has revealed a rich variety of opportunities for everyone to make their lives safer, longer and – above all – more fulfilled; we should avoid presenting it as a collection of disempowering, capricious threats.

2. Although this evidence base is important, slavish adherence to it gets in the way of clear and strategic thinking. Intuition and vision have a place at the decision-making table, alongside data.

3. Communications are only a small part of the game. Glossy advertising campaigns – especially isolated ones – are not the answer.

4. By the same token, ad hoc campaigns of any sort cannot bring about the kind of social change we are seeking.

5. Progress will depend on a deep and sustained understanding of people's real needs, recognizing that these may be more complex than a disease- and accident-free long life. This understanding has to be used to build long-term relationships with our clients and stakeholders.

6. Good health and safe communities are the product of many complex factors – including Government policy, commercial marketing, education and wealth – as well as individual lifestyle choices, and progress will depend on action on all these fronts. Stakeholders are a key target group in social marketing.

7. Competitive analysis is a crucial tool – one of the principle reasons we have so many binge drinkers, smokers and unhealthy eaters is that the commercial sector has been better at marketing than we have. This has to change.

8. This is a long and complex game which demands a sustained strategic response. The Marlboro brand has remained largely unchanged for 50 years, Coke is a centenarian – our efforts need similar continuity.

9. We do not know best – indeed, sometimes it may be that no one knows best – but this is not a problem provided we level with people, adult to adult. It is more important that our clients trust us than obey us.

10. Success will come when people are given – and experience – a measure of genuine control over their own destiny.

Sadly, the powers that be are unlikely to follow these guidelines to the letter. Social marketing principles will not be universally applied in ideal circumstances. Nonetheless, there is still reason for optimism. All we have to do is get better at marketing than the tobacco industry, to build better relationships with the smoker than Philip Morris or Imperial Tobacco. I am sure we can manage that.

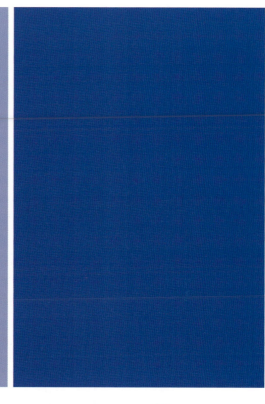

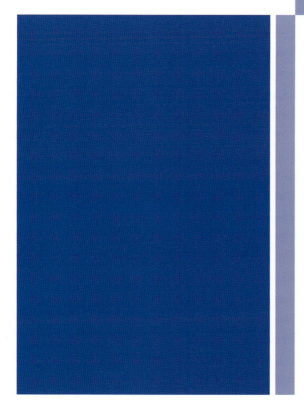

Case Studies

CASE STUDY 1

A marketing strategy to reduce UK prison numbers

Martine Stead, Laura McDermott and Gerard Hastings

1. Introduction

'Rethinking Crime and Punishment' (RCP) was a four-year initiative (2001–2005) in the UK to raise the level of debate about how to deal with offenders and to reduce the rising prison population. A detailed social marketing strategy (Hastings *et al.*, 2002) was developed to guide the initiative's priorities and planning. This case summarizes some of its key components.

2. Problem definition

The UK prison population is disproportionately high compared to other countries with similar crime rates and is continuing to rise at an unsustainable rate. In 2000, before the start of the initiative, the England and Wales prison population was projected to reach 80 000 and the current projection is actually higher: between 90 250 and 106 550 by 2013 (de Silva *et al.*, 2006). Likewise, the prison population projections for Scotland are between 6700 and 8500 by 2010 – an upward trend in comparison to former levels (Scottish Executive, 2002). This places great pressure on the prisons, and the service finds it increasingly difficult to offer rehabilitative programmes. Some estimates suggest that prison numbers would fall by one-third if elderly, young and minor offenders were decarcerated.

The rising prison population cannot be fully explained by crime trends, and is also influenced by other political, social and cultural factors:

- *Sentencing policy and practice.* Successive changes in sentencing policy have made the courts more punitive in many areas, resulting in increased use of custody even for minor offences.
- *Crime is a political football.* Both major political parties in the UK have exploited and sustained public concern about crime. This has resulted in punitive and reactive policies, short-term political oneupmanship and a chronic lack of vision.
- *Public fear of crime.* Surveys show public fear of crime, support for prison and a lack of faith in the criminal justice sector. Qualitative

research suggests a more complex picture, with a less punitive public than the surveys imply.

● *Sensationalist media*. Dramatic and unrealistic coverage of crime in the entertainment and news media have helped to sustain public demand for prison.

Reoffending rates among those released from prison are high, and many offenders leave prison 'no better equipped to fit into society than when they entered it', suggesting prison is ineffective for many offenders (Esmée Fairbairn Foundation, 2004). It is increasingly argued among criminal justice experts that community sentences, particularly those based on restorative justice principles that give a voice to the victim, represent a better way forward for non-serious offenders.

3. Competitive analysis

The main competitive barrier was public opinion: the public demands increasingly harsh approaches to crime, constraining how politicians, judges and magistrates respond, leading them to fear a media and public backlash if they are seen to be too 'soft on crime'. To address this, there was a need to convert the public's, and many other stakeholders', existing ambivalence about prison into dissonance: to strengthen already held perceptions that prison is a meaningless and ineffective response for many offenders, and weaken current attachment to it as a solution. At the same time, there was a need to improve the image of non-custodial alternatives.

4. Stakeholder analysis

The key stakeholder groups are shown in Figure CS1.1. The closer a group's proximity to the centre of the circle, the more direct its influence on imprisonment rates.

All the stakeholders have a role to play, and the full marketing plan analysed each of their needs, the benefits to each of a reduction in prison numbers and their potential role in the reduction process. For the sake of brevity, in this case we will concentrate on the inner circle of Decision Makers who comprise the judiciary and politicians, as well as the Primary Influencers who comprise the media and general public.

5. Aims and objectives

One overall aim of the Rethinking Crime and Punishment initiative was to *reduce society's attachment to the use of prison as a response to crime*. As the competitive analysis highlighted, this divides into two complementary

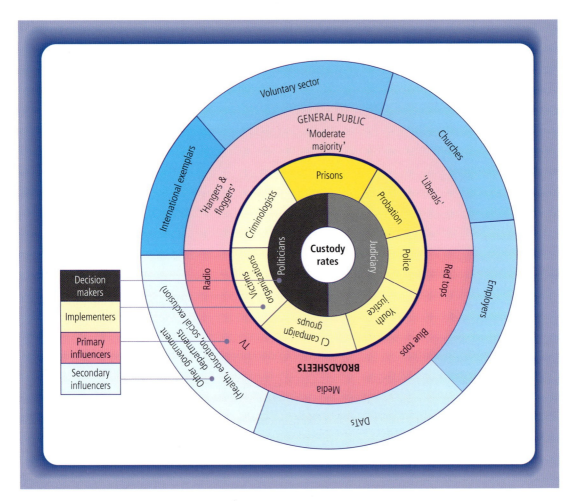

Figure CS1.1
Stakeholder groups.

marketing aims: (i) demarketing prison and (ii) marketing non-custodial alternatives to prison.

For our target groups, these devolved into three marketing objectives:

(a) Encourage consensus on the cause of rising prison numbers and examine the role of sentencing.
(b) Increase dissonance about prison as a sentencing option for many offences.
(c) Improve the perceived and actual effectiveness of non-custodial solutions.

6. Formulation of strategy

A marketing offering was then devised to meet each objective (Table CS1.2).

Table CS1.1 Stakeholder needs and benefits

Stakeholder	Needs	Benefits from reducing prison numbers	Potential role in RCP
Politicians	• Public confidence in CJS. • Deliver on CJS performance pledges. • Belief in electoral and media advantage in 'softer' approach.	• Solution to prison crisis. • Bigger budget for more popular measures. • De-escalation of law and order debate.	• Legislate to reduce prison numbers. • Set media and public agendas.
Judiciary	• Deliver effective sentencing. • Independence. • Robust, efficient sentencing 'products'.	• Rewarding feedback on sentencing decisions. • Making a difference.	• Send fewer people to prison. • Communicate rationale for non-custodial sentences to public through speeches, media pronouncements and other PR.
Media	• Commercial success. • Good stories.	• Compelling human stories (redemption, payback, transformation).	• Threat and opportunity (agenda setting, crusading journalism).
Public	• Safety rather than vengeance. • Support for prison. • Simple solution to serious issue.	• Feel safe because something effective is being done. • Offer real justice for the victims of crime.	• Influence politicians, the media and sentencers. • Strengthen perceptions that prison is meaningless for some offenders. • Weaken attachment to prison as the sole solution to crime.

7. Research and evaluation

The development of the marketing plan was guided by three stages of research:

- A literature review on the history and causes of the rising prison population and the evidence for the effectiveness of different sentencing options.
- Stakeholder research, comprising 41 interviews with politicians, sentencers, criminal justice professionals, police, journalists and social change experts.
- Consumer research, comprising 12 focus groups to explore concerns, priorities and hopes about sentencing and the criminal justice system.

The evaluation comprised interviews with 27 key commentators from parliamentary, civil service, judicial and media backgrounds.

Table CS1.2 Examples of marketing offerings devised to meet each objective

Objective	Marketing offering
Create consensus that current sentencing practice is increasing prison numbers	*Price*: Grants awarded to respected academics to research and publish on this issue, thereby showing the high cost of current system; active dissemination of conclusions through peer-to-peer channels.
Increase dissonance about prison as a sentencing option for many offences	*Marketing communications*: Independent enquiry led by senior judge into the drawbacks of community sentences and the adequacy of alternatives; restorative justice seminar held in Downing Street; senior ministers invited to visit community sentence projects; RCP-funded research on women, children, problem drug users and the mentally ill in prison to demonstrate the costs to society of imprisoning these groups and the role of alternatives to custody, such as drug treatment and testing orders.
Improve the perceived and actual effectiveness of restorative solutions	*Product*: 2002 Sentencing Review (independent of RCP) created a single, flexible community penalty; funded and disseminated demonstration projects; major cost-effectiveness review commissioned; public awareness and education.

8. Outcomes

Assessing the impact of complex long-term interventions, particularly those like the RCP, which seek to influence public policy and social norms, is always challenging (Stead *et al.*, 2002). Furthermore, such changes typically have multiple causes (Clark and McLeroy, 1998) and it is difficult to disentangle the contribution of any single initiative or event.

Official statistics suggest that the UK prison population has continued to rise, but so too has the number of non-custodial disposals given out by the courts. These general data also mask some interesting variations: there has been a decline in the number of short-term prison sentences (a key contributor to the large prison population – see 'Problem definition') and fewer women are being sent to prison (the focus group research revealed the imprisoning of women was one area in which the public are anti-incarceration).

An independent evaluation of RCP (Braggins, 2005), comprising 27 stakeholder interviews, suggested that politicians' thinking about short-term sentences had shifted towards the view that they were costly and ineffective, and that the language around crime and punishment was softening. The RCP was felt to have helped to 'create a climate in which politicians are enabled to be a bit braver'. Informants also welcomed RCP's creation and dissemination of several key pieces of evidence and reports that were felt to move the debate on and give campaigners greater confidence in their arguments. Nevertheless, there was strong acknowledgement by informants that it was difficult to isolate the impact of RCP because many other initiatives and events over the period had contributed to changes in the same direction: 'If you're pushing at an open door, it's more difficult to attribute cause than if you're going against the flow.'

Two RCP recommendations have had an impact on raising the profile of community penalties – the need for greater community involvement and the need for more residential drug treatment. Also, many of the RCP-funded projects have been successful in helping to empower community members and build capacity. *Local Crime, Community Sentence* is one example of such a programme, in which probation officers and magistrates give presentations to community groups (http://www.lcs.org.uk).

A follow-up RCP is currently being implemented – Rethinking Crime and Punishment Phase 2 (RCP2), which aims to put into practice the recommendations from RCP. The project comprises a focused programme of practical work in one region of the country, the Thames Valley, plus an effort to identify and disseminate what works best through an annual awards scheme.

References

Braggins J. (2005). *Rethinking Crime and Punishment: An external evaluation*, February. London: Centre for Strategy and Communication.

Clark N.M. and McLeroy K.R. (1998). Reviewing the evidence for health promotion in the United States. In *Quality, Evidence and Effectiveness in Health Promotion* (Davies J.K. and MacDonald G., eds), pp. 21–46. London: Routledge.

de Silva N., Cowell P., Chow T. and Worthington P. (2006). *Prison Population Projections 2006–2013, England and Wales*. London: Direct Communications Unit.

Esmée Fairbairn Foundation (2004). *Rethinking Crime and Punishment: The Report*. London: Esmée Fairbairn Foundation.

Hastings G.B., Stead M. and MacFadyen L. (2002). Reducing prison numbers: does marketing hold the key? *Criminal Justice Matters (CJM)*, **49**: 20–21, 43.

Scottish Executive (2002). *Scottish Prison Service Estate Consultation Paper*. Edinburgh: Estates Review Team, Scottish Prison Service Headquarters.

Stead M., Hastings G.B. and Eadie D. (2002). The challenge of evaluating complex interventions: a framework for evaluating media advocacy. *Health Education Research Theory and Practice*, **17**(3): 351–364.

Lessons learned

1. Social marketing need not be limited to health behaviour change, but can also be effectively applied to other arenas. The RCP demonstrates how it can be applied to the criminal justice system.
2. The type of competition faced by social marketers differs from that faced by commercial marketing and often requires social marketers to think creatively to address competitive barriers to behaviour change.

In the RCP case, a unique and particularly complex type of competition was addressed – public opinion that prison is the only effective solution for criminals.
3. It is important to analyse the stakeholder environment in every social marketing strategy. In this case, politicians were concerned about a media and public backlash if they were seen as too soft on criminals. The use of a strategic marketing offering successfully addressed this fear.

Case study questions

1. **Q:** List two factors that contribute to the UK's public perception that prison is the only effective solution for criminals and explain why.

   A: (i) Sensationalized media – dramatic/unrealistic coverage of crime in the news and entertainment industry. (ii) Fear – fear of crime or lack of faith in the criminal justice system.

2. **Q:** What role did the RCP-funded research play in an effort to increase dissonance about prison and of what component of the overall marketing offering was this a part?

   A: Four population groups were identified as candidates for alternative solutions to custody – women, children, problem drug users and the mentally ill – for the marketing communications offering.

3. **Q:** Based on the evaluation results of the RCP social marketing programme, what is an important consideration when measuring the success of this programme, as well as other social marketing programmes aimed at influencing behaviour change?

   A: Behaviour change as a direct result of a social marketing initiative is difficult to isolate. Although the evaluation results found changes in politicians' thinking, the direct impact of RCP is difficult to determine due to other initiatives and events that occurred during the time of the strategy, which may also have contributed to behaviour change. This points up the challenges of evaluation and the need to think flexibly about methodology.

CASE STUDY 2

A marketing strategy to increase awareness of oral and bowel cancer

Douglas Eadie and Lisa Cohen

1. Introduction

The 'West of Scotland Cancer Awareness Project' (WoSCAP) was a three-year social marketing programme designed to increase awareness of oral and bowel cancer, and encourage individuals with signs and symptoms to present earlier to the National Health Services (NHS). This case summarizes some of its key components.

2. Problem definition

Five Scottish health boards (Argyll and Clyde, Ayrshire and Arran, Forth Valley, Greater Glasgow, and Lanarkshire) acknowledged the need for a cancer *early detection* campaign.

Oral and bowel cancer were selected as the campaign focus, guided by a review of the following criteria:

- *It is a common problem.* Approximately 530 new mouth cancer cases and over 3500 new bowel cancer cases are diagnosed in Scotland each year (NHS Argyll and Clyde, 2005).
- *Early detection is effective*: If detected early, mouth cancer can be treated successfully and survival rates can improve by over 30%. Likewise, if bowel cancer is detected early there is an 80% chance of cure (NHS Argyll and Clyde, 2005).

- *Public awareness and knowledge* about the signs and symptoms of mouth and bowel cancer are generally poor (NHS Argyll and Clyde, 2005).
- *Value for money.* It was hypothesized that a successful oral and bowel cancer campaign could save lives of people 'at risk' of getting these diseases.
- *Feasibility of service provision.* The campaign was supported by the West of Scotland Cancer Advisory Network (WoSCAN), and links with the Managed Clinical Networks (MCNs) for head and neck and colorectal cancer. A small management team was also established.

3. Competitive analysis

Two competitive barriers existed. First, there was resistance from some health professionals who feared the impact the campaign would have on already swamped health services. To address this resistance, relationships were built with various professionals and they were reassured of the campaign quality. For instance, the role of research was emphasized in developing a thorough and considered approach.

Second was the reluctance from the target group to present to the NHS about potential signs and symptoms of mouth and bowel cancer for several reasons: embarrassment (particularly among those with bowel cancer signs and symptoms); fear to confront cancer issues; limited awareness and understanding of the signs and symptoms of mouth and bowel cancer; limited awareness of the importance of early detection. To address this form of competition, the focus for WoSCAP was to inform the target group of 'new' health information in a relevant, non-threatening and non-patronizing way by focusing on early detection and where to present to the NHS.

Other forms of competition, including competing health and cancer messages, were not a major concern.

4. Stakeholder analysis

Three stakeholder groups are shown in Table CS2.1. The marketing plan analysed each stakeholder need, the benefits from increasing awareness of oral and bowel cancer, and their potential role in the WoSCAP campaign.

Table CS2.1	Stakeholder needs and benefits		
Stakeholder	**Needs**	**Benefits from increasing awareness of oral and bowel cancer**	**Potential role in WoSCAP**
Public	• Limited knowledge and awareness of oral and bowel cancer.	• Increased life expectancy. • Better quality of life.	• Targets for research and monitoring awareness, knowledge and attitudes of oral and bowel cancer.
Professionals	• Deliver effective services.	• Raise professional profile. • Achieve improved results in partnership versus NHS Boards in isolation.	• Active partners through Implementation Teams in each NHS Board area. • Primary and secondary staff training on mouth and bowel cancer issues. • Impact local and national agendas for the provision of services.
Media	• Newsworthy editorial events and stories. • Tight deadlines.	• Portray WoSCAP message to a hard-to-reach audience. • Influence regional cancer services.	• Showcase WoSCAP in wide-reaching newspapers, magazines, radio stations or TV channels.

5. Aims and objectives

Aims and objectives were developed for WoSCAP elements during the early project stages.

Two specific marketing objectives existed:

(a) Spontaneous awareness of the campaign materials, and of the signs and symptoms of oral and bowel cancer.
(b) Early and appropriate presentation of oral and bowel cancer within the West of Scotland.

Additional objectives were set for research and evaluation and the impact of WoSCAP on services.

6. Formulation of strategy

A marketing offering was devised to meet the WoSCAP objectives (Table CS2.2).

Campaign resources are shown in Figures CS2.1 and CS2.2.

Table CS2.2   Marketing offerings to meet each WoSCAP objective

Objective	Marketing offering
Understand and effectively reach both the 'at-risk' population as well as primary and secondary professionals involved	*Targeting and segmentation*: men and women aged 45+ living in deprived areas as well as smokers and heavy drinkers were the primary mouth cancer target group; men and women aged 50+ living in deprived areas were the primary bowel cancer target group; GPs, dentists, pharmacists, primary and secondary care staff and cancer networks were the secondary target group.
Communicate affiliated campaign organizations	*Branding*: WoSCAP brand represented the five health boards involved; presentation of the NHS Health Scotland logo and Big Lottery Fund in all campaign materials.
Offer tangible objects and services to 'at-risk' individuals	*Product*: educational packs and other materials.
Distribute materials in channels and settings suitable to those 'at risk'	*Place*: distribution of WoSCAP communications and educational materials through various channels, including GP surgeries and pharmacies.
Communicate signs and symptoms of oral and bowel cancer to a hard-to-reach audience	*Promotion*: Advertising (TV, radio, press, photographic exhibition); community events (public launches); PR (over 80 articles in local, regional and national press, and covered by the CCB, Scottish Television and all national radio stations).
Train professional in contact with 'at-risk' individuals (GPs, dentists, pharmacists)	*People*: 25 Symposia on Oral Cancer; 17 Symposia on Bowel Cancer; collaborative partnership work with stakeholders.
Gain involvement and support of health professionals	*Exchange*: raise cancer profile nationally; robust business plan; project development participation by professionals; clarification of stakeholder roles and responsibilities; research to guide decision making; £100 000 marketing budget given to colorectal cancer services to cope with anticipated demand.

7. Research and evaluation

The development of the marketing plan was guided by three research stages:

- Independent research, to assess public awareness and knowledge of the signs and symptoms of the different cancers, and extensive consultation with health professionals.
- A literature review, to identify best practice for communicating with the public about cancer and case studies of previous oral and bowel cancer prevention campaigns.
- Consumer research, comprising eight focus groups with seven respondents per group ($N = 57$) to explore the public's knowledge, perceptions and attitudes towards the relevant cancers; plus six further focus groups to pre-test creative treatments.

**Don't let mouth cancer take away
life's little pleasures.**

You can get mouth cancer on your tongue, gums, lips, cheeks and floor or roof of your mouth.
Early signs are sometimes not sore, so look out for:

> An ulcer or sore that doesn't heal after three weeks
> Swelling
> A lump or bump on your lips, gums or inside your mouth
> A white, red or dark patch
> Ongoing soreness in your mouth or throat

See your dentist, doctor or pharmacist.

 NHS SCOTLAND   **West of Scotland
Cancer Awareness Project**   *New Opportunities Fund
funded*   **If in doubt, get it checked out.**

Figure CS2.1
Oral cancer poster.
Source: West of
Scotland Cancer
Awareness Project
(WoSCAP), photo: Paul
Hampton,
Twobobrocket.
Reproduced with
permission.

The evaluation comprised the following:

● Tracking surveys, undertaken by the Institute for Social Marketing, on awareness and knowledge of the cancers.
● Survey research, undertaken by University of Glasgow, to assess the campaign's impact on primary care.
● A review of Local Implementation Teams (LITs).
● Evaluation of training events.

Put your bottom at the top of your list

BOWEL CANCER – WHAT YOU SHOULD LOOK OUT FOR:

→ A recent change in bowel habit that goes on day in day out for over 4 weeks without returning to normal

→ Looser stools/motions – like diarrhoea (constipation is much less likely to be serious)

→ Bleeding from your bottom not caused by constipation, pain or itching

→ Going to the toilet for a number two several more times a day than usual

→ Feeling that your bowel is not empty after going to the toilet

If you have any of these symptoms, go and see your doctor. The chances are unlikely that you will have bowel cancer but the disease can be treated successfully if detected early.

IF IN DOUBT, GET IT CHECKED OUT.

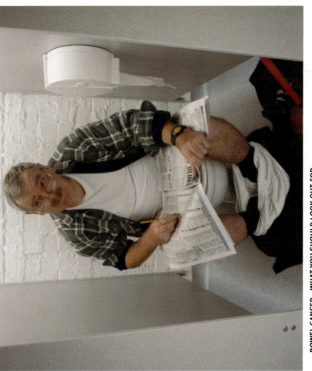

Put your bottom at the top of your list

BOWEL CANCER – WHAT YOU SHOULD LOOK OUT FOR:

→ A recent change in bowel habit that goes on day in day out for over 4 weeks without returning to normal

→ Looser stools/motions – like diarrhoea (constipation is much less likely to be serious)

→ Bleeding from your bottom not caused by constipation, pain or itching

→ Going to the toilet for a number two several more times a day than usual

→ Feeling that your bowel is not empty after going to the toilet

If you have any of these symptoms, go and see your doctor. The chances are unlikely that you will have bowel cancer but the disease can be treated successfully if detected early.

IF IN DOUBT, GET IT CHECKED OUT.

Figure CS2.2

Bowel cancer posters.

Source: West of Scotland Cancer Awareness Project (WoSCAP), photo: Paul Hampton, Twobobrocket. Reproduced with permission.

8. Outcomes

The overall evaluation results indicate that the project successfully achieved its objectives. Some key results are presented below:

- *Oral cancer tracking survey results*. Campaign awareness was variable, with the TV advert achieving extremely impressive awareness levels in the intervention area and the radio advertising failing to achieve the media presence anticipated. Strong evidence was provided for the campaign having a clear and positive impact on awareness of the signs and symptoms of mouth cancer. There is also evidence for the campaign increasing both salience and propensity to act upon key symptoms of the disease, with intention to visit the most popular source, a GMP, increasing markedly following the campaign (Eadie *et al.*, 2005b).
- *Bowel cancer tracking survey results*. The bowel cancer TV advert achieved high awareness levels in the intervention area, with other support advertising attaining consistent awareness levels with what might be expected. The TV advert was found to be realistic and impactful, and there was a sympathetic response to the advert's central character. Evidence for the campaign affecting target audience attitudes towards early detection of bowel cancer and perceptions of the disease's prevalence and survivability showed no change. However, prevailing attitudes towards acting on one of the main symptoms, a change in bowel frequency, were largely positive (Eadie *et al.*, 2005a).
- *Impact on primary care (GPs)*. Interviews with GPs found they expressed generally positive campaign views. This, together with their experiences of other campaigns, led them to believe that public campaigns are capable of producing awareness of cancers (NHS Argyll and Clyde, 2004a).
- *Impact on secondary care (screening)*. As a result of the oral cancer campaign, there was a significant increase in patients attending clinics: one-third of malignant conditions and almost half of pre-malignant conditions were detected in people who came forward as a direct result of the campaign. For the bowel campaign, survey research demonstrated that 62% reported that the WoSCAP advertising had encouraged them to see their GP sooner (NHS Argyll and Clyde, 2005).
- *Review of LITs*. The project was considered to have successfully established operational LITs in the five relevant health board areas and that majority fulfilled their objectives. Strengths of the LIT 'model' include increasing local ownership and involvement in the campaign, and establishing good communication between primary and secondary care, and coordinating high-quality training events (NHS Argyll and Clyde, 2004c).
- *Training events*. The training events were considered successful, with very high reported attendance. Participants described the events as relevant, worthwhile and interesting (NHS Argyll and Clyde, 2004b, d).

The authors would like to acknowledge the research and evaluation work by Susan Anderson, then Research Coordinator and Anne Marie MacKintosh, Senior Researcher of the Institute for Social Marketing, on this project.

References

Eadie D., Anderson S. and MacKintosh A.M. (2005a). *West of Scotland Cancer Awareness Project, Bowel Cancer Mass Media Campaign: Findings from First Follow-up.* Stirling: Institute for Social Marketing. Online at http://www.woscap.co.uk/pdf.pl?file=woscap/file/11_CSM_Bowel_First_FollowUp.pdf (accessed 19 June 2006).

Eadie D., Anderson S. and MacKintosh A.M. (2005b). *West of Scotland Cancer Awareness Project, Oral Cancer Mass Media Campaign: Findings from First Follow-up.* Stirling: Institute for Social Marketing. Online at http://www.woscap.co.uk/pdf.pl?file=woscap/file/09_CSM_Oral_First_FollowUp.pdf (accessed 19 June 2006).

NHS Argyll and Clyde (2004a). *An Impact Evaluation of the West of Scotland Oral Cancer Awareness Campaign on Primary Care Dentistry and Community Pharmacy over Three NHS Board Areas.* Paisley: NHS Argyll and Clyde. Online at http://www.woscap.co.uk/doc.pl?file=woscap/file/08_Oral_Pharm_Impact.doc (accessed 19 June 2006).

NHS Argyll and Clyde (2004b). *West of Scotland Cancer Awareness Project: Bowel Cancer Symposia, Autumn – November 2004 – Evaluation Report.* Paisley: NHS Argyll and Clyde. Online at http://www.woscap.co.uk/doc.pl?file=woscap/file/Event%20Analysis.doc (accessed 19 June 2006).

NHS Argyll and Clyde (2004c). *West of Scotland Cancer Awareness Project: Review of Oral Cancer Local Implementation Teams – Final Report.* Paisley: NHS Argyll and Clyde. Online at http://www.woscap.co.uk/doc.pl?file=woscap/file/06_JC_LIT_Report.doc (accessed 19 June 2006).

NHS Argyll and Clyde (2004d). *West of Scotland Cancer Awareness Project: Symposia on Oral Cancer – Evaluation Summary.* Online at http://www.woscap.co.uk/doc.pl?file=woscap/file/Evaluation%20Summary.doc (accessed 19 June 2006).

NHS Argyll and Clyde (2005). *West of Scotland Cancer Awareness Project 2002–2005.* Paisley: NHS Argyll and Clyde.

West of Scotland Cancer Awareness Project (WoSCAP) photography by Paul Hampton, Twobobrocket, 9/11 Harvie Street, Glasgow, GS11BW.

Lessons learned

1. It is important to develop specific and measurable aims and objectives in the early stages of planning a social marketing campaign. For WoSCAP, specific and measurable objectives existed, allowing the campaign team to monitor each objective in an effort to measure success during and after programme implementation.

2. The four Ps of 'product', 'price', 'place' and 'promotion' need not be the only Ps that a social marketing strategy addresses. The WoSCAP

case study is a prime example of how other Ps, such as 'people', can be a vital component of the marketing mix. Indeed, training of professionals in contact with 'at-risk' individuals for oral and bowel cancer was a fundamental component of building local capacity for this social marketing strategy.

3. Social marketing can play a fundamental role in the prevention and early detection of disease, as demonstrated in the WoSCAP case. By honing in on the competitive barriers faced by both the health professionals and public, the WoSCAP campaign was able to increase awareness of the signs and symptoms of oral and bowel cancer and help at-risk individuals take action by presenting earlier to the National Health Service (NHS).

Case study questions

1. **Q:** What was the significance of research in designing and implementing the WoSCAP campaign strategy and what marketing offering was this a part of?

   A: Research played a fundamental role in gaining the support of key stakeholders and guiding the overall campaign approach. The use of research to guide decision making for the WoSCAP campaign addressed exchange, in this case to gain involvement and support of health professionals.

2. **Q:** Describe how the WoSCAP campaign used the social marketing principle of targeting and segmentation, and what impact this may have had on stakeholder concerns about health screening services.

   A: Targeting and segmentation allowed the campaign to appeal to narrowly defined primary and secondary target audiences. This strategy helped to offset concerns that the campaign would result in unnecessarily swamped health services.

3. **Q:** Using WoSCAP as an example, describe the beneficial role that media as a stakeholder can play for the fourth P – 'promotion' – in a social marketing campaign.

   A: The media was beneficial for WoSCAP because the overall campaign message was showcased in a variety of wide-reaching media sources, such as newspapers, magazines, radio stations and TV channels. This helped to portray the message to a hard-to-reach target audience using a multimedia public relations strategy.

CASE STUDY 3

A social advertising strategy to reduce speeding

Martine Stead and Douglas Eadie

1. Introduction

'Foolsspeed' was a five-year campaign to reduce speeding in Scotland. Although it focused solely on the promotional P, it was informed to some extent by social marketing principles. The campaign was guided by the Theory of Planned Behaviour (TPB), a model that uses psychological determinants to explain and predict behaviour (Ajzen, 1988).

2. Problem definition

Speeding is a major road safety concern in Scotland and most offences occur within built-up 30 m.p.h. speed limit areas. Being young, male, in a higher social class and income bracket, driving a powerful car, and doing higher mileage are characteristics associated with speeding (Manstead, 1991; Stradling, 1999).

Psychological factors related to speeding also include:

- *Social norms*. Compared to drink-driving, speeding attracts less stigma and may be seen as a normative and majority behaviour (Stradling, 1999).
- *Beliefs*. Speeders, in comparison to non-speeders, rate adverse speeding consequences as less likely to occur and less undesirable (Stradling, 1999).
- *Emotional factors*. Speeders are more likely to associate instrumental benefits (getting to a destination quicker) and emotional benefits (the pleasure in driving fast) with speeding (Stradling, 1999).
- *Exaggerated feelings of control and confidence*. Many speeders have an illusory sense of control over their driving (Simon and Corbett, 1991).

The TPB model has accounted for significant variances in speeding intentions (Manstead, 1991; Parker *et al.*, 1992, 1995; Stradling and Parker, 1996) and claims that behaviour is established by *behaviour intention*, determined by:

(a) *Attitude to the behaviour* (AB), predicted by *instrumental beliefs* (beliefs about behaviour consequences, such as *affective beliefs* about the *positive* or *negative* emotions experienced while performing the behaviour) and *outcome evaluations* (evaluations of the desirability of those consequences).

(b) *Subjective norms* (SN), predicted by *normative beliefs* (if significant 'referents', such as family members, friends or partners, will approve of the behaviour) and *motivation to comply* (degree of motivation to meet with referent's approval).

(c) *Perceived behavioural control* (PBC), predicted by *control beliefs* (one's ability to perform or refrain from a particular behaviour in various circumstances) and *control frequency* (how often one is in those circumstances).

3. Competitive analysis

Many urban speeders, although aware of speeding dangers, continue to speed with the belief that speeding saves time, they are in control of their car and it is easy to stop quickly. External pressures can also encourage drivers to speed (e.g. running behind schedule, being stressed, dealing with impatient drivers, listening to music, etc.).

4. Stakeholder analysis

Limited attention was given to stakeholders. The main group was the Scottish Executive (Government), who requested logo placement on all Foolsspeed messaging. Formative consumer research results discouraged this and a Foolsspeed campaign logo was used instead. Police and private sector also had a minor role in promoting and supporting the initiative.
Stakeholder needs and benefits are shown in Table CS3.1.

Table CS3.1 Stakeholder needs and benefits

Stakeholder	Needs	Benefits from reducing speeding	Potential role in Foolsspeed
Government	● Public support shortly after devolution.	● Fewer road casualties.	● Foolsspeed campaign funding.
Police	● Reduce speeding instances.	● Fewer road casualties.	● Collaborate to raise awareness of key road safety messages and support for police service initiatives.
Private sector	● Consumer trust through responsible business practices.	● Corporate responsibility.	● Expose drivers to Foolsspeed through products or business materials.

5. Aims and objectives

Foolsspeed's aim was to reduce inappropriate speed (within the legal limit but inappropriate for the conditions) and excessive speed (over the legal limit) on urban Scotland's roads, and was the first UK attempt to develop a large-scale driving behaviour intervention informed by the TPB.

6. Formulation of strategy

A social advertising strategy was devised to meet each objective (Table CS3.2).

Table CS3.2 Social advertising strategy for each objective

Objective	Social advertising offering
Understand and effectively reach drivers with a speeding tendency	*Targeting and segmentation*: the general driving population in Scotland were the overall target group; men 24–44 years in social classes ABC1 (professional, white-collar and clerical workers) were a core target group within this.
Create a unique and meaningful brand to challenge drivers to think about speeding	*Branding*: Foolsspeed brand and identity. Play on words (fools speed/full speed)
Address costs of adopting responsible driving habits for speeders	*Price*: the 'Mirror' TV advert addressed temporal costs (saving time); the 'Doppelganger' TV advert focused on emotional costs (pleasure in driving fast).
Distribute materials in channels and settings suitable to drivers in Scotland	*Place*: distribution of communication and educational materials through various channels – urban roads, Glasgow cinemas, homes and businesses in Scotland.
Design memorable communication materials that influence behaviour intentions, attitudes, subjective norms and PBC for urban speeding	*Promotion*: advertising (six 10-second campaign launch TV adverts, four TPB TV adverts); outdoor media (bus backs, petrol pump advertising, parking ticket advertising, vehicle decals); PR (adverts and articles featured in the *Herald*); unpaid publicity (use of Foolsspeed by the Association of Chief Police Officers Scotland Road Policing Strategy, road safety units, Scottish Councils); corporate sponsorship (display of logo on some Tesco, Safeway and Transco vehicles, Foolsspeed message on Robert Wiseman's Dairies milk cartons); website; newsletters.
Offer benefits to voluntarily engage speeders in responsible driving habits	*Exchange*: TPB TV adverts promoted the intangible benefits of driving responsibly – time saving, more safe, more socially acceptable and more pleasurable.

The four TV adverts were linked to the TPB as follows:

- *The 1999 'Mirror' advert – attitudes.* The first advert addresses the TPB attitudes component. Beliefs about inappropriate speeding – that speeding saves time, that a speeder is fully in control of the car and that a speeder is able to stop quickly if necessary – are challenged by demonstrating that the legal speed (30 m.p.h.) is too fast in certain circumstances. The advertisement also sought to challenge the belief 'I'm a better driver than most'. It features a male in his thirties driving in an urban residential environment. The driver's conscience or alter ego appears in the rear-view mirror and points out the foolishness of urban speeding by noting that a car from which the driver previously raced away has caught up with him at the traffic lights. As the driver nears a school, the conscience argues about the appropriateness of his speed, to which the driver retorts that 'he is a better driver than most' (implying that he can handle speed safely). The driver's attention is distracted by a young woman walking along the pavement with a small child, and when he looks back at the road he is shocked to realize the car in front has stopped at a school crossing. The driver comes to a noisy halt and the conscience shakes his head in the mirror. The strap-line reads 'Take a good look at yourself when you're driving'.

- *The 2000 'Friends and Family' advert – subjective norms.* The second advert addresses the TPB subjective norms component. It sought to highlight the possible mismatch between a driver's own view of his or her behaviour and how it is seen by passengers, and to illustrate to drivers the possible concern, irritation and anxiety that significant others may feel about their driving. The driver is a male in his thirties, while the significant others are a female spouse/partner and a male friend/work colleague. A baby is also present in the advert, in a child seat in the back of the car. The advertisement begins with the female partner, at home, describing how her partner becomes 'a different person, totally unrecognizable'. The family are then shown in the car, with the driver speeding and his partner protesting as the speed of the car jolts the baby's neck. She says she wishes her partner could see things through her eyes. A male friend/colleague of the driver then addresses the camera, also expressing his disapproval of his friend's speeding. The two friends are shown in the car, with the driver again speeding. The friend spills juice down his sweater when the driver accelerates to race another car away from the lights and expresses annoyance. The advertisement closes by showing the driver alone in the car, to the voice-over 'Put yourself in the passenger seat. If you don't, others won't.'

- *The 2001 'Simon Says' advert – PBC.* The third advertisement addresses PBC – drivers' perceptions of how easy or difficult it is to increase their control over speeding. The advertisement seeks to challenge drivers with the sentiment 'you're responsible for the way you drive' by depicting typical internal and external pressures that encourage drivers to speed, and demonstrating that it is possible and desirable to withstand such pressures. Three different drivers and scenarios are depicted, illustrating the pressure of being in a flow of traffic going at 40 m.p.h. in a 30 m.p.h. limit, the pressure of being late for work, and the more direct pressure of an impatient driver (a 'white-van man') behind. In the latter scenario, the driver nearly hits a cyclist as a result of being distracted and pressurized by the white-van driver. The ad closes with the strap-line 'Be your own man'.

- *2004/05 'Doppelganger' advert – attitudes (affective beliefs)*. The final advert focuses on the positive emotional benefits of calmer driving. In keeping with the realistic approach to everyday driving, the advert contains no accidents or crashes. Instead, it focuses on a man and his doppelganger's journey to work. We see the attitudes and behaviours of the 'two' drivers as they undertake the journey to the office. One character drives calmly and without incident, arriving at his work in a relaxed state, finding a car parking space and getting a cup of coffee. The second character is impatient, takes unnecessary chances (although he is not involved in any incident as such) and ends up being 'lectured' by the police at the side of the road. Consequently, he arrives at the office stressed and frustrated, and unable to find a parking space, while his doppelganger observes him through the window, calmly sipping on his coffee.

Campaign resources are shown in Figures CS3.1 and CS3.2.

Figure CS3.1
Foolsspeed logo.
Reproduced with
permission from the
Scottish Road Safety
Campaign.

Evaluating the impact of Foolspeed

The Centre for Social Marketing at the University of Strathclyde was commissioned by the SRSC to evaluate the impact of the Foolspeed campaign.

This was the first time that a high profile road safety television campaign had avoided the 'blood & guts' approach.

From an advertising viewpoint the big challenge was how to produce memorable road safety TV advertising without a crash. The evaluation was designed to provide feedback on this issue as well as many other variables. The evaluation is still ongoing, however the initial findings of the research have been very encouraging.

Firstly driver awareness of the campaign has been high. The Foolspeed logo continues to remain high profile achieving a 95% awareness level amongst those drivers surveyed.

Awareness of the new Simon Says TV advert was low compared to the previous two adverts, however at the time of the survey the advert had only been screened for one month and it is anticipated that awareness will rise with successive screenings.

Secondly the evaluation has tracked changes in attitudes amongst the target group (males, 25–44year olds) in respect of speeding during the period of the campaign. It has found that Foolspeed has had a positive impact on those mostly likely to speed, concluding that *"Most encouragingly the evaluation suggests that it is possible, with such advertising, to make favourable changes in some of the key psychological mechanisms which motivate people to speed"*.

A final evaluation report of the Foolspeed campaign will be published in mid 2002.

Foolspeed sponsors The Herald

Foolspeed adverts and articles by the Scottish Executive Minister for Transport Sarah Boyack were featured in the Herald's Executive Car supplement in June and the Motoring supplement in September.

Each page was branded with the 'Only Foolspeed' logo along with a quarter page advert in each issue. The articles by Sarah Boyack talked about the theory behind the Foolspeed campaign and the current debate on speed cameras.

Orkney Buses take Foolspeed

Orkney's Road Safety promotion group has persuaded their local bus companies to carry the Foolspeed decals.

The photo shows Orkney coaches with the decals in place. Causeway coaches & the Islands Council's Direct Services have agreed to follow suit.

TESCO display more Decals

Tesco Distribution has recently taken delivery of a further 35 HGV trailer reflective decals. These will be displayed on new trailers operating out of Livingston distribution depot.

The Scottish Road Safety Campaign,

Heriot Watt Research Park, Riccarton,Currie, Edinburgh. Tel: 0131 472 9200   www.srsc.org.uk

---

foolspeed **update**

October 2001

The Foolspeed Campaign- the story so far

Foolspeed was launched in November 1998. Approaching three years on and we can confidently say that the Foolspeed campaign is well established with over 90% of Scottish drivers being aware of the logo.

The campaign began with a number of short television adverts designed to launch the logo and to establish Foolspeed in the minds of Scottish drivers. These short adverts were followed in April 1999 with the launch of the first full-length (40 seconds) television advert 'Mirror'.

This advert showed a driver looking foolish as a result of the beliefs he held regarding his choice of speed. In April 2000 'Friends & Family' was launched. This second full-length advert featured a male driver and showed how his driving had a detrimental effect on his family & one of his friends.

The latest Foolspeed advert is called 'Simon Says'. This was launched in June 2001 and it addresses the third part of the behaviour change model on which the Foolspeed campaign is based.

The advert shows how drivers allow everyday pressures to dictate the way they drive rather than take full control of their choice of speed. It ends with the caption 'Be your own man'.

BE YOUR OWN MAN

Future Activity

The Foolspeed campaign will continue to be promoted over the coming year. 'Simon Says' advert will be screened on TV during February 2002. Later in the year all three adverts will be screened on a rotation basis.

This activity will be supported with outdoor media such as busback and petrol pump nozzle advertising. Longer term plans for the campaign include the production of a fourth TV advert in 2003. The advert will look at the benefits of driving at appropriate speeds.

Foolspeed TV adverts on video

All three Foolspeed TV adverts are now available on video. For more details please contact the SRSC.

Figure CS3.2
Foolspeed newsletter. Reproduced with permission from the Scottish Road Safety Campaign.

7. Research and evaluation

The social advertising plan was guided by three research stages:

- A literature review, comprising a review of previous TPB driving violation studies to identify salient beliefs in forming attitude, subjective norms and PBC.
- Formative consumer research, comprising eight male and female focus groups to explore speeding beliefs and norms, and gauge feelings about road safety advertising.
- Pre-test consumer research, comprising six focus groups each year for three years to examine reactions to each TV advert concept.

The evaluation comprised a four-year longitudinal survey of 17- to 54-year-old drivers with a baseline and three-yearly follow-up surveys (Stead *et al.*, 2005).

8. Outcomes

Foolsspeed was fundamentally a social advertising campaign and could have incorporated a more structured social marketing framework; nevertheless, the campaign was effective in changing speeding attitudes. Evaluation results suggest that road safety campaigns underpinned in a psychological model can be successful without using fear-arousing approaches (Stead *et al.*, 2005).

The main findings were:

- *TPB and speeding variance*. TPB predicted between 47% and 53% of the variance in intentions to speed, and 33–40% of the variance in reported speeding (Stead *et al.*, 2005).
- *Communication outcomes*. Spontaneous and prompted awareness was high for campaign elements: between a fifth and a third of respondents spontaneously mentioned seeing Foolsspeed TV adverts and high awareness levels were found for other media. The 'Mirror' advert received the highest prompted recall level (Stead *et al.*, 2005). All adverts were rated as easy to understand and did not 'talk down to' participants. They were also successful in generating identification and empathy at spontaneous and prompted levels (Stead *et al.*, 2005).
- *Attitude*. The attitude 'Mirror' advert had a moderately favourable effect on beliefs and attitudes. Negative and positive affective beliefs became significantly more anti-speeding, associated with the 'Mirror' advert (Stead *et al.*, 2005).
- *Subjective norms or PBC*. Subjective norms and PBC were stable (Stead *et al.*, 2005).
- *Behaviour intentions and reported behaviour*. Behaviour intentions were stable. Although not associated with campaign awareness, reported

speeding frequency appeared to decrease significantly between the baseline and third survey, as well as the baseline and fourth survey.

References

Ajzen I. (1988). *Attitudes, Personality and Behaviour*. Milton Keynes: Open University Press.

Manstead A.S.R. (1991). Social psychological aspects of driver behaviour. Invited paper presented at the meeting *New Insights into Driver Behaviour*, organized by the Parliamentary Advisory Council for Transport Safety, London. Manchester: University of Manchester.

Parker D., Manstead A.S.R., Stradling S.G., Reason J.T. and Baxter J.S. (1992). Intention to commit driving violations: an application of the theory of planned behaviour. *Journal of Applied Psychology*, **77**: 94–101.

Parker D., Manstead A.S.R. and Stradling S.G. (1995). The role of personal norm in intentions to violate. *British Journal of Social Psychology*, **34**: 127–137.

Simon F. and Corbett C. (1991). A small roadside study of drivers caught breaking speed limits. Paper given at the *Seminar on Behavioural Research in Road Safety*, Manchester University.

Stead M., Tagg S., MacKintosh A.M. and Eadie D. (2005). Development and evaluation of a mass media Theory of Planned Behaviour intervention to reduce speeding. *Health Education Research*, **20**: 36–50.

Stradling S.G. (1999). Changing driver attitude and behaviour. Presented at *DETR Speed Review Seminar*, London.

Stradling S.G. and Parker D. (1996). Extending the Theory of Planned Behaviour: the role of personal norm, instrumental beliefs and affective beliefs in predicting driving violations. Presented at *International Conference on Traffic and Transport Psychology*, Valencia.

Lessons learned

1. Although not a social marketing campaign, Foolsspeed demonstrated how social advertising grounded in psychological theory can be used to effectively change speeding attitudes without using the traditional fear approaches that are commonly present in road safety campaigns.

2. Foolsspeed is also a good example of the distinction between the two components of 'promotion' – the media channels and the media message – and how these can impact change. The Foolsspeed strategy leveraged both components – for instance, by incorporating a variety of media channels to promote the campaign (advertising, PR, unpaid publicity, website and newsletters), as well as the TPB to guide the development of the media message shown in the TV adverts.

3. Because Foolsspeed was fundamentally a social advertising campaign versus a social marketing one, limited attention was paid to key stakeholders. If a social marketing approach had been taken, a more in-depth analysis of the key stakeholder groups could have played a fundamental role in the campaign strategy.

Case study questions

1. Q: Describe how Foolsspeed used targeting and segmenting to understand and reach drivers with a known tendency to speed.

   A: The campaign was designed to appeal to two target groups: the general driving population in Scotland as well as men 24–44 years of age in social classes ABC1 (professional, white-collar and clerical workers).

2. Q: Name and describe the three determinants of behaviour intention encompassed in the TPB model.

   A: Attitude to the behaviour (AB), subjective norms (SN) and perceived behavioural control (PBC). AB is predicted by instrumental beliefs (beliefs about behaviour consequences) and outcome evaluations (evaluations of the desirability of those consequences). SN is predicted by normative beliefs (if significant 'referents' will approve of the behaviour) and motivation to comply (degree of motivation to meet with referent's approval). PBC is predicted by control beliefs (one's ability to perform or refrain from a particular behaviour in various circumstances) and control frequency (how often one is in those circumstances).

3. Q: Choose one determinant of behaviour intention from the TPB model and describe how it was addressed in the Foolsspeed campaign using one of the TV adverts as an example.

   A: For example, the 'Friends and Family' advert addressed the SN component of the TPB by highlighting the difference between how the driver viewed his driving behaviour versus how significant others did. The advert demonstrated the mismatch between his own view in contrast with how a female spouse/partner and a male friend/work colleague felt about his driving behaviour.

CASE STUDY 4

A marketing strategy to review the effects of food promotion to children

Laura McDermott, Martine Stead and Gerard Hastings

1. Introduction

In 2002, the UK Government's Food Standards Agency (FSA) commissioned the Institute for Social Marketing (ISM) to conduct a review of existing research on the effects of food promotion on the dietary choices of children (Hastings *et al.*, 2003). The review has had a significant impact on public policy, underpinning the introduction of tighter regulations on the marketing of energy dense – so-called 'junk'– foods to children. This case summarizes the key research findings and policy implications resulting from the review.

2. Problem definition

Young people's dietary patterns are causing concern in the UK. The National Diet and Nutrition Survey conducted in 2000 reported that a vast majority of 4- to 18-year olds consume more than the recommended amount of saturated fat, sugar and salt (Food Standards Agency, 2000). The Chief Medical Officer's report confirms that, between 1996 and 2001, the proportion of overweight children between six and 15 years increased by 7% and obesity rates increased by 3.5% (Department of Health, 2003).

Questions were raised about the causes of these trends. One obvious answer was that individual behaviour – people eating too much and doing too little – was to blame. On the other hand, a broader situation analysis threw up the possibility that the commercial promotion of energy dense foods (such as burgers and fried chicken) was at least partly responsible.

However, there was a lack of evidence on the existence, nature and extent of any effect food promotion might be having on children's food knowledge, preferences and behaviour. As a result, many conflicting

views were being expressed by the different stakeholders, including the food and advertising industries, consumer/health advocates and public health advisors, about what the Government should do.

A review of the evidence was therefore commissioned.

3. Stakeholder analysis

Stakeholder needs and benefits regarding the review are shown in Table CS4.1.

Table CS4.1 Stakeholder needs and benefits

Stakeholder	Needs	Benefits from the ISM review	Potential role in the FSA review
Politicians	• Approve appropriate policy options. • Fund effective programmes.	• Context to legislate food promotion policies.	• Accept or refute Regulators recommendations. • Provide resources to institutions (e.g. schools) for food and nutrition education.
Regulators	• Recommend, develop and advise on policies. • Governed by laws, political realities, public sentiments, budgets, licensing, etc.	• Research evidence for the effects of food promotion on children.	• Recommend, develop and advise on food promotion policies.
Food and advertising industries	• Produce and advertise food products for society. • Commercial objectives.	• Balanced perspective on industry's role in children's dietary habits.	• Key players in the childhood obesity solution. • Successfully shift children from unhealthy to healthier eating.
NGOs/consumer advocates	• Lobby, persuade, or direct action. • Non-commercial objectives.	• Support legislative action against commercial promotion of food to children.	• Lobby, persuade or direct action for food promotion policies.
Public health professionals	• Develop and evaluate health programming.	• Guide childhood obesity programme planning.	• Programme planning to prevent and reduce childhood obesity. • Evaluation of childhood obesity programming.

4. Who, What, How?

The key stakeholder group was the Government, which had the ultimate responsibility to protect its citizenry. Its need was for incontrovertible evidence on the role, if any, of food promotion in the obesity epidemic. Specifically they needed a rigorous and thorough review of the evidence base.

5. Aims and objectives

A team of independent academics, led by ISM, was commissioned to examine current research evidence on:

(a) The extent and nature of food promotion to children.
(b) The effect, if any, that food promotion has on children's food knowledge, preferences and behaviour.

6. Formulation of strategy

The vital need was for rigorous and reliable results, so *systematic review* procedures were employed. These are borrowed from medical science, where challenging, consensual decisions about a contested evidence base have to be made on a regular basis, and great care is taken to ensure particular treatments are safe and effective, and that every possible source of evidence is identified and rigorously evaluated. The search methods and evaluation process also incorporate a detailed protocol to allow easy replication and review of key conclusions. In addition, the work was exposed to regular peer review.

The Systematic Review identified 30 000 potentially relevant papers, one hundred of which were deemed reliable, valid and hence capable of shedding light on the issue.

7. Findings

This first UK systematic review of the research literature found:

- *There is a lot of food advertising to children.* Food, more than any other product, is promoted to children, with the exception of toys during Christmas.
- *The advertised diet is less healthy than the recommended one.* Television, the principal medium for food promotion, mostly supports the 'big five' (pre-sugared breakfast cereals, soft drinks, confectionery, savoury snacks and fast food).

- *Children enjoy and engage with food promotion*. Fun and fantasy or taste, versus health and nutrition themes are used to promote the advertised diet to children.
- *Food promotion is having an effect*. Food promotion is affecting the food children express a preference for, buy and ask their parents to buy. Weaker evidence also suggests that food promotion impacts children's long-term diet and health.
- *The effect is independent of other factors and operates at both a brand and category level*. Advertising can shift children's preferences not just between brands, but also food categories (e.g. chocolate biscuits and crisps versus apples).

These findings were actively disseminated by the research team in academic outlets, but also at practitioner conferences and in the general media. As a result there was wide discussion of the research, which fed public debate about the issue.

8. Outcomes

Following the release of these results, the study was immediately put to the test. The Food Advertising Unit of the Advertising Association (FAU) commissioned both a rival review, which argued that commercial promotion of foods does *not* influence children (Young, 2003), and a critique of the FSA review (Paliwoda and Crawford, 2003).

The FSA assembled a seminar of leading academics under the chairmanship of Professor Nicholas Mackintosh of Cambridge University to discuss the conflicting assessments. The limited coverage of the FAU review was noted, as well as its contradiction of a review conducted by the same author in 1996 and its rejection of virtually all social science research as either too artificial (experimental studies) or too little control (observational studies) (Food Standards Agency, 2003a). It also rejected the critique (Food Standards Agency, 2003b). It was concluded that the FSA review provided sufficient evidence concerning a link between food promotion and children's food knowledge, preferences and behaviours.

But the sterner test was whether the review was considered robust enough by the Government for them to act. The answer is yes; at the end of 2006 its regulatory authority, Ofcom, proposed detailed proposals for significantly curtailing television advertising of energy dense foods to children (Ofcom, 2006). Other media sectors have agreed to follow suit.

The rigour and quality of the systematic review was critical to this outcome. Perhaps more importantly, from a social marketing perspective, it has also changed behaviour.

The authors would like to acknowledge the other members of the team who worked on the ISM-led review: Mike Rayner at the University of Oxford, Martin Caraher at City University London, Christine Godfrey at the University of York and Maria Piacentini at Lancaster University.

References

Department of Health (2003). Obesity: defusing the health time bomb. In *Health Check: On the State of the Public Health. Annual Report of the Chief Medical Officer, 2002*, pp. 36–45. London: Department of Health.

Food Standards Agency (2000). *National Diet and Nutrition Survey of Young People Aged Four to 18 years*. London: HMSO.

Food Standards Agency (2003a). *Outcome of academic seminar to review recent research on food promotion and children. Held 31st October 2003*. Online at: http://www.food.gov.uk/multimedia/webpage/academicreview (accessed 19 June 2006).

Food Standards Agency (2003b). *Outcome of the review exercise on the Paliwoda and Crawford paper: An Analysis of the Hastings Review: "The Effects of Food Promotion on Children"*. Online at: http://www.food.gov.uk/multimedia/pdfs/paliwodacritique.pdf (accessed 19 June 2006).

Hastings G., Stead M., McDermott L., Forsyth A., MacKintosh A., Rayner M., Godfrey C., Caraher M. and Angus K. (2003). *Review of Research on the Effects of Food Promotion to Children – Final Report and Appendices*. Prepared for the Food Standards Agency. Stirling: Institute for Social Marketing.

Ofcom (2006). *Television Advertising of Food and Drink Products to Children – Options for New Restrictions*. London: Office of Communications. Online at www.ofcom.org.uk/consult/condocs/foodads/ (accessed 19 June 2006).

Paliwoda S. and Crawford I. (2003) *An Analysis of the Hastings Review*. Commissioned by the Food Advertising Unit (FAU) for the Advertising Association. Online at www.adassoc.org.uk/hastings_review_analysis_dec03.pdf (accessed 19 June 2006).

Young B. (2003). *Advertising and Food Choice in Children: A Review of the Literature*. London: Food Advertising Unit, The Advertising Association. Online at: http://www.fau.org.uk/brian_youngliteraturereview.pdf (accessed 19 June 2006).

Lessons learned

1. Situational analysis is a vital step in defining any social marketing problem.
2. Social marketing can seek to change the behaviour of professionals, retailers and – in the case of the FSA systematic review – policymakers and legislators.
3. One of the most important components of the FSA systematic review was the dissemination phase. By actively disseminating the results of the study to stakeholders, media and practitioners, the review played a key role in helping to shape policy responses to food marketing and obesity, both in the UK and internationally.

Case study questions

1. **Q:** How does the FSA review of the existing research on the effects of food promotion demonstrate the challenges of using social science research to reach conclusions about health and how was this challenge addressed?

  A: The FSA review demonstrates that a challenge with relying on social science research to reach health conclusions is that it can never provide final proof. In the FSA review, isolating the possible influence of promotion, only one of the many complex and dynamic factors governing food knowledge, preferences and behaviour is challenging. However, social science research does reduce uncertainty by testing hypotheses and judging the balance of probabilities. Thus, the challenge with social science research was addressed by balancing evidence rather than trying to reach an absolute truth.

2. **Q:** How did the views of stakeholders about the most suitable policies for commercial promotion of foods to children vary?

  A: There was a great variation in perspective. At one extreme the food and advertising industries rejected the idea of food adverting being implicated in childhood obesity; at the other the NGO community was already convinced there was a need for regulation. This made it all the more important for the review to be as rigorous and transparent as possible.

3. **Q:** How does the FSA review demonstrate the challenge faced by many social marketers when disseminating evidence to stakeholders, particularly ones with opposing agendas, and how was this challenge addressed?

  A: The FSA review demonstrated the challenge of disseminating social marketing evidence to stakeholders because the food and advertising industries commissioned researchers to produce a critique of the research results. This challenge was dealt with by holding an independent seminar of leading academics to discuss the different assessments.

CASE STUDY 5

Changing consumption of sugared liquid oral medicines

Raymond Lowry

1. Problem definition

Dental decay remains a serious problem in the North-East of England, especially in socially deprived children, in spite of raised public awareness of the causes of dental decay and access to fluoridated toothpaste. Newcastle North Tyneside Health Authority decided to reduce the consumption of sugared liquid oral medicines as a contribution to better oral health.

2. Sugared medicines

Dental decay remains a problem in the North-East of England and the consumption of sugared medicines makes a small but significant contribution to this problem. Specifically, there is concern that their long-term use increases dental disease in children, especially those with chronic illness.

There is ample evidence to suggest that non-sugar sweeteners do not produce dental decay. There has been a steady increase in the availability and use of such alternative sweeteners in liquid oral medication over the years. As a result, there has been a slow but sustained increase in the supply of sugar-free alternatives to the sugar-containing liquid oral medication. Nonetheless, sugared medicines continue to be commonly used: a survey in the Northern Region of England showed that 59% of prescribed liquid oral medication was sugar based.

With the high rates of dental decay in the North-East, there is a desire to promote the use of sugar-free medications. In 1994, a conventional communication approach to the problem was tried in the North-West of England. It was aimed at all the groups who might have an influence on behaviour: general medical practitioners, pharmacists, health visitors, dentists and parents of young children. The evaluation of the campaign showed a marked attitude change in favour of sugar-free medication by the health professionals, but no sustained change in prescribing behaviour took place.

It was therefore decided to tackle the problem in the North-East of England using a social marketing approach.

3. The solution: a social marketing initiative

Objective

The objective of the initiative was to produce a significant reduction in the consumption by young children of sugar-containing, liquid, oral medication obtained by prescription, with the long-term aim of improving their dental health.

Development

Four potential target groups were identified: pharmaceutical manufacturers and distributors, pharmacists, parents, and general medical practitioners (GPs). However, limited resources meant that only one initiative was possible, so these groups had to be prioritized. Qualitative research was therefore conducted with each group (segment) to establish which showed the greatest potential and guide the development of an appropriate offering for this group.

Research with pharmaceutical manufacturers and distributors revealed that the industry is demand led, and that attempts to impose sugar-free medicine through the supply chain would meet resistance and be prohibitively expensive. Pharmacists are also demand led. Their job is to fill the prescription as determined by the general practitioner. Furthermore, sugar-free alternatives are generally more expensive, so if the pharmacist changes the prescription they have to bear the difference in price.

Attention therefore focused on the two remaining targets: parents and GPs. Over-the-counter medicines were excluded because qualitative research indicated a resistance to change beyond the means of the initiative to influence. The attitude of parents to the sugar-free issue was related to social class: social class IV and V mothers expected their general medical practitioner to prescribe the sugar-free alternative without prompting if it was available and appropriate; social class I and II mothers were more engaged with the issue, although some were wary of artificial sweeteners.

This suggested that family doctors were the key: if they could be persuaded to prescribe sugar-free alternatives, pharmacists and most parents would cooperate. Furthermore, research showed that the doctors were open to persuasion and pre-testing made it possible to develop an appropriate marketing mix:

- *Product*. This was 'the prescribing by general medical practitioners of sugar-free medicines'. It was basically acceptable to the GP, especially if backed by appropriate evidence of effectiveness. However, they had many other priorities and concerns, with the resulting danger that it would get overlooked.
- *Price*. It was therefore very important to keep the price low by making prescribing the sugar-free version of any medication as easy as possible.

Information helped here (see 'Promotion' below), but perhaps more important was the adjustment of prescribing software to favour sugar-free alternatives.

● *Place*. Information and prescribing alternatives were needed at the point of prescription to provide convenient reminders and cues.

● *Promotion*. This helped highlight the issue, by providing information on mothers' views and dental decay in the area, as well as ease change by suggesting and cueing alternatives. A personal selling approach was adopted, using a specially trained health authority 'representative' to promote sugar-free options on a one-to-one basis, backed up by targeted written materials. This mimicked the standard way that GPs learn about new medicines.

4. The evaluation

Method

Test and control areas were chosen for the intervention, matched for population size and socio-economic characteristics, GP and pharmacist numbers. The initiative took place over three years: 1995 pre-intervention, 1996 the intervention year, 1997 post-intervention.

The campaign was evaluated in two ways: by questionnaires distributed before and after the campaign, and by quantitative analysis of prescription and sales of target medicines before and after the campaign, in both the test and control areas (for full details, see Evans *et al.*, 1999; Maguire *et al.*, 1999).

Agreement was obtained from the health authorities and their medical and pharmaceutical advisors for the circulation of pre- and post-campaign questionnaires to GPs and community pharmacists in both the test and control areas. In addition, agreement was obtained for access to 'prescribing analysis and cost' (PACT) data for GPs in both areas. Questionnaires were sent to the principals in 80 medical practices and 107 principal community pharmacists in the test area, and 82 principals in medical practices and 92 principal community pharmacists in the control areas in March/April 1995 before the campaign and February/March 1996 after the campaign. Reminders and a further questionnaire were sent to all non-responders three weeks after the initial questionnaire was posted. Response rates were as follows: GPs, test area 65%, control 60%; pharmacists, test 66%, control 63%. Pharmacists and GPs in deprived areas returned fewer questionnaires than in the test.

All returned questionnaires were coded and entered into a computer for processing. Statistical analysis using the standard chi-square test was carried out on the data, with alpha set at 5%, which did not take account of the pairings before and after the campaign. A separate analysis was undertaken of responses from GPs and pharmacists in the five most deprived wards in Newcastle and North Tyneside, compared with those in the remaining wards.

Results

The questionnaire analysis showed there was a non-statistically significant increase in the knowledge and awareness of both pharmacists and general medical practitioners in relation to the role of sugared medicines in dental caries, and the desirability of using sugar-free substitutes in both the test and control areas. So, for example, the percentage of GPs who thought sugar in medicines was important in relation to dental decay rose from 63% pre-campaign to 66% post-campaign.

Quantitative analysis of the PACT data showed there was an overall increase in the prescribing of sugar-free medicines in both test and control areas between 1995 and 1997 ($P < 0.01$), and this increase was significantly greater in the test area ($P < 0.0001$). Full details are given in Evans *et al.* (1999) and Maguire *et al.* (1999).

5. Conclusion

This is a modest case study concerning relatively minor improvements to public health, but it does serve to demonstrate that social marketing is not limited to either the individual citizen or mass media campaigns.

Target groups are selected by determining who is most likely to have an impact on the public health threat in question, which may be the individual citizen or people further upstream. In our case it was GPs. Interventions are then designed to best meet the needs of the chosen target group or groups. The rubric of the marketing mix helps us to think about this, but no assumptions are made as to its final form. Specifically, the mass media need not dominate or even be part of the final offering. In our case the mass media were not used and, although communications were important, the key element of the campaign was the enhanced prescribing software – which reduced the price of behaviour change.

The case study also shows that social marketing is both efficient and effective. The focus on behaviour change itself, rather than intermediate effects, such as improvements in knowledge and awareness, ensured that resources were applied where they were most needed. The delivery of sustained behaviour change shows that it worked.

References

Evans D.J., Howe D., Maguire A. and Rugg-Gunn A.J. (1999). Development and evaluation of a sugar-free medicines campaign in north east England: analysis of findings from questionnaires. *Community Dental Health*, **16**: 131–137.

Maguire A., Evans D.J., Rugg-Gunn A.J. and Butler T. (1999). Evaluation of a sugar-free medicines campaign in North East England: quantitative analysis of medicines use. *Community Dental Health*, **16**: 138–144.

Lessons learned

1. A common misconception about social marketing is that it only involves the fourth P, 'promotion', of which the marketing offering is mass media based. This case is an excellent example of how a social marketing framework can be effectively used to promote behaviour change without the use of mass media-based social advertising.

2. Although it would be ideal to design a social marketing campaign that appeals to all groups in need, often it is not feasible to do so. The current case outlines how research can be used to successfully narrow and segment the target audience so that campaign efforts are reasonable and effective.

3. Information technology can often play a fundamental role in social marketing campaigns. In this case, the second P, 'price', was addressed in an unconventional way – by adjusting the prescription software to sugar-free alternatives.

Case study questions

1. **Q:** Describe the four target groups that were originally identified for the campaign.

   A: Pharmaceutical manufacturers and distributors, pharmacists, parents and general medical practitioners (GPs) were originally identified as target groups for the campaign.

2. **Q:** Identify the two target groups that were not used in this campaign as a result of qualitative research and explain why.

   A: The two groups that were not used in this campaign were pharmaceutical manufacturers and distributors, as well as pharmacists. These groups were not targeted because research demonstrated that both groups encounter resistance when trying to impose sugar-free medicine due to the demand-led nature of the industry and also the increased cost of sugar-free alternatives.

3. **Q:** Describe the personal selling approach used in the marketing offering to sell sugar-free options to GPs.

   A: In conjunction with cueing alternatives, specially trained health authority staff were recruited to promote sugar-free options to GPs. This was done on a one-to-one basis and was aligned with the standard way that GPs learn about new medicines.

CASE STUDY 6

Using social marketing to increase recruitment of pregnant smokers to smoking cessation service

Raymond Lowry

1. Introduction

Although long established that smoking in pregnancy is harmful, many women still find it difficult to quit for pregnancy, and many health professionals find it frustrating that they cannot help more. So pioneering work in the UK has examined the barriers to cessation in an innovative way (using role play with stakeholders), and produced important improvements in the interest shown in smoking cessation by both pregnant smokers and health professionals. The intervention followed years of research and development. Focus groups provided insights into the issues facing smoking pregnant women, which were used to overcome barriers to smoking cessation using the principles of social marketing. The number of women recruited into a specially designed smoking cessation support initiative was compared to women recruited into comparable groups in the North-East. This innovative intervention has been a success: in generating ideas, guiding development of a client-friendly service and encouraging women to come forward for smoking cessation during their pregnancy. The target population have welcomed the approach, and health professionals have enjoyed and benefited from the role play with professional actors.

2. Problem definition

The impacts of smoking in pregnancy are well documented (Health Education Authority, 1997), and include a higher rate of miscarriage, perinatal mortality, low birth weight and sudden infant death syndrome (Blair, 1996). Approximately 30% of women who smoke in Great Britain continue to smoke during pregnancy (Lowry *et al.*, 2004). Funding in the UK city of Sunderland was used to appoint a local champion to coordinate services for pregnant women who want to give up smoking. In Sunderland between April 2001 and March 2002, only 19 women set a quit date and eight successfully quit smoking at the four-week stage through the mainstream service.

3. Competitive analysis

The promotion activities of the tobacco industry are well known and no exclusive analysis of activities in the target area were carried out. However, the generic, health service-supplied smoking cessation services locally were aware of the impact of tobacco marketing on the local population.

4. Stakeholder analysis

Detailed work was done with stakeholders in the pregnancy-smoking condition: with the women themselves and their 'significant others' (partners, parents, friends); health professionals (obstetric, medical, health promotion), as well as service providers, clinical managers and support groups. At the time the intervention was being planned, background work was being done developing the social marketing foundations, including research with many stakeholders in this and other areas of health-related issues.

5. Aims and objectives

The aim of the intervention was to increase the number of women in Sunderland who were accessing smoking cessation services and achieving formal quitting targets.

The objectives were to:

- Use social marketing to design a user-friendly service
- To re-engineer the local service to meet client needs
- To implement the service and achieve targets
- To record activity accurately and feed back to service providers
- To adjust practice in relation to feedback.

6. Formulation of strategy

The four Ps were used:

- *Product*. A customer-focused smoking cessation service.
- *Price*. Ease of access for the target (including free of charge).
- *Place*. Concentrating on the target population preferred locations.
- *Promotion*. Enthusing and skilling up health professionals.

Other considerations were:

- *Consumer research*. Focus groups with target audience, in-depth interviews, with professionals.
- *Testing*. Materials and approach in groups.
- *Specific channels*. Antenatal clinics.

- *Paid and voluntary agents.* Clinicians and supporters of target women.
- *Incentives.* Health and self-esteem related.

7. Research

Although it has long been known that smoking during pregnancy is undesirable and that many women still find it difficult to abstain, many health care professionals are at a loss to help. Therefore, to start the social marketing process, we undertook wide-ranging market research with the target population. Extensive developmental work was undertaken with the Centre for Social Marketing, Strathclyde University. Under the auspices of the Northern Regional Health Authority, the social marketing process was applied to a number of issues, including smoking in pregnancy. Once the skills in social marketing had been acquired, formative research was initiated. The research adopted a qualitative focus group method. Subjects were recruited to take part in one of 12 focus groups on a door-to-door basis by trained and experienced market research interviewers according to a strict code of conduct. The research spans 10 years from 1992. The majority of focus groups took place at the beginning and the final two more recently. A total of 12 groups were segmented in relation to age, social class, smoking behaviour/history and cohabitation status. In order to avoid any possible bias, participants were not informed of the exact nature of the research, but were told that the discussion would be centred on the topic of 'health and illness'. The moderator ensured that the aims of the research were covered, without restraining the discussion, with the help of a discussion guide. Data were analysed by the group moderators: an audio recording was made of each group and contemporaneous notes were made be a trained observer. Using the audio recordings as an *aide-mémoire*, and with the observer and notes, key themes were extracted and developed. The findings were used to develop the intervention, with feedback from participating target women at each stage of development.

Table CS6.1 Analysis of barriers and interventions to overcome them

Barrier	Intervention
Difficulty recruiting women	Proactive recruiting, dedicated worker, home visits
Poor existing information	Design and pre-test new marketing/information material with target population
Health professionals lack of engagement	Role play to engage health professionals
Nagging/make them feel worse	Consumer-friendly cessation support (including dedicated worker)

8. Outcomes

Recruitment of pregnant (and non-pregnant) smokers to the new smoking cessation intervention increased 10-fold during the intervention phase, and the Sunderland stop smoking service is now one of the top performers in the UK (Table CS6.2).

Recruitment of pregnant smokers also increased after actor/role-play sessions with health care professionals (especially midwives) (Figure CS6.1) and was higher than the neighbouring services (in which different

Table CS6.2 Sunderland stop smoking service assessment at end of 2005
Sunderland pregnancy stop smoking service highlighted in Department of Health 'Best practice in smoking cessation services for pregnant smokers' (November 2005)
One of the *top three* beacon services in England
The *most cost-effective* (quitters per member of staff, clarity of data collection and reporting procedures)

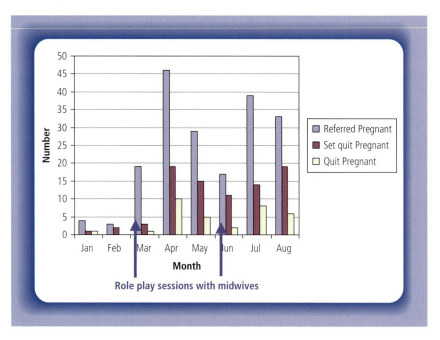

Figure CS6.1
Sunderland Smoking Cessation Activity (Pregnancy) by Month
(Referral to Service, Quit Date and 4 Week Quit Rates)

Table CS6.3 Activity of Sunderland smokers cessation support April–June 2002 compared to control areas (other Primary Care Trusts in North-East England)

Progress	PCT A	PCT B	PCT C	PCT D+E	Sunderland	North-East
Set quit date	18	10	26	6	47	107
Success quit four weeks self-report	2	3	10	2	17	34
Not quit four weeks self-report	8	5	10	4	19	46
Not known/lost	8	2	6	0	11	27
Quit four weeks validated CO analyser	2	3	9	0	15	29

smoking cessation interventions targeted at pregnant women were being undertaken) in all the parameters measured (Table CS6.3).

9. Discussion

Market research identified a number of barriers that women face in relation to smoking cessation during pregnancy: unsatisfactory information, lack of enthusiasm/empathy from health care professionals, short-term support, all showing as a reluctance to be recruited.

The difficulty of recruiting women to take part in smoking cessation meant we had to concentrate effort where women might be recruitable (in this case, in the antenatal clinic at first booking). Support was designed to be consumer friendly by using information from focus groups, recruitment of skilled and empathic dedicated workers, and using feedback techniques. Apart from designing and pre-testing posters and leaflets that would meet women's needs, a full-time worker was specially recruited to provide long-term, home-based, user-friendly support. The major barrier to overcome was health care professional enthusiasm/empathy, and to do that we used professional actors/role players.

By studying the transcripts of the focus groups, actors/role players were able to bring to groups of health care workers the chance to interact with the target women as they had never before. Using active participation in group work, professional staff were able to get direct feedback on what it felt to be the target women and what approaches might work more effectively. These sessions evaluated highly with participants and proved to be very effective in the intervention.

The undoubted success of the intervention shows how social marketing can bring about behaviour change in a hard-to-change population. These techniques are not foolproof: it is only by diligent application and hard work by the participants that the success has been achieved.

References

Blair P.S. (1996). Smoking and sudden infant death syndrome. *British Medical Journal*, **313**: 195–198.

Health Education Authority (1997). *Action on Smoking and Pregnancy*. London: Health Education Authority.

Lowry R., Hardy S., Jordan C. and Wayman G. (2004). Using social marketing to increase recruitment of pregnant smokers to smoking cessation service: a success story. *Public Health*, **118**: 239–243.

Lessons learned

1. A similarity between social marketing and commercial marketing is that the consumer is put at the heart of the process. This case demonstrates how the needs of the target consumer can be put at the forefront of all behaviour-change efforts from the onset through to the completion of a campaign.

2. Aligned with the campaign's consumer focus, this case demonstrates the vital role that research can play in helping to design and implement a successful social marketing campaign. By engaging in years of qualitative social marketing research, campaign planners were able to design strategies to successfully overcome barriers to smoking cessation that met the needs of the target women.

3. The use of actors/role players was particularly beneficial in getting health practitioners to understand and put themselves in the shoes of the target women. By training key professionals about the target women and more effective intervention approaches, this actor/role-play session proved to be extremely effective.

Case study questions

1. **Q:** What were the barriers identified by market research that caused the target women to be reluctant about participating in smoking cessation programmes?

   A: Formative market research identified unsatisfactory information, lack of enthusiasm/empathy from health care professionals and short-term support as causing reluctance among the target to be recruited to smoking cessation programmes.

2. **Q:** Choose one of the barriers from Question 1 and describe how the social marketing intervention overcame this barrier.

   A: For example, to address the finding that women felt unsatisfactory information existed for smoking cessation during pregnancy, posters and leaflets were pre-tested and designed to meet women's needs and preferences.

3. Q: Using the smoking in pregnancy case study as an example, describe the role of the third P, 'place', in the design and implementation of a social marketing campaign.

   A: Place in social marketing is used to identify when and where a customer will consume the product and carry out the behaviour. In the case of the smoking in pregnancy campaign, women were recruited in the antenatal clinic at their first booking and home-based support was also provided to them. This allowed the intervention to be convenient and accessible.

CASE STUDY 7

The VERB™ Summer Scorecard

*Carol A. Bryant, Anita Courtney, Julie A. Baldwin,
Robert J. McDermott, Jen Nickelson and
Kelli R. McCormack Brown*

1. Introduction

The VERB™ Summer Scorecard is a physical activity promotion programme that offers tweens (9- to 13-year-olds) opportunities to be active
in their community during the summer months. Initially developed by a
community coalition in Lexington, Kentucky, the programme is now
being adapted for use in multiple communities around the USA. This case
study describes how community-based prevention marketing (Bryant
et al., 2000) was used to develop an intervention that encourages youth to
try new physical activities and facilitates their participation. Community-
based prevention marketing blends the wisdom of community control
and direction with the effectiveness of social marketing in designing interventions to promote socially beneficial behaviours and services.
Community representatives learn to use marketing principles and practices to analyse local problems, set goals, develop marketing plans, and
implement and evaluate them.

2. Problem definition

Over the past 30 years, the prevalence of obesity has more than tripled for
youths aged 6–11 years and more than doubled for youths 12–19 years of
age (Committee on Prevention of Obesity in Children and Youth, 2005).
According to the 2003–04 National Health and Nutrition Examination
Survey (NHANES), 18.8% of 6- to 11-year-old youths were overweight
(BMI greater than or equal to the 95th percentile for age and gender) and
37.2% were at risk for overweight (BMI at or above the 85th percentile but
less than the 95th percentile for age and gender). Rates are even higher for
12- to 19-year-old youths – 17% were overweight and 34.3% were at risk of
being overweight (Ogden *et al.*, 2006).

As the extent and consequences of the childhood obesity epidemic
become clear, many communities are searching for local solutions. Physical
activity promotion is considered one of the most promising strategies for

obesity prevention among youths, yet physical activity levels decrease significantly as children grow older (Ritchie *et al.*, 2006).

3. Competitive analysis

Although no industry intentionally promotes a sedentary lifestyle for tweens, television, computer use, hand-held video games and many other activities compete for tweens' time and attention. Efforts to promote physical activity must find ways to compete with the enjoyment these activities provide youths.

4. Stakeholder analysis

A wide variety of individuals and organizations are invested in young people's health, well-being and economic expenditures. In addition to understanding the needs and benefits these stakeholders have in reaching youths, community-based prevention marketing invites stakeholders to participate in designing the intervention to promote physical activity among youths. Among the 55 organizations and individuals recruited to participate in a community coalition to prevent childhood obesity were the county health department, the YMCA, the county parks and recreation department, public school food service personnel, faith-based organizations, community centres, a children's museum, various businesses (especially ones serving a youth audience), other civic organizations, and concerned principals, teachers, coaches, physicians and parents. Interviews were conducted with representatives from each of the participating coalition organizations to determine their perception of the benefits and costs of participating in a childhood obesity prevention coalition. Whereas most coalition members were motivated by a strong desire to prevent the health and emotional problems associated with childhood obesity, many doubted a coalition's effectiveness in tackling the problem and feared they would waste time on fruitless planning meetings. As a result, agendas for coalition meetings were carefully organized to ensure that members felt a sense of achievement in the short run as well as progress towards their long-term goal.

5. Aims and objectives

The overall aim of the coalition's activities was to prevent childhood obesity. To this end, the coalition selected several protective behaviours to promote – physical activity in community settings, incorporation of physical education in public schools, regular breakfast consumption, reduced sweetened beverage consumption and parental involvement in promoting healthy eating. The coalition also selected tweens as the target population, with an emphasis on those in middle school. They selected this age group because physical activity levels are beginning to decline as youths reach middle school and become more independent. The remainder of this case study focuses on the first objective: the coalition's efforts to promote physical activity outside of the school setting.

6. Formulation of strategy

The marketing plan developed to achieve this objective is summarized in Table CS7.1.

7. Research

In addition to the stakeholder analysis, the formative research included a literature review, 10 individual interviews with principals and other programme partners, six focus groups with tweens, and two focus groups with parents. High school students were trained to conduct the focus groups and provide advice and assistance throughout programme development and implementation (McCormack Brown *et al.*, 2003). Programme evaluation included follow-up telephone interviews with a sample of parents whose tweens participated in the programme, as well as surveys of students in public elementary and middle schools. Interviews were also conducted with representatives of business and community organizations that participated in the programme, as well as coalition members.

8. Outcomes

Although it was not possible to document how many families participated in the programme or completed Scorecards, approximately 950 people attended an event held on the 'Longest Day of Play' (in reference to 21 June, the first day of summer and longest day of sunlight), an estimated 1000 people attended the VERB™ Summer Scorecard Grand Finale and 335 tweens submitted completed scorecards for the grand prize draw in 2004. The following year, approximately 900 cards were submitted and 1200 attended the Grand Finale in August of 2005.

Of the 35 parents who participated in the follow-up telephone interview (Autumn 2005), 65% said that their child's physical activity increased during VERB™ Summer Scorecard, 56% of parents believed that their children were more active after VERB™ Summer Scorecard, 47% of parents indicated that other children in the house were more active as a result of VERB™ Summer Scorecard and 70% reported they were more aware of their child's physical activity levels since the inception of the VERB™ Summer Scorecard (Skeen-Morris, 2006).

A survey of 2974 students conducted in 27 elementary schools in May 2005 revealed that 42.6% of the students had seen, read or heard messages

Table CS7.1 The marketing plan

Strategic component	Marketing plan
Audience segmentation	The project focused on *moderately active* tweens (i.e. those who are active but not yet passionate about any of the physical activities in which they participate) and *passives* (i.e. those who are uninvolved in physical activity and do things mostly out of boredom). It did not attempt to reach *high*-risk youth who lack parental support and other resources needed to participate in physical activities outside of school. The project also attempted to address differences between boys and girls and younger (8–10 years of age) and older (11–13 years of age) tweens.
Product strategy	Activities are designed to satisfy tweens' primary motivators: have fun, spend time with friends, and explore new and adventurous activities. Health messages are strictly avoided.
Pricing strategy	Project activities are designed to overcome tweens' fear of embarrassment in front of peers, their parents' fears about their children's safety, and provide free or discounted opportunities to be active.
Promotion	A VERB™ Summer Scorecard is used to encourage tweens to monitor their physical activity throughout the summer and try new ways to be physically active. The Scorecard has 24 squares that can be stamped each time a tween is physically active at one of the Summer Scorecard sites that offer special deals to cardholders (e.g. free admission to public pools, reduced admission prices to commercial facilities, free sports clinics for beginners, etc.). Parents and other adults also may initial as many as 12 squares to acknowledge when tweens are physically active for at least one hour. Tweens who get all 24 squares stamped or initialled before the end of summer receive a prize, gain entrance into an exciting Grand Finale event and become eligible for the grand prize draw that features desirable items that promote physical activity (e.g. bicycles, scooters and karate lessons). Free and paid media are used to promote the programme and the Scorecard, and all promotional materials include the VERB™ logo and follow its branding guidelines.
Placement strategy	A wide variety of action outlets (special opportunities for tweens to be physically active with friends and try new activities) are offered around the community throughout the summer months. Special efforts are made to provide free or low-cost opportunities in or near economically disadvantaged neighbourhoods. Scorecards are distributed by schools, at McDonald's restaurants,[a] at the YMCA, day camps, faith-based organizations, and other non-profit and private business partners.

[a] The coalition struggled over the decision to distribute Scorecards through McDonald's outlets because of the restaurant's reputation for contributing to obesity. Some members noted the efforts McDonald's has recently made to improve its offerings (e.g. adding nutritious items and eliminating the supersizing practices). In the end, they felt the benefits gained in reaching the target audience outweighed the costs of partnering with this organization.

or ads about the VERB™ Summer Scorecard and 31.3% had participated during the summer of 2004. More than nine out of 10 youths (90.3%) reported that they had seen, read or heard messages about the national VERB™ programme. However, those youths exposed to both VERB™ and VERB™ Summer Scorecard programmes reported higher levels of vigorous physical activity than those students who had been exposed to only one of these programmes. Further research is needed, but these results suggest an additive effect of implementing a locally tailored intervention in conjunction with a national media campaign (Baldwin *et al.*, 2006).

Recommendations of parents, site partners and tweens for programme improvement are part of the lessons learned from the pilot project. They have been used to revise the programme for implementation in 2006, and to develop a manual to assist communities in designing and implementing a scorecard-type intervention. As of summer 2006, the programme had been adapted by 15 other communities in the USA to promote physical activity during the summer months, over the winter vacation and during other time periods.

References

Baldwin J., Bryant C., Courtney A., Nickelson J.E., Alfonso M., Phillips L.M., McCormack Brown K.R. and McDermott R.J. (2006). Physical activity and *VERB™* awareness among elementary school children. Presentation at the *International Congress on Physical Activity*, Atlanta, GA.

Bryant C.A., Forthofer M., McCormack Brown K., Landis D. and McDermott R.J. (2000). Community-based prevention marketing: the next steps in disseminating behavior change. *American Journal of Health Behavior*, **24**: 61–68.

Committee on Prevention of Obesity in Children and Youth (2005). *Preventing Childhood Obesity: Health in the Balance*. Washington, DC: Institute of Medicine.

McCormack Brown K.R., McDermott R.J., Bryant C.A. and Forthofer M.S. (2003). Youth as community researchers: the Sarasota County demonstration project. *Community and Youth Development Journal*, **4**(1): 40–44.

Ogden C.L., Carroll M.D., Curtin L.R. *et al.* (2006). Prevalence of overweight and obesity in the United States, 1999–2004. *Journal of the American Medical Association*, **295**: 1549–1555.

Ritchie L., Ivey S., Masch M., Lopez G.W., Ikeda J. and Crawford P. (2006). *Pediatric Overweight: A Review of the Literature*; http://www.cnr.berkeley.edu/cwh/activities/position.shtml

Skeen-Morris K. (2006). *VERB™ 2005 Follow-up Survey Results: What did parents think of the program*. Data collected and analysed by the Kentucky Prevention Research Center. Lexington, KY: University of Kentucky.

Lessons learned

1. Social marketing does not need to apply solely to individual behaviour change. The VERB™ Summer Scorecard is one example of how

social marketing is evolving, in this case by applying the framework to community-based prevention marketing.

2. The VERB™ Summer Scorecard was instrumental in helping to build community capacity. A campaign strength was the involvement of a wide range of stakeholders and individuals in the design of the physical activity intervention. With 55 organizations and individuals with varying expertise participating in the campaign strategy design, each of the stakeholders were able to be actively involved and take a sense of ownership over short- and long-term campaign goals.

3. The VERB™ Summer Scorecard illustrates one of the challenges associated with community-based prevention marketing – the struggle that a coalition may face during decision making. For instance, the decision to use McDonald's to reach the campaign's target audience was particularly contentious.

Case study questions

1. **Q:** Why were tweens (9- to 13-year-olds) chosen as the target audience for the VERB™ Summer Scorecard?

   A: Tweens were chosen because levels of physical activity are beginning to decline in this age group, yet at the same time they are starting to make their own physical activity-related choices.

2. **Q:** What psychographic and demographic variables were used in the VERB™ Summer Scorecard campaign to further segment tweens?

   A: The campaign segmented the tweens by age (tweens in middle school), activity level (moderately active tweens) and passives (those uninvolved in physical activity and doing things mainly out of boredom). Differences between boys and girls as well as older tweens were also addressed during campaign efforts.

3. **Q:** By avoiding the use of health messages to promote the VERB™ Summer Scorecard initiative, campaign planners demonstrated that they had a keen understanding of the target audience. Explain what motivators were used instead of health messages to gauge the physical activity interests of tweens.

   A: Instead of using health messages to gauge the physical activity interests of tweens, campaign planners chose having fun, spending time with friends, and exploring new and adventurous activities as key motivators to appeal to.

CASE STUDY 8

Quit&Win New Zealand

Kiri Milne, Sue Walker and Iain Potter

1. Introduction

Quit&Win is an international smoking cessation contest that has been coordinated by the National Public Health Institute (KTL) in Finland since 1994, and is supported by the World Health Organization. Participants stop using tobacco for at least the contest period of four weeks and, if they succeed, they are eligible to win prizes. The most recent contest in May 2006 attracted 700 000 smokers from 85 countries.

This case study describes New Zealand's experience of implementing Quit&Win in 2002.

2. Problem definition

Tobacco smoking is a leading risk factor causing preventable deaths in New Zealand, and is responsible for approximately 15% of all deaths. Smoking rates remain high in New Zealand, despite a comprehensive tobacco control programme that incorporates the internationally recommended strategies of legislation, taxation, health promotion and smoking cessation services. In 2002, 25% of all adult New Zealanders smoked. Smoking rates are even higher among Maori, New Zealand's indigenous people, especially young Maori women. In 2002, one in two Maori (49%) smoked cigarettes. For Maori women aged 15–24 years, the rate was 58%, compared with 42% for men in this age bracket (Public Health Intelligence, 2003).

Competitions are popular in New Zealand, and Quit&Win was seen as a new way to motivate people, including young Maori women, to stop smoking.

3. Competitive analysis

Smoke-free and quitting messages compete with the tobacco industry's promotion of its products. Although tobacco advertising and sponsorship are banned in New Zealand, the tobacco industry continues to market its products using techniques such as below-the-line marketing. Audiences, particularly young audiences, continue to encounter substantial media

content depicting smoking across virtually all media channels. Much of this content is non-promotional, incidental portrayals of tobacco. However, there is increasing evidence to suggest that tobacco companies are responsible for some of these media portrayals (Health Sponsorship Council, 2006).

At an individual level, for many smokers calls to stop smoking compete with an addiction to nicotine, the enjoyment of smoking, and family and peer influences, i.e. their family and friends smoke as well.

Quit&Win aims to counter this competition by motivating people to quit smoking using a tangible incentive – a prize draw. Even people who do not win contest prizes are winners, as everyone who quits gains the health benefits of being smoke-free.

4. Stakeholder analysis

Quit&Win's stakeholders share the common goal of minimizing the harm from tobacco, and range from the international Quit&Win organizers to the families and friends of participants, who support them to quit their smoking habit. Stakeholders in New Zealand include policy and funding agencies, principally the Ministry of Health, and the tobacco control and public health agencies that implemented Quit&Win. From a marketing perspective, the HSC (Health Sponsorship Council) and regional public health units acted as the 'head and regional offices', coordinating the contest, while the local health promoters and primary health care providers acted as the retailers, delivering the intervention to the 'customers', the people who smoke. Local pharmacies also acted as sales outlets by promoting the contest and enrolling participants.

5. Aims and objectives

Quit&Win's overall aim, like that of all tobacco control measures, is to reduce the major burden of tobacco-related disease. More specifically, it aims to provide a cost-effective, evidence-based smoking cessation method for population-wide public health use. Quit&Win has demonstrated that it is capable of reaching more smokers, at a lower cost, than most smoking cessation interventions. It also appeals to people of different cultures.

The specific marketing objective was to motivate quit attempts among smokers in the areas participating in the contest in New Zealand.

6. Formulation of strategy

Quit&Win was selected as an intervention because it was seen as an innovative product that would appeal to adult smokers, particularly

Table CS8.1 Components of the Quit&Win campaign

Components of marketing	How Quit&Win delivered these components
Product	Quit&Win provides tangible products, i.e. the motivation to quit in the form of a prize draw and a set date for a quit attempt.
	Supporting products are available in the form of personal support from a nominated person and cessation support (e.g. the Quitline and nicotine replacement therapy).
	Quit&Win also offers added value by allowing people to feel they are not alone, but are sharing in a quit attempt with other smokers – this is similar to the way many commercial products sell an image or lifestyle, as well as a product.
Price	Quit&Win offers a clear 'exchange' or benefit, i.e. make a quit attempt and be rewarded by entering a prize draw and being supported to stop smoking. The exchange is formalized by a documented, witnessed commitment (the enrolment form) to making the attempt by the agreed time.
Place	The intervention is delivered directly to the customer, i.e. at a community level. Multiple points of sale are used, ranging from pharmacies to people's workplaces.
Promotion	Advertising and promotional resources were developed and coordinated nationally and distributed to a regional sales force (public health units), who, in turn, 'sold' it on to the retailers (the local coordinators and public health workers who enrolled the entrants – cessation providers, doctors, child-health nurses).
	A range of communication channels was used, targeted at the key audiences – e.g. *iwi* (Maori) radio, local newspapers, entry forms, posters, advertisements, display stands, prizes and giveaways.

among key audiences that were proving hard to reach with existing cessation programmes – Maori and young Maori women.

Quit&Win fits well with a social marketing model, with clear parallels to the 'four Ps' of commercial marketing – product, price, place and promotion – as Table CS8.1 illustrates.

Sales targets were set for local coordinators, with the aim being to enrol 1.5% of smokers in each area into the contest. Selling techniques included visiting workplaces, education establishments (particularly Maori pre-schools) and community events (particularly Maori community activities), and encouraging smokers to enrol. This technique was useful as it helped coordinators meet their targets.

7. Research and evaluation

Quit&Win is an evidence-based intervention that is assessed by the International Coordinating Centre in Finland using standard approaches

(Sandström *et al.*, 2006). Quit&Win in New Zealand was subject to a three-stage evaluation:

1. *Formative research.* As well as drawing on the international research, the intervention was piloted in one region of New Zealand in 2000. Following a positive evaluation, Quit&Win was implemented in a further four regions in 2002 (Forsyte Research, 2001).
2. *Process evaluation.* Key informant interviews were used to provide feedback from stakeholders on the implementation of Quit&Win (Gravitas Research and Strategy Ltd and Stokes, 2002; Milne, 2003).
3. *Impact evaluation.* Quantitative research was used to assess short-term and longer-term impacts of the intervention on participants (Gravitas Research and Strategy Ltd, 2002, 2003).

8. Outcomes

1796 people entered the contest that was run in the five regions in 2002. The entrant numbers represented 1.8% of the regions' smoking population, well in excess of the average international participation rate of 1.25%.

The impact evaluation reported a range of positive outcomes:

- Just over one-half of the people surveyed (55%) reported quitting smoking for the entire contest (four weeks).
- Twelve months after the contest finished, just over one in 10 (12%) people reported not smoking at all. One in 10 people were not smoking at the 12-month follow-up but had relapsed at some stage during the year. Overall, therefore, 22% of participants were not smoking at the 12-month follow-up, which is consistent with the average rates reported by the international studies.
- Quit rates were similar for males and females, and Maori and non-Maori.

The evaluation did not measure the potential secondary benefits of Quit&Win, such as people cutting down the number of cigarettes they smoked during and after the contest.

Key lessons from the impact evaluation included:

- Preparation of participants was important, with contest quit rates higher among those 'ready to quit'.
- People who were not ready to quit may have been encouraged to sign up for the contest by the 'sales technique' used, i.e. coordinators visiting locations in their community and encouraging people to enrol. This approach may have led some people to sign up because their friends and family were enrolling, rather than because they were ready to quit smoking. Higher quit rates might be achievable in future contests if more participants are ready to quit.
- Supporting products were important and contest quit rates were higher among those using other cessation methods.

The rate of relapse among those managing to quit for the whole contest was highest in the months immediately after the contest, indicating a need for continuing support. Stress was the main reason why people relapsed, suggesting that support should include stress management techniques.

The process evaluation also provided useful lessons. Overall, Quit&Win was seen as a valuable option as part of a range of cessation products. Efficacy could be improved by product enhancement – for example, continuing support after the contest, especially stress management skills – and by workforce development, with both the regional 'sales force' and the local retailers saying they needed more training and support from 'head office' (HSC) to use the intervention to its full potential.

New Zealand did not take part in Quit&Win in 2004 and 2006, but it is considering profiting from its earlier experience and re-entering in 2008.

References

Forsyte Research (2001). *Quit&Win Pilot Competition Participant Evaluation: Twelve-month follow up*. Unpublished report to the Health Sponsorship Council.

Gravitas Research and Strategy Ltd (2002). *Quit&Win 2002: Initial follow-up of competition participants*. Unpublished report to the Health Sponsorship Council.

Gravitas Research and Strategy Ltd (2003). *Quit&Win 2002: 12-month follow-up of competition participants*. Unpublished report to the Health Sponsorship Council.

Gravitas Research and Strategy Ltd and Stokes K. (2002). *A Qualitative Study of Quit&Win 2002 in Tairawhiti*. Unpublished report to the Health Sponsorship Council.

Health Sponsorship Council (2006). *Tobacco in the Media and Youth Smoking. A Summary of Key Literature*. In preparation.

Milne K. (2003). *Stakeholder Perspectives on Quit&Win 2002*. Unpublished Health Sponsorship Council Research and Evaluation Unit report.

Public Health Intelligence (2003). *Tobacco Facts 2003*, Occasional Report No. 20. Wellington, New Zealand: Ministry of Health.

Sandström P., Vartiainen E.R. and Pyykönen M. (2006). *International Quit&Win 2002 and 2004*. Report on behalf of the Working Group of the International Quit&Win. Helsinki: KTL-National Public Health Institute.

Lessons learned

1. The first P, 'product', in a social marketing strategy can be tangible or intangible. The Quit&Win intervention outlines how a social marketing campaign can encourage healthy behaviour using both tangible and intangible products. Specifically, a prize draw, set quit date and supporting products are examples of the tangible product offerings used to encourage smoking cessation among programme participants. On the other hand, the value of allowing people to feel they are not alone in quitting smoking is an example of the intangible product offering.

2. The use of impact evaluation was particularly valuable for the Quit&Win intervention. By measuring both short- and longer-term programme impacts, the campaign team was able to assess the longevity of this social marketing intervention.
3. The evaluation used for Quit&Win did not measure other smoking behaviours besides quitting, such as cutting down of the number of cigarettes smoked after the contest. A measure of such intermediate behaviours may have shed more light into the potential impact of the Quit&Win intervention.

Case study questions

1. **Q:** Identify the three lessons learned from the impact evaluation for the Quit&Win intervention.
   A: 'Ready to quit' participants demonstrated a higher contest quit rate, suggesting that preparation of participants prior to programme involvement was important. Results also indicated that if more 'ready to quit' participants took part in the programme, higher quitting rates might have been achieved. Also, supporting products were found to be particularly useful among those with higher quit rates, suggesting that multiple smoking cessation methods are valuable.
2. **Q:** What is one potential challenge in using tangible objects to promote behaviour change as outlined in the Quit&Win case?
   A: A challenge with using tangible objects to promote behaviour change is that long-term change can be difficult to sustain. As outlined in the Quit&Win case, the rate of relapse among those managing to quit for the whole contest was the highest in the months immediately after the contest.
3. **Q:** Describe one mechanism identified in the Quit&Win case that could be used to address the difficulties in using tangible objects to promote behaviour change.
   A: Continued support for smoking cessation could have been provided to Quit&Win programme participants. For instance, stress management techniques could have been a useful way to manage relapse rates following the months when the contest ended.

CASE STUDY 9

Quit&Save Scotland: linking social marketing and social enterprise

Neil McLean

1. Introduction – quit smoking services in Scotland

Smoking levels in Scotland currently equate to almost one in three of the adult population (http://www.healthscotland.com). NHS cessation services increase people's chances of quitting four-fold compared with an unsupported quit attempt (http://www.healthscotland.com) and the provision of such a service is one of the cheapest 'interventions' available; it is cheaper than the aspirin a day prevention of myocardial infarction (Parrot and Godfrey, 2004). And yet these services will have only a negligible impact on Scotland's smoking prevalence (Milne, 2005) because they cannot meet demand. Even at near full capacity, only 50 000 of Scotland's 1.3 million smokers will get access to the service.

If this is such an excellent and cost-effective treatment, why do so few people ultimately benefit from it? Why too is there no incentive to grow these services beyond their current capacity? This case study will present an alternative service structure which has growth through social marketing at its core. Quit&Save Scotland is a social enterprise that aims to deliver cessation services in a flexible, customer-focused way.

2. Problem definition

Targets set for the NHS cessation services are based on throughput and not outcome. That is, the focus is on exposing as many people as possible to the intervention and hope that the rates of success are maintained. In a scientifically driven discipline such as the NHS, standardization is extremely important, and it is an excellent system for delivering hip replacements. But for something as deeply personal as tackling an addiction, a more flexible and human approach is needed. One size will not fit all, and the chronic relapsing rate of smokers compels us to look beyond the short term.

Self-limiting nature of current services

A harsh judge might liken the current focus on target setting within the NHS to a planned economy: the Central Committee know that if you deliver service X to 100 people, then 15 will quit; they therefore set targets and provide resources for service delivery to 100 people. Those who only deliver to 99 people get criticized; on the other hand, those who deliver to 101 are under-resourced. In addition, the 15% conversion rate becomes equally set in stone – if you fail to achieve it you will be criticized, so best follow the rules exactly so that you do not get the blame. In short, the system punishes initiative, and minima and maxima converge.

Thus, the service provider is not incentivized to grow the service because if they do they hit resource problems or create waiting lists.

Dispensing treatments, not encouraging behaviour change

By focusing on the treatment, it underestimates the complexity of human behaviour in two ways. First, as noted above, cessation services at their best only double the quitting success of the smoker acting on their own (assuming use of a patch or gum). This suggests that the smoker has a lot of expertise to offer to the quitting process and they should be an active participant in – not a passive recipient of – the service.

Second, the service provider needs to be able to respond flexibly to the smoker's needs. A recent Quit&Save client was amazed but delighted that there was the flexibility in the programme to allow her to choose when she would quit. This contrasted with her experience of the NHS service, which worked principally in groups of around 20 – very cost-effective and convenient for the service provider, but with built-in inflexibility for the client.

3. Aims and objectives

(Organic) sustainable growth

Quit&Save's mission is to produce 'sustainable growth by creating delighted customers – not satisfied patients'. We know from numerous studies that around 90% of smokers wish they had never started; 70% want to quit and around 30% of smokers will make a quit attempt in any one year (West, 2005). Why then do only one in 20 access 'best practice' smoking cessation services?

A quit smoking service in Liverpool, called Fag Ends, set up and run by lay people on behalf of the Roy Castle Foundation, consistently equals or outperforms NHS services. So successful has this service been that it now delivers most of the services in the area. It shows that we do not need to have trained nurses delivering our services in this area, and indeed the customer orientation of the Fag Ends project has seen word-of-mouth referral now exceed GP referrals.

It is clear, then, that excellence is not defined by nursing qualifications and that there is a huge potential market of people wanting to quit. We just need a vehicle to allow our population to become involved in solving the problem, what Derek Wanless called 'fully engaged' – rather than leaving the experts to dispense ready-made but undifferentiated solutions.

Social enterprise as a form of social marketing

How would a business approach this problem? Probably, as the Allen Carr organization has, by top-slicing the potential market and targeting the most affluent clients who can pay. However, there is a third alternative to public sector and private sector solutions – the social enterprise, which 'bridges an important gap between business and benevolence; it is the application of entrepreneurship in the social sphere' (Roberts and Woods, 2006, p. 45).

Taking a look at the private sector again for a moment, the Weight Watchers organization has some interesting parallels with the opportunities that exist in the smoking cessation arena. Here is an organization that is encouraging behavioural change, using trained lay people who have succeeded in a similar fashion to achieve a particular goal. Over time, Weight Watchers have gained credibility, are now sponsored by the British Heart Foundation and have recently been positively reported upon in the *British Medical Journal* (Truby *et al.*, 2006).

In this type of operation, individuals are invited to grow the business by becoming a leader and setting up their own weight-loss support class. People are motivated to help others achieve their goals, but also to maintain their own behavioural change. A degree of standardization occurs – the Weight Watcher brand and support materials are used, for instance – but individuals are treated as customers and mutually beneficial exchange takes place. The leaders are highly incentivized to grow their own groups, as it increases both income and satisfaction.

Social enterprise takes this thinking a stage further, and any profits from the operation are ploughed back into the purpose of the firm.

But making profits from a habit that is dominated by disadvantage is surely both impractical and immoral. Quit&Save is navigating a way through:

● A recent Institute of Directors study showed that employers gain between £700 and £800 per annum when an employee quits smoking successfully because of reduced absence, fewer breaks and increased concentration levels. This obvious business opportunity could subsidize services in areas where people could not so easily afford to pay.
● Alternatively, more sophisticated business models can be employed in deprived areas – for example, where the customer (the payer) is not the same person as the client (the service recipient).

4. Strategies

Quit&Save aims to engage clients in the process or journey of quitting, supporting them towards a day where they do not want to smoke any more. We will treat smokers as a whole human being who has the ability to make a choice, and use feedback and focus groups to ensure that every part of the organization is devoted to keeping the clients delighted.

Products

Figure CS9.1 shows our three operational sectors – the corporate, commercial and community – and each will have a bespoke range of products.

For example, in the corporate sector we will offer:

- *Smoking awareness workshops* for managers who are managing people during quit attempts. There are many individual experiences with

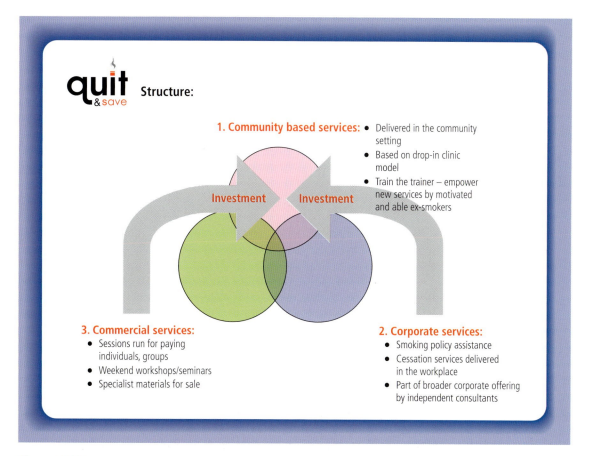

Figure CS9.1
Operational sectors. Reproduced with permission of McLean and Quit&Save.

smoking and it is helpful to provide insight for managers to allow them to provide a consistent and supportive message to employees who are embarking on a major life change.

- *Quit smoking classes.* Ten weeks made up of six two-hour and three one-hour sessions, finishing up with a two-hour session including 'graduation'.
- *'Don't want to quit' smoking classes.* Four weeks made up of four two-hour workshops. Research and experience have shown that people who declare they do not want to stop smoking are just as successful in actually quitting permanently as those who embark on a course with the stated objective of actually stopping.
- *Quit smoking clubs.* Once a number of quit smoking classes have been completed, individuals can be invited to help set up a peer-based 'quit club' which would continue to run in the workplace (outside of working hours) to support people who are quitting. During this period, Quit&Save would provide training and support to those individuals wishing to participate.

Price

This will vary by sector. Corporate clients are willing and able to pay, if only because, as the IOD report shows, they stand to make financial gain from quitters. Low-income communities, on the other hand, will get a subsidized service either through internal cross-subsidy or through building relationships with external funders.

Place

Locations that suit the target audience: workplace programmes for employees during working hours and community centres where people can access services and avoid a medicalized approach.

Promotion

Based largely on relationship marketing, where the focus is on generating delighted customers, word-of-mouth marketing is employed to gain referrals from companies and individuals to allow people to recommend the programme to their friends. As Reichhield said: 'The one number you need to grow: would you recommend us to a friend?' (Hastings and McLean, 2006).

5. Outcomes to date

Any new business faces challenges, and I am sure we have got some aspects of the marketing mix wrong. However, as a social enterprise, it is both our job and our passion to create a world-class service that can grow to satisfy the needs of all smokers.

So far, we have had mixed results in getting people to participate in the programme, but once there, the results have been excellent. Feedback and outcomes are tremendous – we have resisted the temptation to create the pass/fail environment of the NHS model, but initial results are extremely encouraging. I am not suggesting we have created a better service in terms of content, but I do believe that our clients will come back if necessary to continue on their journey in a way that they do not appear to be doing in the NHS. Recent anecdotal evidence suggests a steady decline (over the past three or four quarters in 14 out of 16 PCTs) of people engaging with NHS services in England (Globalink correspondence referring to PCT self-monitoring of results for England, August 2006).

We also provide telephone, text and email support to our clients when they need it and ask them to enter into a contractual arrangement whereby they agree to call their 'quit coach' if they feel tempted to have a puff. In many cases this has avoided relapse – our nursing colleagues tell us that this is simply not practical. 'What if you're not on duty?' If you want to grow your business and make it successful, you will make yourself available. This single, fairly simple feature of our service is cited in most evaluations by clients as very important to them. It is what they want, and they believe it helps get them over certain 'humps' during the first two or three weeks.

One disappointing area was in the arena of the 'quit club' in the high street – we got something wrong: much effort went into market research, programme development, getting the right venue for drop in, the right advertising and editorial coverage in local newspapers, and word-of-mouth referral wherever possible. Everything was done to coincide with the introduction of the smoking ban in Scotland, but people did not engage so we had to go back to the drawing board.

Consequently, we have had to focus more on the areas where we are pushing at an open door – and this tends to be responsible employers who assist by taking on the administrative burden of arranging the logistics of getting staff to come along to the sessions. Once there, it is down to us to engage the individuals in the process or journey of quitting. This is more about excellent facilitation than expertise (although also important) in the subject, as we want to support the individual, who after all is the only person who can ever be an 'expert' in their own quit attempt. We hope to revisit the high street model, but in the meantime, we are focusing on growing our business and marketing our service to people by trying to create delighted customers. Hopefully, if they are delighted, they will quit smoking somewhere along the way too. We are also in the process of creating a community model on a voluntary basis funded by profits made from corporate clients. Indeed, corporate clients are very receptive to the idea that for every three or four corporate classes we run, we can afford to run one free of charge in an area of deprivation. And if that does not work, we will try something else!

References

Hastings G. and McLean N. (2006). Social marketing, smoking cessation and inequalities [Editorial]. *Addiction*, **101**: 303–304.

Milne E. (2005). NHS smoking cessation services and smoking prevalence: observational study. *British Medical Journal*, **330**: 760.

Parrott S. and Godfrey C. (2004). Economics of smoking cessation. *British Medical Journal*, **328**(7445): 947–949.

Roberts D. and Woods C. (2006). Changing the world on a shoestring: the concept of social entrepreneurship. *University of Auckland Business Review*, **8**(1): 45–51.

Truby H., Baic S., deLooy A., Fox K.R., Livingstone M.B.E., Logan C.M., Macdonald I.A., Morgan L.M., Taylor M.A. and Millward D.J. (2006). Randomised controlled trial of four commercial weight loss programmes in the UK: initial findings from the BBC "diet trial". *British Medical Journal*, **332**: 1309–1314.

West R. (2005). Presentation at the *UK National Smoking Cessation Conference*, London, 9–10 June.

Lessons learned

1. The Quit&Save social marketing campaign demonstrates how the fourth P, 'promotion', need not be limited to conventional promotion channels such as advertising, PR, media advocacy, information materials, direct mail, etc. In this case, relationship marketing was used to communicate the benefits of quitting smoking. This word-of-mouth strategy demonstrates that, in certain cases, non-traditional approaches to promotion can be particularly effective.

2. Consumer orientation places a strong emphasis on the consumer at the heart of all processes, and is a key component of both social marketing and traditional marketing campaigns. In the case of the Quit&Save social marketing programme, a bottom-up empowerment approach where the lay person is involved in solving the problem was used. This strategy is very different from a top-down, health professional service delivery approach.

3. Social marketing interventions seek to change behaviour. The current case demonstrates how smoking cessation programmes do not need to be solely treatment based. Instead, by engaging the individual to explore and examine their own smoking habits, the Quit&Save social marketing campaign demonstrates how a smoking cessation intervention can be driven by behaviour change.

Case study questions

1. **Q:** Using the existing NHS Health Scotland smoking cessation programmes as an example, explain why a top-down, service delivery

approach to quitting smoking has largely been unsuccessful in getting programme participants to quit over the long term.

A: A top-down, service delivery approach to quitting smoking, such
as the UK NHS service, uses a one-size-fits-all method for smoking
cessation. Not only does the approach rely on service delivery versus behaviour change, but little flexibility is provided to meet the
needs of each and every individual smoker.

2. Q: Describe the three operational sectors at which the Quit&Save
products are aimed.

A: (i) Community-based services: drop-in clinic model delivered in a
community setting by ex-smokers. (ii) Corporate services: services
offered in the workplace, including smoking policy assistance. (iii)
Commercial services: pay-based services for individuals and
groups involving smoking cessation workshops or seminars.

3. Q: Explain the financial cost of the Quit&Save programme for corporate and community operational sectors.

A: Corporate clients will pay for the programme if they save financially from getting staff to quit. On the other hand, community-
based services will be subsidized or funded by external bodies.

CASE STUDY 10

Physicians Taking Action Against Smoking

François Lagarde, Michèle Tremblay and Violaine Des Marchais

1. Introduction

Physicians Taking Action Against Smoking was a five-year intervention programme introduced by the *Direction de la Santé publique de Montréal* (Montreal Public Health Department) in 1998 to improve the smoking cessation counselling practices of general practitioners (GPs) in Montreal (Quebec, Canada). Programme development was guided by the precede–proceed model, as well as by behaviour-change models. The programme was an integral component of a comprehensive province-wide initiative for smoking prevention, protection and cessation, which calls for health care professionals, and physicians in particular, to deliver smoking cessation interventions (Tremblay *et al.*, 2001). This case study describes how social marketing principles were applied in the development of this initiative.

2. Problem definition

Smoking is considered one of the worst enemies of public health, because its consequences are devastating. In fact, half of all regular smokers die of a smoking-related illness and half of these individuals will die in middle age (between 35 and 69 years) (Doll *et al.*, 2004). At the time of the project design, an estimated 12000 Quebecers (3000 Montrealers) died every year from smoking-related causes. Yet over one-quarter (26.9%) of Montrealers aged 12 years and up were still smoking in 2000–2001 (Statistique Canada, 2002).

The health benefits of smoking cessation are well established, and physicians are acknowledged as the health care providers of choice for provision of cessation counselling (Fiore, 2000). However, according to a Health Canada survey (1995), only 41% of smokers who consulted a doctor during that year said that the doctor had advised them to quit smoking. Clearly, many doctors do not make the most of the opportunity to advise patients who smoke to quit smoking.

3. Contextual analysis

This programme was introduced in a favourable social and policy environment. Many provincial, national and international medical and governmental agencies had established policy positions recommending that general practitioners engage in smoking cessation counselling. In addition, the Quebec public health sector introduced many tobacco control initiatives, including mass-mediated campaigns and smoking cessation challenges. Two other significant events that could influence patient demand for smoking cessation support arose at the time the programme was introduced: in August 1998, a new smoking cessation drug called Zyban was introduced on the market and, in October 2000, smoking cessation therapies were included in the public drug insurance plan (with a medical prescription only).

4. Aim and objectives

The overall aim of the Physicians Taking Action Against Smoking initiative was to optimize smoking cessation counselling practices among general practitioners (GPs) in Montreal. More specifically, the behavioural objectives were to have GPs:

- Determine the smoking status of all their patients aged 9 and over
- Enter the information in the patient's file
- Motivate smokers to quit smoking and provide them with actionable information.

5. Formulation of strategy

The social marketing plan developed to achieve these objectives is summarized in Table CS10.1.

6. Resources

The programme was developed and implemented by a project team composed of three public health doctors, with input from an internal communications professional, a social marketing consultant, an advertising agency and an internal evaluation team. The human resources required for the intervention were the equivalent of one full-time public health doctor. The modest annual out-of-pocket budget was approximately CAN $34 000.

Table CS10.1 The social marketing plan

Strategic component	Marketing plan
Audience segmentation	The programme focused on GPs who were *not actively engaged in smoking cessation counselling* but who would be relatively *easy to convince* if we managed to eliminate their real and perceived barriers. The initiative consisted of identifying barriers that hindered smoking cessation counselling and adapting the programme to overcome the barriers. The main barriers identified were patients' lack of interest and compliance, as well as physicians' lack of time and cost (no refund on therapies). The project team agreed that the programme should provide doctors with quick and simple counselling tools, along with interesting and appealing documentation and a full range of interesting resources in the area to help patients quit smoking. A separate segment of more reluctant GPs could potentially be reached when provided with proof of a clearly demonstrated new social norm founded on the increased adoption of desired practices by the priority segment.
Product strategy	The desired behaviours were made as simple as possible to address barriers – and particularly the time required. Based on formative research, the recommended practices and support materials were designed to ensure that the call to action could be accomplished within (but not limited to) approximately two minutes. The other significant enabling factor identified in the literature was the physicians' perceived ability to communicate, listen and establish a relationship with patients, while providing effective smoking cessation counselling. To that end, interactive workshops (of 1–2 hours) were held and involved discussion of clinical cases. A list of constantly updated local resources that GPs could recommend to patients was drawn up. Guidelines were also developed with and confirmed by several medical health organizations.
Price strategy	A key incentive for encouraging the desired behaviours is the financial reimbursement to physicians for smoking cessation counselling. The *Direction de Santé publique de Montréal* worked with numerous stakeholders to advocate for a provincial policy that would enable physicians to bill for smoking cessation counselling. The policy was adopted in 2006 by the *Régie de l'assurance-maladie du Québec* (RAMQ). Physicians had to order programme materials, but they were available free of charge.
Promotion strategy	Between 1997 and 2000, the following promotional activities were held: two 30-minute medical conferences on smoking cessation counselling, an advertising campaign in professional journals, a personalized direct marketing campaign to all GPs, a word-of-mouth recruitment strategy, 11 articles on smoking cessation counselling in the most widely distributed and popular professional interest journals in Quebec. Patient materials were made simple and attractive (in a format that looked like a cigarette pack). Partnerships with several medical and health organizations were established to provide further credibility to the programme. An annual public advertising campaign ran to encourage smokers to ask their GP for advice on smoking cessation.

7. Evaluation and outcomes

Two cross-sectional surveys were conducted to monitor trends in the smoking cessation practices of Montreal GPs, as well as trends in factors related to counselling (Tremblay *et al.*, 2001). The first survey was conducted between April and July 1998, and the second between April and September 2000. Data were gathered through self-administered mailed questionnaires, which included socio-demographic characteristics, beliefs and attitudes related to cessation counselling, self-perceived ability to provide effective smoking cessation counselling, perceived importance of selected barriers, and use of counselling behaviours relevant at each stage of readiness to quit.

Results from the surveys showed that more positive changes were noted among female than male GPs between 1998 and 2000. More specifically, the percentage of female GPs who felt that GPs should schedule specific appointments to help patients quit smoking increased from 1998 to 2000. Ratings for two of the three indicators of self-perceived ability to provide effective counselling improved by approximately 12–16% respectively among female GPs, and the perception of the importance of several barriers to cessation decreased (e.g. perceived lack of patient education and perceived lack of impact on patients). However, the perceived importance of lack of time as a barrier to counselling increased over time among both male and female GPs.

The greater changes among female GPs and their increased involvement in smoking cessation counselling relative to male GPs is consistent with the results of previous research, which indicates that women are more likely to be involved in patient education (Woodward *et al.*, 1996). Results also suggested that male GPs may focus attention on patients who are at a more advanced stage of readiness to quit. The introduction of new products and incentives (such as access to nicotine replacement therapy and reimbursement for smoking cessation counselling) will likely encourage more GPs (particularly male GPs) to engage in educational efforts aimed at improving their smoking cessation counselling skills.

References

Doll R., Peto R., Boreham J. and Sutherland I. (2004). Mortality in relation to smoking: 50 years' observations on male British doctors. *British Medical Journal*, **328**: 1519.

Fiore M.C. (2000). A clinical practice guideline for treating tobacco use and dependence. *Journal of the American Medical Association*, **283**: 3244–3254.

Health Canada (1995). *Survey on Smoking in Canada: Cycle 4*. Ottawa: Health Canada.

Statistique Canada (2002). *Enquête sur la santé dans les collectivités canadiennes 2000–2001*. Statistique Canada.

Tremblay M., Gervais A., Lacroix C., O'Loughlin J., Makni H. and Paradis G. (2001). Physicians Taking Action Against Smoking: an intervention program to optimize smoking cessation counselling by Montreal general practitioners. *Canadian Medical Association Journal*, **33**: 601–607.

Woodward C.A., Hutchison B.G., Abelson J. and Geoffrey N. (1996). Do female primary care physicians practise preventive care differently from their male colleagues? *Canadian Family Physician*, **42**: 2370–2379.

Lessons learned

1. The Physicians Taking Action Against Smoking social marketing case study is a good example of how the fourth P, 'promotion', can encompass many different activities: skills training, advertising, direct marketing, word of mouth, public relations, patients' materials and partnerships.

2. This case demonstrated that social marketing is not limited to individual behaviour change, but it can also be applied to the policymaking process. Indeed, as part of the price strategy to address the cost of adoption, the *Direction de Santé publique de Montréal* (in conjunction with key stakeholders) played a key role in the adoption of a provincial policy to enable physicians to bill for smoking cessation counselling.

3. A key strength associated with the Physicians Taking Action Against Smoking social marketing campaign was the use of a multi-disciplinary team of professionals to implement the intervention: public health doctors, a communications professional, as well as a social marketing consultant.

Case study questions

1. **Q:** Briefly describe three characteristics that helped to make the social and policy environment favourable to the Physicians Taking Action Against Smoking intervention.

   A: (i) Policy recommendations that GPs engage in smoking cessation counselling were established among medical and government agencies at local, national and international levels. (ii) The public health sector in Quebec introduced many tobacco control initiatives. (iii) Zyban was introduced as a smoking cessation drug. (iv) Smoking cessation therapies were included in the public drug insurance plan.

2. **Q:** Describe the target audience for the current case study.

   A: The target audience included GPs that were not engaged in smoking cessation counselling. This audience was considered easy to convince if real and perceived barriers (e.g. patients' lack of interest and compliance, as well as physicians' lack of time and cost) were addressed.

3. **Q:** Using the product strategy in the Physicians Taking Action Against Smoking intervention as an example, describe how the perceived time and communication barriers to physicians informing patients about smoking cessation services were addressed.

   A: Support materials were developed that allowed physicians the flexibility to complete the call of action in a simple and timely manner. Training workshops were also organized to further enable physicians' abilities to communicate, listen and establish a relationship with patients.

CASE STUDY 11

The challenges of using social marketing in India: the case of HIV/AIDS prevention

Sameer Deshpande

In India, 5.7 million adults and children were estimated to be living with HIV/AIDS in 2005, an increase from 5.3 million in 2003. The number of adults and children who died due to HIV/AIDS during the same period was in the range of 270 000–680 000 (UNAIDS, 2006). The primary driver of the epidemic is heterosexual activities between commercial sex workers (CSWs) and their male clients, including truck drivers and migrant workers, who then spread it to their housewives and/or lovers.

Since the mid-1990s, there has been a strong effort to create awareness and promote behaviours that would prevent HIV/AIDS infection and stem the epidemic. Since a cure to HIV is expensive, long and not completely effective, preventing the infection is a superior option. Due to these reasons, HIV/AIDS efforts have been more or less on the preventive end. However, social marketers have faced numerous problems and challenges in this effort. This report discusses the key problems and challenges that social marketers have faced while addressing male groups such as truck drivers, migrant workers, youths and men from the general population; these are categorized into individual factors, the immediate environment and the wider environment.

Several individual characteristics pose challenges to social marketers. Approximately 55% of the entire Indian population is not aware of HIV/AIDS (Chattopadhyay and McKaig, 2004). Due to both the lack of discussion about sexual matters and the lack of sex education in the society, male groups do not have the proper knowledge about what causes, prevents and cures AIDS. For example, several male groups also believe that condoms should be used only when having sex with a CSW and not with a trusted friend or good-looking person. Even among those who are aware, regular condom use remains low (Chattopadhyay and McKaig, 2004). There are numerous reasons for this.

First, condoms are considered to interfere with sexual pleasure. Second, the hard, unpredictable and risk-prone lifestyle creates a sense of helplessness and, combined with acculturated fatalism, high-risk groups such as truck drivers, migrant workers and slum youths lack the motivation to practise safe sexual and drug use. Third, they continue to deny the severity and the susceptibility to HIV/AIDS and thus avoid paying attention to prevention campaigns. Instead, they consider others to be more susceptible to HIV infection. Rural youths, for example, consider it to be an urban problem, street children believe it to be an adult problem and housewives think it affects only men, while men from the general population believe truck drivers and migrant workers are at risk. Men do not readily perceive the preventive benefits of condoms, since these benefits are not immediate and are never obvious – making it difficult to promote safe sex practices (Singhal and Rogers, 2003).

Fourth, being a patriarchal society, Indian men impose their manhood by discouraging women to wear condoms (Chattopadhyay and McKaig, 2004), thus exposing housewives and CSWs to risks of HIV infection (Singhal and Rogers, 2003). CSWs fear that insistence on condom usage could result in loss of clientele and monetary gains (Chattopadhyay and McKaig, 2004). Even if male groups are aware and convinced about condom use, their distribution has been far from effective. Condoms are still largely sold in urban areas, through chemist shops and not through mainstream retail outlets, which limits consumer access to condoms. The availability is especially low in critical areas such as brothels in Mumbai. Retailers also avoid displaying condoms prominently.

Other than poor condom usage, the issue of prejudice against people living with HIV/AIDS (PLWHs) also poses challenges to social marketers. PLWHs experience severe discrimination at the workplace, by the community and many times by their own families. Being a moralistic society (Singhal and Rogers, 2003), Indians in general believe that people who get infected indulge due to immoral behaviours and deserve this penalty. Thus, high-risk individuals are not willing to test themselves for HIV and/or to declare themselves as HIV-positive due to fear of discrimination and rejection (Singhal and Rogers, 2003). This has resulted in underreporting of HIV prevalence in India (Solomon *et al.*, 2004).

Existing stigma against PLWHs and the discomfort with sexual matters creates an unfavourable environment for social marketing campaigns. For example, the Balbir Pasha Campaign in Mumbai – which aimed to create awareness that, although men may have sex with only one CSW, she may have numerous regulars – was criticized for its frankness ('bringing the bedroom into the living room'), thus negatively impacting on its effectiveness.

In addition to individual and societal barriers, the wider environment also presents its own set of challenges. The geographical and population size as well as socio-cultural and economic diversity, combined with lack of resources, makes the task of conducting HIV/AIDS prevention efforts in India very difficult (Solomon *et al.*, 2004). India supports 16% of the world's population over 3.3% of the total land area (Observer Research Foundation, 2001–02). However, the resources do not match the population size. A substantial amount of the population lives in absolute poverty and one-quarter of the population cannot afford an adequate diet (Solomon *et al.*, 2004). Although in recent years the economy has grown rapidly and poverty has been reduced (Dhongde, 2004), the growth has been uneven. Rich states such as Maharashtra and Tamil Nadu, which have witnessed an economic boom, attract migrant workers leaving their wives behind in rural areas, thus attracting CSWs and the resulting HIV/AIDS epidemic.

Lack of resources also influences the state of health care in India. According to a report by the Confederation of Indian Industry–McKinsey (2002–03), only 15% of the total population is covered by any form of insurance. Furthermore, government spending on health care is low (0.9% of GDP), resulting in poor infrastructure. India has 1.5 beds and 1.2 registered physicians per 1000 people as compared to 4.3 and 1.8 in countries like China and Brazil respectively. In addition to poor coverage and infrastructure, the purchasing of health care is inefficient (because 60% of health care delivery is financed by out-of-pocket spending) and the delivery of health care is undertaken mostly by the private sector, which puts a financial burden on the individual seeking medical aid. These factors limit the extent of government coverage and negatively impact health outcomes – for example, the majority of PLWHs lack access to anti-retrovirals and other forms of medical support (Singhal and Rogers, 2003).

Other macro factors such as illiteracy, socio-cultural diversity and corruption also create barriers to HIV/AIDS prevention efforts. India is struggling to achieve a respectable literacy rate, currently standing at 52% (Observer Research Foundation, 2001–02). The female literacy rate of 39% is alarming, since it is inversely related to fertility rates, population growth rates and other important social indicators (Sharma, 2000). India is a hugely diverse country with long-standing traditions – for example, 24 languages are spoken by at least a million people (Solomon *et al.*, 2004), combined with numerous religious practices and lifestyles. It is difficult to create campaigns that can address a sizeable group in any part of the country. India also suffers from widespread corruption at all levels of government. In the past, these corrupt practices have created distrust towards any government contraceptive social marketing campaigns among Indian consumers.

Government efforts have also suffered from other weaknesses (Chattopadhyay and McKaig, 2004). By denying the existence of the HIV/AIDS epidemic, the government and the country lost valuable time and opportunity to address the problem in its early stages. Furthermore, the government has tended to centralize campaign management, thus creating huge bureaucracy, inefficiency and stifling of individual efforts (Singhal and Rogers, 2003). The current government prevention policy also lacks clarity on how to reduce socio-cultural barriers and increase acceptance of condoms. Adman Alyque Padamsee provides an example:

> 'The government condom, Nirodh, acted as a deterrent to sex, because as soon as you thought of Nirodh, you lost your erection! If you lose your erection, you can't put on a condom. The logic is simple, but nobody seemed to have stumbled upon it. So I said, "How can the male think of the condom as a pleasure enhancer?" Nobody wants to sit down to a sumptuous meal, and then be told that you have to take medicine before it kills your appetite.'
>
> (Mazzarella, 2003, p. 65)

NGOs, on the other hand, have lacked the expertise and the resources to develop effective campaigns, since they rely on both in-house marketing programmes and donated commodities (Armand, 2003). This is reflected in a variety of ways. For example, NGOs in India, especially those funded by the Department for International Development (DFID), failed to develop a strategic approach, lacked knowledge about secondary audiences, failed to sensitize the community to gain general support, and used limited numbers of media materials and creative abilities. Campaigns have also been criticized for their emphasis on knowledge rather than behaviour change, for failing to use peer educators as outreach workers (Singhal and Rogers, 2003) and for poor choice of media. Finally, the materials lack research rigour, since they were not adequately pre-tested or evaluated. In response to these weaknesses, attempts have been made to partner with commercial enterprises to market contraceptives (Armand, 2003). While these campaigns may have been effective in the short term, once the partnership contract ended, commercial partners have tended to revert back to their earlier practices to increase prices, reduce the distribution coverage and focus on the higher income sections of society.

In conclusion, even if male groups are aware of benefits, critical individual and societal barriers discourage them from practising safe sex. Wider environmental factors also pose challenges that intertwine with the individual and societal barriers, and present a very messy situation for social marketers. This case study has tried to illustrate that unless these real-world complexities are recognized and worked upon, social marketers will not succeed in their HIV/AIDS prevention efforts in India.

With thanks to Family Health International for their four 2001 reports on HIV/AIDS-related studies conducted in the State of Maharashtra and Population Services International for their 2003 report on the Balbir Pasha case study.

References

Armand F. (2003). *Social Marketing Models for Product-Based Reproductive Health Programs: A Comparative Analysis*. Washington, DC: Commercial Market Strategies.

Chattopadhyay A. and McKaig R.M. (2004). Social development of commercial sex workers in India: an essential step in HIV/AIDS prevention. *AIDS Patient Care and STDs*, **18**(3): 159–168.

Confederation of Indian Industry–McKinsey & Company (2002–03). *Healthcare in India: The Road Ahead*.

Dhongde S. (2004). *Measuring the Impact of Growth and Income Distribution on Poverty in India*. Online: http://www.economics.ucr.edu/seminars/fall04/10-27-04.pdf (Accessed 4 August 2006).

Mazzarella W. (2003). *Shoveling Smoke: Advertising and Globalization in Contemporary India*. Durham, NC: Duke University Press.

Observer Research Foundation (2001–02). *Observer Statistical Handbook*.

Sharma R.C. (2000). *Communication and Advocacy Strategies: Adolescent Reproductive and Sexual Health (Case Study: India)*. Bangkok: UNESCO.

Singhal A. and Rogers E.M. (2003). *Combating AIDS: Communication Strategies in Action*. New Delhi: Sage.

Solomon S., Chakraborty A. and D'Souza-Yepthomi R. (2004). A review of the HIV epidemic in India. *AIDS Education and Prevention*, **16**(Suppl. A): 155–169.

UNAIDS (2006). *2006 Report on the Global AIDS Epidemic*, UNAIDS 10th Anniversary Special Edition.

Lessons learned

1. The current case demonstrates that health cannot be viewed solely in terms of individual behaviour; it also needs to be considered in terms of broader social and environmental factors. Without a doubt, social marketers working in the field of HIV/AIDS in India need to examine how individual, societal and wider environmental factors contribute to this epidemic.

2. The government of India is a major player in addressing the HIV/AIDS problem. This case shows that not only is it necessary for key government officials to acknowledge the serious health issue of HIV/AIDS in India, but the centralized campaign management also needs to be addressed. Clarity should also be established in the government prevention policy with regards to addressing the socio-cultural barriers that play a key role in the acceptance of condom use.

3. As outlined in the case, previous HIV/AIDS prevention efforts in India have not used basic social marketing principles such as clear behavioural goals, consumer orientation and research to guide programme planning and implementation.

Case study questions

1. **Q:** What is the primary driver for the spread of HIV/AIDS in India?

   A: The primary driver of the HIV/AIDS epidemic in India is heterosexual activities among commercial sex workers and their male clients, who are often truck drivers and migrant workers, who then spread HIV to their housewives and/or lovers.

2. **Q:** Describe three individual factors that contribute to the spread of HIV/AIDS in India.

   A: (i) Inhibitions about discussing sex. (ii) Negative attitudes to condoms. (iii) Prejudice towards people living with HIV/AIDS.

3. **Q:** Describe three challenges from the wider environment that contribute to the spread of HIV/AIDS in India.

   A: (i) Financial burden on individuals seeking medical aid due to a large monopoly of privatized health care. (ii) Alarmingly low literacy rates, which are inversely related to a variety of social indicators. (iii) Diversity of the culture in India in terms of language, religious practices and lifestyles, making it difficult to design wide-reaching prevention campaigns.

CASE STUDY 12

The case of the evolution of the March 21 Anti-Racism social marketing programme[1]

Judith Madill and Frances Abele

1. Introduction

The Canadian Heritage March 21 Anti-Racism programme was set up in 1988 by the Canadian Government to respond to the United Nations' International Day for the Elimination of Racial Discrimination. The over-all goal of the programme is to reduce and eliminate racism in Canadian society. In the early years, the goal of the programme was more focused on raising awareness concerning racism and to educating Canadians (mainly youth) about the negative impacts of racism on society. In later years, the goal of the programme was more focused on eliminating behaviours related to racial discrimination.

   This case illustrates how a large-scale Canadian social marketing pro-gramme – the 'March 21 Canadian Heritage Anti-Racism Campaign' mor-phed over a 12-year period from its inception as a public education programme until the turn of the millennium in 2000, when it had become a fully fledged social marketing programme.

2. The evolution of the March 21 Campaign from public education to social marketing

The programme's evolution was characterized by two important phases or stages – Phase I: Getting Started: The Public Education Years 1988–1993 and Phase II: The Shift from Public Education to Social Marketing 1994–1999.

   In the early years, the programme designers really had not heard of social marketing, and designed and implemented a public education programme.

[1] This case is based on an article to be published by the authors (Madill and Abele, forthcoming, 2007).

Over time, the ideas of social marketing began to surface and diffuse, and the managers of the programme adopted many of the social marketing ways of thinking and approaches. A number of highlights emerged over each phase, as outlined below.

Consistency and change

Management and staff remained highly committed to the goals of eliminating racism in Canada. Many of the tools and approaches used to achieve these goals shifted.

Discernible phases

The March 21 Campaign began in 1989 as a relatively conventional public awareness programme and at the beginning of its inception distribution channels concentrated on the public sector, educational institutions and NGOs. However, the programme expanded its reach each year. In the mid-1990s it defied early expectations by expanding activities and adopting more social marketing tools, motivated largely by the straitened circumstances of a period of Federal Government cutbacks and a widespread review of all programmes under the purview of the Federal Government of Canada. Nonetheless, many of the elements designed and introduced during the early public education phase continued on throughout the 1990s, even as the language and tools of social marketing began to appear in the programme materials, strategy and evaluation documents.

Social marketing techniques and practices evolved

Over time, social marketing principles (and the language of social marketing) were incorporated in the Campaign, so that by 1999–2000, many of the most important features of a social marketing approach were integral to the programme's activities. From its inception, the March 21 Campaign shared some characteristics of a social marketing campaign (such as the aspiration to change behaviour as well as attitudes). After 1994–5, programme staff made more extensive and more self-conscious use of social marketing techniques. The incentive for increased adoption of social marketing appeared to be twofold:

1. Increased expectations regarding the reach of the programme accompanied by a period of significant resource constraints. Under these conditions, senior managers became more aware of the concept and approaches of social marketing and viewed it as attractive in these circumstances.
2. The first external evaluation of the programme showed many elements of success within the context of a public education programme. This external evaluation made recommendations to adopt social marketing

approaches. The social marketing features that were incorporated included increased emphasis on clear and specific target identification as well as increased development of marketing strategy around all of the four Ps, with the exception of pricing.

Development of strategy and thinking around the four Ps

More extensive distribution approaches were developed, as well as considerable development of all aspects of promotion. For instance, distribution grew from the public sector, educational institutions and NGOs to include the private sector. This allowed the reach of the programme to be extended through the development and distribution of promotion items (i.e. Benetton re: T-shirts, Royal Bank re: posters, Roots, etc.) by the private sector. Distribution channels also became more intensive, including a 1-800 phone number and website. The promotion element became more sophisticated and messages more actionable on the part of targeted groups. Professional advertising agency assistance was engaged to develop promotional messages and making messages more consistent over time, and between different media types, such as radio and television.

In the early years, product was conceived as consisting of posters, brochures and competitions that promoted the message of working together and building inclusive communities. In social marketing frameworks, these are regarded as promotional vehicles rather than as products. As social marketing ideas, tools and thinking began to take hold, the notion that the product was intangible (anti-racist behaviour on the part of Canadians) began to take hold. Furthermore, recognition that one needs to try to understand the benefits consumers are really seeking (Andreasen and Kotler, 2003, p. 313) began to be observed. Products and promotional vehicles were designed with the needs of specific target markets in mind (i.e. it was recognized that if teachers were going to request and utilize kits designed to conduct school projects and videos involving discussion of the benefits of inclusion of all racial groups in schools and communities, developing such products to meet the specific needs of teachers was required).

Also, during the mid-1990s, March 21 began to be recognized and referred to as a brand. Multi-year consistency was considered as important in supporting this brand. The symbol of the raised hand started to become a symbol associated with the March 21 brand. Terms such as 'positioning' began to be observed within the strategy documents referring to product strategy.

As discussed previously, the development of relationships/partnerships increased markedly and attempts at partnership development incorporated both organizations from public sectors as well as the private sectors. Indeed, partnerships became a key cornerstone of the March 21 programme in the face of declining government resources. Examples of new partners included the Canadian Teachers' Federation, Canadian Broadcasting Corporation, Much Music, Musique Plus, The Royal Bank,

Benetton, Roots Panasonic, Sympatico (not after 1998), Tribute Teen, Famous Players, Vik Recording and the Canadian Film Centre.

The use of marketing research increased and evaluation became more embedded in the campaign over time. Eventually, an increase in the use of marketing research resulted in a shift in the promotion messages – members of ethnic groups felt the softer images were inappropriate and idealistic. This led to changes in the product and the accompanying images, which became much harder. Market research also showed the need for stronger branding.

Some social marketing practices are still absent

As discussed previously, some of the major social marketing features that are still absent include:

- Explicit definition of the nature of the proposed exchange(s) with the target market (although the notion of clearly identifying an explicit exchange with the target market is emerging, the benefit to targeted groups for engaging in anti-racism behaviours is still not explicitly a part of the strategy).
- A clear understanding of the pricing component and the development of a strategy concerning price.
- Consistent tailoring of products and communication to specific target markets and further development of a strategic plan.

How social marketing was diffused

One of the key agents of change was outside consulting groups engaged by the programme management to provide evaluation of the programme and recommendations for future strategy development. Several key managers within the unit managing the March 21 Campaign (the Multiculturalism Secretariat) also acted as change agents in promoting the adoption of social marketing. These managers organized training for managers in the unit on the broader topic of marketing generally and how it could be used in the Secretariat, as well as social marketing specifically. One manager in the unit in the mid-1990s had some professional training in marketing, but the majority of the managers and staff within the unit were not highly knowledgeable about marketing or social marketing. However, management and staff were more than willing to use these tools to achieve goals within their unit.

This case study shows that the March 21 programme began as an internally funded Canadian Federal Government public education programme that gradually took on many (but not all) of the characteristics of a social marketing programme. This study suggests that it may be possible for a social marketing programme to evolve from a more traditional public education campaign. However, even after 12 years, a number of the important characteristics of a social marketing programme were still absent from the March 21 programme. Lack of understanding of social marketing on the part of senior management may still exist and this may explain why several key aspects of social marketing are still missing. It is also possible that programme managers do not believe that all elements of a social marketing programme are appropriate in the context of a government-sponsored anti-racism programme.

References

Andreasen A.R. and Kotler P. (2003). *Strategic Marketing for Nonprofit Organizations*, 6th edition. Upper Saddle River, NJ: Prentice-Hall.

Madill J. and Abele F. (forthcoming in 2007). From public education to social marketing: the evolution of the Canadian Heritage Anti-Racism social marketing program. *Journal of Non Profit and Public Sector Marketing*, **17**(1/2).

Lessons learned

1. The March 21 Anti-Racism programme demonstrates that public education approaches can evolve into successful social marketing strategies and, in doing so, they do not need to undergo drastic changes. In the case of the March 21 Anti-Racism programme, key elements designed and introduced during the early programme planning phases were incorporated throughout the programme's evolution.

2. Partnerships can play a fundamental role in programme success. As described in the March 21 Anti-Racism programme, by expanding partners to include not only the public sector, educational institutions and NGOs, but also the private sector, distribution channels became wider reaching.

3. The use of branding and positioning by social marketers can be significant for relationship building. The March 21 Anti-Racism programme did just that. By increasing its recognition and brand orientation through the use of symbolic meanings, such as the raised hand, the programme demonstrated that it was evolving from its original inception of simply a public awareness approach to a social marketing programme rooted in meaningful relationship building.

Case study questions

1. **Q:** What two incentives contributed to adopting a social marketing approach for the March 21 Anti-Racism programme?

   A: (i) Increased awareness of the concept of social marketing during a period of significant programme resource constraints. (ii) Recommendations from the first external evaluation to adopt more social marketing approaches.

2. Q: Describe how the use of marketing research helped to improve the March 21 Anti-Racism programme.

 A: Marketing research helped shift the promotional messages to those more consistent with ethnic group ideologies. Market research also shed light into the need for the programme to have a stronger brand position.

3. Q: Identify the three social marketing characteristics that are still absent from the March 21 Anti-Racism programme and identify how programme managers may have contributed to these absences.

 A: (i) Lack of explicit definition of exchange for anti-racism behaviour among targeted groups. (ii) Underdeveloped pricing strategy. (iii) Lack of consistency in tailoring products and communication efforts for target markets. These absences may have been caused by the lack of understanding of social marketing on the part of senior management or from programme managers questioning the appropriateness of including all elements of a social marketing approach in a government-sponsored anti-racism programme.

CASE STUDY 13

The World Anti-Doping Agency: the case of barriers to the adoption of social marketing[1]

Norm O'Reilly and Judith Madill

1. Introduction

Sport plays an important social and economic role in virtually every country of the world. Examples of the influence of sport globally range from the estimated 3.7 billion people from over 220 countries who watched in excess of 36 billion hours of television coverage of the 2000 Summer Olympic Games from Sydney, Australia (IOC, 2000), to the 60.3% of men and 39.7% of women who attended sporting events in 2002 in Canada, to estimates that 35 million people worldwide played at least one round of golf in 2000 (World Golf Foundation, 2004). At the national level, countries use sport to promote nationalism (Palmer, 2001) and there are endless examples of star athletes who influence millions of people as role models in their local markets (Shanklin and Miciak, 1996).

Sport currently faces an enormous threat from doping. In recognition of this threat, numerous sport organizations and governments from around the world founded (1999) and continue to support the World Anti-Doping Agency (WADA) and its mission to eradicate doping from sport. WADA was formed with a 'somewhat unique' structure based on equal representation of the Olympic Movement and public authorities, with a funding model of 50% provided by the Olympic Movement and 50% provided by various governments around the world (Pound, 2004). WADA defines doping as 'the occurrence of one or more of the anti-doping rule violations' (WADA, 2003) as outlined in eight articles of its World Anti-Doping Code. These rules are broad, including 'the presence of a prohibited substance or its metabolites or markers in an athlete's bodily specimen' (WADA, 2003), 'tampering, or attempting to tamper, with any part of doping control' (WADA, 2003), and 'administration or attempted administration of a prohibited substance or prohibited method to any athlete, or

---

[1] This case study is based upon an article by the authors (O'Reilly and Madill, forthcoming).

assisting, encouraging, aiding, abetting, covering up or any other type of complicity involving an anti-doping rule violation or attempted violation' (WADA, 2003).

Doping and anti-doping and sport

Improving performance is inherent in the nature of competitive sport. Throughout the history of sport, athletes, trainers and coaches have applied various methods towards improving athletic performance. Some approaches have been legal (i.e. nutrition, training practices, coaching, equipment improvements) while others have been illegal (i.e. drug use, blood doping, bribery). One of these aspects that has been deemed 'illegal' and in need of sanction is doping, or the use of performance-enhancing substances and techniques. The movement to eliminate doping is known as 'anti-doping' and it has required some element of control ever since Thomas Hicks won gold in the 1904 Olympic marathon with the help of a dozen raw eggs, injections of strychnine and doses of brandy adminis-tered to him during the race (WADA, 2004a).

Target markets: high-performance sport

Sport, as an industry, is not homogeneous and this is particularly import-ant from an anti-doping perspective. The segment of sport that is most likely to be impacted by doping is the high-performance stream of sport. High performance refers to sport where performance is the principal goal (i.e. Olympic Games, professional sport), as opposed to development or participation. This stream is not limited to just elite international athletes; it also includes any athlete who is on the 'track' to high performance, beginning at quite young ages depending upon the sport. In practical terms, the stream includes varsity athletes, national-level athletes, devel-opment-level athletes and participation-level athletes in high-perform-ance training environments with the objective of achieving performance success (i.e. junior national athletes). An important point is the consider-ation of the athlete's entourage (e.g. coach, trainer, family, doctor, masseuse, etc.) as part of the equation. WADA's programmes must target an athlete and their entourage.

2. WADA: current strategy and approaches to behaviour change

WADA's business activities include conducting unannounced out-of-competition doping control among elite athletes, funding scientific research to develop new detection methods, observing the doping control and results management programmes of major events, and providing anti-doping education to athletes, coaches and administrators. WADA has a physical presence in four cities: headquarters in Montreal, Canada, and regional offices in Lausanne, Switzerland, Tokyo, Japan and Cape Town, South Africa.

WADA works through National Olympic Committees, government authorities and National Anti-Doping Organizations (NADOs) to administer its programmes. In terms of funding, WADA's 2004 budget is based on US $21 438 000, of which $10.1 million comes from the Olympic movement, $10.1 from public authorities, as well as $1.2 million from other sources (WADA, 2004b).

WADA's *raison d'être* is to eradicate doping from sport, which involves changing behaviours at many levels in over 200 nation states and dozens of sports. WADA's 2004 budget reveals that sanctions (law) and education are WADA's priority. Of the 2004 budget of $17 304 220, $10 507 400 (or 61%) is allocated to administration, finance, salaries, regional offices and operations, including research. The remaining $6 796 820 (or 39%) is allocated primarily (34%) to sanctioning (law) initiatives and secondarily (5%) to educational pursuits. WADA's 2004–2009 strategic plan further demonstrates WADA's focus on the legal and education approaches to social change. Also, the tenants of WADA's World Anti-Doping Code are strongly rooted in, primarily, the law and, secondarily, education as ways to affect behaviour change.

3. Social marketing: barriers to use at WADA

The social marketing literature suggests that eight barriers influence the adoption of social marketing, seven of which have had a significant role in limiting the consideration of social marketing as part of WADA's overall strategy to social change (Table CS13.1).

4. The potential role of social marketing in WADA strategy

A social marketing strategy offers the potential to complement educational and legal approaches to behaviour change, both at WADA and for broader application. A number of potential roles for social marketing can be considered:

1. Doped athletes may experience 'negative demand' where they may not see a problem with their doping behaviour. Negative demand

Table CS13.1 Barriers to the adoption of social marketing

No.	Barrier	Source	Description	WADA situation
1	Reliance on education and the law as approaches to social change	Rothschild (1999)	Need to show relevance of social marketing as a complement to education and the law.	Analysis of WADA documents described previously support this barrier.
2	There is a difficulty in distinguishing social marketing from education	Rothschild (1999)	Education can suggest an exchange but cannot deliver the benefit of the exchange explicitly. Targets must figure out how to meet their own needs.	'Yes [we consider our education programmes to be a form of social marketing], because they are designed to alter behaviour and bring about certain outcomes' (comment by WADA CEO).
3	Managers lack formal marketing training	Rothschild (1999)	Lack an appreciation for the self-interest of the client, the benefits of an exchange, and an understanding of power and competition.	'Less than 10% [of WADA's directors and managers have formal marketing training]' (comment by WADA CEO).
4	The ethics of social marketing	Rothschild (1999)	Trade-off between the rights and responsibilities of the individual and the society.	No related comment.
5	There is a lack of appreciation of social marketing at top management levels	Andreasen (2002)	Research has shown acceptance of social marketing primarily at the practitioner level.	'I haven't the faintest idea [what social marketing is]' (comment by WADA CEO).
6	The field has poor 'brand positioning' and some perceive it as manipulative and not 'community based'	Andreasen (2002)	Fuzzy image, no clear definition and no differentiation from other approaches to change.	No related comment.
7	There is a lack of formally documented and publicized successes	Andreasen (2002)	There is a need to demonstrate the effectiveness of social marketing, superior to its alternatives.	No evaluation and evidence available at WADA.
8	Social marketing lacks academic structure	Andreasen (2002)	There is a lack of courses, programmes, faculties and journals.	'Not as such but I don't often get into that level of curriculum' (comment by WADA CEO when asked 'are you aware of any universities that offer courses in social marketing?')

Barriers adapted from Rothschild (1999) and Andreasen (2002).

means that the doping athlete has no need or want for changing his/her behaviour (i.e. an exchange, in marketing terms, will not take place). Marketing would encourage a doping athlete to recognize the significant 'costs' of their doping behaviour. Such costs might include potential health risks as well as the risks associated with a positive doping test. The damage that would follow from experiencing a positive doping test may include the termination of one's career, the disgrace and loss of prestige and status, loss of potential and/or current sponsors and government support. Further, in losing one's career or incurring a suspension, the athlete's concept of self is significantly altered and/or damaged.

2. A marketing strategy would develop a programme to enhance the benefits that could accrue to an athlete who engages in anti-doping behaviours. Benefits might include not experiencing a positive doping test and reducing health risks (presently and in the future). The marketing approach would require that marketing research be done to understand what drives an athlete to adopt an anti-doping approach (both the costs of doping and the benefits of anti-doping), as well as the best ways to reach this group. Such information would be used to design marketing strategy.

3. Marketing would be used to complement the legal and education approaches currently being used by WADA. Akin to smoking, it is possible that a doped athlete may downplay the risks of doping to their health. Used in collaboration with education, a marketing approach would undertake marketing research to truly understand athletes' thinking concerning the risks and rewards they face, leading to strategy based on this understanding. Marketing, in conjunction with a legal approach, will ensure the athlete understands that all athletes who dope will get caught. This is a critical point because the athletes who engage in anti-doping behaviour, as well as those who currently dope, need to be assured of a level playing field. Marketing can play an especially critical role in this context – education and legal approaches probably cannot succeed on their own.

4. Adoption of social marketing will enhance or clarify thinking about the WADA 'product'. A social marketing framework positions the WADA product as 'anti-doping behaviour'. An important part of what athletes want in engaging in anti-doping behaviour is a level playing field – the understanding that no competitors in any country or at any competitive level will be doping. Therefore, an effective testing procedure is necessary, making it part of the product of WADA.

5. At least two major competitors to WADA's product (including both the alternate behaviour (doping) and commercial marketing, which fosters an environment where performance is highly valued) exist. Innovative strategies to behaviour change (that legal and educational approaches cannot offer) are required to compete effectively. For example, personal selling as a social marketing tactic to convince athletes to change to (or continue) doping-free behaviour could be implemented by former top athletes following training in social marketing.

References

Andreasen A. (2002). Marketing social marketing in the social change marketplace. *Journal of Public Policy and Marketing*, **21**(1): 3–13.

International Olympic Committee (IOC) (2000). *The Sydney 2000 Olympic Games*. Report online at http://multimedia.olympic.org/pdf/en_report_249.pdf

O'Reilly N. and Madill J. (forthcoming). The World Anti-Doping Agency: the role of social marketing. *Journal of Non Profit and Public Sector Marketing*, **17**(1/2).

Palmer C. (2001). Outside the Imagined community: Basque terrorism, political activism, and the Tour de France. *Journal of the Sociology of Sport*, **18**(2): 143–161.

Pound R. (2004). In-depth CEO interviews, Montreal, Quebec, 16 March and 7 April.

Rothschild M. (1999). Carrots, sticks, and promises: a conceptual framework for the management of public health and social issue behaviours. *Journal of Marketing*, **63** (October): 24–27.

Shanklin W.L. and Miciak A.L. (1996). Selecting sports personalities as celebrity endorsers. *Journal of Promotion Management*, **4**(1): 1–11.

World Anti-Doping Agency (2003). *The World Anti-Doping Code*; http://www.wada-ama.org

World Anti-Doping Agency (2004a). *A Brief History of Anti-Doping*; http://www.wada-ama.org

World Anti-Doping Agency (2004b). *WADA 2004 Budget*; http://www.wada-ama.org

World Golf Foundation (2004). *Industry Report*; http://www.golf2020.com

Lessons learned

1. The adoption of social marketing as a behaviour-change tool faces a number of barriers. In the current case, social marketing was given limited consideration for WADA's overall strategy due to a number of factors: reliance on education and law, grouping education programmes in the same category as social marketing, inadequate managerial training in social marketing, lack of managerial knowledge about social marketing, few formally documented successes, and a lack of academic structure.

2. One of the prevalent discrepancies in social marketing is an assumption that it is analogous with education. As outlined in the current case, although education can suggest an exchange, the target audience must engage in their own pursuits of the benefits or punishments associated with behaviour change. On the other hand, social marketing incorporates the use of product, price, place and promotion to facilitate an explicit exchange.

3. Another main challenge with social marketing is the limited knowledge and training of basic social marketing principles. In the case of WADA, because top managers may not appreciate social marketing and a lack of social marketing training at both the managerial and academic levels exists, social marketing risks being properly implemented.

Case study questions

Take the position of the Executive Director of WADA. You and your education committee (there is no formal social marketing structure currently) are discussing how to improve your strategies and tactics given the continued growth in funding and support from governments and the sporting community. The topic of social marketing comes up as a potential strategy to embark upon. Many are interested, many do not understand what it is and many are hesitant as they express concerns over its effectiveness and, more importantly, the time-frame to effectiveness. Many questions emerge:

1. What do you do?
2. Can social marketing work here?
3. Think of your targets. How diverse are they? Can they all be reached?
4. If you were to include a social marketing effort, what would you do? Where do you start?

CASE STUDY 14

Using the Internet to reach upstream and downstream in social marketing programmes

Josephine Previte

1. Introduction

Typically, social marketing's domain is dealing with 'problem people', which results in many social marketers 'telling people what's right and wrong' in their lifestyle practices. This case study takes a different approach by outlining how not-for-profit organizations in Australia are using Internet technology to engage and empower youth to make positive social change. This is not to say that the Internet is the panacea for dealing with social problems that affect young people. Rather, the aim of the case study is to illustrate that the Internet is more than just a simple information channel. The following case study demonstrates how the characteristic features of the Internet (i.e. interactivity, accessibility, anonymity and online sociality) have been used to facilitate persuasive strategies targeting a young person's progress towards positive behaviour change and/or to mobilize individuals and community groups to advocate for structural change to improve society.

2. Problem definition

Social marketers primarily think of the Internet as an information source (Previte, 2006). This is a narrow conceptualization of the Internet, which limits its strategic application to targeting behaviour change. In addition to its information characteristics, the Internet also offers diverse forms of interactive transactions and participation. New styles of proactive engagement with youth audiences online have been adopted by innovative not-for-profit organizations in Australia.

The following discussion draws on two Internet-based social change strategies: ReachOut!, an online information, support and referral service programme established in 1998 in response to rising rates of youth suicide in Australia; and Bursting the Bubble, a campaign launched in 2003 during the 'Week without Violence' event, which targeted teenagers experiencing incidences of domestic violence against their mother or stepmother, and other experiences of 'direct' physical, emotional or sexual abuse from a parent or caregiver (McKenzie, 2005).

3. Stakeholder and competitor analysis

In Australia a variety of individuals, business and social service organizations, and government institutions influence young people's health and well-being. Many of these public and private sector organizations have an online presence and make information available online to youth audiences. They have established a presence online because the Internet is a site where much needed information and assistance about social and personal issues is in a format that appeals to young people. As the ReachOut! website explains, the Internet offers an anonymous and stigma-free way to get help, explore issues and to discover how other young people have got through difficult times.

In commercial marketing competitors are more easily defined; this is not as simple for health and social marketers. Online and offline, two competitor types can influence the youth audiences who engage in ReachOut! and Bursting the Bubble.com. First, there are competitors defined by beliefs and values that generate disagreement and conflict in society (Donovan and Henley, 2003). The freedom to publish and act anonymously has encouraged hate groups and fundamentalist organizations to build a presence online. The negative influence of these organizations can be countered through online and offline media providing responsible reporting of suicide and domestic violence issues. Second, there are competitors in terms of socio-cultural beliefs and values; many of these competitors sustain unhealthy lifestyles and behaviours that inhibit societal well-being (Donovan and Henley, 2003, p. 182). For example, societal beliefs about the submissive role of women in society contribute to sexual and physical violence against women, and beliefs that economic factors and market forces have priority in Australia inhibit community welfare allocations to social services organizations that aim to support young people. These competitor forces need to be taken into account when developing online social marketing.

4. Setting realistic Internet aims and objectives

Both ReachOut! and Bursting the Bubble.com share a similar overall aim: to increase the number of young people seeking support. It is unrealistic to assume that this aim can be met simply through online exchanges at the organization's website. To this end, both organizations promote offline social services and national telephone helpline services to respond to young people in crisis. At Bursting the Bubble.com, the service information provided online includes more than a simple list of service names and telephone numbers, and also provides links and information about the organization. This is important because organizational values influence the support provided to young clients. For example, different solutions may be offered to a young woman escaping violence when seeking support from a feminist women's service, compared to religious funded organizations.

5. Formulation of strategy

Three major campaign strategies – to educate, motivate and advocate (Donovan and Henley, 2003, p. 12) – are used in the following section to illustrate the role of the Internet in online social marketing. Education and persuasion are aimed at downstream individual behaviour change. Advocacy is an upstream strategy that focuses on socio-political action, which can be used to mobilize individual policymakers and/or community groups to change social structures that negatively impact young people.

Educational strategies focus on the provision of information – facts, figures and dispassionate information – to assist the target audience in making informed choices. For example, on the ReachOut! website (http://www.reachout.com.au), young people can download fact sheets about health and social issues. On Bursting the Bubble.com, online competitions and quizzes use 'cool' graphics as an interesting way to pass on factual information using entertainment as a tactic to engage and create information exchanges with youth audiences (DVIRC, 2005).

The ReachOut! website was originally launched in response to a target audience of young people aged 16–24 at risk of suicide. Over time, a secondary audience, of young people experiencing life challenges (e.g. depression, eating disorders, etc.) has also been reached. They have achieved this through exploiting the interactive potential of the Internet to persuade young people to engage in dealing with life challenges by talking about the problems they are experiencing. Storytelling and 'scream it/dream it' are online tactics that motivate explicit actions in the target audience. Young people can self-select relevant information in an appropriate format and personalize their online presence. This makes the ReachOut! website a safe place that they return to frequently. Storytelling can also improve dissemination of the social and/or health message by making the issues discussed less confronting and more realistic to the target audience, because the message is delivered via a credible source (i.e. ReachOut!) using the language and experience of the target audience. A young person who has used Bursting the Bubble.com illustrates this point in stating:

> 'What I liked about this website is that people express their feelings and I don't feel alone – there are people like me'.
>
> (DVIRC, 2005)

Figure CS14.1
The ReachOut!
website is a web-
based mental health
service that provides
information,
support and
referrals to help
young people get
through tough
times.
Source: ReachOut!

Online advocacy is typically integrated with offline strategies to drive policy change. Recently, DVIRC has used its website to drive a 'call to action' in government to change its approach to domestic violence campaigns. At the website they have criticized the government's entrenched educational approach focused on public awareness campaigns. DVIRC is advocating a new approach to violence prevention, which positions strategies on reducing the incidence of domestic violence by 'building healthy relationships'. This is different to the Australian Government's characteristic approach, which concentrates on violence *after* it has occurred (DVIRC, 2006).

6. Research and evaluation

Evaluation of online social marketing involves more than reporting the number of 'hits' a website achieves at a certain time. A recent evaluation

Figure CS14.2
Storytelling and 'scream it/dream it' on the ReachOut! website.
Source: ReachOut!

of Bursting the Bubble.com revealed that their online campaign has motivated young people to seek help and support. For example, 72% of young people who participated in the evaluation stated they would use the information to act on violence happening to them or someone else at home. Other recommendations for using social change websites to motivate young people included:

- Selective use of illustration – avoid exaggerated or self-conscious use of graphics. One focus group participant pointed out: 'A lot of government websites, they're trying too hard … They have bad cartoons and stuff.'
- Tone is important and organizations should not try too hard to achieve a tone that *might* appeal to young people. A self-conscious use of 'cool' and other youth nomenclature can disengage a teen audience.

7. Outcomes

The Internet is being used successfully in ReachOut! and Bursting the Bubble.com to motivate the youth audience to seek help and social support. Their success is based on active engagement of the target audience, and providing opportunities via the building of long-term relationships between the target audience and the not-for-profit organization. Building and sustaining relationships is a core strategy for ReachOut!. They achieve this by providing programmes where ReachOut! participants elect to become

Figure CS14.3
The Bursting the
Bubble.com
website.
Source: http://www.
burstingthebubble.com
with permission from
the Domestic Violence
and Incest Resource
Centre.

'youth ambassadors' for the programme, and participate in decision making, developing new ideas for the service and promotional activities.

The Internet offers social marketers an opportunity to build new and different relationships with target audiences. The progress made by ReachOut! and Bursting the Bubble.com provide exciting evidence on how social marketers can adopt and use the Internet as an integrated element in social marketing programmes that reach upstream to change agents and downstream to the individual. These campaigns also demonstrate that social marketers can move beyond campaigns that only focus on telling young people what is right and wrong in their lifestyle practices.

References

Domestic Violence and Incest Resource Centre (DVIRC) (2005). Young peoples' views on designing effective websites: learnings from Bursting the Bubble.com. Online: http://www.dvirc.org.au

Domestic Violence and Incest Resource Centre (DVIRC) (2006). Online: http://www.dvirc.org.au

Donovan R. and Henley N. (2003). *Social Marketing: Principles and Practice*. Melbourne: IP Communications.

McKenzie M. (2005). Young people's views on developing effective websites: learns from bursting the bubble.com. *Domestic Violence and Incest Resource Centre Newsletter*, **2**(Winter): 24–26.

Previte J. (2006). *Understanding Everyday Internet Experiences: Applications to Social Marketing Theory and Practice*. Unpublished doctoral dissertation, Queensland University of Technology, Australia.

Lessons learned

1. The Internet can help social marketers to build capacity and empower youth in an anonymous and stigma-free way.
2. One of the key characteristics of a social marketing campaign is that the consumer is put at the core of all social marketing processes. By tapping into the Internet as a communication vehicle that is not only appealing to youth, but also offers a channel that youth can feel comfortable using when dealing with personal issues, both the ReachOut! and Bursting the Bubble.com campaigns demonstrate a strong consumer orientation.
3. Social marketing campaigns can be particularly successful if long-term relationships are built with key target groups. In the current case, the ReachOut! and Bursting the Bubble.com campaigns were able to do just that. For example, by using youth ambassadors to participate in decision making as well as the overall programme planning of the ReachOut! campaign, a strong relationship was built between the youth target group and the not-for-profit organization.

Case study questions

1. **Q:** Discuss the two types of competition relevant to both youth suicide and domestic violence for programme participants in the ReachOut! and Bursting the Bubble.com initiatives. Give an example of how this type of competition can be addressed.
   A: (i) Online presence of hate groups and fundamentalist organizations. (ii) Problematic socio-cultural beliefs and values related to youth suicide and domestic violence. One way to address these competitive barriers is by providing responsible reporting of issues related to suicide and domestic violence using online and offline media.
2. **Q:** Describe the primary and secondary target audience that the ReachOut! website was geared towards.
   A: The primary target audience is young people aged 16–24 who are at risk of suicide. The secondary audience is young people who experience life challenges, such as depression, eating disorders, etc.
3. **Q:** Name and describe the three campaign strategies outlined in the case study.
   A: (i) Education. (ii) Persuasion. (iii) Advocacy. Education and persuasion are aimed towards downstream individual behaviour change, while advocacy is aimed towards policymakers and/or community groups in an effort to influence upstream socio-political action, such as changes in policy or social structures.

CASE STUDY 15

Be Well, Know Your BGL: Diabetes Australia's diabetes awareness campaign

Sandra Jones and Danika Hall

1. Introduction

Diabetes is a chronic disease estimated to affect over 1 million Australians. The most common and fastest growing form of diabetes is Type 2 (85–90% of diagnosed cases), which usually has its onset in adults over 45 years of age. The Australian Diabetes, Obesity and Life Study (AusDiab, 2001) found that, on average, 150 people are diagnosed with diabetes every day. The number of diagnoses is estimated to have trebled over the past 20 years, making diabetes Australia's fastest growing chronic disease (AIHW, 2002). While over 500 000 Australians have currently been diagnosed, it is estimated that at least this number again have undiagnosed diabetes (AusDiab, 2001), which equates to almost 7% of the population. It is estimated that close to 2 million Australians will have diabetes by 2010. The complications and consequences of diabetes are severe, and it is rated as the seventh highest cause of death in Australia (AusDiab, 2001).

2. The Be Well, Know Your BGL campaign

Diabetes Australia is a not-for-profit organization that provides resources and assistance for people with diabetes, including research, services and products. It also acts as an advocacy service, and aims to create greater public awareness of the disease, its causes, impacts and prevention. Be Well, Know Your BGL was a national awareness campaign launched by Diabetes Australia on 14 July 2002.

The Be Well, Know Your BGL campaign was designed by the New South Wales state branch of the organization, in line with the key goals of Diabetes Australia and the National Diabetes Strategy 2000–2004. It built on the 2000 Community Awareness Diabetes Strategy (CADS), which created general awareness regarding Type 2 diabetes. The evaluation of CADS identified the need for more specific community messages, a sense of urgency and a call to action – specifically, to communicate to at-risk people the need to know their blood glucose level (BGL) to detect diabetes or, ideally, as an important step in preventing its onset.

The Be Well, Know Your BGL campaign did not receive federal funding, despite an approach by Diabetes Australia in April of 2002. Diabetes Australia spent $AUD167 000 on the campaign, while corporate sponsorship from Alphapharm and Abbott Australia plus in-kind sponsorship provided an additional $AUD200 000.

According to Diabetes Australia, the key message of the campaign was:

> 'Just as people accept the need to know their cholesterol and blood pressure, they should know their blood glucose level – which is an indicator of their health.'

This message was directed to the general public, but more importantly to those with one or more of the following risk factors:

- Over 35 years with Aboriginal, Torres Strait Islander, Chinese, Indian or Pacific Islander heritage
- Over 45 years with family history of diabetes
- Over 45 years and overweight or with high blood pressure
- All other Australians over 55 years
- Previous heart attack or heart disease
- Overweight and suffered polycystic ovarian syndrome
- Previous gestational diabetes.

The campaign proposal also identified general practitioners and health professionals as important partners in the campaign, as well as 'gatekeepers' to the screening process. The campaign aimed to provide these groups with tools and support for the early diagnosis, prevention and ongoing management of diabetes.

Be Well, Know Your BGL comprised four phases: Phase 1 targeted general practitioners (GPs) and health professionals; Phase 2 comprised the actual launch of the campaign, targeting the general public via the mass media; Phase 3 was the mass media advertising campaign targeting at-risk groups; and Phase 4 included a handful of outdoor advertisements to maintain general public awareness.

The marketing mix

While Diabetes Australia did not formally consider the four Ps in their campaign proposal or evaluation, they can be deduced from the campaign proposal and have been set out in Table CS15.1.

Target audience segmentation

In the Be Well, Know Your BGL campaign, Diabetes Australia segmented their market by the measure of those most at risk of diabetes. This

Table CS15.1	Application of the four Ps	
Product	Core	Being well, taking control of your health.
	Actual	BGL, which is a measurement or indicator of health.
	Augmented	BGL can help to diagnose risk of diabetes, so checking your BGL can provide early prevention, diagnosis and management.
	Branding	BGL is branded as a common and important indicator of health, like blood pressure or cholesterol level.
Price	Action	Visiting the general practitioner or health practitioner and arranging a blood test.
	Financial	The price in financial terms depends on the billing policy of the GP or health professional, but generally would be small.
	Non-financial	The non-financial cost included time and effort in making appointments, travelling to surgery and pathology clinic, waiting times, consultation times, follow-up requirements.
	Psychological and physical	There may also be psychological and physical costs, including pain in having blood taken, fear of diagnosis.
	Negative outcomes	An important price to consider would be a high BGL reading and lifestyle changes relating to that, or a subsequent positive diabetes diagnosis and ongoing management and lifestyle changes that may then be required.
Place	Distribution channels	Patients are recommended to obtain their BGL via their GP or other health professional, who provides a referral to a local pathology clinic plus follow-up.
	Controlling channels	Kits seeking cooperation of GPs and health professionals were mailed or taken directly by sponsoring pharmaceutical company representatives, and while cooperation was assumed it was not guaranteed.
Promotion	Four-phase campaign	BGL was promoted via a general awareness mass media campaign (detailed activities outlined in the text), including television and radio advertising, outdoor advertising and public relations, plus direct marketing to general practitioners and health professionals, and the provision of point-of-purchase advertising to patients.

included the estimated 500 000 Australians currently suffering undiagnosed diabetes, plus people with one or more of the various risk factors previously outlined. They also targeted current (diagnosed) diabetes sufferers and those who know they are at risk as secondary markets. Ideally, in this type of campaign, the primary and secondary markets would be further segmented and targeted in more specific ways. Kotler and Roberto (1989) recommend specific marketing efforts or activities for each market segment. For example, the National High Blood Pressure Education Program in the United States (1997) divided their target groups into those that were aware of their hypertension and those unaware; for the latter group, they further segmented using demographics. They then designed specific advertising campaigns targeted to demographic groups, e.g.

younger African-American males (Roccella, 2002). Diabetes Australia acknowledged the need for dedicated campaigns for special groups such as Indigenous Australians and Torres Strait Islanders, but state that the campaign ran as 'an "umbrella" campaign designed to cover all Australians'.

Diabetes Australia also identified family and friends and the general community as secondary target markets. These secondary markets, however, could be more accurately seen as having special roles to play in relation to the primary target market's behaviour (Jones and Rossiter, 2002). For example, the general community, family and friends may initiate or influence an at-risk person to see their GP or health professional. The GPs and health professionals, considered partners in the campaign by Diabetes Australia, can also be seen as important initiators and influencers in the decision-making process.

Ideally, in social marketing practice, once target markets have been segmented and the key role players defined, action objectives should be assigned (Jones and Rossiter, 2002). Franklin (2000) stresses that social marketing objectives should be specific, measurable, achievable, and in line with the organization's mission and other objectives. While the objectives previously outlined by Diabetes Australia were in line with organizational goals and that of the National Diabetes Strategy, more specific and measurable behavioural objectives were not devised for the primary target market and for secondary audiences such as influencers.

Creative idea and execution tactics

The Diabetes Australia campaign made use of an emotional portrayal in their television and radio advertisement, and this creative concept carried through most of their print material. The portrayal comprised a man and woman in their mid-forties discussing BGL in a typical Australian social setting. Jones and Rossiter (2002) stress the importance of the target audience identifying with the characters and the genuineness of the emotional portrayal. Unfortunately, neither of the characters appeared to typify the target market – those most at risk of Type 2 diabetes with the previously outlined risk factors (overweight; Aboriginal, Torres Strait Islander, Chinese, Indian or Pacific Islander heritage; over 55 years, etc.) – and the scene itself and conversation that unfolded seemed somewhat staged.

The conversation between the two characters introduced BGL as a new brand of health indicator, where high BGL can lead to serious health problems. The motivation provided to the audience was control over low to moderate BGL and fear of a high BGL. The use of a fear appeal, according to Kotler and Roberto (1989), can be effective as it can help target markets realize that they are at risk and therefore adopt the desired behaviour. Unfortunately, however, the television advertisements failed to target those most at risk and may consequently have motivated the wrong group (people in their early forties who are not overweight and already concerned or proactive with respect to their health). The commercial continued with the man modelling the desired behaviour of discussing his BGL with his GP. The commercial demonstrated the desired behaviour to be achievable, and it was described as 'easy' in the conversation between the two characters; however, it failed to overcome many perceived barriers of the target market, such as price considerations (e.g. fear of diagnosis and the subsequent need for medication and/or substantial lifestyle changes).

Interestingly, the pre-testing of the television commercial by a focus group found that 86% of the at-risk group found 'a message to be clearly communicated'; however, there is no reference in their findings as to what they perceived to be the message. Importantly, 80% of the at-risk group said they 'would ask about their BGL at their next visit to the GP', while 93% said they 'wanted to know more about BGL'.

3. Evaluation

Diabetes Australia conducted post-launch surveys to evaluate the effectiveness of the campaign; however, these surveys were only available via the Diabetes Australia website that featured the campaign material or at Diabetes Australia branch offices, where there was also considerable campaign material available. For this reason, it is doubtful that the surveys measured the effectiveness of the mass media campaign on the target population. There are no figures relating to the number of web surveys completed; however, the Research Report described that 50% of respondents already had diagnosed diabetes and were evenly spread over all age groups. The web survey found that 83% of respondents had heard of BGL. Of those who said they had seen the campaign material, 64% said they saw the television commercial, 15% saw media coverage of public relations activities, 11% via the Diabetes Australia website, while the remaining 10% spoke with health professionals.

Diabetes Australia plans to conduct further evaluation into the effectiveness of the campaign via general practitioners and monitoring registrations with the National Diabetes Services Scheme. They plan to build further on their campaign and the branding of BGL over the next three years.

4. Conclusion

While Diabetes Australia consider the initial Be Well, Know Your BGL campaign to be an outstanding success, there are several areas that could be improved in the campaign planning, execution and evaluation in light of best practice in social marketing. Achievable and measurable objectives should be developed, and should be formally and scientifically evaluated at the conclusion of the campaign. The target market needs to be more carefully segmented and advertising material needs to be tailored to each segment. Finally, additional resources would be required to ensure a more controlled and effective implementation of the campaign, as well as a thorough evaluation of the campaign components to increase the likelihood of success of future campaigns.

References

AusDiab (2001). *Australian Diabetes, Obesity and Life Study & Associated Disorders in Australia 2000*. International Diabetes Institute, and Department of Health and Ageing.

Australian Institute of Health and Welfare (AIHW) (2002). 'Introduction'. *Diabetes: Australian Facts 2002*; available at: http://www.aihw.gov.au/publications/cvd/daf02/daf02-c01.pdf

Franklin D. (2000). *Social Marketing for the New Millennium: A practical, 'do-it-yourself' manual for non-government organizations and community and voluntary associations*. Sydney: The Australian Youth Foundation.

Jones S.C. and Rossiter J.R. (2002). The applicability of Commercial Advertising Theory to social marketing: two case studies of current Australian social marketing campaigns. *Social Marketing Quarterly*, **8**(1).

Kotler P. and Roberto E.L. (1989). *Social Marketing, Strategies for Changing Public Behaviour*. New York: The Free Press.

Roccella E.J. (2002). The contributions of public health education toward the reduction of cardiovascular disease mortality: experiences from the National High Blood Pressure Education Program. In *Public Health Communication: Evidence for Behaviour Change* (Hornik R.C., ed.). Mahwah, NJ: Lawrence Erlbaum Associates.

Lessons learned

1. In addition to the traditional four Ps social marketing mix, an additional P – 'people' – can also encompass the mix. For instance, as part of the marketing strategy, training can be provided to intervention delivery agents. In the case of the Be Well, Know Your BGL campaign, the campaign aimed to provide general practitioners and health professions with tools and support for early diagnosis of diabetes, prevention and ongoing management.

2. Good social marketing objectives are considered to be measurable (e.g. easily evaluated) and realistic (within the organization's capabilities). In the case of the Be Well, Know Your BGL campaign, objectives were consistent with those of the National Diabetes Strategy; however, none were developed to measure the campaign impacts on the primary and secondary audiences in order to properly evaluate the programme.

3. Both primary and secondary target markets were identified for the Be Well, Know Your BGL campaign. A potential campaign improvement would be to further segment the target markets in order to adequately tailor key communication materials for specified segments.

Case study questions

1. **Q:** Describe the weaknesses with the Be Well, Know Your BGL creative concept and execution tactics present in the television, radio and print materials.

A: The characters did not adequately resemble the target market, and both the scene and conversation were not considered realistic. For instance, the television advertisement specifically failed to target those that were the most at risk for getting diabetes and may have actually motivated the wrong group of people.

2. **Q:** What type of cost did the Be Well, Know Your BGL television advertisement fail to address?

   A: The advertisement failed to address the psychological and physical costs to diagnosis, such as fear of diagnosis, need for medication and lifestyle changes.

3. **Q:** Given one of the weaknesses of the Be Well, Know Your BGL campaign is that the target audience could have been more carefully segmented, if you were given the opportunity to further segment the primary target market, how would you do so?

   A: As an example, those most at risk could be further segmented based on ethnicity, such as Aboriginal, Torres Strait Islander, Chinese, Indian or Pacific Islander heritage. Campaign materials could then be designed to specifically appeal to different ethnic groups.

CASE STUDY 16

Development of a primary school curriculum for the control of trachoma in Tanzania

Chad MacArthur and Manisha Tharaney

1. Introduction

Helen Keller International (HKI), an international non-governmental organization (NGO), and the World Health Organization (WHO) collaborated to develop a methodology for the design and implementation of a primary school curriculum to increase knowledge and change behaviours among schoolchildren to help protect them and their families from the blinding disease of trachoma. The goal of the project was stated as such: to develop a global model for the design and implementation of a school curriculum for the effective prevention of trachoma. The main objectives were: (1) to design an effective curriculum for the elimination of blinding trachoma and (2) to ensure that the methodology could be replicated in other countries with a minimum of adaptation.

This case study describes the process implemented in the East African country of Tanzania to develop this model and the eventual integration of the resulting curriculum into the national primary-level school curriculum.

2. Problem statement

Trachoma is the largest cause of infectious blindness in the world, affecting the very poor living in rural areas with limited access to water and sanitation. Endemic in 55 countries, 84 million people are estimated to be affected by the active form of the disease and over 7 million have been blinded.

The active infection is particularly common among children aged 1–9 years. Repeated infections throughout childhood lead to inflammation and scarring of the conjunctiva lining the underneath part of the eyelid. The scarring leads to the turning in of the eyelid, a condition known as trichiasis, in which the eyelashes begin to rub and eventually abrade the cornea of the eye, causing intense pain and leading to irreversible blindness.

To control trachoma and to eliminate it as a cause of blindness, the WHO has endorsed the SAFE strategy, an integrated strategy with four components to prevent, control and treat the disease. These components are S for the Surgical correction of trichiasis, A for treatment of the active disease with Antibiotics, F for Face washing as the main behaviour to prevent infection and interrupt transmission, and E for Environmental change, which looks at increasing access to water (to support face washing) and promoting the construction and use of latrines.

As active disease is most common among 1- to 9-year-old children, school health offers an opportunity to reach a large number of this target group to educate and develop the necessary life skills that will help these children prevent being infected themselves, as well their families and communities. The F and E components of this strategy are particularly conducive to being taught in the classroom, focusing on increasing students' knowledge of the disease and practising the appropriate behaviours, particularly face washing and latrine use.

Tanzania is one of the most highly endemic countries in the world, with an estimated 1–2 million children bearing the active infection. Tanzania, however, has a primary school enrolment rate of 70%, enabling a large proportion of the target group to be reached through schools.

3. Competitive analysis

In international development, sustainability of initiatives requires governments and other stakeholders to eventually assume responsibility of the programmes, incorporating them into their own strategic plans as well as in their annual budgets. Like many developing countries, Tanzania has a plethora of different health issues to confront and is assisted in this by various NGOs vying for government attention and buy-in to their programmes. In the health arena, trachoma competes against a number of diseases, including HIV/AIDS, tuberculosis, malaria and malnutrition.

4. Stakeholder analysis

HKI conducted a situational analysis of the national school health programme, as well as the national efforts to eliminate trachoma as a blinding disease. Through this analysis, the key stakeholders were identified. They included the Ministry of Health (MOH), the Ministry of Education and Vocational Training (MOEVT, formerly the Ministry of Education and Culture), the Tanzania Institute of Education (TIE) and the National Eye Care Programme (NECP). The International Trachoma Initiative (ITI), an NGO dedicated to the control and elimination of trachoma, was also identified as a potential partner. From the analysis, the TIE was recognized as the key player in this process, as it is responsible for all curriculum development and review throughout the country. The TIE's involvement was motivated by its institutional mandate, its desire to partner with an international NGO and the possible resources that such a partnership might bring to the table. Like many government institutions in the developing world, adequate budgets to meet the needs of their constituents are sorely lacking. The other stakeholders were more passively involved, though recognizing that such an initiative would assist in meeting their own organizational objectives, i.e. the strengthening of school health programmes and the control of trachoma.

5. Formulation and implementation of strategy

Prior to initiating country-level activities, the implementers from the WHO and HKI and two external experts in childhood education and behaviour change developed a matrix outlining the key aspects of trachoma on one axis, with knowledge, attitudes, skills, policy (policies needed by the school or system to support trachoma control) and indicators on the other axis.

This matrix was the only externally driven component of the project. It was recognized that for the curriculum development process to be successful, the need for ownership of in-country partners would be critical and that a curriculum imposed from the outside would not be sustainable. As education has a strong cultural component, it was also then necessary for Tanzanians to do the actual development.

In Tanzania, a technical workshop was organized of curriculum developers from the TIE, representatives from the Ministries of Health and Education at national and regional levels (Dodoma and Singida regions), as well as NGO partners and representatives from the local offices of the WHO and UNICEF. The matrix was presented to the participants to be filled out as described above. The completed matrix then served as the basis for the development of the actual curriculum.

A stakeholders meeting was originally planned to garner more buy-in from a broader spectrum of organizations and individuals, but it was found to be impossible to gather the necessary people at one time due to competing demands on many of these figures' time. Person-to-person meetings were arranged and a small steering committee established with those who were closely involved in trachoma and school health.

HKI and the TIE signed a Memorandum of Understanding to formalize the collaboration of the two organizations. This document outlined the steps of curriculum development, pre-testing and teacher training. HKI remunerated the TIE for developing the curriculum and particularly the time of their developers engaged in the project.

A second workshop was then convened using the completed matrix as a guide to develop the actual curriculum. Participating in this workshop were TIE curriculum developers, HKI school health staff, school and zonal inspectors, and coordinators of the school health programme from the central regions of the country where trachoma is highly endemic and where the curriculum would be pre-tested. To accompany the curriculum, the TIE was also commissioned to develop a teacher's manual and learners' guides.

The products developed for the project included:

- The trachoma school curriculum, which consisted of a trachoma syllabus for grades I–VII and a scheme of work for teachers.
- A teacher's manual and learners' guides were developed to facilitate the teaching and learning process, and to serve as technical and resource materials. These documents were developed for each grade from I to VII. A local artist was hired to draw the illustrations for the learners' guides.
- A pre-test questionnaire and focus group discussion guide was developed to pre-test the curriculum and teachers' and learners' guides in the Kongwa district of the Dodoma region. The teachers in the district have had considerable experience teaching school health and trachoma through a previously supported school health programme and were able to provide invaluable feedback.
- A supervision and monitoring tool to assess the effectiveness of the syllabus and the ease in teachers' use.

The TIE and the curriculum team pre-tested the curriculum in Kongwa district, where teachers had already been implementing the school health curriculum. The objective of the pre-test was to solicit their feedback on the new trachoma curriculum. Based on the feedback from teachers and school inspectors, appropriate changes were made to the curriculum. The pre-testing followed the minimum TIE requirements for new curricula.

A validation workshop of the curriculum by key stakeholders was held in Dar es Salaam to finalize the changes. During this workshop, members of the project steering committee were invited to review the curriculum and provide their feedback.

6. Research

The steering committee and TIE decided that the finalized curriculum should be further tested for its effectiveness in another district of Tanzania. A number of criteria were used to select the district: prevalence of trachoma, minimum school health interventions in that district, relatively fewer number of NGOs working there. The Manyoni district in the Singida region in the central part of the country was chosen as the area for piloting. It is characterized by high school enrolment rates of 70%, but is one of the poorest districts in the country, with chronic food insecurity and frequent droughts. A prevalence survey was carried out in 30 schools in the district. Twenty schools with the highest trachoma prevalence were then chosen as a subset from the 30 schools surveyed. These 20 schools were randomly assigned to programme and control schools. In all the 20 schools, a KAP (knowledge, attitudes and practices) survey was conducted among teachers and school pupils. One year later, an endline survey was conducted.

Overall, the data showed an increase among the children in programme schools in key indicators of knowledge and practices before and after, as well as in comparison with the control or non-programme schools.

Though the differences among teachers were not as statistically strong as among children, perhaps due to the small number of study subjects, more positive changes were noted among those teachers in the programme schools.

7. Outcome of project

In Tanzania, the timing of the curriculum project was ideal as it occurred when Tanzania was in the process of reviewing its primary school curriculum. The decision by the TIE to make their new primary school curriculum competence based also fitted well with the project's needs to emphasize life skills and active learning methods to promote decision-making skills among schoolchildren.

The trachoma curriculum developed under this project has been accepted into the new primary school curriculum. As mentioned above, the timing of the project was one contributing factor, but more important was the willingness of the implementers to follow the host institution's lead, meeting its needs both technically and financially, and providing the TIE with a clear sense of ownership.

Once the new curriculum is rolled out and all teachers trained in its use, the final result of this project will be that every child living in one of the 40-plus endemic districts of Tanzania enrolled in primary school will learn about trachoma and the behaviours necessary to prevent it.

Lessons learned

1. Social marketing campaigns need to analyse the role of competing forces to behaviour change. In the case of social marketing campaigns being implemented in developing countries, often competing health messages and campaigns need to be considered. The current case outlines how a campaign for blinding trachoma in Tanzania competed with the plethora of other diseases in Tanzania, such as HIV/AIDS, tuberculosis, malaria and malnutrition.
2. It is increasingly important to consider the role of mutually beneficial relationships in a social marketing strategy. In the case of the development of a primary school curriculum for blinding trachoma, a mutually beneficial relationship was established between HKI, the WHO and the TIE. Specifically, the TIE was recognized as the important player in curriculum development and review, while the TIE was able to benefit from partnering with an international NGO in an effort to expand future resources.

3. Social marketing can be applied not only to individual behaviour change, but also to policy change. For instance, the school curriculum strategy for blinding trachoma in Tanzania included policy control as a key consideration of blinding trachoma.

Case study questions

1. **Q:** What are the various components of the WHO-endorsed strategy for control of blinding trachoma?

   A: The WHO has endorsed the SAFE strategy. (i) S for Surgical correction of trichiasis. (ii) A for Antibiotic treatment of the active disease. (iii) F for Face washing to prevent infection and interrupt transmission. (iv) E for Environmental change, which looks at increasing access to water and promoting the construction and use of latrines.

2. **Q:** Which elements of the various components of the WHO-endorsed strategy for control of blinding trachoma are particularly favourable to classroom education and why?

   A: The last two components (F and E) are favourable to classroom education because they focus on increasing students' knowledge of the disease and practise of appropriate prevention behaviours.

3. **Q:** Why was the school environment chosen as the site where prevention efforts would take place?

   A: The school environment was chosen because it was the best way to access the target group. Since the disease is active most commonly in children between the ages of 1 and 9 years, the school environment is an ideal avenue to reach this group. Also, since the primary school enrolment rate is as high as 70%, a large portion of Tanzanian children can be reached.

CASE STUDY 17

Community-based social marketing to promote positive mental health: the Act–Belong–Commit campaign in rural Western Australia

Robert J. Donovan, Ray James and Geoffrey Jalleh

1. Introduction

The Mentally Healthy WA Act–Belong–Commit campaign provides a conceptual and practical framework for health professionals to communicate with and gain the cooperation of potential partners and stakeholders for mental health promotion programmes. The campaign is based on the results of quantitative and qualitative research with community members about their perceptions of mental health, and on concepts of positive mental health as described by psychologists and others in the literature (Donovan *et al.*, 2006).

The intervention described here targets individuals to be proactive about their own mental health and at the same time targets appropriate 'partner' organizations to promote their activities as beneficial to mental health. The 'A–B–C' message provides a simple mnemonic of relevant concepts.

The campaign is being piloted and evaluated in six communities in regional Western Australia. After an initial six-month consultation period with organizations in the six communities, there was a six-month preparatory period for development of campaign materials, recruitment of staff and collection of baseline data. The campaign was launched in the six demonstration towns progressively through October and November 2005. The campaign employs one full-time or two part-time project officers in each town, and a full-time project director, a part-time research officer and a part-time administration officer in Perth, the state's capital city.

2. Problem definition

Governments in developed countries around the world are confronted with increasing rates of mental health problems and complex psychosocial disorders, such as substance misuse, violence and crime. These outcomes are associated with significant personal, social and economic costs (WHO, 2004). Using measures of disability adjusted life years, Murray and Lopez (1996) have shown that mental health disorders emerge as a highly significant component of global disease burden when disability, as well as death, is taken into account. Their projections show that mental health conditions could increase their share of the total global burden by almost half, from 10.5% of the total burden to almost 15% by 2020.

Mental health problems and disorders have significant implications in a broad range of areas (WHO, 2004). For example: depression can lead to excess alcohol consumption or drug abuse, which can then result in a vehicular accident; unresolved anger can result in violence against women partners and children, with considerable psychological and physical costs; mental problems can result in poor nutritional habits and physical inactivity; and so on.

It is now widely acknowledged that the growth of mental health problems and disorders is outstripping the capacity of mental health services to meet the demand for traditional, individually based, treatment services. This has led to growing international interest in promotion, prevention and early intervention for mental health.

3. Competitive analysis

To date, most of the 'mental health' work has been related to de-stigmatizing mental illness problems such as depression, bipolar and schizophrenia. The mental health field has not turned its attention towards preventing mental disorders or promoting positive mental health.

Positive mental health relies on people keeping physically, socially and mentally active, participating in group activities, keeping up social interactions, getting involved in community activities, and taking up causes or setting goals and achieving them. We are therefore competing with current trends in our society that contribute little to good mental health (e.g. passive, non-challenging activities), or in fact might harm a person's mental health (e.g. illicit drugs, excess alcohol).

4. Segmentation and targeting

In this campaign we targeted: (i) office holders and owners of community organizations or businesses that offered activities conducive to good mental health, to increase their awareness that the activities they provided were in fact good for participants' mental health (e.g. libraries, sporting and recreational clubs, tourism operators, volunteer associations, walking groups, educational institutions, eco-environmental groups, arts and craft groups, etc.); and (ii) individual members of communities to increase their awareness of what they could and should do to increase or maintain good mental health.

In the first year of the intervention, most organizations who became involved did so via direct contacts, briefings and organizational meetings. Hence a variety of demographic and interest subgroups were accessed through these partners (youths, young men and women, older women, sports people, theatre groups, artists, etc.). Project officers were encouraged to target individuals and groups that might be isolated or could particularly benefit from inclusive activities. However, each town set its own specific objectives.

This has resulted in some towns targeting Indigenous groups or older adults or women's networks to participate in community activities. Others have formed partnerships to increase access to sporting and physical activities for people with a disability. A third communication strategy has been the sponsorship of arts and cultural events.

5. Behavioural objectives

Given that people rarely considered what they could or should be doing for their mental health (in contrast to the salience and proactive intentions about their physical health), Donovan *et al*. (2003) concluded that a primary objective for mental health promotion in Western Australia was to reframe people's perceptions of mental health away from the *absence* of mental illness, to the belief that people can (and should) act proactively to protect and strengthen their mental health.

The specific objectives were:

1. To increase individuals' awareness of things they can (and should) do to enhance or improve their own mental health.
2. To increase individuals' participation in individual and community activities that increase mental health and reduce vulnerability to mental health problems.
3. To build cohesion in communities by fostering links between organizations around a unifying theme of positive mental health.
4. To build links between those in the community dealing with mental health problems and those in the community with the capacity to strengthen positive mental health.

Our objectives for individuals are threefold, representing the Act–Belong–Commit message:

- *Act*. Maintain or increase levels of physical activity (e.g. walk, garden, dance, etc.), cognitive activity (e.g. read, crossword puzzles, study, etc.) and social activity (e.g. say hello to neighbours, have a chat to shopkeeper, maintain contacts with friends, etc.).
- *Belong*. Maintain or increase level of participation in groups if already a member or join a group, maintain or increase participation in community events, and with family and friends.
- *Commit*. Take up a cause or challenge (e.g. volunteer for a good cause, learn a new, challenging skill, etc.).

For example, a person can *Act* by reading a book, *Belong* by joining a book club, *Commit* by becoming the secretary/organizer for the book club, or by occasionally reading challenging books rather than just 'pulp fiction'. The A–B–C project officer has assisted library staff to co-promote and organize book clubs until the library is able to continue unassisted (although still using the Act–Belong–Commit banner and mental health benefit message).

6. Formulation of strategy

Our two primary target groups were individuals ('end-consumers') and partners ('retailers'), who could not only provide access to end-consumers for messages but also provide the products we wished end-consumers to 'purchase' (i.e. adopt or participate in). A third target group was the journalists of the local media in each town, primarily the newspapers.

Our primary communication objectives related to mental health promotion literacy – for both end-consumers and community organizations. Our primary behavioural objectives were for end-consumers to increase or maintain their levels of Acting–Belonging–Committing, and for organizations to promote appropriate activities and events under the Act–Belong–Commit banner.

A media advertising and publicity campaign was developed to inform and encourage individuals to engage in activities that would enhance their mental health, while a direct approach to potential partners simultaneously encouraged community organizations offering such activities to promote their activities under a mental health benefit message.

In exchange for partners ('retailers') promoting their activities under our banner, we offered merchandise resources (T-shirts, water bottles, stickers, hats, etc.), paid advertising support and promotional expertise that many community organizations did not have. The media budget for each town was $30 000, a not inconsiderable amount in a small town. Our project officers also offered expertise in assisting community organizations apply for funding from grant bodies (e.g. government and charity arts and sporting funding bodies) in return for their partnership cooperation.

In return for our paid advertising, we expected – and generally received – good use of our press releases and coverage of local events held under the Act–Belong–Commit banner. In all such cases we attempt to make the releases interesting to the paper's readers and provide good-quality photos. Other mutually beneficial newspaper features have been negotiated in some towns (e.g. one town's newspaper features a 'club of the month', describing the club's activities and contact details, along with the Act–Belong–Commit logo and message).

7. Research and evaluation

Prior to the campaign, focus group discussions were held with a broad range of individuals about their understanding of mental health and mental

What does it mean to be mentally healthy?

It means that most of the time you feel good about yourself, good about what you do, and good about others. You enjoy the simple things in life, feel fairly optimistic about the future, and are interested in what's going on in the world.

Being mentally healthy also means you are able to cope with the normal problems and tragedies that occur in life – usually with a little help from friends or relatives when things get really tough. Good friends make the good times better and the bad times tolerable.

In this day and age when there is much to feel depressed about, it is more important than ever to do things to keep ourselves mentally healthy so we can enjoy life and cope with the demands and pressures of everyday living.

Most of the things we do to keep physically healthy are also good for our mental health like being physically active, eating a healthy diet, avoiding drugs and using alcohol in moderation.

But we can do much more for our mental health – and it's as easy as A-B-C

Act – keep mentally, physically and socially active: take a walk, say g'day, read a book, do a crossword, dance, play cards, stop for a chat ...

Belong – join a book club, take a cooking class, be more involved in groups you are already a member of, go along to community events ...

Commit – take up a cause, help a neighbour, learn something new, set yourself a challenge, help out at the school or meals on wheels ...

Being active, having a sense of belonging, and having a purpose in life all contribute to good mental health.

If you want to know more, visit www.mentallyhealthywa.org.au Phone Amberlee Laws on 9690 1674 or email Amberlee.Laws@health.wa.gov.au

www.mentallyhealthywa.org.au

Figure CS17.1
A–B–C publicity.
From Mentally
Healthy W.A.

illness (excluding the psychoses) (Donovan *et al.*, 2003). The qualitative research indicated that people rarely thought proactively about their mental health and that the term 'mental health' had connotations primarily of 'mental *illness*' (e.g. schizophrenia, psychiatry, manic depression,

depression, etc.). However, the term 'mentally healthy' had primarily positive or 'good health' connotations (e.g. alert, happy, able to cope, socially adept, emotionally stable, etc.). The campaign was therefore named the 'Mentally Healthy WA' campaign (WA: Western Australia).

The formative research delineated a number of factors that people perceived to impact on positive mental health: ranging from economic and socio-cultural factors to individual personality and lifestyle factors. There was near universal support for the concepts that remaining active (physically, socially and mentally), having good friends, being a member of various groups in the community and feeling in control of one's circumstances were necessary for good mental health. There was also widespread agreement that having opportunities for achievable challenges – at home, school or work, or in hobbies, sports or the arts – are important for a good sense of self. Helping others (including volunteering, coaching, mentoring) was frequently mentioned as a great source of satisfaction, as well as providing a source of activity and involvement with others.

Forums were held with mental health professionals to assess their reactions to a mental health promotion intervention of this type and to ensure there would be no major criticisms of the campaign by these stakeholders. Mental health professionals were supportive of the campaign, although cautious that the campaign would not increase workloads.

Community-wide impact will be assessed by benchmark (September 2005) and independent sample follow-up surveys (September 2006 and 2007) of $N = 1200$ respondents chosen randomly from the six intervention towns, and $N = 1000$ non-intervention respondents chosen randomly from the metropolitan area and non-intervention country towns. Partner organizations will be surveyed in September 2006 and 2007 to assess the impact that collaboration with Act–Belong–Commit has had on their organization, including general support, membership participation, funding applications and grants received. The intervention's impact on the health system will also be gauged in September 2007 in terms of the extent to which mental health promotion becomes a major activity of the Division of Mental Health within the Health Department of Western Australia. We have already seen the reorientation of six part-time (0.5 FTE) positions towards mental health promotion in the six demonstration sites.

Overall, the intervention activities are designed to be self-sustaining. At the end of two years intervention, we hope to leave a network of collaborating organizations in each town who have the capacity to obtain sufficient funding to maintain their activities under the Act–Belong–Commit banner, with the support of not just the Department of Health but other government sectors (such as Sport and Recreation, Conservation and Land Management, Education, Office of Seniors Interest, etc.).

8. Outcome

In the first year, we established over 40 ongoing partners across the six towns, holding co-branded major events at least once a month. Project officers have assisted a number of organizations to apply for funding and this is expected to increase substantially in the coming year.

There are no data available yet from the first follow-up community-wide survey or the partner organization survey. Where available, we are recording immediate impacts. For example, following a club-of-the-month newspaper feature for a club for mothers of pre-school children, the number of members went from around 20 (and 57 children) to about 50 (160 children). There was clearly a substantial number of mothers wanting to meet others in the same situation. Our feature not only made them aware of such a club, but provided a welcoming feel and a personal contact for the club. The newspaper performed a community service (good for its community image) and we achieved increased social connections via participation in an organization beneficial to mothers' mental health.

References

Donovan R.J., Watson N., Henley N. *et al.* (2003). *Report to Healthway: Mental Health Promotion Scoping Project*. Perth: Curtin University, Centre for Behavioural Research in Cancer Control.

Donovan R.J., James R., Jalleh G. and Sidebottom C. (2006). Implementing mental health promotion: the 'Act–Belong–Commit' Mentally Healthy WA campaign in Western Australia. *International Journal of Mental Health Promotion*, **8**(1): 29–38.

Murray C.J.L. and Lopez A.D. (1996). *The Global Burden of Disease*. Cambridge, MA: WHO.

World Health Organization (WHO) (2004). *Prevention of Mental Disorders: Effective Interventions and Policy Options*. A report of the WHO and the Prevention Research Centre.

Lessons learned

1. Positive interventions can be used to tackle an important but overlooked health problem.
2. Stakeholders and individual citizens can be successfully targeted in one programme, and this can increase its effectiveness. In particular, partner organizations were able to increase the reach of the campaign to minority and disadvantaged groups.
3. Formative research can be immensely helpful in devising interventions.

Case study questions

1. **Q:** How was the idea of positioning used in this case?
   A: The programme adopted a radical new view of mental health, defining it as a positive state of well-being, rather than the more usual absence of illness and symptoms.

2. **Q:** How was exchange used to encourage partners to participate?

   A: Local partners were offered something of real value – up to $12 000 worth of paid advertising, along with communications expertise. As a result, they were happy to deliver good publicity and PR in return. It was a genuine 'win–win'.

3. **Q:** How did formative research help?

   A: It gave a clear insight into people's current views about mental health. In particular, whilst these tended to link in with the negative framing the topic tends to have, the term 'mentally healthy' also had many positive connotations.

CASE STUDY 18

Combating obesity: eight principles for programme planners

Michael Harker, Debra Harker and Robert Burns

1. Introduction

People around the world are getting bigger (Organization for Economic Cooperation and Development, 2005). Malnutrition is affecting people at both ends of the weight spectrum. In 2000, for the first time in human history, the number of overweight people in the world equalled the number of underfed, with 1.1 billion in each group (Gardner and Halweil, 2000). Childhood obesity is a growing problem (see Case Study 7).

According to the OECD, the top three most obese member nations are the USA, Mexico and the UK. China, however, has laid claim to the 'fat capital of the world', with an estimated 200 million of the country's 1.3 billion population classified as overweight (Asia Case Research Centre, 2006).

2. Problem definition

Despite the escalating and costly obesity problem, many of the intervention strategies to combat the 'disease' over the past two decades have been unsuccessful. In her work on the impact of television on childhood obesity, Livingstone (2006, p.15) concludes that the 'effectiveness of a range of policy interventions are inconsistent or unclear'. Likewise, Flynn *et al.* (2006, p. 29), in their systematic review of the literature on obesity and intervention programmes, found that the onward and upward march of obesity is 'testament to a deficiency in obesity prevention and treatment approaches'. Flynn *et al.*'s rigorous research provides some valuable insights into some 147 programmes.

Whilst some successful programmes have been reported by Doak *et al.*, Flynn *et al.*, Livingstone and Guittard (all 2006), the aim of the most comprehensive study undertaken by Flynn *et al.* (2006) was to identify a 'best practice' programme. Regrettably, none was found. Some of the important shortcomings were:

- Inadequate and inappropriate research designs used to conduct the research

- Stakeholders were not heavily involved in programme development and evaluation, and 30% of programmes lacked 'feasibility'
- Programmes were generally of short duration and evaluation periods were short or non-existent
- Over two-thirds of interventions scored low on 'upstream investment', or government and policymaker involvement
- Less than 3% of intervention strategies took place in the home setting.

In order to get a clearer insight into the effective management of intervention strategies, the successful programmes reported by Doak *et al.*, Flynn *et al.*, Livingstone and Guittard (all 2006) were also analysed. Consideration of the 'good' as well as the 'failing' interventions has enabled us to develop a tentative, positive model for effective intervention strategies.

3. Principles for effective intervention

(i) Relevance

The factors that have a significant effect on obesity, especially in young people, need to be understood and evaluated. To date, much of the debate surrounding obesity has been based on spuriously accurate data, anecdotal evidence and dogma. There is a need for clear evidence-based data to guide decision making (Hastings *et al.*, 2003; Doak *et al.*, 2006).

(ii) Rigour

There is clear evidence that many existing programmes are methodologically flawed.

Rigorous research designs, statistical and qualitative analyses, and careful evaluation should be used to obtain results that stand up to scrutiny. There must be provision for some programmes for longer interventions and multiple measures, as well as further development of programmes to show long-term effects. Health interventions take time to take root in the minds, attitudes and norms of a culture.

(iii) Obesogenic environment

A key feature of an intervention for obesity must be to effect some change in the surrounding obesogenic environment that makes healthy choices easier. An environmental approach to obesity prevention takes all influences on obesity (individual, physical, economic, social, technical and policy) into consideration when planning an intervention. It also focuses more on the changeable aspects of an environment rather than the changeable aspects of an individual. Environment-based interventions do not tell people how to eat or exercise, or present dire warnings for non-compliance, they simply try to make it easier for people to eat, exercise and live in healthy ways.

(iv) Home foundation

It is important to involve the home setting in intervention programmes, as early behavioural habits and routines to do with food and exercise are learned there. Parents control the purse strings.

However, access to the home is fraught with difficulties and is perhaps best accessed via the school as part of the school community. It is important to note that food eaten at school is often brought from home, so that the lunchbox from home influences the school food environment greatly. Again, this reflects the importance of including a range of settings, not one in isolation. The most investigated home issue is TV watching, and some home intervention studies hold promise by demonstrating that reducing sedentary behaviours and increasing activity levels pays dividends for weight loss (Robinson, 1999).

(v) Involvement

Behaviour change is a complex and challenging process, and there is need for commitment to, and support for, the process from multiple stakeholders, including parents, siblings, teachers, clinicians, food/beverage companies and restaurants, health officials, and local and national governments.

At the programme level, it is important to involve the participants actively in the intervention so that they are taking appropriate action in a supervised, controlled and public manner.

(vi) Congruence

Intervention must take account of the person(s) in their environment to enable behaviour change to be congruent with changes in the surrounding environment.

There are three target levels for intervention in this field:

1. *Individuals*. Individual interventions are difficult to control without close supervision, and therefore are most common in clinical settings for severely obese persons seriously at risk of health deterioration.
2. *The general population*. Population intervention programmes generally focus on information, educational and facilities provision approaches to modifying diet and levels of exercise/activity. Population interventions usually stem from government/national campaign initiatives, and are funded and managed by governments or their proxies.
3. *Aggregates of individuals*. This is a middle road in terms of interventions. These usually exist already as intact formal groups (subsets of population such as schools, school class, guides/scouts/youth groups,

employee groups, parents). Outcome measures are usually the same as for population studies, but may also include psychosocial measures.

People do not live in a sterile vacuum, yet many mass and individually targeted interventions seem to ignore this fact. This growing awareness is leading to the exploration of interventional approaches that leverage Social Marketing Theory, Social Cognitive Theory and other social epidemiology theories that place a greater emphasis on the social, institutional and cultural contexts that affect an individual's behaviours.

(vii) Epidemiological framework

The need to consider the obese person as an integrated part of their obesogenic environment points the way to the epidemiological model as an appropriate basis for generating an obesity prevention intervention. The epidemiological triad of *host*, *vector* and *environment* is a traditional medical approach to looking at the origin and spread of infectious diseases. A range of epidemics have been reversed by joint general public health and individual clinical effort, including HIV/AIDS, cot death and some cancers, and non-biological ones such as smoking and car accidents.

The epidemiological model consists of three components:

- *Host*. Since the host is a person in this epidemic, host-based strategies are generally informational, educational and psychological, trying to change behaviour, self-beliefs, knowledge and attitudes. Other host factors include medical/genetic and metabolic characteristics of the person.
- *Vector*. Main vectors in weight increase are energy-dense foods and drinks with increasing portion size, coupled with low-energy expenditure through decreasing physical activity and increasing amounts of sedentary behaviours. Vector-based strategies modify eating habits, introduce healthy diets and encourage activity that is more physical.
- *Environment*. The environment is increasingly obesogenic, and strategies must try to alter that through economic, policy, cultural and social environments. Environmental changes require positive action from political and social change agents who can alter such items as food marketing rules and labelling regulations, and provide funding for physical activities and recreational facilities/equipment (Swinburne and Egger, 2002).

(viii) Enlightened accessible settings

Educational institutions are a most viable setting for controlled interventions, as they also provide links to other important settings like the home and are foci for upstream policy and regulatory input.

Ready-made group settings for interventions employing experimental and control designs on obesity, particularly focusing on dietary patterns, nutrient intake, nutrition knowledge and physical activity, are schools and similar settings, like day-care and after-school care services

(Gortmaker *et al.*, 1999; Sahota *et al.*, 2001). The Centres for Disease Control (CDC) (2001) provides an evidence-based review that recommends school-based curricula and policies to increase physical activities. School settings also permit the linkages between individuals and a range of other settings, as well as overarching policy and regulatory bodies at a regional or national level.

The multiple functions that schooling involves have been relatively ignored. Schools are a critical setting, as obesity, exercise, fitness and other health status indicators can be directly impacted in a sustained and controlled way on large numbers of children and youths. Children spend half their lives there. Good health should be part of education and learning. Schools can identify and intervene with children at risk, and by developing health in the school community strengthen, enrich and reinforce the promotion of health-enhancing behaviour in the neighbourhood outside.

The authors would like to thank the University of the Sunshine Coast and the Foundation for Advertising Research for their support of this research group.

References

Asia Case Research Centre (2006). *Traditional Chinese Medicine: Emerging Market of China*. HKU; http://www.acrc.org.hk.promotional (accessed 9 April 2006).

Centers for Disease Control (2001). *Increasing Physical Activity*. Atlanta: Centers for Disease Control and Prevention.

Doak C.M., Visscher T.L.S., Renders C.M. and Seidell J.C. (2006). The prevention of overweight and obesity in children and adolescents: a review of interventions and programs. *Obesity Reviews*, **7**: 111–136.

Flynn M.A.T., McNeil K.A., Maloff B., Mutasingwa D., Wu M., Ford C. and Tough S.C. (2006). Reducing obesity and related chronic disease risk in children and youth: a synthesis of evidence with 'best practice' recommendations. The International Association for the Study of Obesity. *Obesity Reviews*, **7**(Suppl. 1): 7–66.

Gardner G. and Halweil B. (2000). *Underfed and Overfed: The Global Epidemic of Malnutrition*, World Watch Paper No. 150. Washington, DC: World Watch Institute.

Gortmaker S., Petersen K., Wiecha J., Sobol A.M., Dixit S. and Laird N. (1999). Reducing obesity via a school-based interdisciplinary intervention among youth. *Archives of Paediatric Adolescent Medicine*, **153**: 409–418.

Guittard C. (2006). On the European Commission's Green Paper – "Healthy Diets and Physical Activities". European Parliament briefing note, Brussels.

Hastings G., Stead M., McDermott L., Forsyth A., MacKintosh A.M., Rayner M., Godfrey C., Caraher M. and Angus K. (2003). *Review of Research on the Effects of Food Promotion to Children*. Prepared for the Food Standard Agency, 22 September. Stirling: Institute for Social Marketing, University of Stirling.

Livingstone S. (2006). *Television Advertising of Food and Drink Products to Children: Research Annex 9*. Prepared for the Research Department of the Office of Communications (Ofcom), Department of Media and Communications, London School of Economics and Political Science, Houghton Street, London, 22 January.

Organization for Economic Cooperation and Development (2005). *OECD in Figures*, 2005 edition. ISBN: 9264013059; http://www.oecd.org/infigures/

Robinson T. (1999). Reducing children's television to prevent obesity: a randomized control trial. *Journal of the American Medical Association*, **282**: 1561–1567.

Sahota P., Rudolf M.C., Dixey R., Hill A., Barth J. and Cade J. (2001). Randomised controlled trial of primary school-based intervention to reduce risk factors for obesity. *British Medical Journal*, **323**: 1029–1032.

Swinburne B. and Egger G. (2002). Preventive strategies against weight gain and obesity. The International Association for the Study of Obesity. *Obesity Reviews*, **3**: 289–301.

Questions and lessons

This is not a case study of a specific campaign. Rather it explores how social marketing can be used to tackle a particular problem: obesity. As such it provides a useful vehicle for reprising many of the ideas discussed throughout the book. Try thinking through how you would convert the principles it discusses into practice. You can stick with the example of obesity or pick an example of your own.

Further Reading

■ Social marketing

Albrecht T.L. (1996). Defining social marketing: 25 years later. *Social Marketing Quarterly*, **3**(3/4): 21–23.

Alcalay R. and Bell R.A. (2000). *Promoting Nutrition and Physical Activity Through Social Marketing: Current Practices and Recommendations*. Prepared for the Cancer Prevention and Nutrition Section, California Department of Health Services, Sacramento, CA, June. Davis, CA: Center for Advanced Studies in Nutrition and Social Marketing, University of California.

Andreasen A.R. (1994). Social marketing: its definition and domain. *Journal of Public Policy and Marketing*, **13**(1): 108–114.

Andreasen A.R. (1995). *Marketing Social Change – Changing Behavior to Promote Health, Social Development, and the Environment*. San Francisco, CA: Jossey-Bass.

Andreasen A.R. (2001). *Ethics in Social Marketing*. Washington, DC: Georgetown University Press.

Andreasen A.R. (2002). Marketing social marketing in the social change market-place. *Journal of Public Policy and Marketing*, **21**(1): 3–13.

Andreasen A.R. (2006). *Social Marketing in the 21st Century*. London: Sage.

Backer T.E., Rogers E.M. and Sopory P. (1992). *Designing health communication campaigns: what works?* Newbury Park, CA; London: Sage.

Department of Health, HM Government, UK (2004). *Choosing Health: Making healthier choices easier*. Public Health White Paper, Series No. CM 6374. London: The Stationery Office.

Donovan R.J. and Henley N. (2003). *Social Marketing: Principles and Practice*. Melbourne: IP Communications. ISBN: 0957861753.

Dubois-Arber F., Jeannin A. and Spencer B. (1999). Long-term global evaluation of a national AIDS prevention strategy: the case of Switzerland. *AIDS*, **13**(18): 2571–2582.

Eadie D.R. and Smith C.J. (1995). The role of applied research in public health advertising: some comparisons with commercial marketing. *Health Education Journal*, **54**: 367–380.

Fine S.H. (1981). *The Marketing of Ideas and Social Issues*. New York, NY: Praeger.

Glanz K., Rimer B.K. and Lewis F.M. (2002). *Health Behavior and Health Education: Theory, Research and Practice*. San Francisco, CA: Jossey-Bass.

Goldberg M.E., Fishbein M. and Middlestadt S.E. (eds) (1997). *Social Marketing: Theoretical and Practical Perspectives*. Mahwah, NJ: Lawrence Erlbaum Associates.

Hastings G.B. (1990). Qualitative research in health education. *Journal of the Institute of Health Education*, **28**(4): 118–127.

Hastings G.B. (2003). Relational paradigms in social marketing. *Journal of Macromarketing*, **23**(1): 6–15.

Hastings G.B. and Elliott B. (1993). Social marketing practice in traffic safety. In *Marketing of Traffic Safety*, Chapter III, pp. 35–53. Paris: OECD.

Hastings G.B. and Leathar D.S. (1987). The creative potential of research. *International Journal of Advertising*, **6**: 159–168.

Hastings G. and McDermott L. (2006). Putting social marketing into practice. *British Medical Journal*, **332**(7551): 1210–1212.

Hastings G., MacFadyen L. and Anderson S. (2000). Whose behaviour is it any-way? The broader potential of social marketing. *Social Marketing Quarterly*, **VI**(2): 46–58.

Kotler P. and Zaltman G. (1971). Social marketing: an approach to planned social change. *Journal of Marketing*, **35**(3): 3–12.

Kotler P., Roberto N. and Lee N. (2002). *Social Marketing: Improving the Quality of Life*. 2nd edition. Thousand Oaks, CA; London: Sage.

Kotler P., Armstrong G., Saunders J. and Wong V. (2005). *Principles of Marketing*, 4th European edition. Harlow: Financial Times Prentice-Hall.

Lazer W. and Kelley E. (1973). *Social Marketing: Perspectives and Viewpoints*. Homewood, IL: Richard D. Irwin.

Lefebvre C. (1992). Social marketing and health promotion. In *Health Promotion: Disciplines and Diversity* (Bunton R. and MacDonald G., eds), Chapter 8. London: Routledge.

MacAskill S., Stead M., MacKintosh A.M. and Hastings G.B. (2002). "You cannae just take cigarettes away from somebody and no' gie them something back": can social marketing help solve the problem of low income smoking? *Social Marketing Quarterly*, **VIII**(1): 19–34.

MacFadyen L., Stead M. and Hastings G.B. (2002). Social marketing. In *The Marketing Book* (Baker M.J., ed.), 5th edition, Chapter 27. Oxford: Butterworth-Heinemann.

Maibach E. and Parrott R.L. (eds) (1995). *Designing Health Messages. Approaches From Communication Theory and Public Health Practice*. Newbury Park, CA: Sage.

McDermott L., Stead M. and Hastings G. (2005). What is and what is not social marketing: the challenge of reviewing the evidence. *Journal of Marketing Management*, **21**(5–6): 545–553.

McDermott L., Stead M., Hastings G.B., Angus K., Banerjee S., Rayner M. and Kent R. (2005). *A Systematic Review of the Effectiveness of Social Marketing Nutrition and Food Safety Interventions – Final report prepared for safe food*, March. Stirling: Institute for Social Marketing, University of Stirling.

McKenzie-Mohr D. and Smith W. (2000). *Fostering Sustainable Behaviour: an Introduction to Community-Based Social Marketing*. Gabriola Island, BC: New Society Publishers.

Morgan R.M. and Hunt S.D. (1994). The commitment-trust theory of relationship marketing. *Journal of Marketing*, **58**(3): 20–38.

National Social Marketing Centre (2005). *Social Marketing Pocket Guide*; www.nsms.org.uk

National Social Marketing Centre (2006). *Social Marketing Works!*; www.nsms.org.uk

National Social Marketing Centre (2006). *It's Our Health*; www.nsms.org.uk

Rangun V.K., Karim S. and Sandberg S.K. (1996). Do better at doing good. *Harvard Business Review*, **74**(3): 42–54.

Rogers E.M. (2003). *Diffusion of Innovations*. 5th edition. New York, NY: Simon & Schuster.

Rothschild M. (1999). Carrots, sticks, and promises: a conceptual framework for the management of public health and social issue behaviors. *Journal of Marketing*, **63**(4): 24–37.

Rutter D. and Quine L. (2002). *Changing Health Behaviour: Intervention and Research with Social Cognition Models*. Buckingham: Open University Press.

Stead M., Hastings G.B. and Eadie D. (2002). The challenge of evaluating complex interventions: a framework for evaluating media advocacy. *Health Education Research Theory and Practice*, **17**(3): 351–364.

Wallack L., Dorfman L., Jernigan D. and Themba M. (1993). *Media Advocacy and Public Health*. Newbury Park, CA: Sage.

Walsh D.C., Rudd R.E., Moeykens B.A. and Moloney T.W. (1993). Social marketing for public health. *Health Affairs*, **12**(2): 104–119.

Wanless D. (2004). *Securing Good Health for the Whole Population*. London: The Stationery Office.

Wiebe G.D. (1951/52). Merchandising commodities and citizenship in television. *Public Opinion Quarterly*, **15**(Winter): 679–691.

Wilkie W.L. and Moore E.S. (2003). Scholarly research in marketing: exploring the 'four eras' of thought development. *Journal of Public Policy and Marketing*, **22**(2): 116–146.

Useful journals

European Journal of Marketing, ISSN: 0309-0566.
Health Education Research, ISSN: 0268-1153 (print) and 1465-3648 (online).
International Journal of Advertising, ISSN: 0265-0487.
International Journal of Nonprofit and Voluntary Sector Marketing, ISSN: 1465-4520 (print) and 1479-103X (online).
Journal of Macromarketing, ISSN: 0276-1467 (print) and 1552-6534 (online).
Journal of Marketing Communication, ISSN: 1352-7266 (print) and 1466-4445 (online).
Journal of Marketing Theory, ISSN: 1470-5931 (print) and 1741-301X (online).
Journal of Public Policy and Marketing, ISSN: 0743-9156 (print) and 1547-7207 (online).
Psychology & Marketing, ISSN: 0742-6046 (print) and 1520-6793 (online).
Social Marketing Quarterly, ISSN: 1524-5004 (print) and 1539-4093 (online).

Websites

www.ism.ac.uk
www.nsms.org.uk
www.socialmarketing.blogs.com
www.social-marketing.com
www.social-marketing.org

■ Behaviour change theory

Stages of Change

Prochaska J.O. and DiClemente C.C. (1984). *The Transtheoretical Approach: Crossing Traditional Boundaries of Therapy*. Homewood, IL: Dow Jones-Irwin.

Prochaska J.O. and Velicer W.F. (1997). The transtheoretical model of health behavior change. *American Journal of Health Promotion*, **12**(1): 38–48.

Prochaska J.O., DiClemente C.C. and Norcross J.C. (1992). In search of how people change. *American Psychologist*, **47**: 1102–1114.

Social Cognitive Theory

Bandura A. (1986). *Social Foundations of Thought and Action: A Social Cognitive Approach*. Englewood Cliffs, NJ: Prentice-Hall.

Maibach E.W. and Cotton D. (1995). Moving people to behaviour change: a staged social cognitive approach to message design. In *Designing Health Messages. Approaches From Communication Theory and Public Health Practice* (Maibach E. and Parrott R.L., eds), Chapter 3, pp. 41–64. Newbury Park, CA: Sage.

Exchange Theory

Bagozzi R. (1975). Marketing and exchange. *Journal of Marketing*, **39**(October): 32–39.

Houston F.S. and Gassenheimer J.B. (1987). Marketing and exchange. *Journal of Marketing*, **51**(October): 3–18.

Theory of Planned Behaviour

Ajzen I. (1991). The Theory of Planned Behavior. *Organizational Behavior and Human Decision Processes*, **50**(2): 179–211.

Ajzen I. and Fishbein M. (1980). *Understanding Attitudes and Predicting Social Behavior*. London: Prentice-Hall.

Social Learning Theory

Bandura A. (1986). *Social Foundations of Thought and Action: A Social Cognitive Theory*. Englewood Cliffs, NJ: Prentice-Hall.

Bandura A. and Walters R.H. (1963). *Social Learning and Personality Development*. New York: Holt Reinhart & Winston.

Miller N.E. and Dollard J. (1941). *Social Learning and Imitation*. New Haven, CT: Yale University Press.

■ Critical marketing and critical thought

Bakan J. (2004). *The Corporation: the Pathological Pursuit of Profit and Power*. London: Constable.

Gladwell M. (2000). *The Tipping Point: How Little Things Can Make A Big Difference*. Boston: Little, Brown & Co.

Gladwell M. (2005). *Blink: The power of thinking without thinking*. London: Allen Lane.

Gordon R., Hastings G., McDermott L. and Siquier P. (2007). The critical role of social marketing. In *Critical Marketing* (Saren M., Maclaran P., Goulding C., Shankar A., Elliott R. and Catterall M., eds). Oxford: Elsevier.

Grant I.C., Hassan L.M., Hastings G.B., MacKintosh A.M. and Eadie D. (2007). The influence of branding on adolescent smoking behaviour: exploring the mediating role of image and attitudes. *International Journal of Nonprofit and Voluntary Sector Marketing*.

Hastings G.B. and MacFadyen L. (2000). *Keep Smiling. No One's Going To Die: An analysis of internal documents from the tobacco industry's main UK advertising agencies*. Centre for Tobacco Control Research and Tobacco Control Resource Centre. London: BMA. ISBN: 0-7279-1600-9.

Hastings G.B., Stead M., McDermott L., Forsyth A., MacKintosh A.M., Rayner M., Godfrey G., Carahar M. and Angus K. (2003). *Review of Research on the Effects of Food Promotion to Children – Final Report and Appendices*. Prepared for the Food Standards Agency. Published on the Food Standards Agency website: www.foodstandards.gov.uk/news/newsarchive/promote

Hastings G., Anderson S., Cooke E. and Gordon R. (2005). Alcohol marketing and young people's drinking: a review of the research. *Journal of Public Health Policy*, **26**(3): 296–311.

Hastings G., McDermott L., Angus K., Stead M. and Thomson S. (2007). *The Extent, Nature and Effects of Food Promotion to Children: A Review of the Evidence*. Technical Paper prepared for the World Health Organization, July 2006. Geneva: World Health Organization. Online: http://www.who.int/dietphysicalactivity/publications/Hastings_paper_marketing.pdf.

Heath J. and Potter A. (2006). *The Rebel Sell: How the Counter Culture Became Consumer Culture*. Chichester: Capstone Publishing.

Klein N. (2001). *No Logo*. London: Flamingo.

Layard P.R.G. (2005). *Happiness: Lessons from a New Science*. London: Allen Lane.

Levitt S. and Dubner S.J. (2005). *Freakonomics: A Rogue Economist Explores the Hidden Side of Everything*. London: Allen Lane.

Lovato C., Linn G., Stead L.F. and Best A. (2004). Impact of tobacco advertising and promotion on increasing adolescent smoking behaviours (Cochrane Review). In *The Cochrane Library*, Issue 2. Chichester: John Wiley.

Mackintosh A. (2004). *Soil and Soul: People versus Corporate Power*. Aurum Press.

Saren M. (2006). *Marketing Graffiti: The view from the street*. Oxford: Elsevier.

Saren M., Maclaran P., Elliott R., Goulding C., Shankar A. and Caterall M. (2007). *Critical Marketing: Defining the Field*. Oxford: Elsevier.

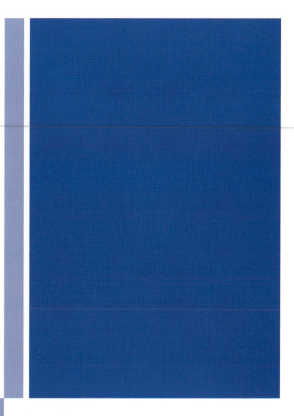

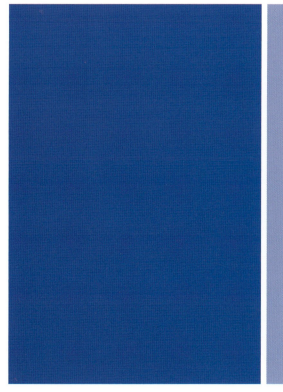

Index